Holly's Ukulele Method™

by Holly Rudin-Braschi
Master of Music, Manhattan School of Music, NYC

To download FREE mp3 music files for the songs and exercises in this book, or to purchase an interactive ebook version that includes the mp3s, please visit: **www.HollyUkulele.com**

Holly's Ukulele Method™

FIRST EDITION
ISBN-13: 978-0996441124
ISBN-10: 0996441123

Library of Congress Control Number: 2016911032, 2016
1. music, 2. musical arrangement, 3. text, 4. compilation of musical exercises, 5. sound recording.

Edited by Charylu Roberts; Initial Edit by Ronny S. Schiff
Music Typography and Interior Design by Charylu Roberts, O.Ruby Productions — www.SelfPublishMusicBooks.com
Cover Design, Proofreading and EBook Production by Phyllis Peterson — www.MagnoliaStudio.com
"Uke Dawg"™ Logo and Drawings by Pete McDonnell — www.McDonnellillustration.com
Illustrations by Ryan Quackenbush — www.RyanQuackenbush.com
Interior Photos by Ed Dudkowski — www.EDudkowski.com
Holly's Cover and Introduction Photograph by Hugh O'Connor — hoconnor@me.com
Ukulele Photograph on Cover Provided by Kala Brand Music Co. — www.KalaBrand.com
Musical Examples Recorded at:
Zone Recording Studios by Blair Hardman — www.ZoneRecording.com
Island Sound Studios by Gaylord Kalani Holomalia — gholomalia@mac.com

PUBLISHED BY:

UKE DAWG
PRODUCTIONS

www.HollyUkulele.com

Manufactured in the United States of America

Table of Contents

TM

Welcome!

Thank you for choosing to study ukulele with me!

There are many ways to play the ukulele. All are valid, particularly if the result is music that is clear, rhythmic and inspired. ***Holly's Ukulele Method*** helps you do all of this and much more. I developed the playing techniques in ***Holly's Ukulele Method*** over ten years of teaching beginners from grade school to grad school. If you have a fire in your belly to make music, plus make a commitment to practice a minimum of 20 minutes 5-days a week with this book, you will be on the road to becoming a ukulele musician, not simply a ukulele player. This comprehensive, information-packed manual transforms your ukulele into a tool to teach you the basics of musicianship… skills that can be applied to any other instrument.

Perfect for both private or classroom study, ***Holly's Ukulele Method*** is organized as a six-lesson course in reading music because I want to encourage ukulele players to learn more than chords and songs. The ability to read music enables you to "sight read" music you have never heard; listen to new music then play the notes and chords "by ear" while recognizing their names and rhythms; write new music, and much, much more.

Using my method, you will learn to:

- **Read music and tablature in the key of C** so you can pick up any piece of music and play it
- **Play melody lines**
- **Play chords** to accompany yourself and others
- **Combine both melody and chords** for dynamite solo playing
- **Fingerpick and strum** for a professional sound

Lessons include:

- String-by-string music reading
- Clear descriptions
- Easy-to-follow photos and drawings
- Songs and chords
- Strumming and fingerpicking technique
- Finger exercises
- Music writing exercises

Each lesson offers loads of extra material so that beginners can have a variety of songs and exercises to hone their skills. I don't expect beginners to learn everything in each lesson within a week, but, depending on your aptitude, prior musical knowledge, and the amount of practicing you do, you may get through all of the material in a couple of weeks, or you might have to work on each chapter for a few months to play it to your satisfaction. Everyone learns differently and at a different pace, so relax, give yourself permission to make loads of mistakes, and have fun making music!

Sincerely,

Holly Rudin-Braschi

Introduction

OMG! You just got your first ukulele and are sooooo excited. But, you don't exactly know how to play and you want to start NOW. Perhaps you were inspired to purchase your ukulele because:

- a friend invited you to their uke group
- one of your favorite musicians plays a song on the uke that you want to learn
- you used to play as a child and want to resume
- you impulsively purchased a uke you saw beckoning you in a shop window

...However you got connected to your ukulele, I have solutions to help get your musical mojo started.

My name is Holly Rudin-Braschi and I have taught hundreds of beginners to successfully make music on their ukuleles with professional-style techniques. I am a master ukulele instructor who has also taught hundreds of people how to play through group and private ukulele classes at Santa Rosa Junior College in Santa Rosa, CA and at the Petaluma School of Music in Petaluma, CA and master classes around the US.

I hold a BA from Vassar College, NY in musicology and a Master's Degree in Music from the Manhattan School of Music, NYC. Trained as a guitarist and singer, little did I know that I would be hooked on an instrument that my husband purchased for me as an anniversary gift!

My ukulele is more than just a "cute" instrument. It is serious fun! Any devoted ukulele student who puts in the time can learn to play any genre of music that "floats their boat"... from folk, to classical, rock, reggae, blues, jazz... you name it, you can play it! Since I am a maverick who couldn't find a text that suited my needs as a musician and teacher, I wrote this book to help students learn to read music, play chords and play solos on this 4-stringed dynamo.

Ukulele 12-Step Jump-Start Guide

Book Organization

To learn basic playing techniques from the get-go, this books starts with a "**12-Step Jump-Start Guide**." This introductory chapter provides you with the know-how to learn and play chords so that you can start singing your favorite songs while playing your ukulele. Following this guide, we get down to the business of reading music, basic musicianship and playing technique. This book pertains to ukuleles tuned G, C, E, A. Have fun learning!

To download FREE mp3 music files for the songs and exercises in this book, or to purchase an interactive ebook version that includes the mp3s, please visit: **www.HollyUkulele.com**

Ukulele Anatomy

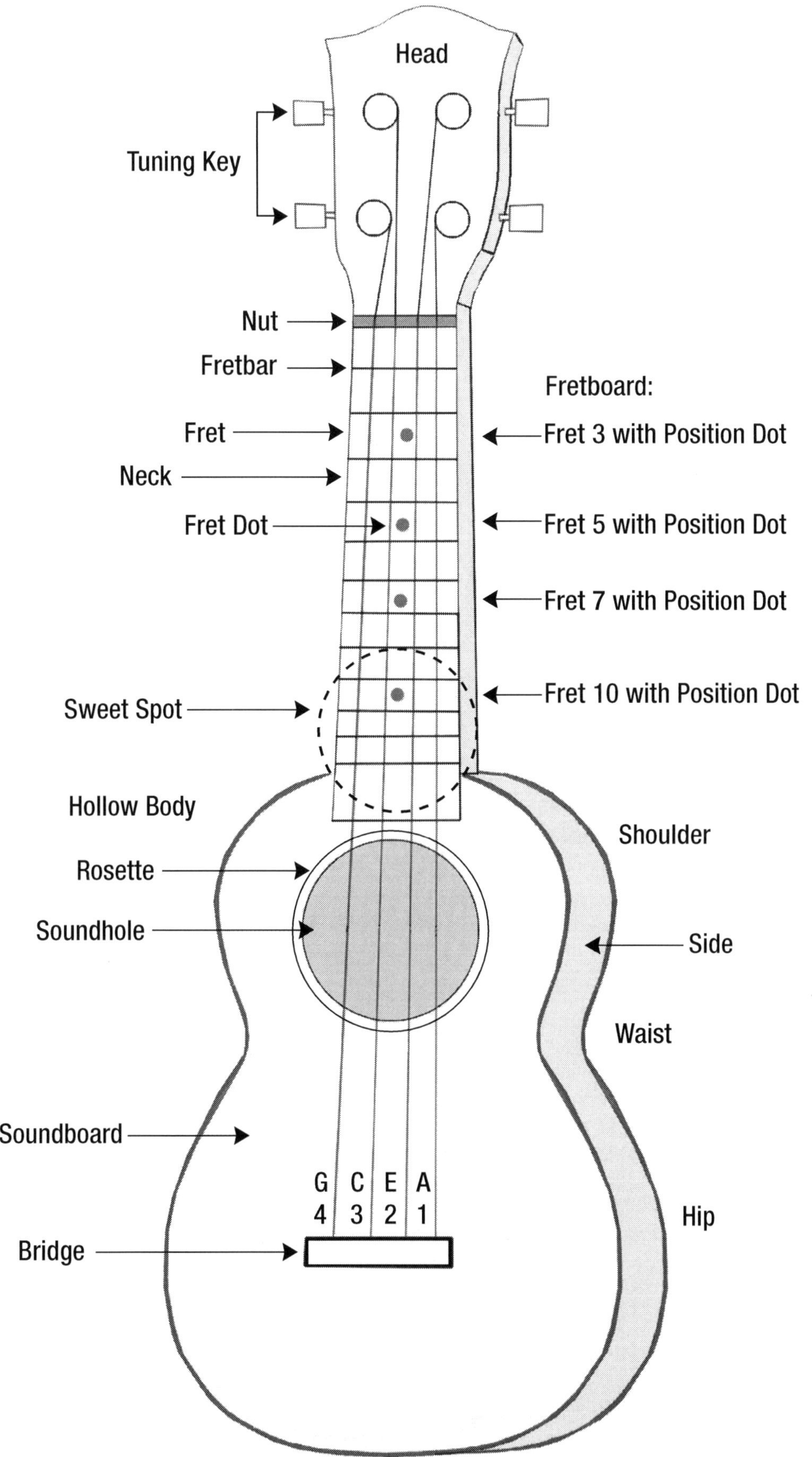

STEP 1. Know Your Ukulele Anatomy

Playing a uke is more than knowing notes and chords. Knowing how all the parts work enhances your technique, enables you to identify anything that may go wrong with your uke and helps you make an informed decision when purchasing.

1. **Back** (not shown on diagram) • Wood on the back of the body. Most ukes have a flat back. Some manufacturers feature a "bowed" or rounded back, which acts like a mini amphitheater giving a deeper and richer sound than a flat-backed ukulele.

2. **Bridge** and **saddle** • Uke strings are first attached to the bridge. The bridge transfers string vibration to the ukulele's body. On top of the bridge is a notched "saddle." The notches separate and hold the strings in place and help them track evenly over the neck and fretboard, through the nut on the bottom of the head, and up to the tuning keys. There are two main types of bridges. Each requires attaching strings in a different way. The ***tie-bar bridge*** has holes that run from top to bottom so strings can be threaded through and secured by winding over themselves. The ***standard bridge*** has small notches on the bottom. A knot must be tied at the end of each string in order to hold it in the notch.

3. **Cutaway** (not shown on diagram) • One uke *shoulder* is "cut away" leaving a *cutout* or half circle so players can easily reach the frets that produce the highest notes nearest the soundhole.

4. **Fretboard**, **fretbars** and **frets** • Located on the front of the neck is the **fretboard**. This piece of wood is divided into sections by metal bars called "**fretbars**." Each section is called a "**fret**" and is the location of an individual note. The larger the uke, the longer the fretboard, the more frets on the uke (giving you more notes), and the wider the frets. Tenor ukes have longer fretboards (and more notes) than soprano ukes (see **"Full Ukulele Fretboard" on page 172**). **When you *fret* a note**, you press your fingertip on a string between two fret bars. This shortens the length of the string. When you pluck a "fretted" note, the string vibrates or resonates to create the note's pitch. The frets near the head produce lower pitched notes. The frets near the body produce higher pitched notes.

5. **Fretbars** • The metal strips that divide the fretboard into frets. The fretbars should be smooth when you run your hand along the side of the fretboard. If the edges are sharp, they can be smoothed by a luthier (person who makes and repairs stringed instruments).

6. **Fret position dots** • These little dots are roadmap markers to tell the players where they are on the fretboard. Fret position dots usually indicate the 3rd, 5th, 7th, 10th, and 12th frets. They may be placed directly on the fretboard in the middle of frets and/or on the side of the neck.

7. **Head** • The top of the uke where the tuning keys are attached.

8. **Label** (not shown on diagram) • Located just inside the sound hole, the label gives information about the manufacturer, model number, serial number, and manufacture date.

9. **Nut** • One of the most important parts of the uke; it has small notches that keep the strings in place above the fretboard. If the notches are too deep, the strings will hit the metal fretbars and make a buzzing sound when they are strummed, a.k.a. "*low action.*" Notches that are shallow make it harder to play because the strings are raised too high above the fretboard, also known as "*high*" or "*raised action.*"

10. **Neck** • A piece of wood that supports the fretboard, frets, head, and strings. String tension gives the neck more stress than any other part of the ukulele. To counteract the tension and to give added strength, the neck is carved from a single piece of wood, and may be made of a harder wood than the main body. The neck is rounded at the back to fit the palm shape of a hand.

11. **Sides** • The curved pieces of wood on the sides of the uke body. These are formed by steaming the wood to fit the shape of the soundboard.

12. **Soundboard** • The top of the uke body, the soundboard supports the bridge. It resonates when the uke strings are strummed and is one of the elements that contribute to the uke's overall tone. The more coatings (lacquer, paint, varnish) on a soundboard, the less it will resonate.

13. **Soundhole** and **rosette** • The opening in the uke's soundboard acts like the uke's speaker system, allowing sound out of the instrument. The "rosette" is a decoration around the soundhole. It can be painted or inlaid with wood, ivory, mother-of-pearl, or abalone.

14. **Strings** • The strings are the uke's sound source. They vibrate at different pitches depending on how they are tuned and where they are fretted when fingerpicked or strummed.

15. **Sweet spot** • Where the neck is glued to the body. This is the place for strumming and/or fingerpicking where the best tone quality is produced.

16. **Tuning key** • There is one tuning key on the head of the ukulele for each string. The tuning keys tighten and loosen the tension of each string for tuning. Ukulele manufacturers install two different types of tuning keys on their ukuleles:

    - **Friction tuning keys** • Stick out of the back of the ukulele head and may be very touchy, making tuning a challenge.
    - **Geared tuning keys** • Stick out of the side of the ukulele head and are attached to a screw at the back of the uke that turns a small-toothed gear. These tuners are easier to adjust and are good choices for beginners.

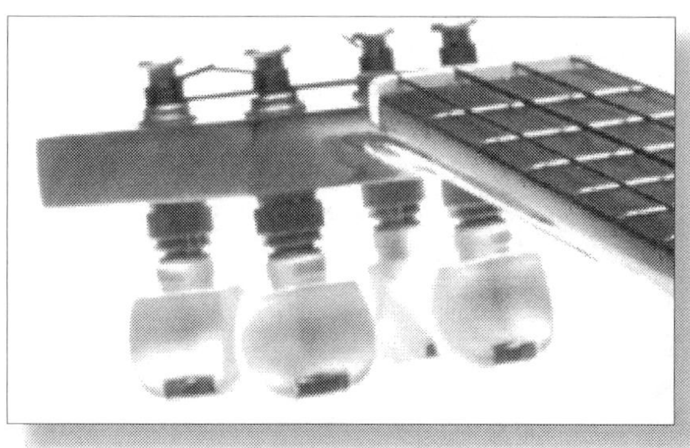

Friction Tuning Keys

Geared Tuning Keys

STEP 2. Set Up Your Ukulele

Strings • No matter how inexpensive or costly your instrument, a good set of strings can make all the difference in tone quality. Whether you play a soprano, concert, or tenor-sized ukulele, consider choosing a high-quality set of strings that includes a Low G string. The Low G gives you three extra low melody notes that aren't available in traditional High-G string sets: the G, A and B notes below middle C (see **"Appendix" on page 170**). These three extra low notes enable you to play a world of lead melodies. In addition, a Low G string provides a more rounded depth of sound for your instrument. You can choose:

- **Low G strings wound with metal:** the metal increases the weight of the string while keeping the flexibility of a smaller string and provides a vibrant sound. Strings that are too thick have a dead, muddy sound.
- **"No wound" Low G strings:** Some musicians don't like metal wound strings because they make a hissing sound when a finger rubs the winding. Both metal and "no wound" are acceptable. But remember that metal can wear out the wood between the fret bars.

Ukulele strap • Uke straps make holding your instrument easier. It puts less pressure on your strumming and fingerpicking arm, allowing it to work freely, and is particularly helpful when you stand and play. Plus, straps keep your uke in the optimal position for ergonomically sound playing. Have a luthier (stringed instrument maker) install one strap button on the bottom of the body and a second button on the base of the neck facing the floor. Many instrument stores have in-house luthiers who can install the buttons in a jiffy. Then, choose a colorful strap that fits your instrument and personality. Many uke manufacturers now sell ukulele straps. You can also choose a guitar strap if you have a large frame.

Base strap button placement

Neck strap button placement

Properly holding uke with a strap

STEP 3. Clock into Your Playing Position

Even though the traditional ukulele looks like a mini guitar, it isn't held or played the same way. This is due to the physics of the sound.

Whether standing or sitting...

- **Uke position:** Imagine your head at the 12 o'clock position within a clock. Then rotate the head of your ukulele slightly below the 2 o'clock position... about a 40° angle.
- **Sit or stand tall:** Shoulders over hips. If sitting in a chair, sit forward, with a space between your back and the back of the chair back. Good spinal alignment is essential for:
  - positioning hands and arms to build the strength and agility required for accurate playing
  - providing unrestricted breathing for maximum vocal support when you sing
- **Strumming arm position:** Secure your uke against your body under your right forearm. Depending on the size of your uke, your height and arm length, you may want to rest the bottom of the uke in the crook of your right arm.

STEP 4. Finding the Strumming "Sweet Spot"

Next, position your strumming hand and arm. ***Do not play over the sound hole.*** The best sound from any ukulele is at a position called the "sweet spot," located just above the spot where the neck and body join. It is ***not*** located over the sound hole like a guitar. Sit in a quiet room and strum over both areas to hear the difference. Depending on the length of your arms and the size of your instrument, the elbow or forearm rests against the lower body of the uke, while the fingers tickle the sweet spot.

STEP 5. Learn the Names of Your Strings

This sounds so obvious, but you would be surprised at how many people don't bother. Knowing your string names helps you:

- tune your instrument
- learn the note names on your fretboard
- purchase strings and restring your uke

I help my students remember string names with this phrase that is so silly, it is hard to forget:

"Good Cats Eat Apples"

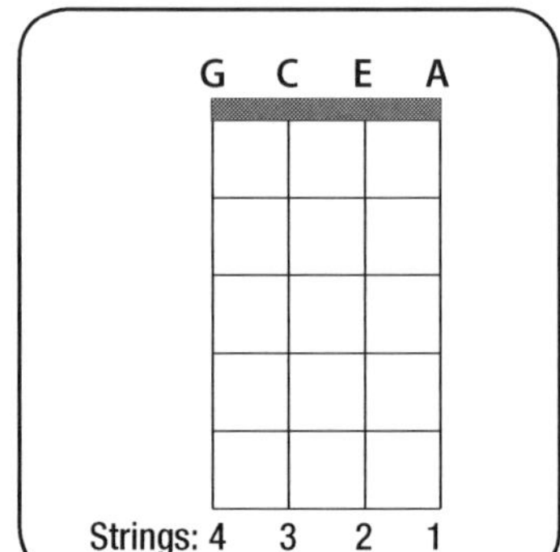

To learn the names of the strings:

- Hold your uke upright so the strings face you.
- The string on the far left is string 4, or the G string.
- The string on the far right is string 1, or the A string.
- To memorize their names, sing the following as you play each string…

String 4: Good **String 3: Cats** **String 2: Eat** **String 1: Apples**

STEP 6. Tune Up

Since ukulele players tend to play in groups, consider purchasing a clip-on tuner. This type of tuner doesn't pick up the ambient sound of other musicians tuning their instruments because they work from the vibrations of your instrument alone. My favorite tuners have a red-light/green-light system. When you get the string perfectly tuned, the light turns from red to green. Many of these tuners can be used on other stringed instruments including bass, cello, and guitar, so make sure you set your tuner to either "chromatic" or "ukulele in C" before tuning.

- **Technique for tuning with clip on tuners:** These little guys have a small computer chip that gets easily "distracted" if you pluck a string too many times in a row, or pluck more than one string at the same time. Grip the tuning peg of the string you are tuning with the fingers of one hand, a finger of the other hand on the string. Pluck the string you are tuning ONCE. As it resonates, simultaneously adjust the tuning peg. After the tuning peg is set, mute the string with your plucking finger to stop the sound and let the minicomputer readjust. Then pluck the string again to test for accuracy.

- **Tuning TIP:** Remember after tuning to turn off your tuner so you don't use up your battery too quickly. But… leave it connected to your ukulele while playing because you may need to retune several times depending on the temperature and age of the strings. Cold weather can cause strings to go sharp, while hot weather can cause them to go flat. If your strings are new, they will constantly go flat. So you will need to retune constantly to stretch them. See **"Tune Me Up and Turn Me Loose!" on page 175** for more help with tuning.

STEP 7. Get a Grip!

Correct fretting-hand positioning and fretting technique is essential for a clear, vibrant sound and ergonomically safe playing. Your left hand fretting fingers are:

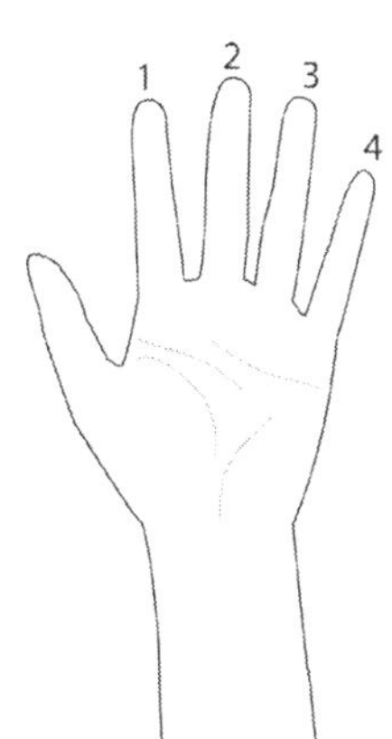

The Left Hand

1 = Index Finger
2 = Middle Finger
3 = Ring Finger
4 = Pinky Finger

Left hand fingernails: Your nails must be short enough to allow the fingertips to hold the strings down without the pad of the fingertip stopping the sound on adjacent strings. That, for most people, is a very short length. You may want to keep an extra set of nail clippers in your uke case.

Left hand wrist position: For maximum dexterity, reach and flexibility in your fingers, your left hand wrist should be a natural extension of the arm… relaxed, yet slightly curved without being forced into position.

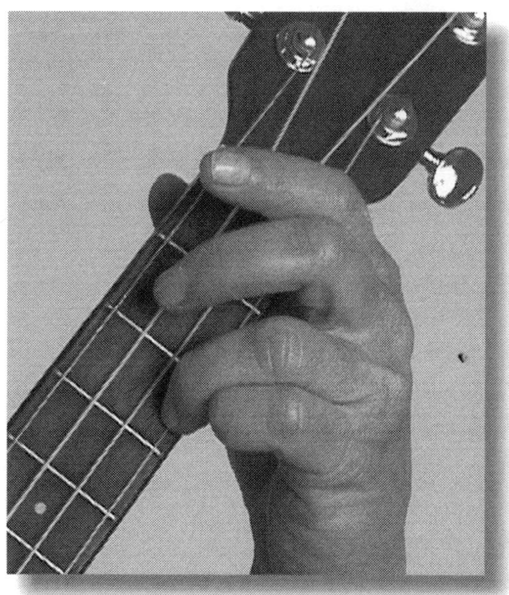

Correct Wrist: *This wrist is relaxed and slightly curved.*

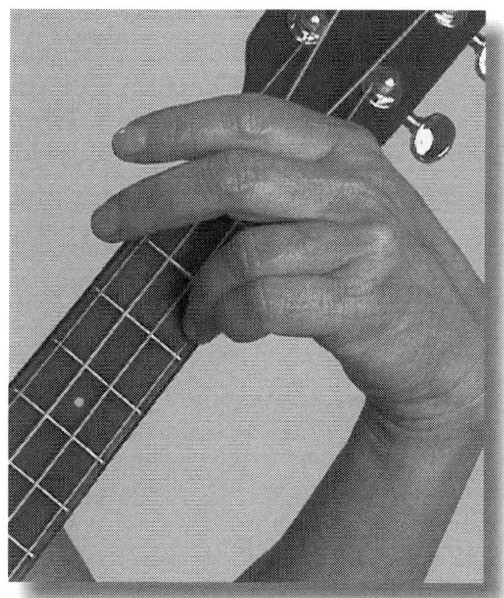

Incorrect Wrist: *This extremely bent wrist makes playing difficult and does not allow the tendons to work easily. Over time this position may cause tendonitis.*

Finger Placement

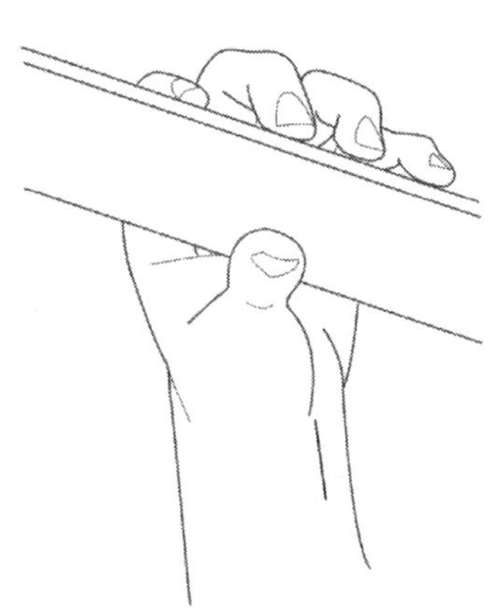

- **Thumb**—Think of the thumb as a vice that helps distribute pressure evenly among the other fingers.
- Place the underside of your thumb at the back of the ukulele neck directly behind the fretboard. Position your thumb just under the second finger at a slight angle, and then point the tip of the thumb toward your nose. Beginners often point their thumb toward the head of the uke, which gives a weak grip. For the cleanest technique, *do not wrap your thumb around the neck of the ukulele.*

Think "little bridges" when pressing down the strings with the fingers on your left hand. The two joints of each finger should make a rounded U-shaped bridge over each string. This gives your hand the most strength and power to get the best sound from your instrument. Collapsed fingers make it hard to hold the strings down.

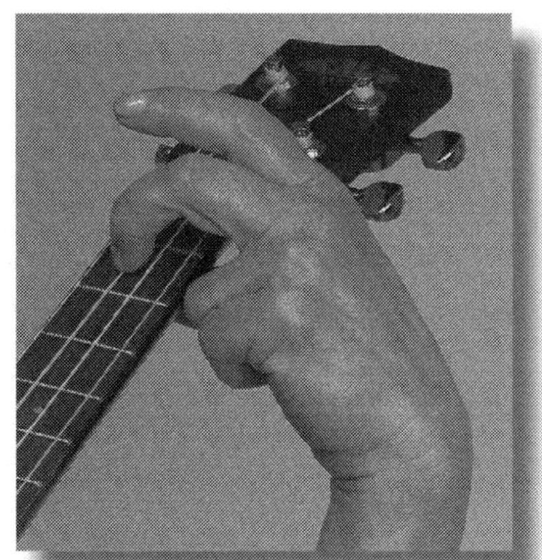

Correct: *Fretting bridge. Notice the strong U form.*

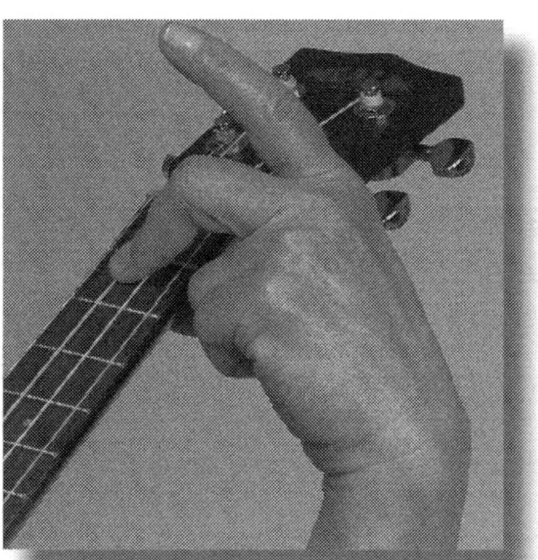

Incorrect: *Collapsed fretting bridge*

Aim for just above the fretbar at the bottom of each fret (toward the uke body) for the clearest sound and maximum tone quality. When playing in the first fret, this is especially important because the strings are slightly higher near the nut and harder to hold down in that position.

Correct: *Proper fingertip placement*

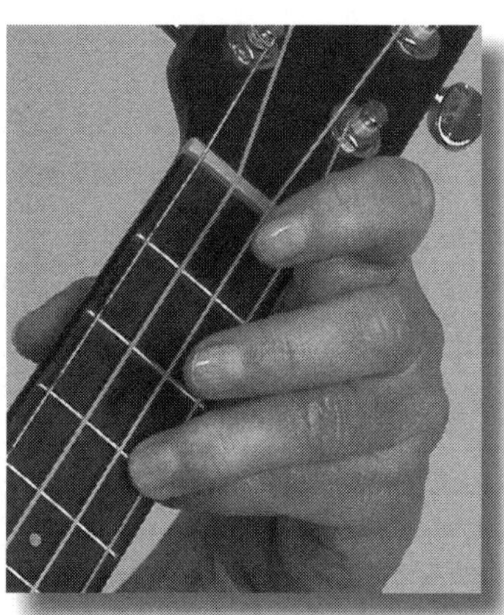

Incorrect: *Fingertip on top of fretbar*

Keep each finger pad away from adjacent strings so that all strings ring freely when played. Fingertip shapes are as individual as fingerprints. The larger the fingertip, the more challenging it is to prevent the finger pad from touching and muting adjacent strings. This can be frustrating at first for big fingers in little frets. But consider this: Some of the largest people in the world play the smallest soprano ukes. The late Israel "IZ" Kamakawiwo'ole weighed in at over 600 pounds and accompanied his angelic voice with a soprano uke.

Your fingers are "hover crafts." Economy of motion is the key for great playing, particularly on the left hand. Beginners often make the mistake of lifting their fingers too far off of the strings after they have "fretted" a note. Instead, think of your fingertips as hover crafts, waiting just above the strings and ready to land firmly in any fret when needed. No fingers should ever rest under the neck of the uke. It will take you too long to fret the next note. Remember, it's only a fraction of an inch between fretting a note and lifting slightly above the string without touching it to let it resonate freely.

Left hand finger placement self-test • To test your fingertip placement, put all the left hand fingers on a single string on consecutive frets starting with the first fret. Press down. You will notice that your fingertips don't fall naturally on the center. You will find that keeping the following positioning when playing individual fingers is easier:

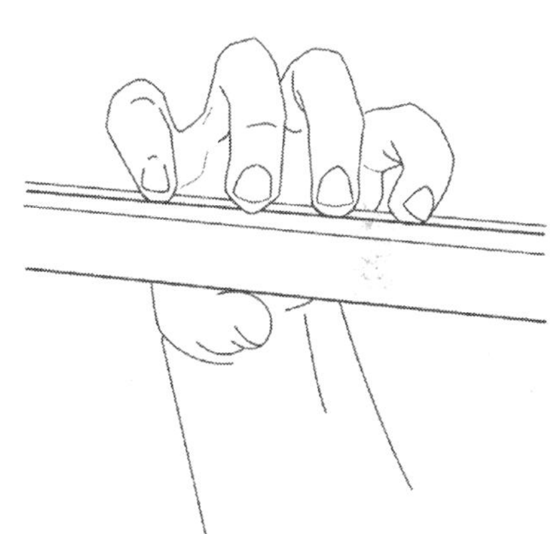

1. **First or index finger**—Plays on the left side of the tip.
2. **Second or middle finger**—Plays just to the left of the tip.
3. **Third or ring finger**—Plays just to the right of the tip.
4. **Fourth or pinky finger**—Makes contact on the right side of the tip.

STEP 8. Learn to Strum

Traditionally, the ukulele is strummed either with the thumb, index, or the middle finger... whatever feels comfortable to you. You can also use a combination of thumb, index and middle finger if you like. Some people find the thumb is better for downstrokes because it is stronger, making it easier to control for dynamics (loud and soft playing); while the index or middle work well for upstrokes. Experiment and practice all the following moves to train your fingers and determine which ones are your strumming favorites.

Strum Movement • Whether you use your thumb, index or middle finger, the movement is economical and comes from a rotating forearm.

- **Downstroke**—movement is down and away from you
- **Upstroke**—movement is upwards and toward you
- **Apply some pressure!** As you experiment, apply some pressure to your strum. Otherwise your playing will sound wimpy and weak. Strumming with pressure brings out the best tone quality your ukulele has to offer. And, let's face it, you only have 4 strings. So practice techniques that bring out as much resonance from your instrument as possible. Whether you are playing "piano" (softly) or "forte" (loudly), you still need some pressure to bring out your ukulele's best sound.

Thumb strumming:

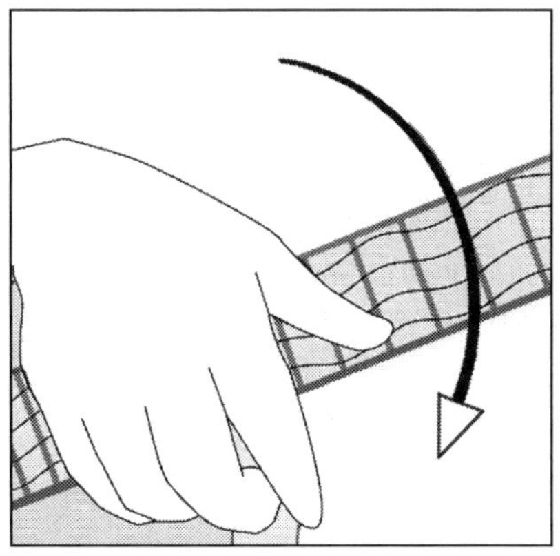

***Downstroke**—use the left under side of your thumb nail*

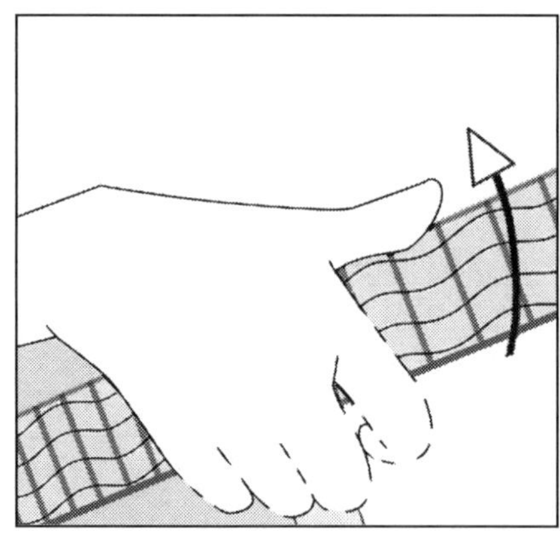

***Upstroke**—use the left top of your thumb nail*

Index or middle finger strumming:

- **Downstroke**—use the top of your fingernail.

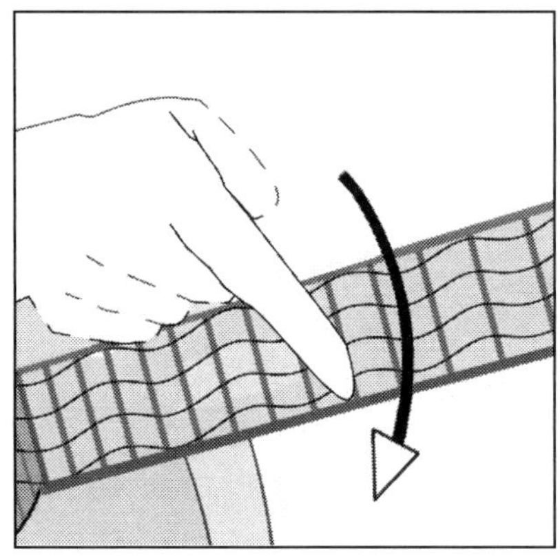

Index Finger Downstroke

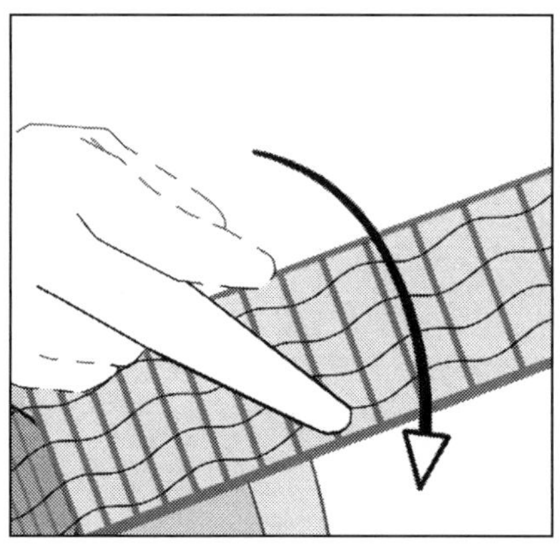

Middle Finger Downstroke

- **Upstroke**—use the underside of your fingernail.

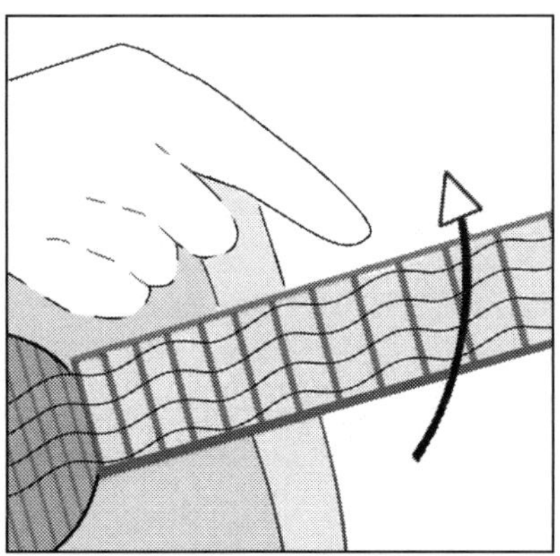

Index Finger Upstroke

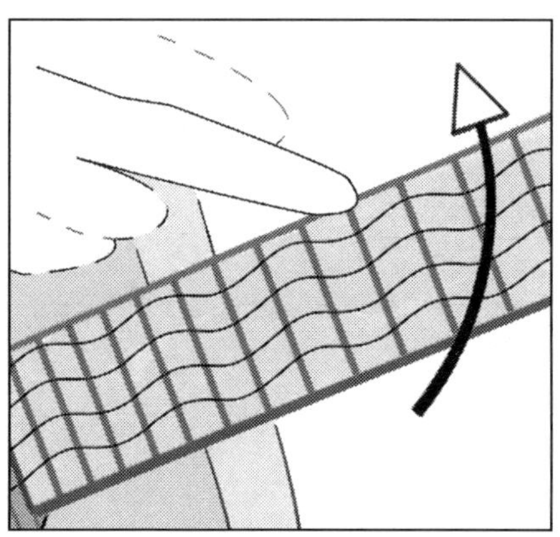

Middle Finger Upstroke

STEP 9. Learn to Read Chord Grids

A *chord grid* is a diagram of three or more frets on the ukulele's fret board. They are used to represent the **fretted (a.k.a. closed) notes** and **non-fretted (a.k.a. open) notes** of a chord. They often appear in songs over a musical staff, directly over a lyric to designate a chord change. The chord grid is drawn as if you are holding your ukulele at arm's length with the fretboard facing you.

Understanding the basic grid:

- The **vertical lines** represent the strings
- The **horizontal lines** indicate the fretbars that delineate the frets (spaces between the fretbars)

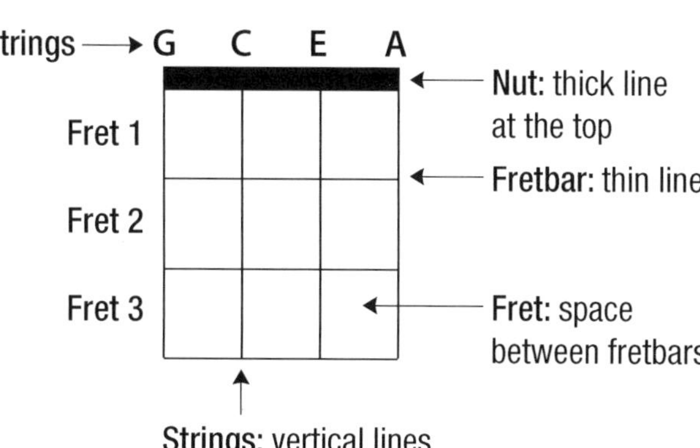

Understanding the grid with fretting indications:

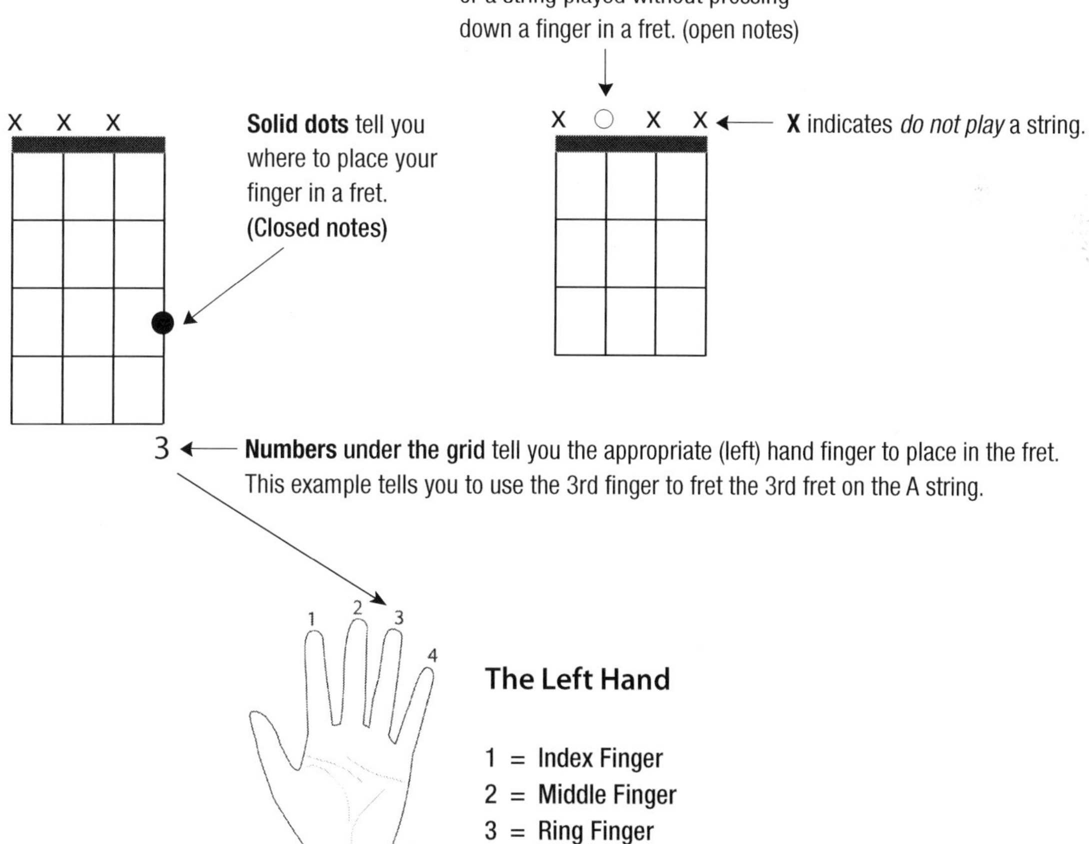

The Left Hand

1 = Index Finger
2 = Middle Finger
3 = Ring Finger
4 = Pinky Finger

STEP 10. Learn the Difference Between a Note and a Chord

A ***note*** is a tone of a definite pitch. When you play a note on the ukulele, one string is played alone. The string can be played two ways:

- **Open**—left-hand finger **does not hold down** a string on the fret board
- **Closed**—a left-hand finger ***does*** hold down a string on the fret board

Notes

First, try playing an *open C note*. This note is known as "middle C" and is played on the open C string.

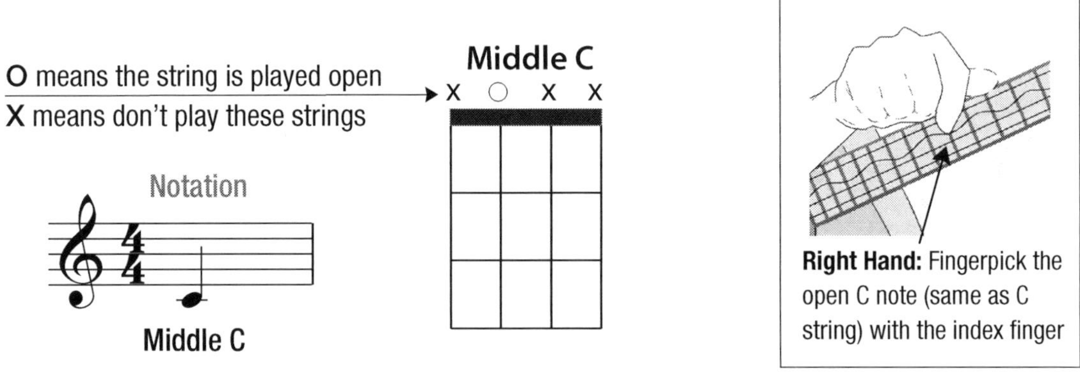

Next, try playing a *closed C note*. This is known as the C above "middle C." It is fretted on the A string and is eight notes, or one octave higher than middle C.

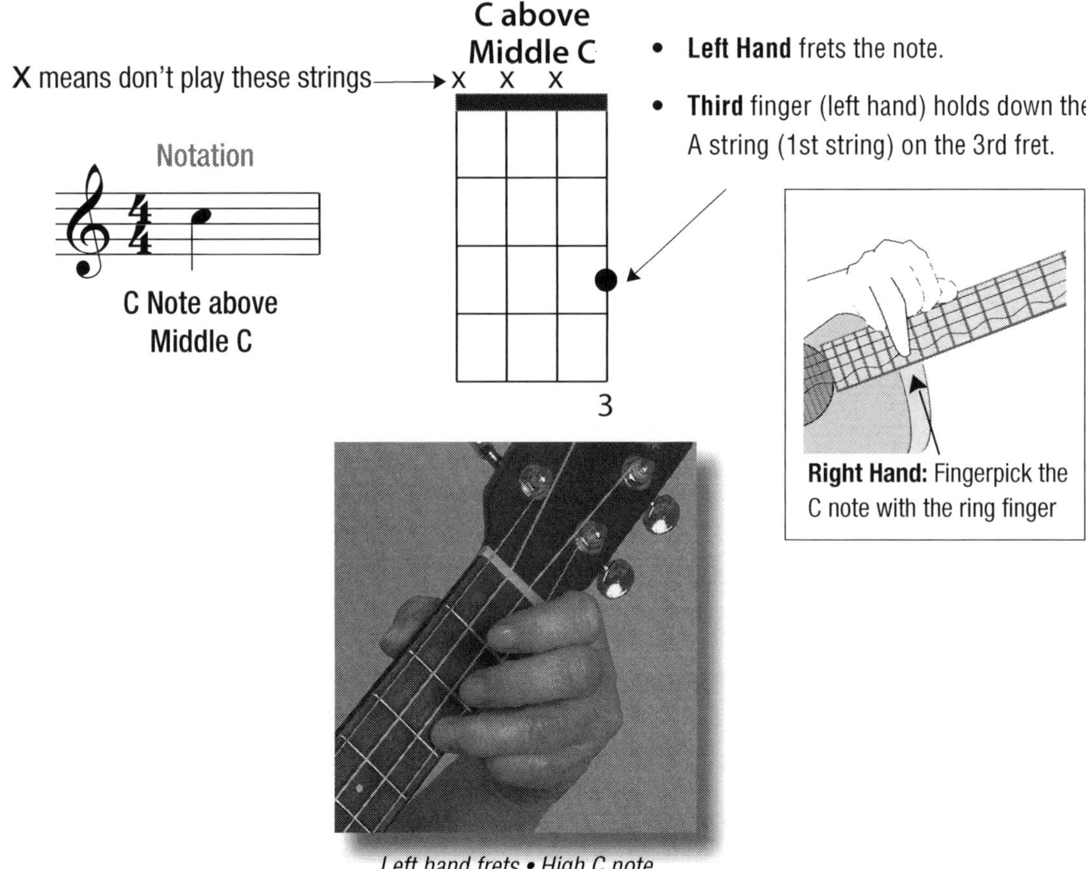

Left hand frets • High C note

Chords

- A ***chord*** is two or more tones or pitches played simultaneously.
- A ***chord*** on the ukulele is two or more strings played together.

Now try playing a C Chord:

- O means these strings are open with no fingers fretting the strings.
- It also means strum all of the open strings.

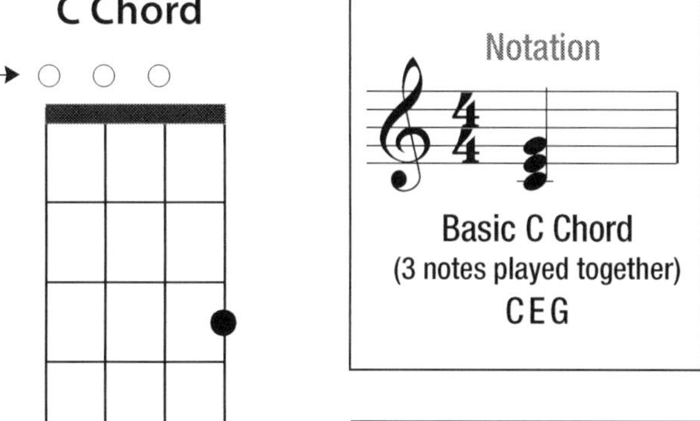

3
G C E C

Note names of the open and fretted strings in the C chord. Notice that the chord has three notes C, E, G. The C note is doubled, but the two C notes are different in sound. Middle C on the open C string is 8 notes or tones lower than the C on the A string (3rd fret). Play the notes individually to hear the difference.

Left Hand Frets the Note: Third finger holds down the A string (1st string) on the 3rd fret.

Left hand frets • C chord

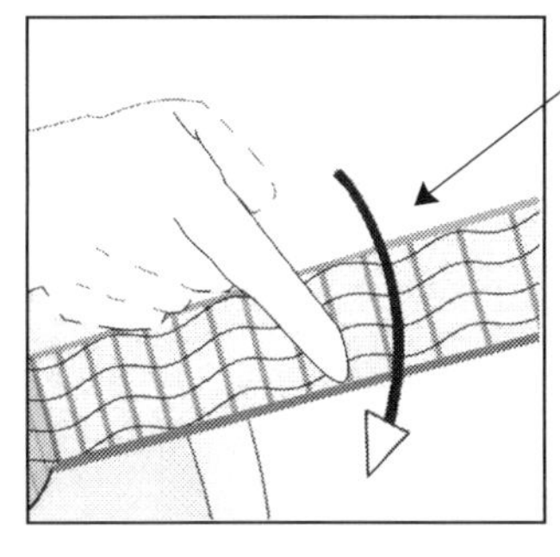

Strum all four strings using any of the following right hand fingers. Try them all and choose the finger that is most comfortable for you:

- **Index Finger**
- **Middle Finger**
- **Thumb**

STEP 11. Learn to Play the C and G7 Chords

Create a roadmap for fretting between chords • The key for accuracy and speed in moving from one specific chord to the next is to do it the same way every time. To find your *route,* identify *fretted* notes between chords that are either common or adjacent, then use *slide, pivot,* or *walking* fingers to *travel* from chord-to-chord. For example, take a look at the C and G7 chords below. There are no fretted notes in common between these two chords. But, they have *adjacent* notes on the A string. The third finger frets a C note (3rd fret, A string) in the C chord. When moving to G7, the third finger slides down one fret to the B note (2nd fret, A string).

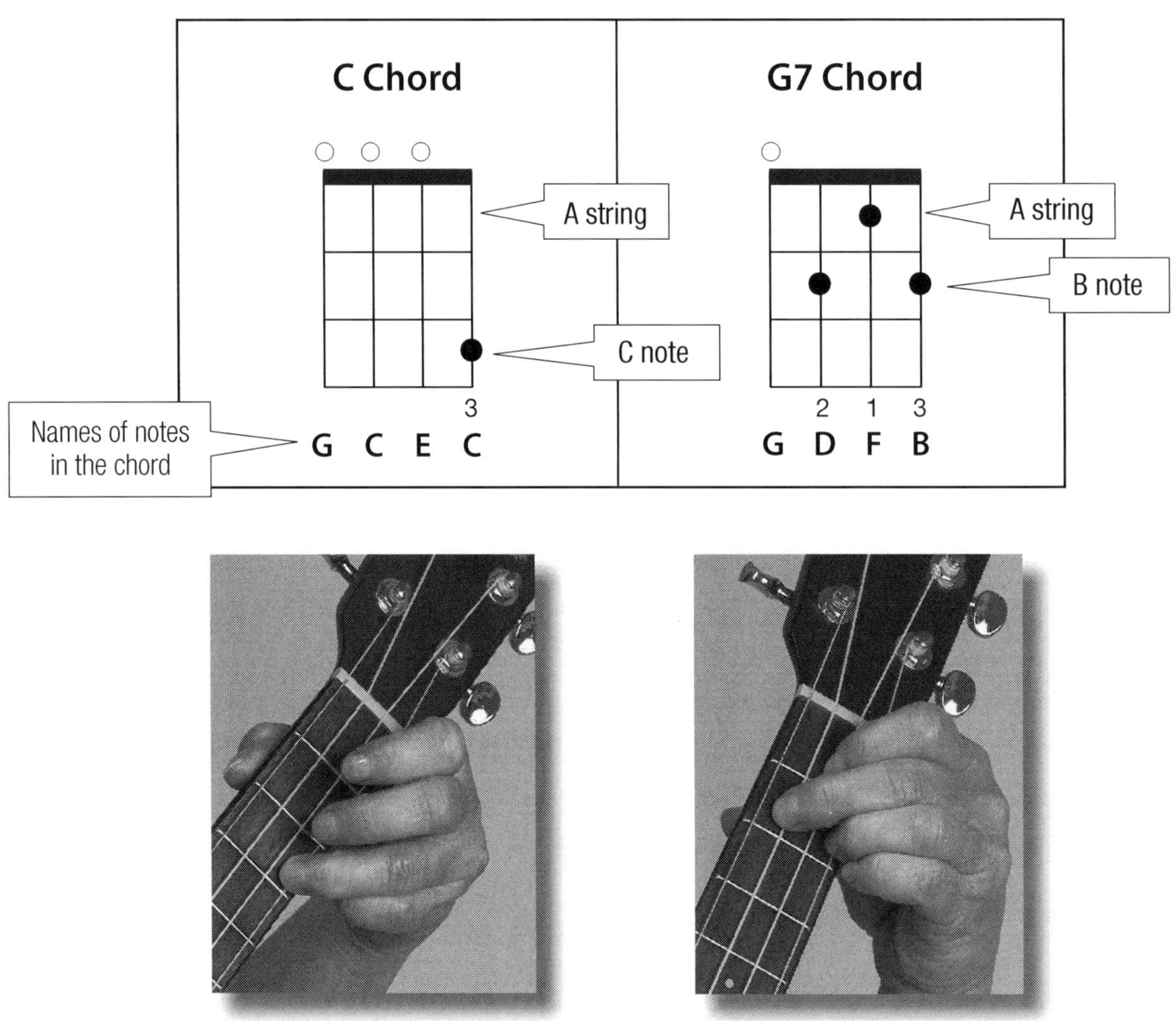

Left hand fretting C chord

Left hand fretting G7 chord

Moving smoothly between C and G7 chords • To keep your place, slide your 3rd finger from the C position (A string, 3rd finger, third fret) up to the second fret. As you slide, continue applying pressure so you feel the fretbar as you move over it. This helps you place your third finger exactly where you want it for good tone quality. Next, place your remaining fingers in the G7 position in this order: 2nd finger (D note, C string, second fret) then 1st finger (F note, E string, first fret).

Learning Tip: Practice this roadmap with your eyes closed to create fretting and strumming hand muscle memory and to train your ear.

STEP 12. Use Your Roadmap to Play Music

From my experience, most beginners purchase a load of ukulele song books to help kick-start their learning. Most have never read a note of music, so when they excitedly open their new purchases, the musical staff looks like hieroglyphics and they panic. *As you progress in this book, you will learn to read everything on the staff. But even though you may not be able to read a note, I have designed this 12-Step Jump-Start Guide to help you start playing.* The following examples are what you will get in most ukulele song books minus the beat numbers and note names (underneath the staff), and the strum marks (above the staff), all of which I include to help my students learn to read music quickly.

Demystifying the music • The example below is a musical staff containing the "melody" notes. Melody notes make up the string of single notes that are sung by a voice or played by a solo instrument. On top of the staff are the chord grids that identify the harmonies that accompany the melody line.

Strum markings • Some beginning books include strum markings. The downstroke sign looks like a small table. The upstroke sign looks like a V. In this example we are only using a downstroke on the 1 and 3 beats of each measure.

How to change chords • Start playing the first chord indicated by the chord grid at the beginning of the staff. Continue playing the first chord designated above the lyrics until a new chord is indicated above a word. Then quickly change chords and do not stop strumming.

When to strum • Fret each chord with your left hand, and then strum downward:

- **3/4 Time**—on the **1st beat of each measure**
- **4/4 Time**—on the **1st and 3rd beat of each measure**

In the following example, keep strumming the C chord until the word "he" when you change to the G7 chord. Strum down on the 1 and 3 beats.

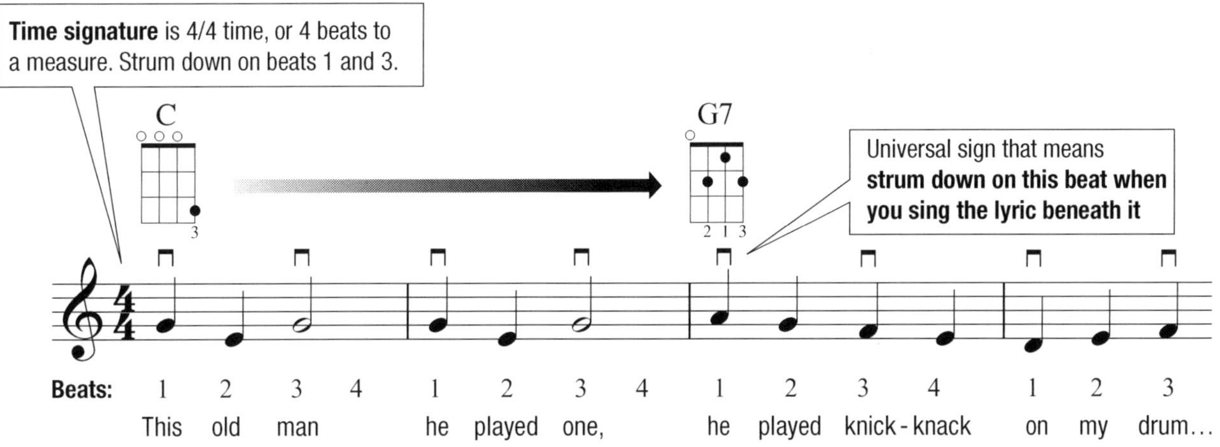

Playing Tip: Don't look at your fretting hand! Constantly looking at your fretting hand can, over time, give you neck problems and will move your ukulele out of optimal playing position. Keep your eyes on the music and not your hands. The moment you take your eyes away from the music to look at your fretting hand, you will be off tempo because it will take time to find the place you left off in the music. Try feeling and listening instead of looking. If the chord doesn't sound right, feel around with your left hand until you find the correct position. If you still can't find the chord, take a peek and readjust your fingers.

Introductory Songs

Songs 1-5 are all about learning to do two things in rhythm:

1. Change chords
2. Strum in rhythm

Don't worry about playing the melody notes in any of these songs because:

- At this point, you don't know any notes.
- Lessons 1 through 4 will teach you to play the C scale. Once you have learned to read the scale, you will be able to revisit these songs and play the melody notes as well as the chords.

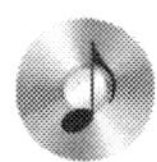

1. Row Your Boat

TRACK 1

Woo-hoo! This is your first song—chosen because it is a one-chord song! It will teach you how to strum the C chord rhythmically in 3/4 time (three beats in each measure). To practice this song:

- Strum down with your thumb, index, or middle finger on beat 1 of each measure.
- Don't worry about playing the notes in this song. We will work on that in later lessons.

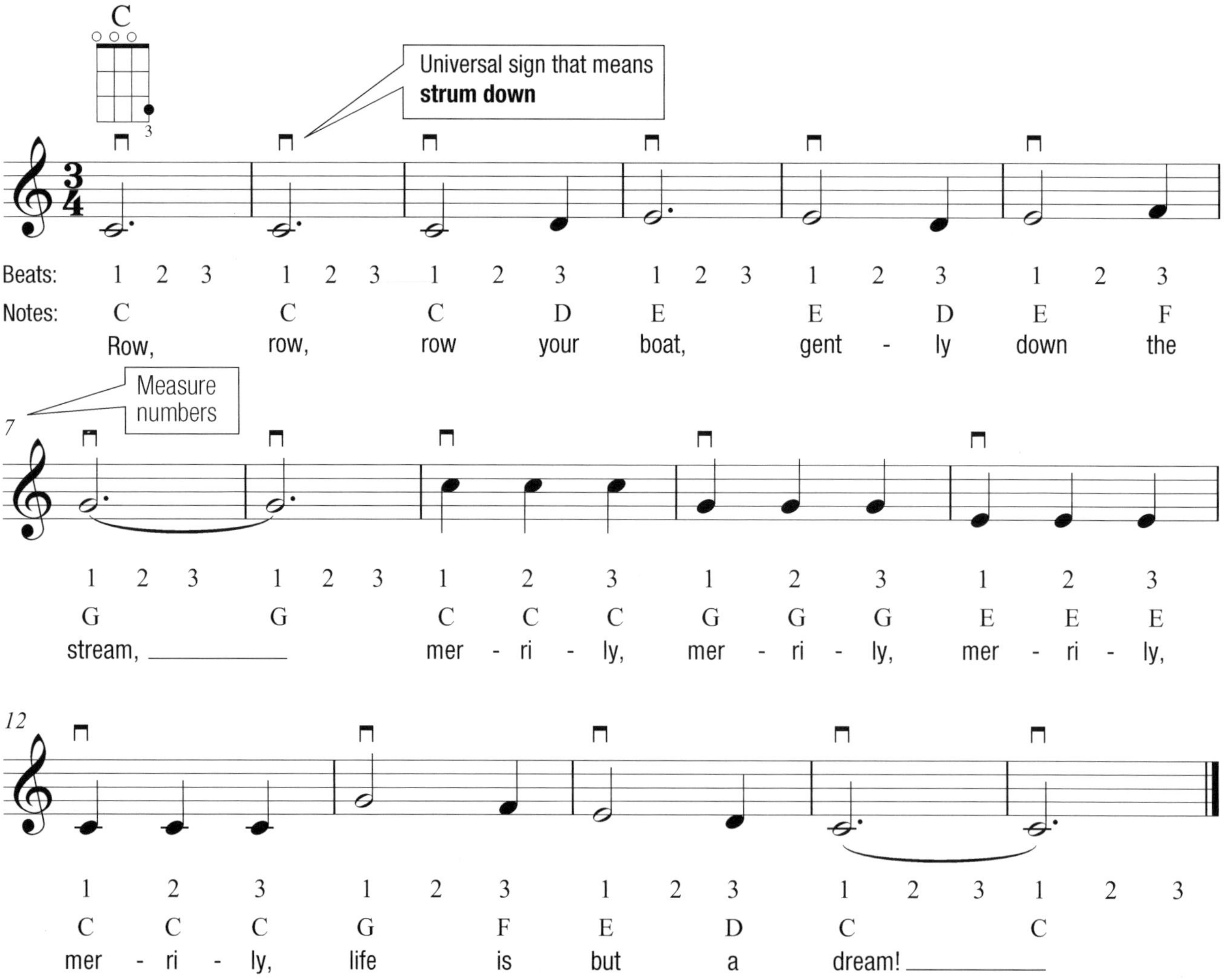

C

Universal sign that means **strum down**

Beats: 1 2 3 | 1 2 3 | 1 2 3 | 1 2 3 | 1 2 3 | 1 2 3

Notes: C | C | C D | E | E D | E F

Row, | row, | row your | boat, | gent - ly | down the

Measure numbers

7

1 2 3 | 1 2 3 | 1 2 3 | 1 2 3 | 1 2 3

G | G | C C C | G G G | E E E

stream, ______ | | mer - ri - ly, | mer - ri - ly, | mer - ri - ly,

12

1 2 3 | 1 2 3 | 1 2 3 | 1 2 3 | 1 2 3

C C C | G F | E D | C | C

mer - ri - ly, | life is | but a | dream! ______ |

2. Frère Jacques

Here is another one-chord song. It will teach you how to strum the C chord rhythmically in 4/4 Time (four beats in each measure).

To practice this song:

- Strum down with your thumb, index or middle finger on beats 1 and 3 of each measure. In this arrangement, instead of putting a C chord at the beginning of the song (like in **"1. Row Your Boat" on page 18**), I put a C chord over each strum down mark. This is to help beginners learn to strum down on beats 1 and 3 in 4/4 time.
- Don't worry about playing the notes in this song. You'll work on that in later lessons.

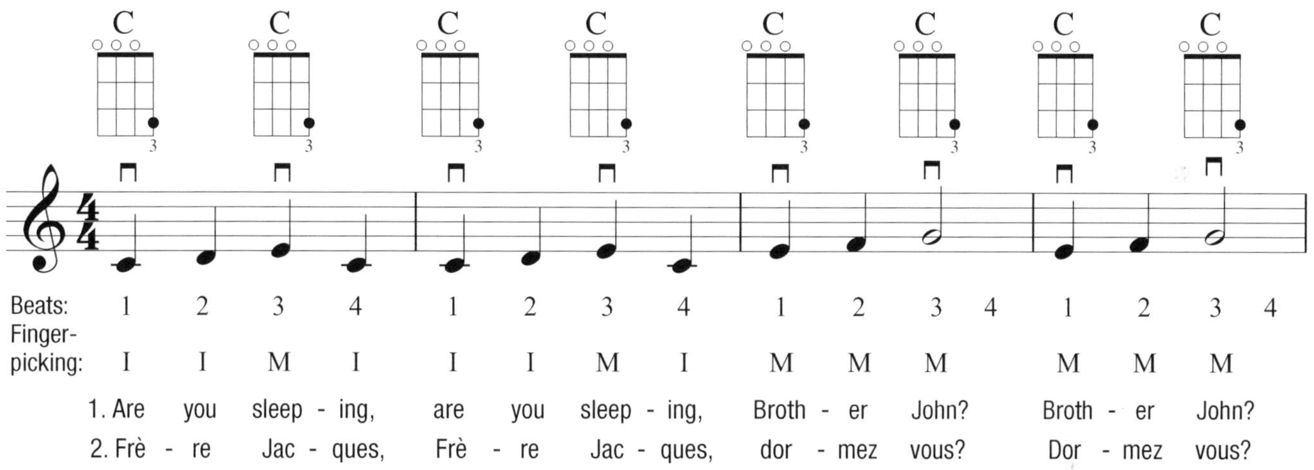

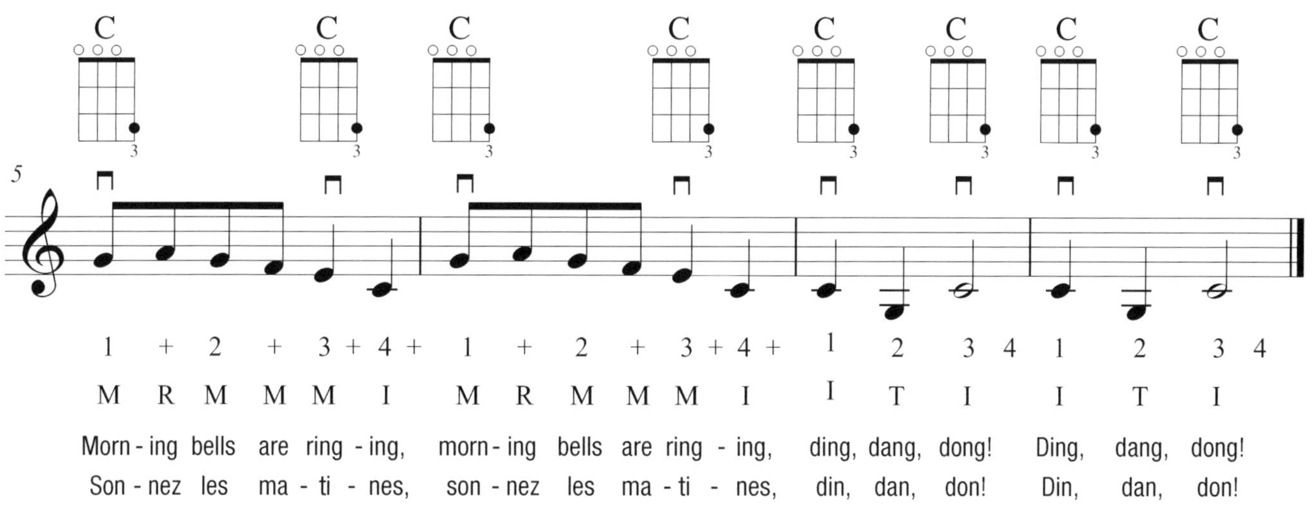

3. This Old Man

TRACK 3

- In this song you will learn to move smoothly from the C to the G7 chord.
- Don't worry about playing the notes. You'll work on that in a later lesson.
- Don't look at your left hand as you change chords. Train yourself to watch the music.
- **Strum down with your thumb, index or middle finger on beats 1 and 3 of each measure.**

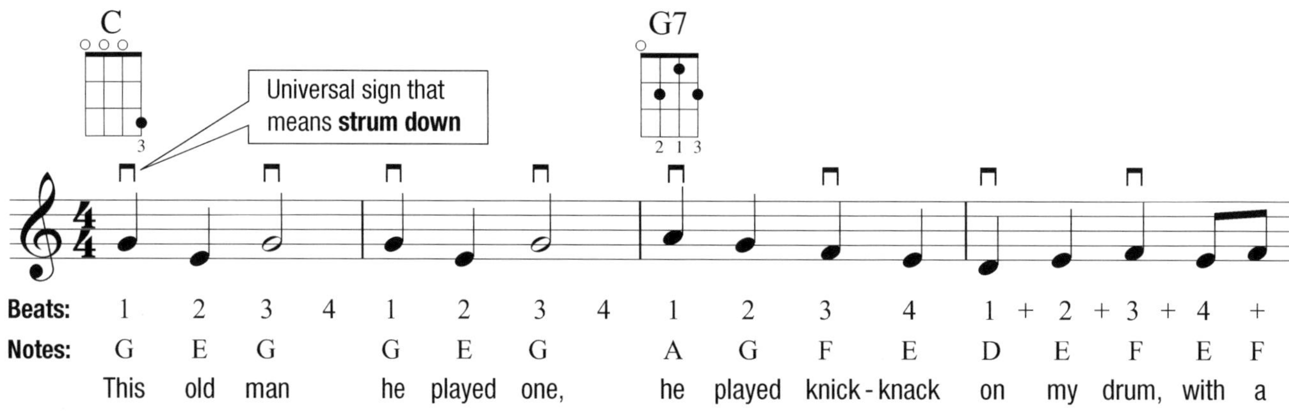

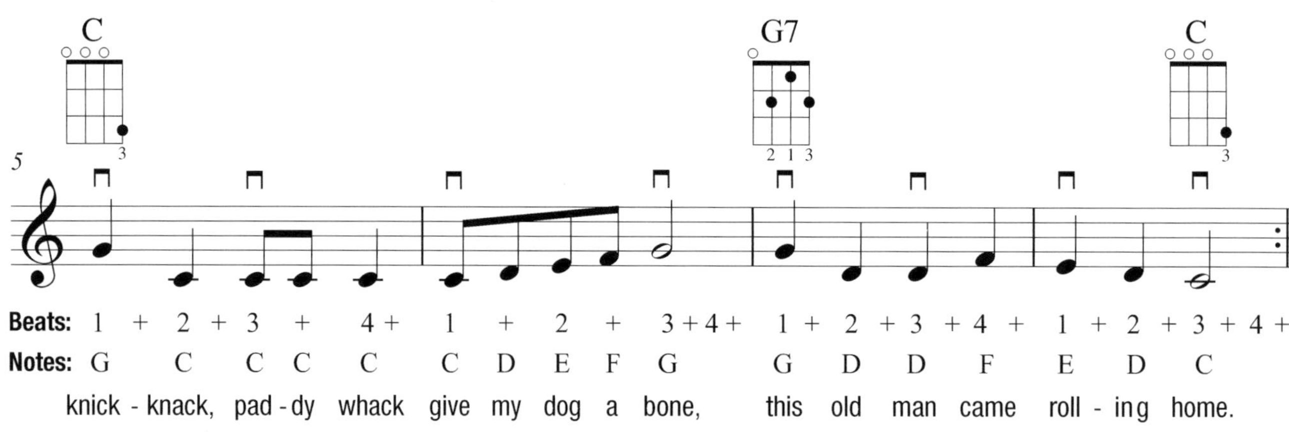

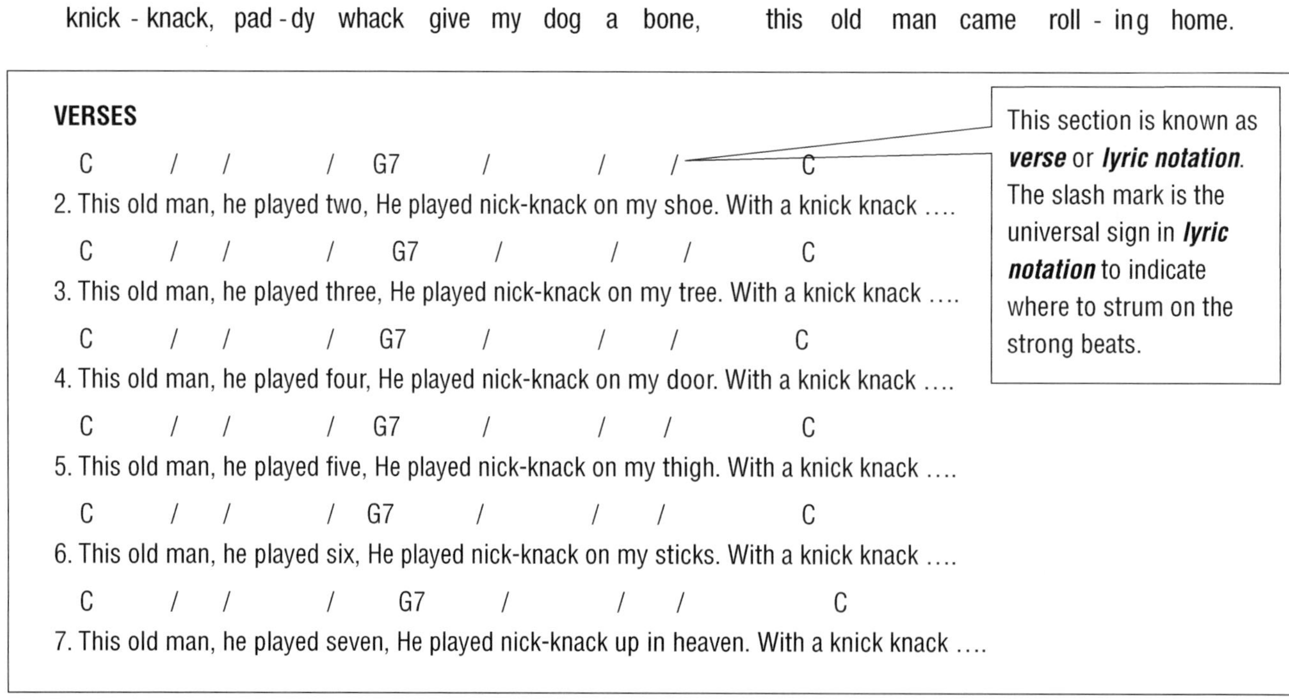

VERSES

C / / / G7 / / / C
2. This old man, he played two, He played nick-knack on my shoe. With a knick knack ….

C / / / G7 / / / C
3. This old man, he played three, He played nick-knack on my tree. With a knick knack ….

C / / / G7 / / / C
4. This old man, he played four, He played nick-knack on my door. With a knick knack ….

C / / / G7 / / / C
5. This old man, he played five, He played nick-knack on my thigh. With a knick knack ….

C / / / G7 / / / C
6. This old man, he played six, He played nick-knack on my sticks. With a knick knack ….

C / / / G7 / / / C
7. This old man, he played seven, He played nick-knack up in heaven. With a knick knack ….

This section is known as ***verse*** or ***lyric notation***. The slash mark is the universal sign in ***lyric notation*** to indicate where to strum on the strong beats.

4. He's Got the Whole World in His Hands

TRACK 4

- In this song you will learn to move smoothly from the C to the G7 chord.
- Don't worry about playing the notes. You'll work on that in a later lesson.
- Don't look at your left hand as you change chords. Train yourself to watch the music.
- **Strum down with your thumb, index or middle finger on beats 1 and 3 of each measure.**

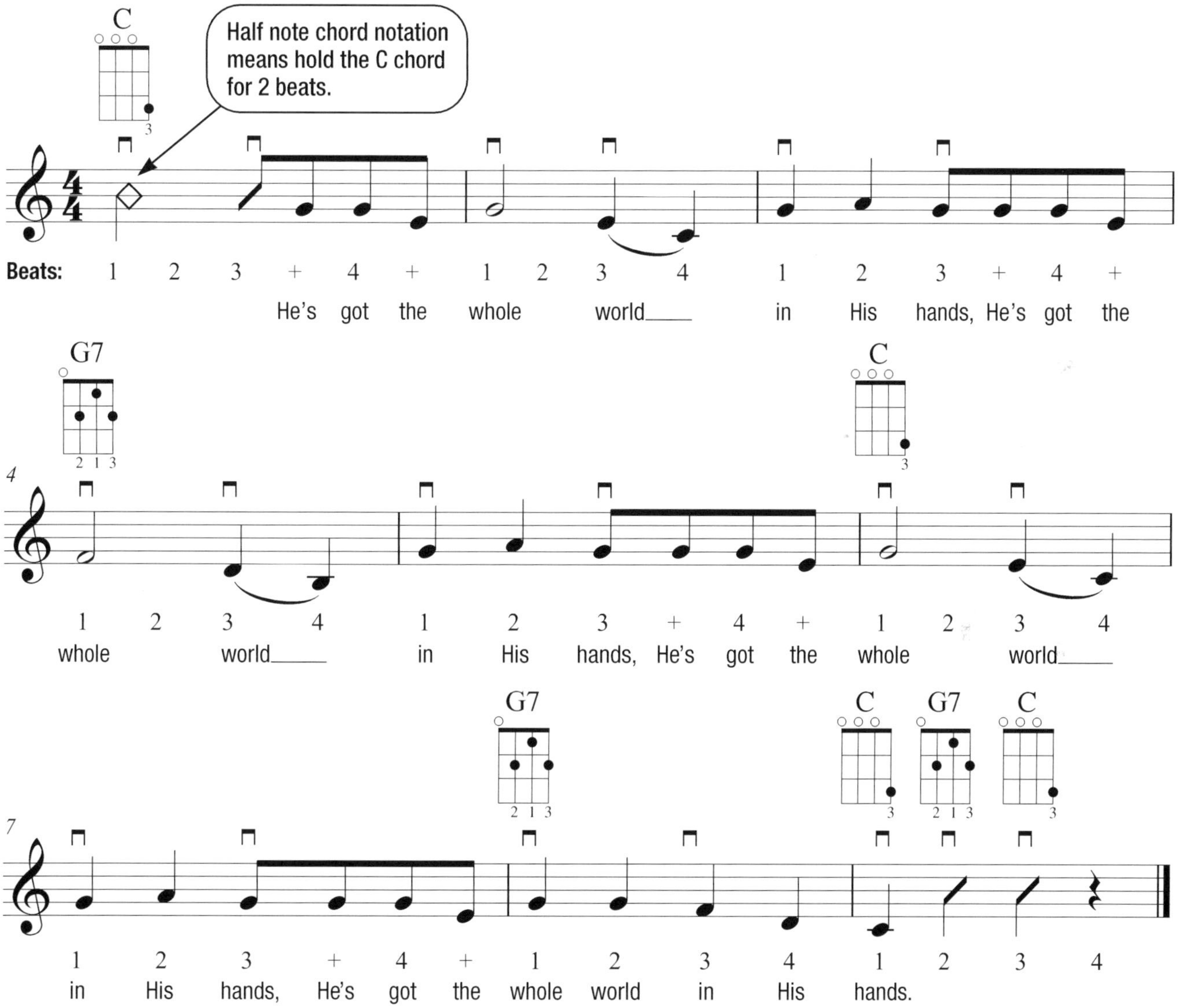

C

Half note chord notation means hold the C chord for 2 beats.

Beats: 1 2 3 + 4 + 1 2 3 4 1 2 3 + 4 +

He's got the whole world___ in His hands, He's got the

G7 C

4

1 2 3 4 1 2 3 + 4 + 1 2 3 4

whole world___ in His hands, He's got the whole world___

G7 C G7 C

7

1 2 3 + 4 + 1 2 3 4 1 2 3 4

in His hands, He's got the whole world in His hands.

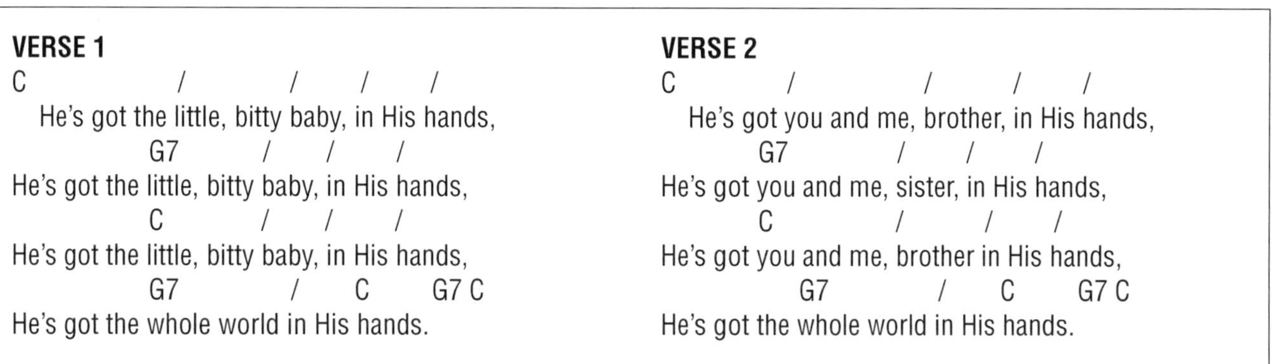

VERSE 1

C / / / /
He's got the little, bitty baby, in His hands,
G7 / / /
He's got the little, bitty baby, in His hands,
C / / /
He's got the little, bitty baby, in His hands,
G7 / C G7 C
He's got the whole world in His hands.

VERSE 2

C / / / /
He's got you and me, brother, in His hands,
G7 / / /
He's got you and me, sister, in His hands,
C / / /
He's got you and me, brother in His hands,
G7 / C G7 C
He's got the whole world in His hands.

5. Hush Little Baby

TRACK 5

- In this song you will learn to move smoothly from the C to the G7 chord.
- Don't worry about playing the notes. You'll work on that in a later lesson.
- Don't look at your left hand as you change chords. Train yourself to watch the music.
- **Strum down with your thumb, index or middle finger on beats 1 and 3 of each measure.**

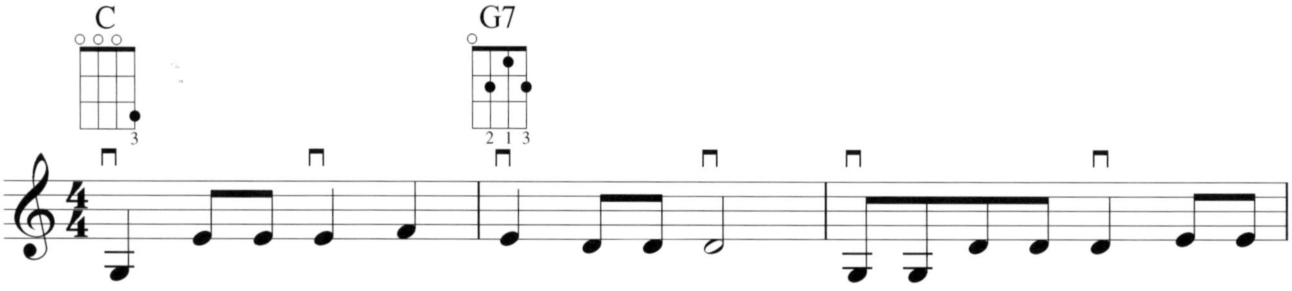

C G7

Beats: 1 + 2 + 3 + 4 + 1 + 2 + 3 + 4 + 1 + 2 + 3 + 4 +

Finger-picking: T M M M M M I I I T T I I I M M

1. Hush lit - tle ba - by, don't say a word, Pa - pa's gon - na buy you a
2. if that dia - mond ring turns brass, Pa - pa's gon - na buy you a
3. if that bil - ly goat won't pull, Pa - pa's gon - na buy you a
4. if that dog named Rover won't bark, Pa - pa's gon - na buy you a

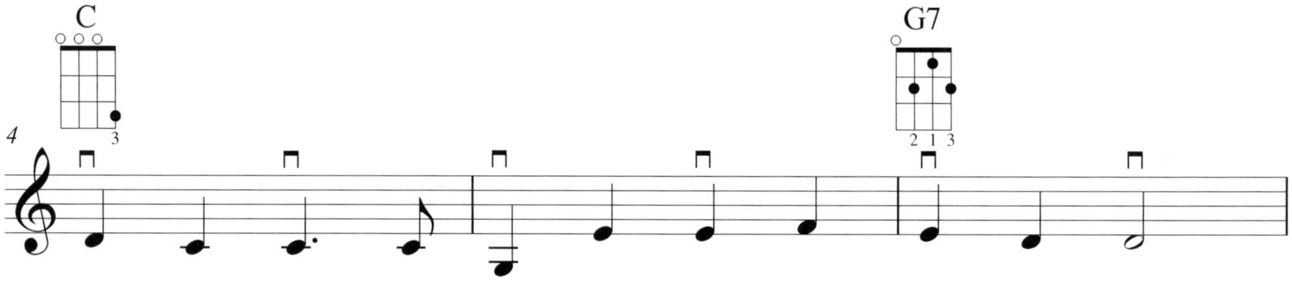

C G7

4

1 + 2 + 3 + 4 + 1 + 2 + 3 + 4 + 1 + 2 + 3 + 4 +

I I I I T M M M M I I

mock - ing - bird. And if that mock - ing - bird don't sing,
look - ing - glass. And if that look - ing - glass gets broke,
cart and bull. And if that cart and bull turn over,
horse and cart. And if that horse and cart fall down,

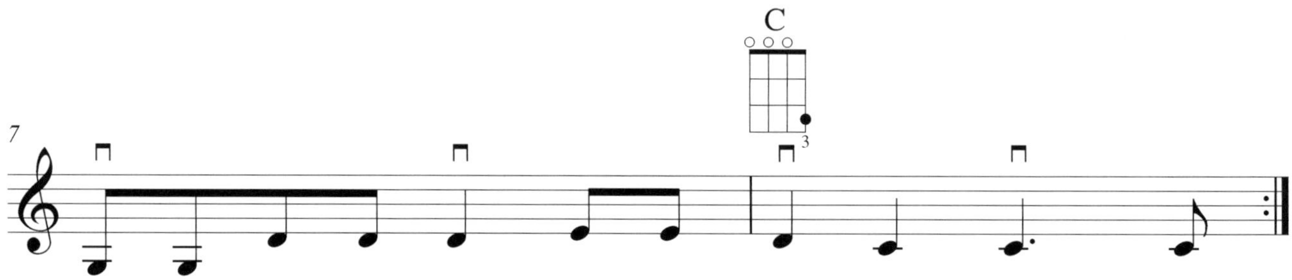

C

7

1 + 2 + 3 + 4 + 1 + 2 + 3 + 4 +

T T I I I M M I I I I

Pa - pa's gon - na buy you a dia - mond ring. 2. And
Pa - pa's gon - na buy you a bil - ly goat. 3. And
Pa - pa's gon - na buy you a dog named Rover. 4. And
you'll still be the sweetest lit - tle baby in town.

Lesson 1

Assignment

Instructor Note: *Depending on the individual student's or class ability, the content in this lesson may be assigned over several weeks. Advise students to keep a Weekly Practice Log* (**page 180**).

1. **Musical Staff and Notation:** Memorize and explain the...
   A. Difference between a note and a chord (**page 14**)
   B. Names of the notes on the lines and spaces (**page 25**)
   C. G Clef—be able to draw it on a staff (**page 27**)
   D. Difference between melody and harmony notes / Notes and their rhythmic values (**page 28**)
   E. Two numbers in a time signature—be able to write a time signature on a staff (**page 29**)
   F. C and D notes—be able to draw them on a staff (**page 40**)

2. **Musical Practice:**
   A. **Learn:**
      1) **C major and G7 major chords fretting road map practice:** Practice fretting without strumming. Do not look at your left hand as you practice switching your left hand fingers between the C and G7 chords. As you do this, make sure to slide your left hand 3rd finger on the 3rd fret (A string, C note) to the 2nd fret (A string, B note) to help guide your fingers to the rest of the notes in the G7 chord. Practice silent fretting until you are confident. Then, strum down every time you change chords (**page 16**).
      2) **Songs in introduction:** As you practice, strum down on the 1 and 3 beat for songs in 4/4 time; on the 1 beat for the songs in 3/4 time. Practice singing and playing simultaneously (**pages 18-22**).
      3) **C and D notes:** (**page 33**)
      4) **Fingerpicking practice:**
         a) Play the C and G7 chords as block chords (**page 36**) using the one-finger-one-string method (**page 30**).
         b) Next practice playing a block C chord. Let it resonate while you use your right hand index finger to pick out the middle C note. Do the same with the G7 chord and the D note (**page 36**).
         c) Combining melody and chords exercises (**pages 36-38**).
      5) **Count while reading music:** (See **"You've Got Rhythm... Out Loud!" on page 31**.)

3. **Written Exercises:** *(Please use a pencil for the following exercises)*
   A. **Write the Treble Clef** (**page 27**)
   B. **Write 4/4 and 3/4 Time** (**page 29**)
   C. **What's My Line?** (**page 39**)
   D. **Note Writing: Middle C and D Notes with Beats** (**page 40**)

READING MUSIC ON YOUR UKE

Reading Music is not Rocket Science!

But, it will blast you off to new worlds of music that you might never have imagined you could visit. Reading music enables you to:

- Play a piece of music you have never *heard* before
- "Sight-read" music, which means play a piece of music the first time you see it as easily as you read a magazine
- Learn a wide variety of musical styles on your uke including Hawai'ian, country western, bluegrass, blues, rock, folk, flamenco, classical, and world music
- Play easily with other musicians
- Write your own music
- Learn to play other instruments

The Musical Alphabet

The musical alphabet has 7 letter names that repeat starting on the letter C:

C – D – E – F – G – A – B
1 2 3 4 5 6 7

If you can say it, you can play it! Memorize the musical alphabet by saying it forwards to represent the notes going up a scale and backwards to represent the notes going down the scale. Memorizing the note names backwards is easy because they spell "bag" and "fed" with C notes surrounding the words.

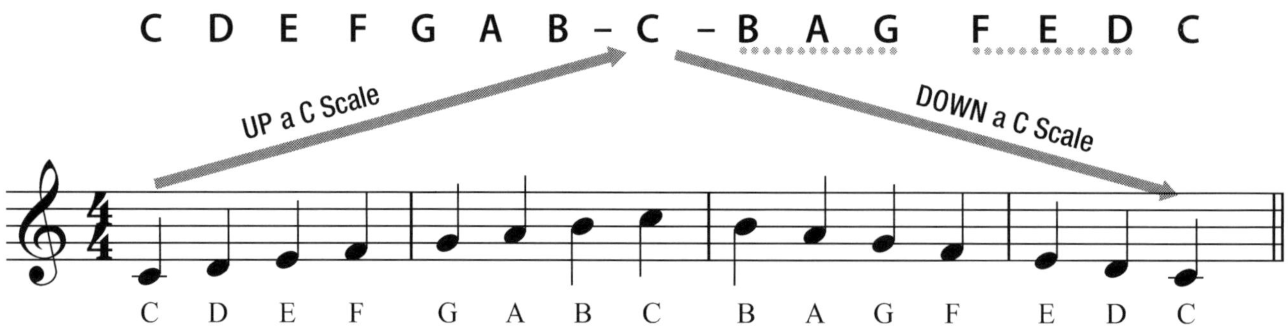

Music Notation

Music notation is a system for writing music that tells the musician two things:

1. **Pitch** or sound of a note
2. **Rhythm** of the note, or how long a note is held

The Musical Staff

Music notation for the ukulele, like all other instruments, is written on either a *musical staff* or in *tablature*. You will learn about tablature in **"How to Read Tablature" on page 45**.

The musical staff for the ukulele is known as a standard staff. The *standard staff* is also used for other fretted instruments including the guitar, banjo, and mandolin.

- **Lines and spaces:** The staff has 5 equally spaced horizontal lines. Musical notes are written on the lines and in the spaces.
- **Lines and spaces have names:** Each line and space has a specific letter name that corresponds to a specific pitch, or sound.
- **Notes:** Notes are placed on a line or in a space to indicate a specific pitch on the staff. Notes also tell us how long to hold each note... 1 beat, 2 beats, etc.
- **How to remember the note names:** The easiest way to memorize note names and their position on the staff is to learn two nonsense acronyms. The first represents the notes on the lines and the second represents the notes in the spaces.

Lines:

Spaces:

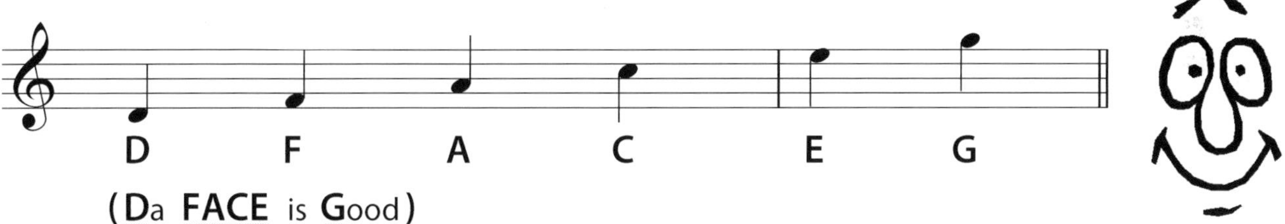

The difference between *high* and *low* notes on the staff

Notes positioned lower on the staff have lower pitches or sound. Notes positioned higher on the staff have higher pitches. Look below and compare the C note on the line under the staff to the higher C note in the third space. Both notes are C notes, but the lower C has a lower pitch and the higher C note has a higher pitch. These notes are eight notes apart, which means they are an "octave" apart.

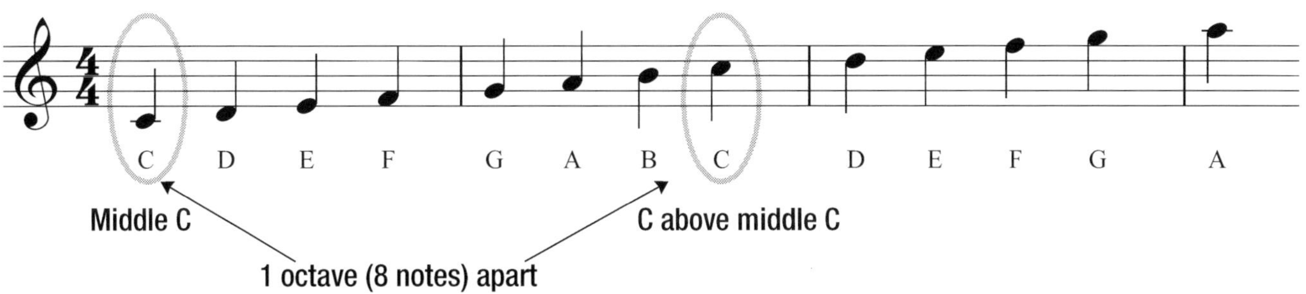

Notes that don't fit on the staff

The 5 lines and 4 spaces of standard staff plus the space underneath the lowest line and the space on top of the highest line represent 11 notes on the ukulele. But the uke also has notes that are higher and lower than those 11. These are written with *ledger lines* above and below the staff. Look at the example below: the C note at the bottom, known as "Middle C" is written on a ledger line below the staff. The high A note is written on a ledger line above the staff.

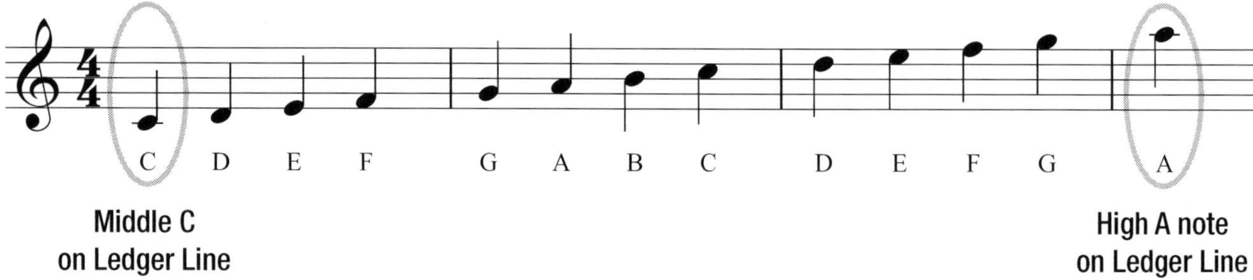

What is a Measure or Bar?

- The musical staff is separated into sections by measures or bars.
- The lines separating the measures or bars are known as bar lines.

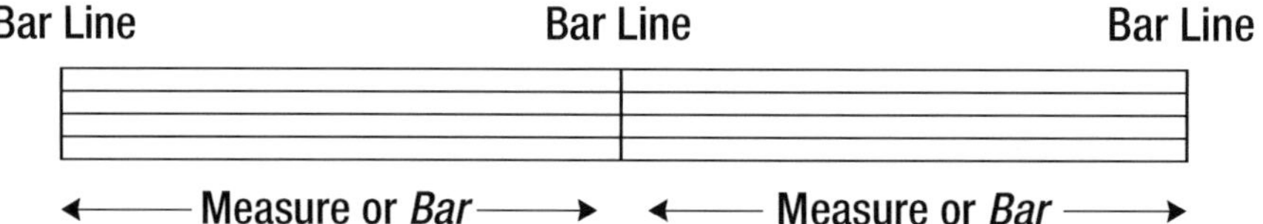

- **Double bar line** at the end of a staff means the song ends.
- **Two dots before a double bar line** means repeat from the beginning of the song.
- **Two repeat signs within a song** mean repeat all the music between the measures.

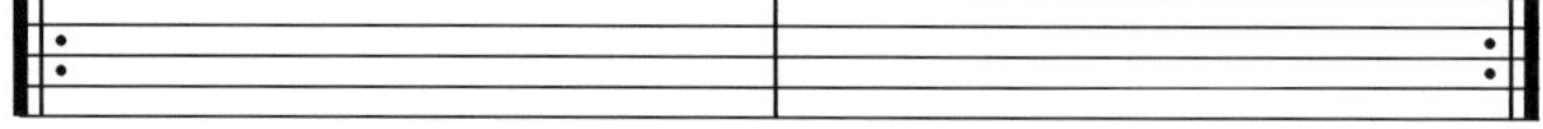

The Clef

"Clef" means "key" in French. The musical *clef* is a figure at the beginning of a staff that gives the starting point for finding notes on the staff.

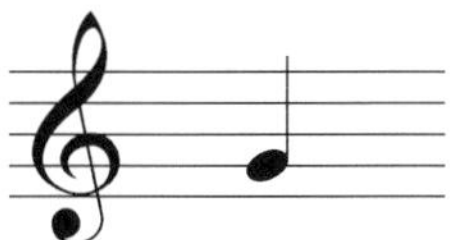

The G Clef: The clef used for ukulele music is known as the G Clef because the bottom half curls around the G line, or second line of the staff.

The G clef curls around the G note line

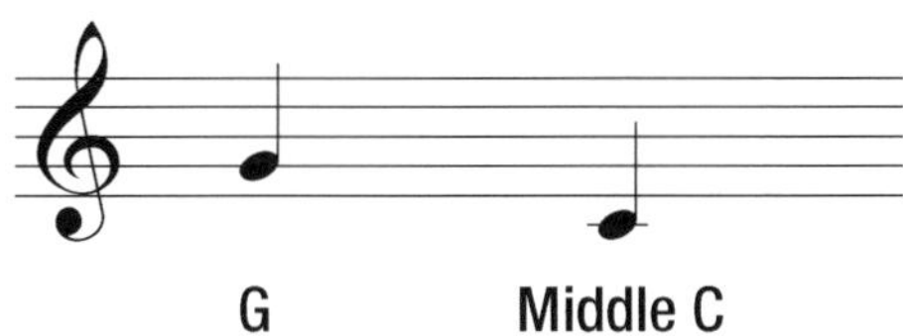

This note position is also known as "G above middle C."

Other G Clef Facts:

- It's also called the soprano or treble clef because it shows the range of notes sung by a soprano or higher voice.
- It shows a range of notes that is above and slightly below middle C.
- Middle C on the G Clef staff is the same pitch as the C string on your ukulele.

EXERCISE: Practice writing the treble clef

Practice drawing a treble clef in each measure below:

1. Trace this treble clef sign.

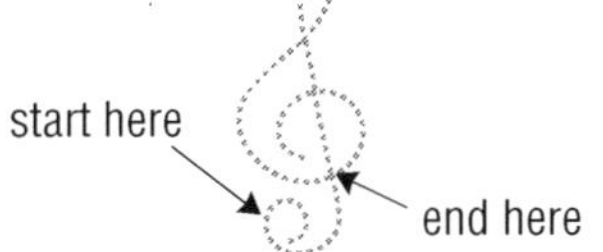

2. Trace these treble clef signs. Begin below the staff. Curl the end of the sign around the G line.

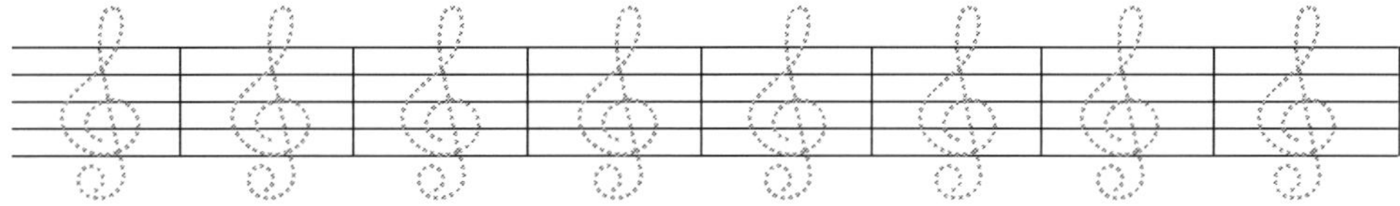

The difference between a melody and a harmony

A ***melody*** is a series of single notes played or sung one after another.

Lyrics: This old man he played one, he played knick - knack on my drum...

A ***harmony*** is a combination of notes sung or played at the same time. The notes in a chord make a harmony. Harmony supports the notes of a melody. For example, when you sing and play chords on the ukulele, your voice is singing the melody and the ukulele supplies the harmony. The "melody line" may also be played by another instrument.

Notes and Their Rhythmic Values

As you have just learned, the position of a note on a line or in a space within the staff gives the letter name and pitch of the note. Notes also tell us how long, or how many beats, to hold a pitch. This is indicated by the type of note used. Each type of note has a specific "rhythmic value":

TYPES OF NOTES	Count the beats as you clap the note values in each rhythm below.
 Count Beats **Quarter Note = 1 beat** (Hold each note for 1 beat.)	 Clap Note Value 1 2 3 4 1 2 3 4 Clap quarter notes each time you count a beat.
 **Half Note = 2 beats** (Hold each note for 2 beats.)	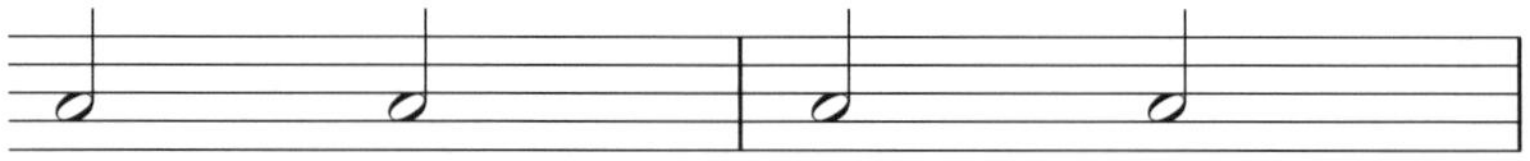 1 2 3 4 1 2 3 4 Clap half notes on the 1 and 3 beats.
 **Dotted Half Note = 3 beats** (Hold each note for 3 beats.)	 1 2 3 1 2 3 Clap dotted half notes on the 1 beat.
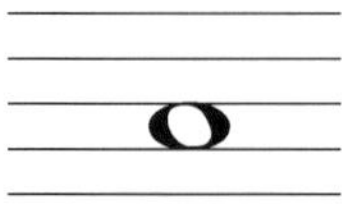 **Whole Note = 4 beats** (Hold each note for 4 beats.)	 1 2 3 4 1 2 3 4 Clap whole notes on the 1 beat.

The Time Signature

A *time signature* is set up like a fraction and appears at the beginning of each piece of music after the clef sign. A time signature tells you two things:

1. The **top number** indicates the number of beats in each measure.
2. The **bottom number** indicates the type of note that gets one beat or count.

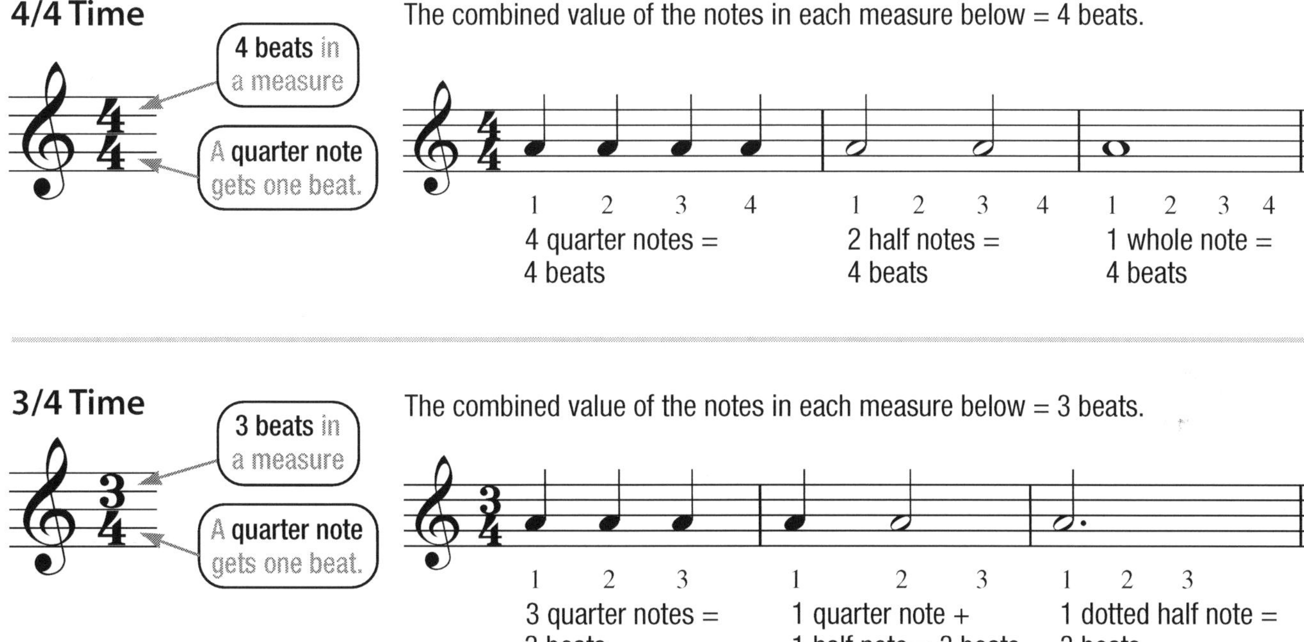

Practice writing time signatures:

1. Practice writing a 4/4 time signature above each 4/4.

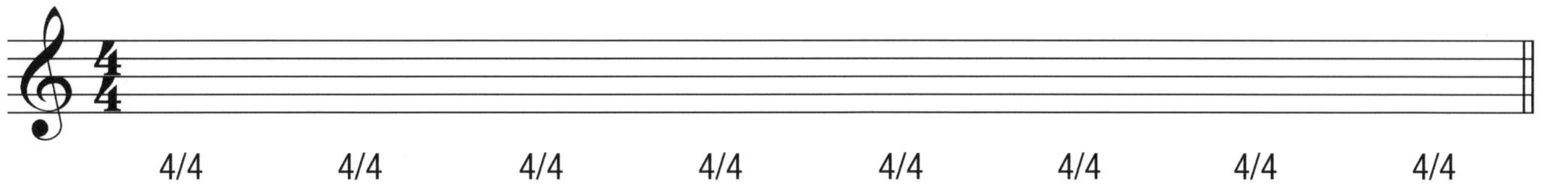

2. Practice writing a 3/4 time signature above each 3/4.

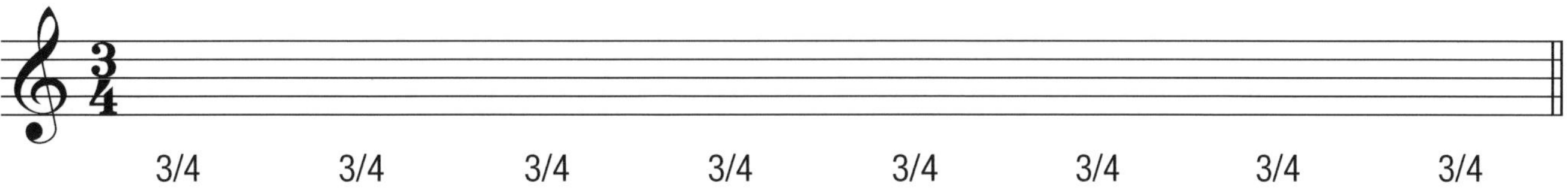

INTRODUCING FINGERPICKING

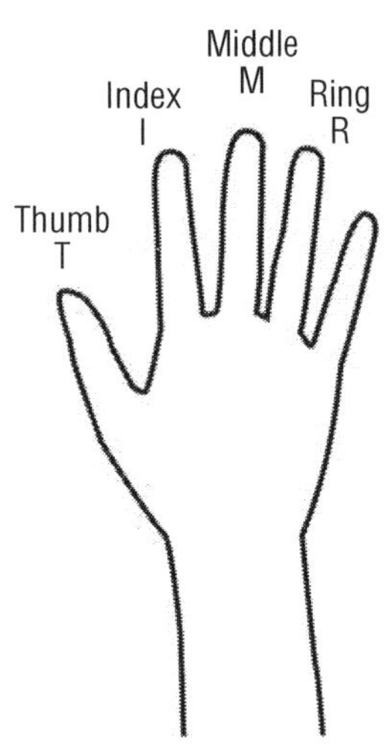

Before you start learning to read notes on your ukulele, I would like to teach you the basics of fingerpicking because learning to pick individual strings with individual fingers enables you to play melody notes, or "lead" ukulele. In this book, I teach classical-style, one finger/one string fingerpicking. There are two other popular ways to fingerpick a uke. Many people fingerpick all the strings with their thumb and hold the uke with their remaining right hand fingers. Others fingerpick all the strings with the thumb and index finger. Both techniques work. But, they don't give you the same technical foundation for speed, agility, and accuracy that classical style does for playing a wide range of musical styles. Classical style fingerpicking puts the "umph" into a variety of genres ranging from Hawai'ian slack key, to blues, pop, reggae, folk, classical, jazz, and much more. Simply put:

Classical-style fingerpicking = economy of motion

In this book the right hand fingers are named: T = Thumb I = Index M = Middle R = Ring

Arm, Wrist and Right Hand Position Do's and Don'ts

Correct: Forearm and Wrist Fingerpicking Position

- **Your wrist flows out of your forearm** in a long, straight line.
- **Hover your palm and wrist above the fretboard** by anchoring your forearm over the ukulele soundboard near the top of the hip.
- **There should always be space** between your wrist and the soundboard.
- **Your forearm, wrist, and hand remain stationary** once your hand position is correct. The only thing that moves are your fingers.

Incorrect: Bent Wrist Position

- **This wrist is unnaturally bent.** Playing this way for an extended period of time could cause tendonitis or carpal tunnel syndrome.

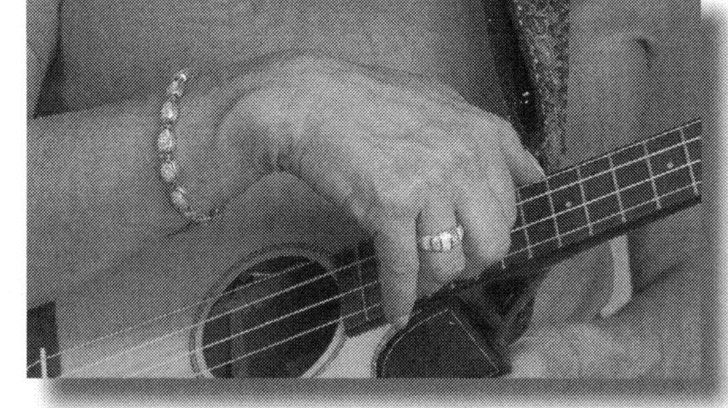

Incorrect: Resting Wrist Position

- **This wrist is resting against the soundboard.** Playing this way for an extended period of time could also cause tendonitis or carpal tunnel syndrome because it puts too much pressure on your wrist.

Right Hand Fingers: How to Position and Play

Right Hand Fingers	Strings
T or Thumb plays the Low **G** string • **Position**: Thumb is always extended and points toward the head of the uke at all times. • **Motion**: Moves only from the joint nearest the palm in a circular, rotating, down-up motion toward the string and then away. • **Pick with the left side of the fingernail.** Do not pick the G string with a bent knuckle.	**Low G**
I or Index finger plays the **C** string • **Position**: Fingertip points toward your wrist. Knuckle aligns with under-side of Thumb knuckle joint. • **Motion**: Move from the knuckle down only. Pick toward the palm of the hand and away from the thumb. • **Pick with the left side of the fingernail**.	**C**
M or Middle finger plays the **E** string • **Position:** Fingertip points toward your wrist. Knuckle slightly behind Index finger knuckle. • **Motion**: Move from the knuckle down only. Pick toward the palm of the hand and away from the thumb. • **Pick with the left side of the fingernail**.	**E**
R or Ring finger plays the **A** string • **Position**: Fingertip points toward your wrist. Knuckle slightly behind Middle finger knuckle. • **Motion**: Move from the knuckle down only. Pick toward the palm of the hand and away from the thumb. • **Pick with the left side of the fingernail**.	**A**

You've Got Rhythm... Out Loud!

You may have heard a musician in a band shout out, "one, two, three, four!" before starting a song. That is called giving "one measure for nothing." The lead musician is acting like a conductor by giving the band the tempo or speed at which they will play. You can also think of the conductor as a live metronome. A metronome is a machine that keeps a beat for musicians.

When you play your uke as a solo instrument, you have to act as your own conductor to keep a steady beat. To do this you must learn to count rhythm. This is particularly important if you want to play with other musicians. Strange as this may sound, playing a wrong note here or there is forgiven by most audiences as long as your rhythm is correct.

***Count the rhythm out loud* when you practice**. This will help you learn to read music faster and become a better sight-reader. It will also help you internalize the rhythm of any piece you learn, and make you a better performer. It really works!

> As one 10-year-old student put it, "Counting while playing is like learning how to walk, chew gum and talk at the same time. But once you learn how, counting makes difficult music easier to play the first time you pick up a piece."

"One Measure for Nothing" Technique:

1. First determine the *time signature*.
2. Then before playing, *count* one measure "for nothing" to set the tempo you will keep throughout the piece. Start at a tempo that will enable you to comfortably play the most challenging passages without slowing down. Playing at an extremely slow tempo while first learning a piece gets you in the habit of playing in good rhythm. As you improve and bring the music up to its proper tempo, you won't slow down when you play sections you previously thought challenging because you will have mastered them.
3. **Before playing in:**
   - **3/4 time say**, "**1, 2, Play**" or "**1, 2, 3**"
   - **4/4 time say**, "**1, 2, 3, Play**" or "**1, 2, 3, 4**"

Introducing Notes on the C String

Middle C and D Notes

Note Diagram Key: o = play the string open, or no fingers on any frets x = do not play the string • = fret with a fingertip

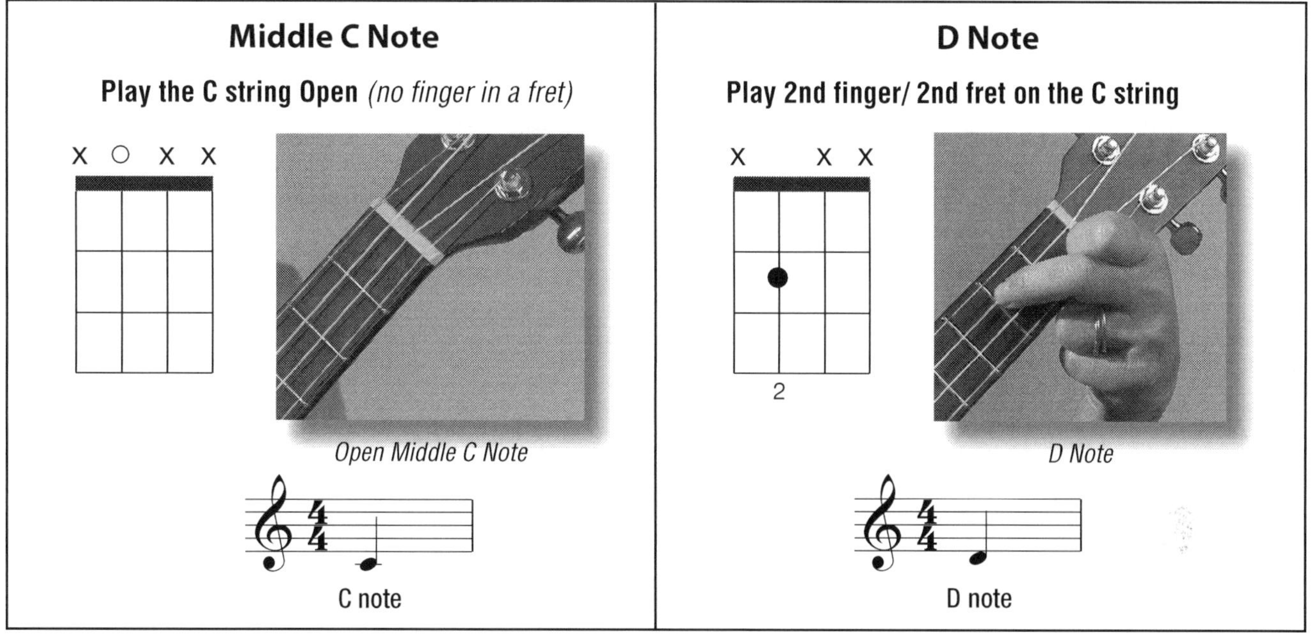

Right hand fingerpicking for C and D notes:

Fingerpicking: I or Index finger plays the C String.

- Index fingertip points toward your wrist. Knuckle aligns with underside of Thumb knuckle joint.
- Play with the left side of index fingernail.

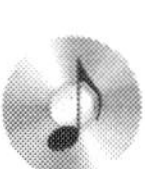

1. C and D Away We Go!

TRACK 6

- Before playing, count four for nothing: 1, 2, 3, Play or 1, 2, 3, 4.
- *Continue counting out loud through the rest of the piece.*

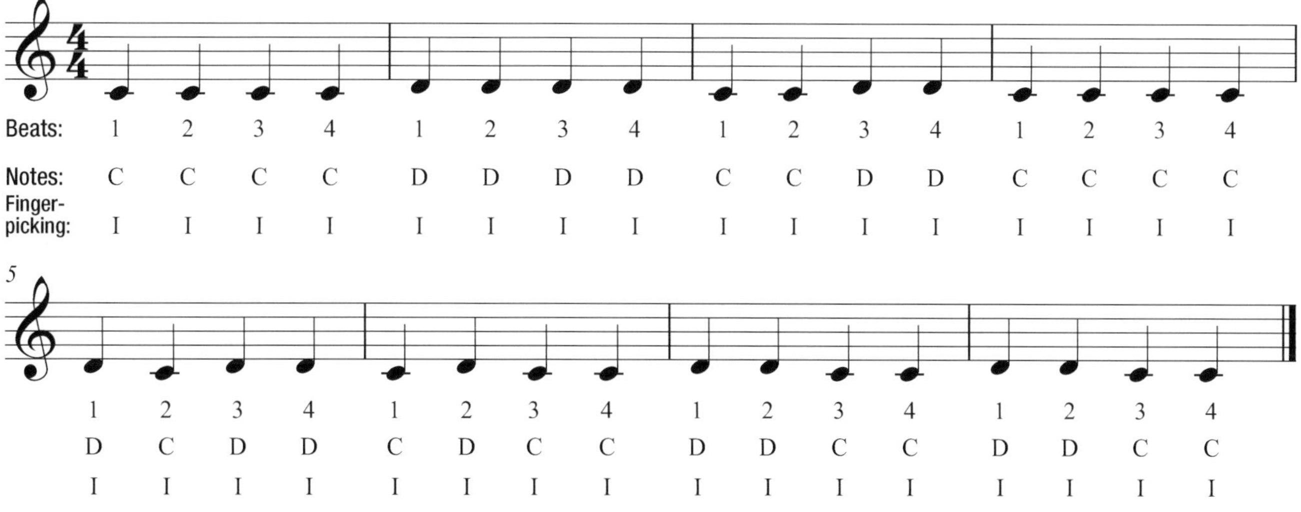

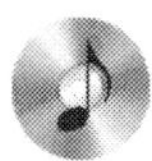

2. Take Three for C and D

TRACK 7

NOTE: Now, you'll learn to recognize and read the notes. If you like, write the names of the notes on the lines. Use pencil so you can erase them later to test yourself.

- Before playing, count three for nothing: 1, 2, Play or 1, 2, 3.
- *Continue counting out loud through the rest of the piece.*

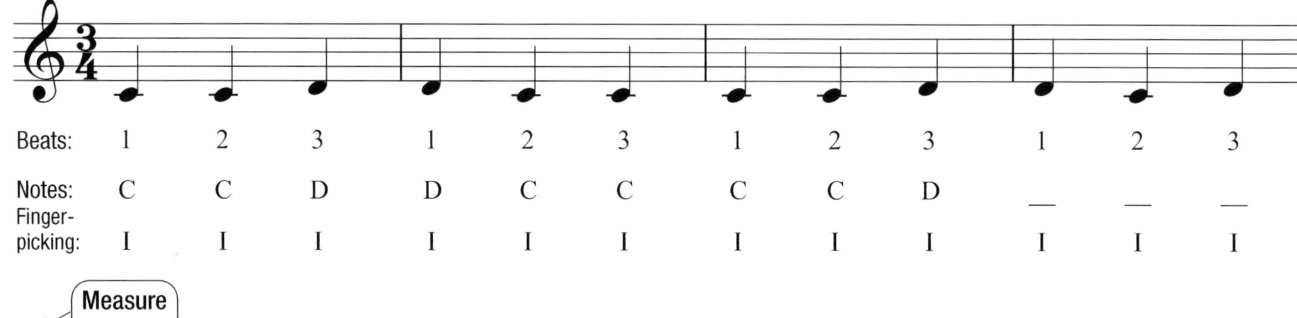

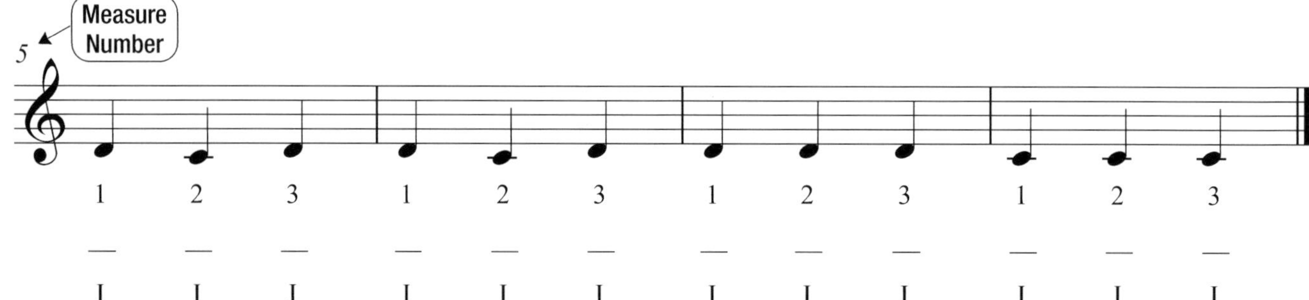

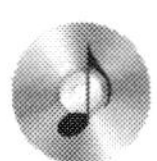

3. More Four Count C and D

TRACK 8

Remember: A half note gets 2 counts.

- Before playing, count four for nothing: 1, 2, 3, Play or 1, 2, 3, 4.
- *Continue counting out loud through the rest of the piece.*

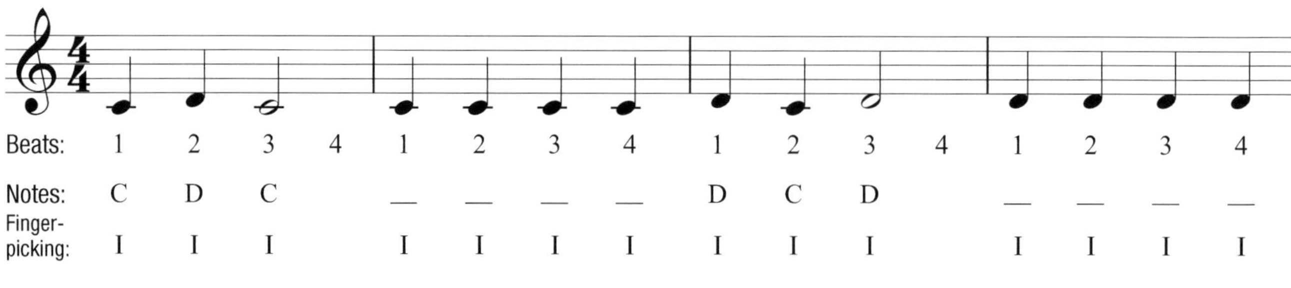

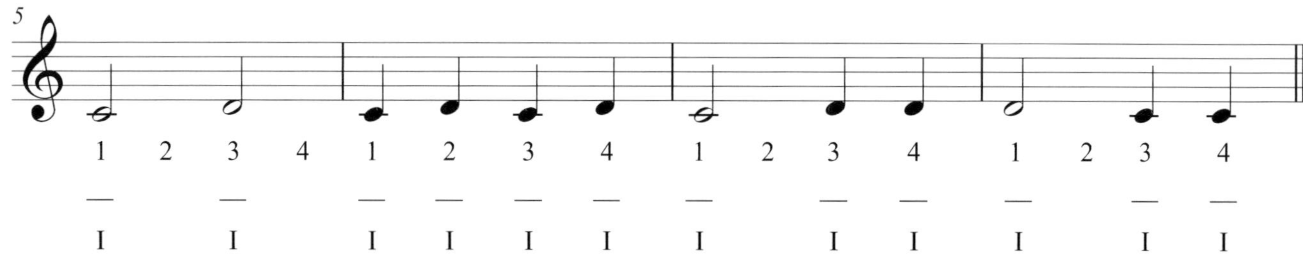

4. Three Count Caper

TRACK 9

- Before playing, count three for nothing: 1, 2, Play or 1, 2, 3.
- *Continue counting out loud through the rest of the piece.*

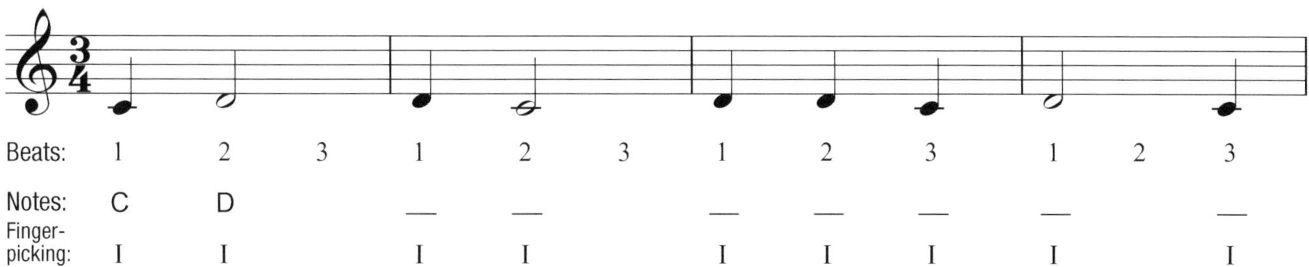

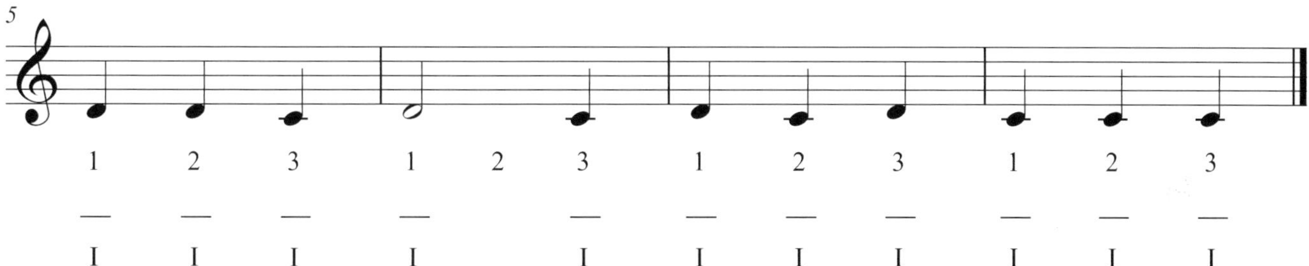

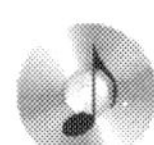

5. Last Call C and D

TRACK 10

- Before playing, count four for nothing: 1, 2, 3, Play or 1, 2, 3, 4.
- *Continue counting out loud through the rest of the piece.*

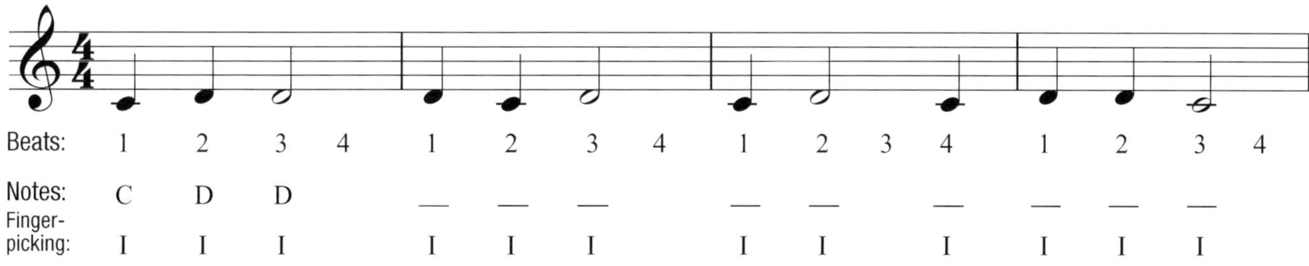

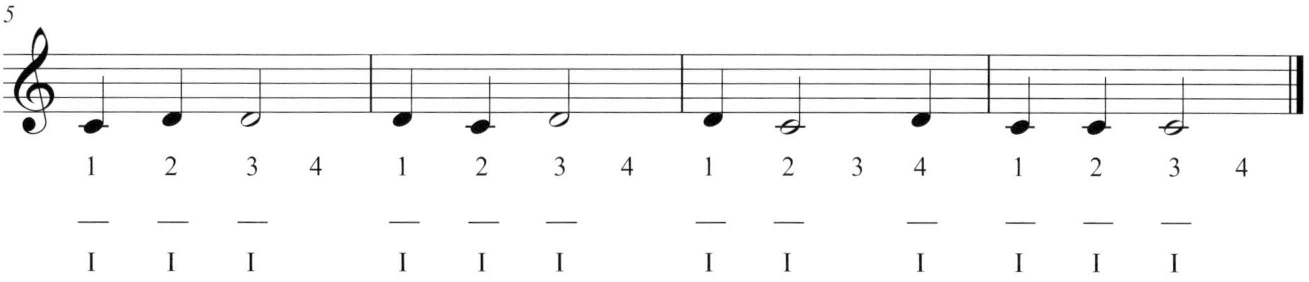

COMBINING MELODY AND CHORDS

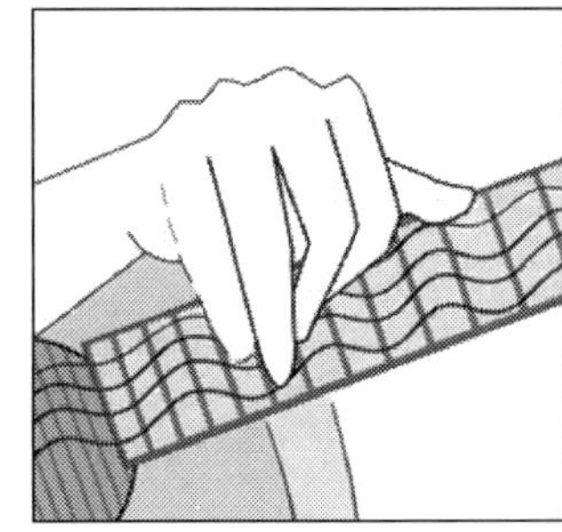

TIMR
Thumb-**I**ndex-**M**iddle-**R**ing
Pluck all strings simultaneously

You can make your uke playing sound professional by sprinkling a melody line with the chords to accompany it. Most of the melody notes are contained in the notes you are fretting for the chord. You'll get to explore this in more depth in a later lesson. Try this technique. Once you get the hang of it, you will see how natural it is to pick out a melody from the chords you are playing.

Step 1—Learn to fingerpick a *block chord:*

- All strings are plucked simultaneously with the **T**humb, **I**ndex, **M**iddle and **R**ing fingers.
- Block Chords are indicated with **TIMR** in this book.
- Position all right hand fingers on the strings:
  - Thumb is extended and points toward the head of the uke at all times.

Step 2—Fret the chord. The melody notes are usually found within:

- Look ahead to see if a chord that follows a melody line includes the note of that melody. If so, fret the chord before playing it so you can play the note, then the chord. So that you understand what to look for when fretting a chord ahead, call-out bubbles give playing technique tips throughout the music. ***The callout bubbles are like a road map for playing, so make sure to read each one when learning to play the arrangements in this book.***
- In the following music:
  - The **C chord** includes the **middle C** note you just learned.
  - The **G7 chord** includes the **D note** you just learned.

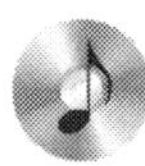

6. Find the Note in the Chord

TRACK 11

- **Chord rhythmic notation**—See **page 38** for explanation.
- The chord to be played is directly above the slash or diamond. Play that chord until a new chord is indicated.
- Before playing, count four for nothing: 1, 2, 3, Play or 1, 2, 3, 4.
- *Continue counting out loud through the rest of the piece.*

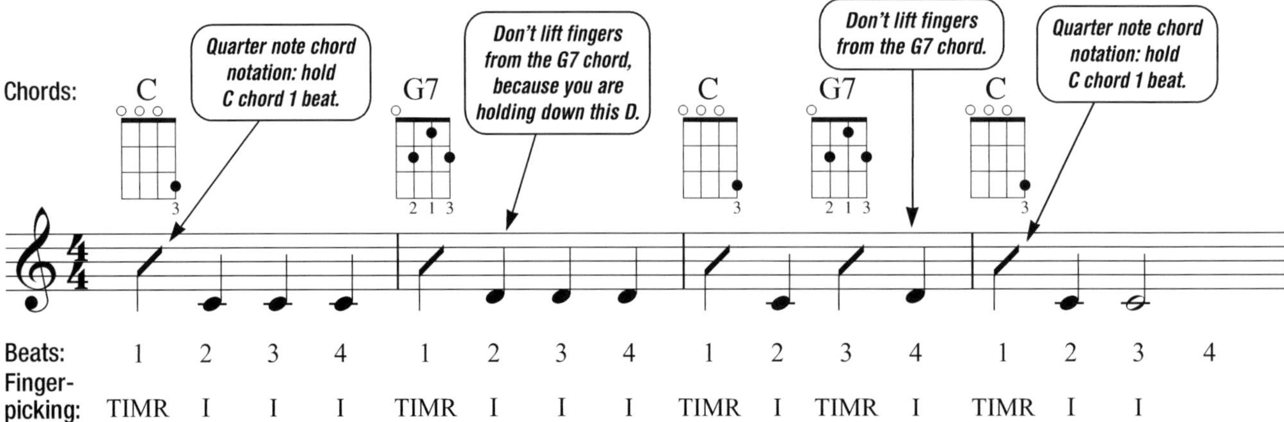

7. Anticipate the Chord in the Melody

TRACK 12

- In this exercise, notes are played before the chords that contain them.
- This exercise trains you to look ahead in the music to plan your left hand fretting for ease and economy of motion. To do this, fret each chord at the start of each measure. Then play the notes that precede the chord before actually playing the chord.
- Before playing, count four for nothing: 1, 2, 3, Play or 1, 2, 3, 4.
- *Continue counting out loud through the rest of the piece.*

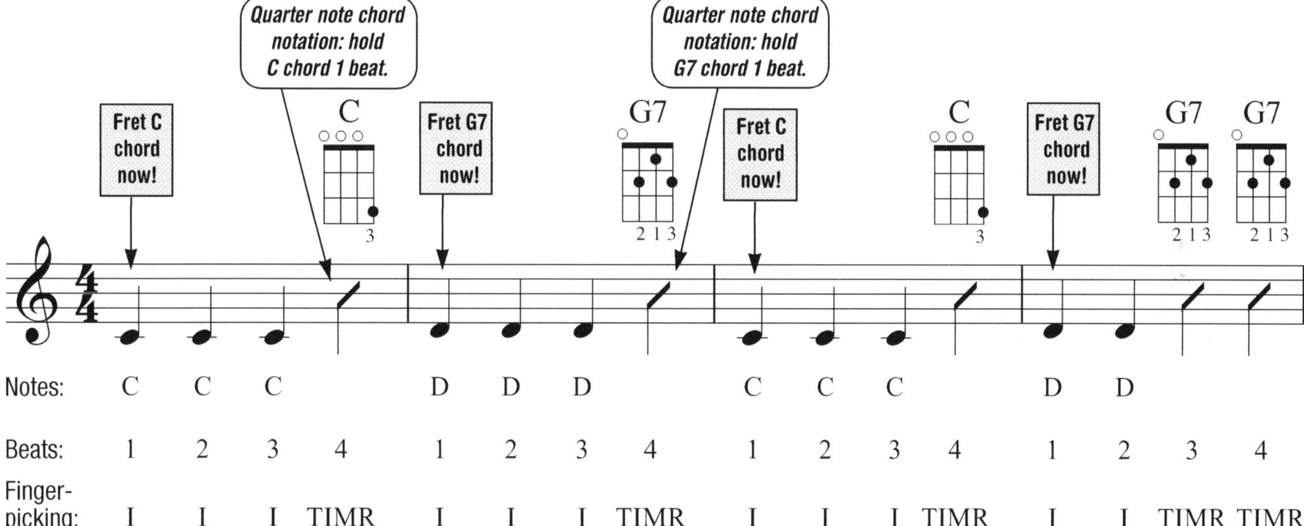

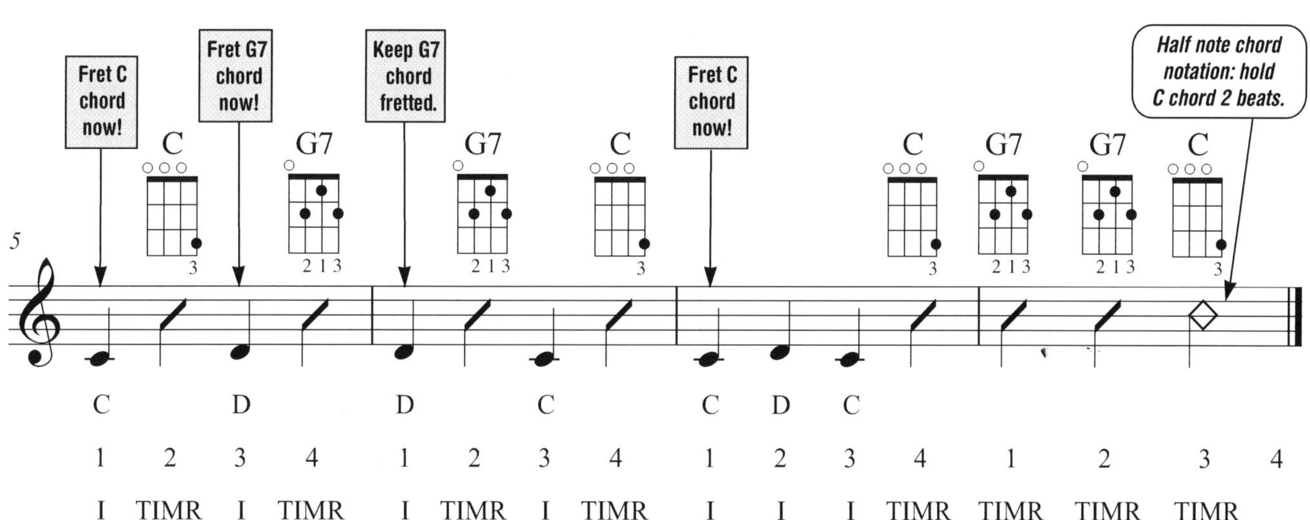

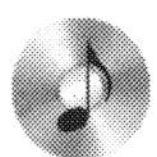

8. Three Count Can-Do

TRACK 13

- Before playing, count three for nothing: 1, 2, Play or 1, 2, 3.
- *Continue counting out loud through the rest of the piece.*

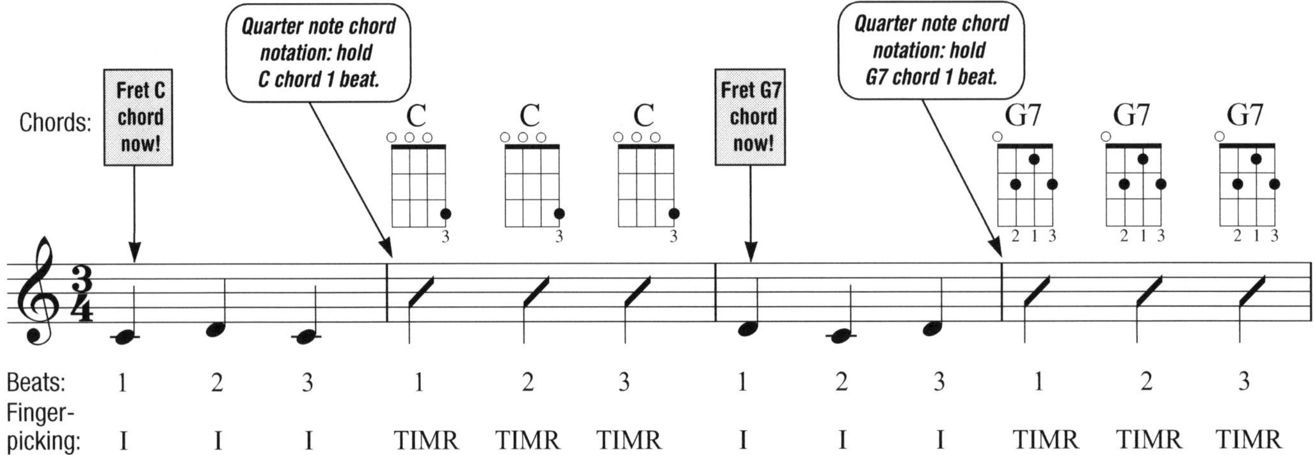

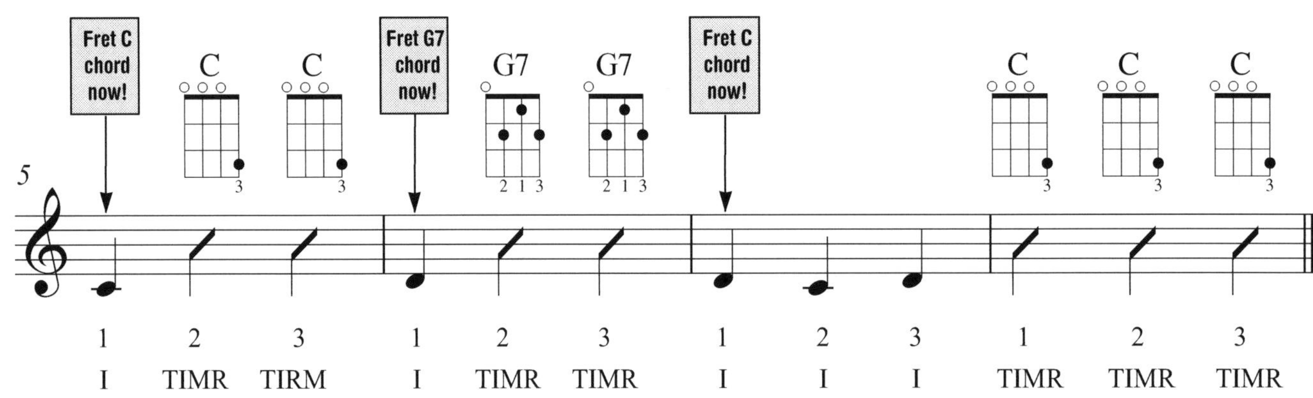

Chord Rhythmic Notation

When chords are combined with melody lines as they are in exercises 6-8 (see **page 36**), they are often notated on the musical staff with slashes and open diamonds to designate their rhythm. These "notes" are called chord notation and appear directly under a fretboard diagram of the chord to be played. The chord notation indicates how many beats to hold the chord. Also see the Appendix, **"Note, Rhythm and Rest Values" on page 173** for a full diagram of rhythmic notation.

Quarter Note = 1 Beat
(Hold each chord for 1 beat)

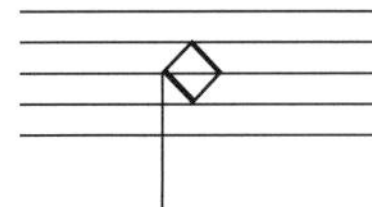

Half Note = 2 Beats
(Hold each chord for 2 beats)

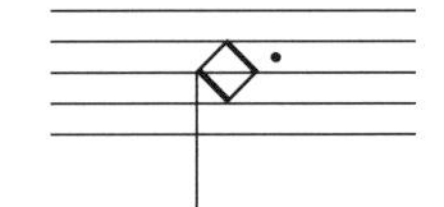

Dotted Half Note = 3 Beats
(Hold each chord for 3 beats)

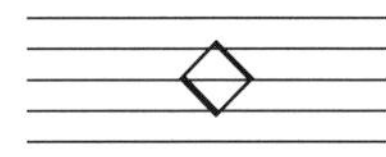

Whole Note = 4 Beat
(Hold each chord for 4 beats)

WRITTEN EXERCISE 1:
What's My Line?

Directions: Using ***pencil***, write the name of each note on the line below.

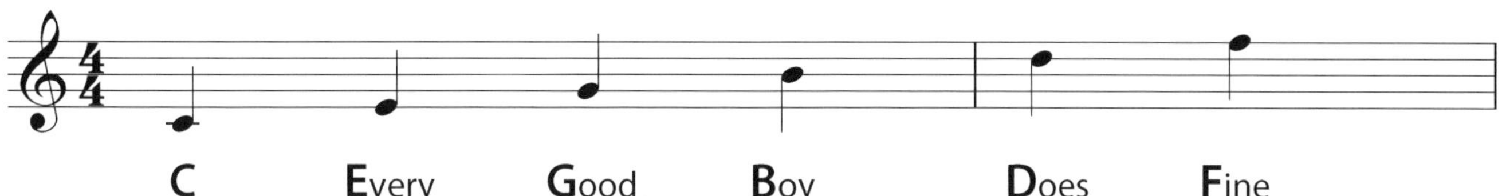

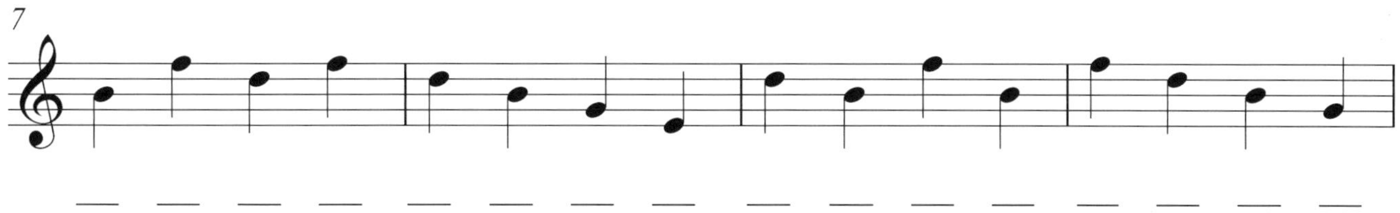

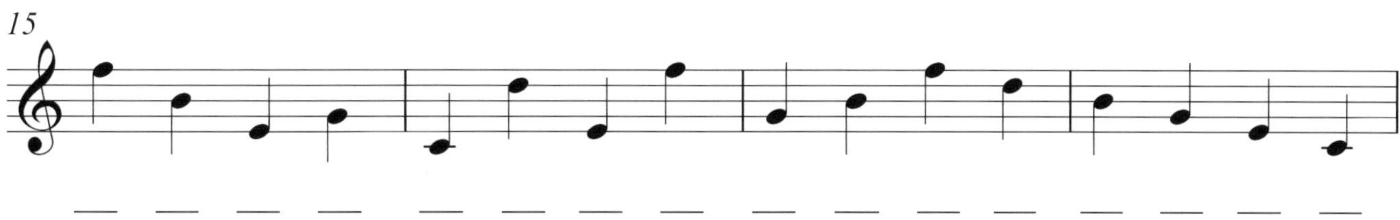

WRITTEN EXERCISE 2:
Note Writing Middle C and D Notes

1. Using a pencil, write the G Clef at the beginning of each staff below.
2. Next, write a 4/4 time signature on the first staff only.
3. Write a quarter or half note above the letter name indicated below the staff. Half note rhythms are notated with a comma between beats, e.g. 1, 2.
4. Draw the stem of each note 3 spaces long.
5. Add the beat number under each note.
6. When you are finished, play the exercise on your uke.

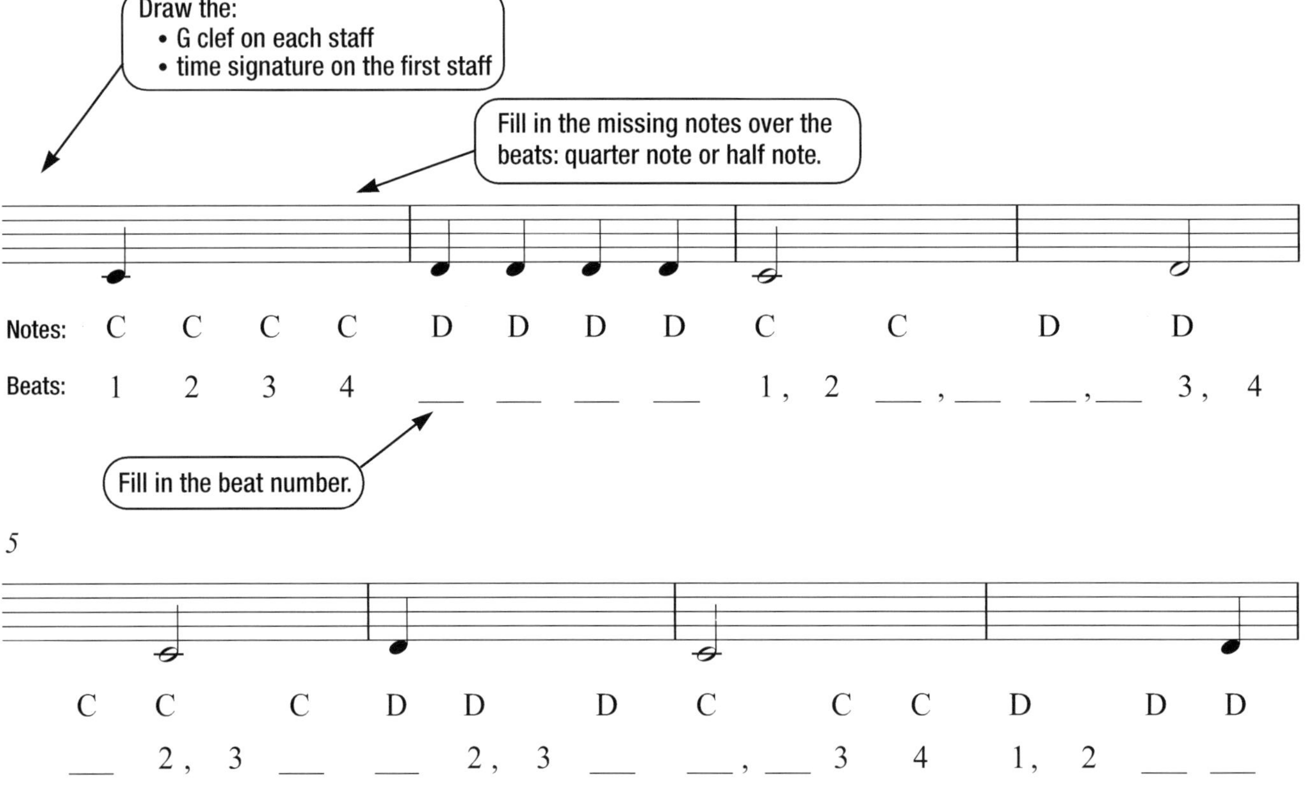

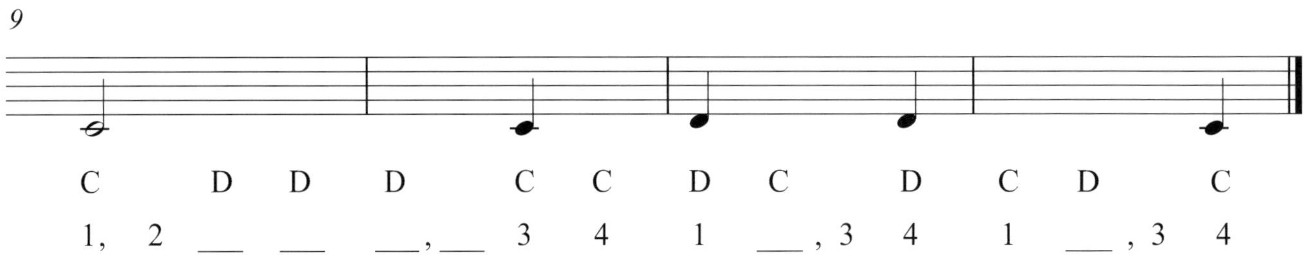

WRITTEN EXERCISE 1:
Answer Key for What's My Line?

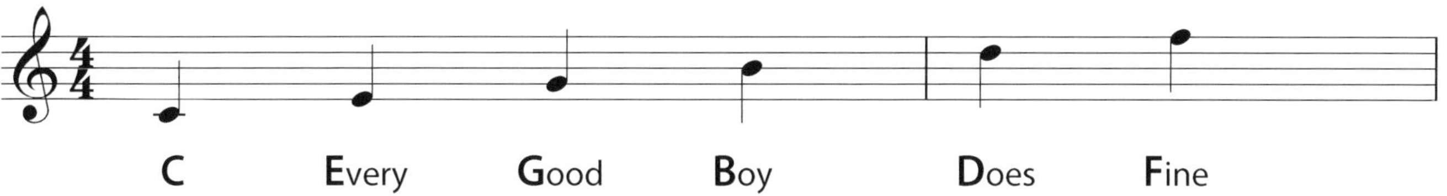

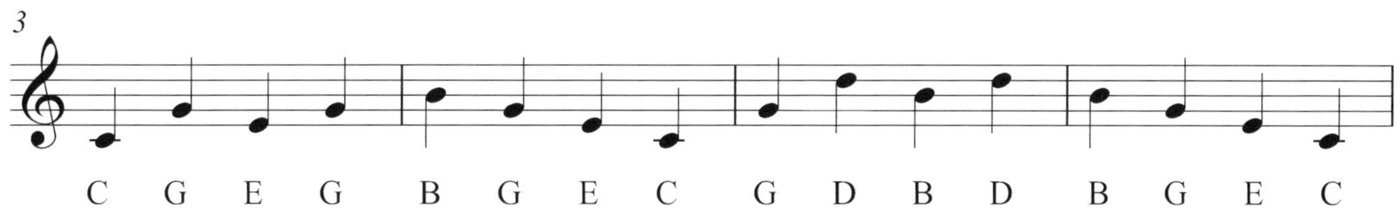

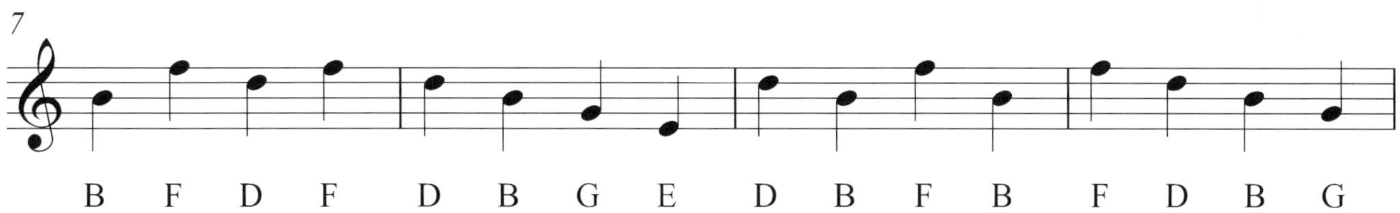

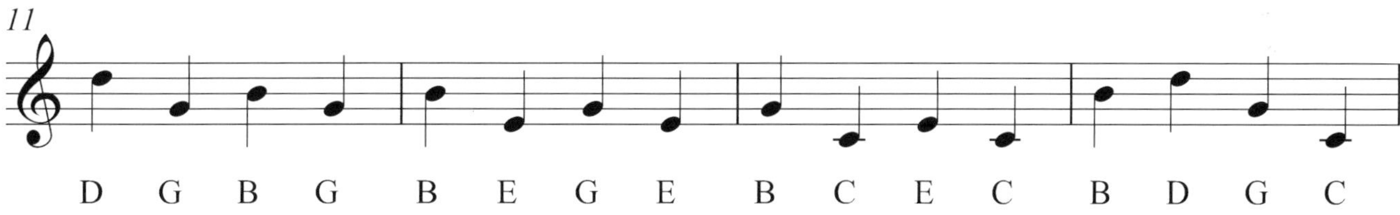

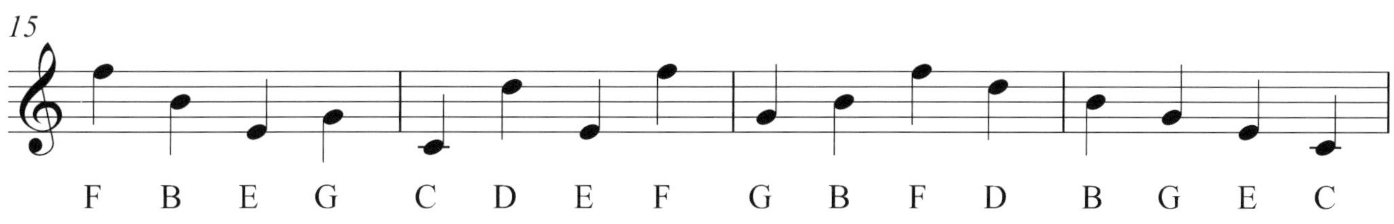

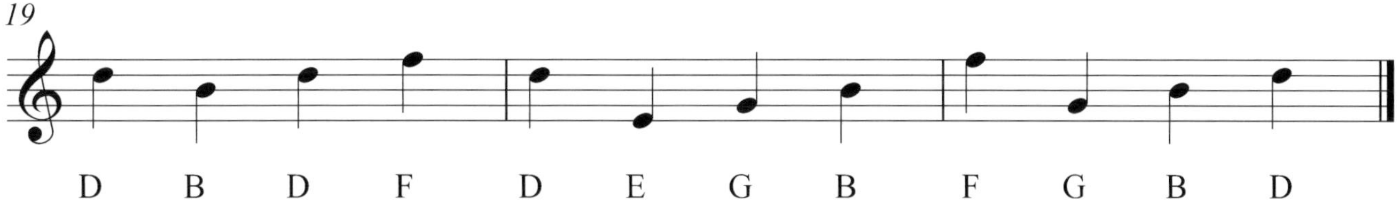

WRITTEN EXERCISE 2:
Answer Key for Note Writing Middle C and D Notes

1. Using a pencil, write the G Clef at the beginning of each staff below.
2. Next, write a 4/4 time signature on the first staff only.
3. Write a quarter or half note above the letter name indicated below the staff. Half notes rhythms are notated with a comma between beats, e.g. 1, 2.
4. Draw the stem of each note 3 spaces long.
5. Add the beat number under each note.
6. When you are finished, play the exercise on your uke.

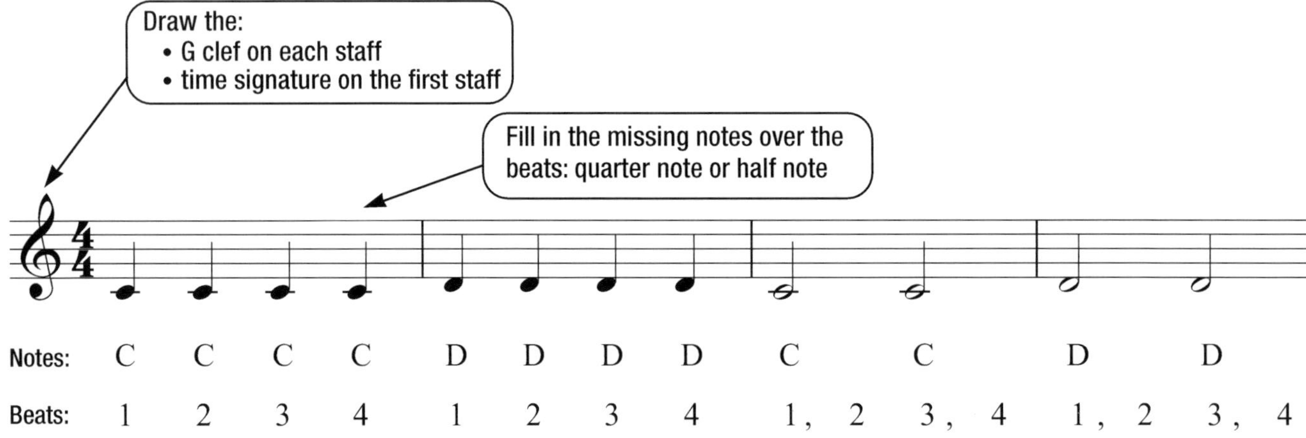

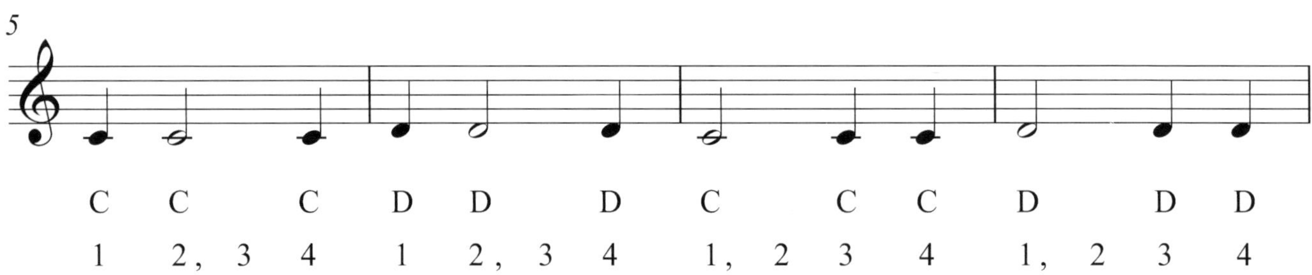

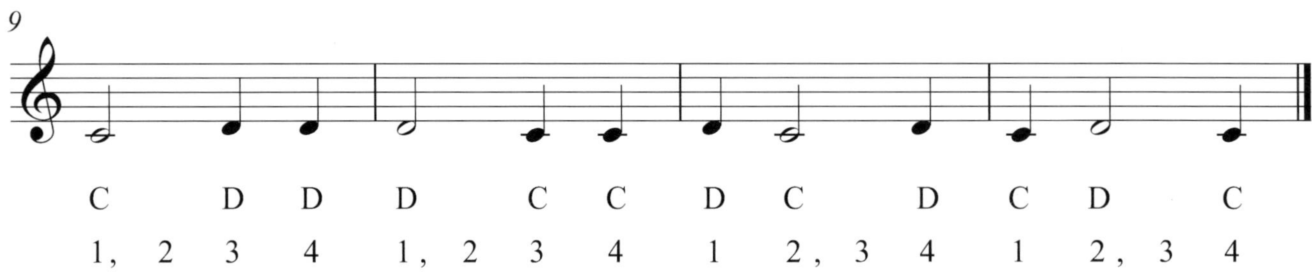

Lesson 2

Assignment

1. **Warm-up:** Each time you sit down to practice, play the following in this order...

   A. **4-Fret half-step chromatic scale exercise:** Practice with a battery operated metronome, or a metronome app (available inexpensively for all electronic devices). Listen closely to your playing to check if you are playing legato and in rhythm. Start with a very slow beat per minute, then increase the speed gradually as you become more proficient. Make sure your right hand plucking fingers are playing one finger, one string, while your left hand fretting fingers are fretting one finger, one fret. The goal of this exercise is accuracy. Speed is not important at this stage (**page 47**).

   B. **Five-note scale exercise and learning to play legato:** Sing or say the names of the notes as you look at the music. Then close your eyes and sing the notes as you play (**page 50**).

2. **Review:** Play through your favorite *Lesson 1* music and songs as a refresher and for reinforcement. Work on anything challenging that you still need to master... a chord change, a musical passage, whatever. Practice while reading the music. Then close your eyes and play short passages to train your memory, ears and fingers.

3. **Learn:**

   A. **E, F and G notes** (**page 48**)

   B. **F major chord** (**page 54**)
   Practice the F major chord by learning the following chord progressions:

   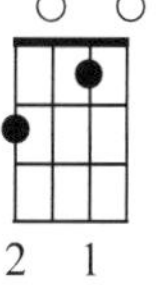

   1) C to G7 to F to C
   2) G7 to C to F to G7
   3) F to C to F to G7
   4) G7 to F to G7 to C

   C. **Combine notes and chords in songs: *Don't try to learn everything in the entire lesson at once***—Like the other lessons in this book, I included a lot of extra material to allow you to take your time mastering the music and techniques.

   1) **Select 1-3 songs and practice them until they are mastered**. When you learn those well enough to play them slowly and in rhythm, learn a couple more until you learn them all (**pages 51-69**).

   2) **If you can say it, you can play it!** Play each piece you are learning 3 ways:

      a) First, count the beats in each measure while reading music.

      b) Second, say the note names while reading the music.

      c) Third, say the right hand finger names while plucking the strings.

4. **Written Exercises:** *(Please use a pencil for the following exercises)*

   A. Get **Spaced! Notes in the Spaces (page 70)**

   B. **Writing Middle C, D, E, F. G Notes (page 71)**

   C. **Kn**ow Your Rests! (**page 72**)

4-FRET, HALF-STEP CHROMATIC SCALE EXERCISE

"**Chromatic**" means going higher or lower in pitch by one fret.

This exercise trains your fingers to ascend (go higher in pitch or sound) and descend (go lower in pitch or sound) one fret at a time.

Why are finger exercises important? Finger exercises develop strength, agility, and accuracy while improving technique and speed in both the right and left hands.

What is the purpose of this exercise? It trains you to:

- Accurately ascend (go up) and descend (go down) the fretboard by half steps (the chromatic scale).
- Play individual strings with individual fingers.
- Play smoothly and in rhythm.
- Maintain good finger technique in both left and right hands.

What should I learn?

At first glance, the musical diagram, on **page 47,** can be daunting. But please, don't panic. I have included something for every ability level in this exercise:

- Musical staff—for people who read music
- Note names and beats—for extreme beginners
- Tab staff—for Tab readers (also for extreme beginners)
- Fingerpicking indication

Learning TIP: Memorizing the names of the notes will help you learn your fretboard in the first 4 frets faster! Sharps (♯), and Flats (♭) after a note are called "accidentals." Sharps raise and flats lower the pitch of a note one half step, or 1 fret. (For more on this, see **"Accidentals" on page 177**.) Whether a note is sharp or flat depends on the scale. All sharp and flat notes have two names which are called "enharmonic equivalents." For example, A♯ is played on the A string first fret, and so is the B♭ note. ***Don't FRET about this! There are no sharps of flats in the key of C.*** So... even though we aren't learning accidentals in this book, try singing the names of all the notes as you look at the music and play. Then close your eyes and do the same with each string. (To help with note memorization, see **"Full Ukulele Fretboard" on page 172**.)

Focus on:

1. Fretting each note correctly with the left hand.
2. Picking correctly with the right hand.

Technique Instructions: The following fretting and playing technique trains your fingers to play "legato" an Italian musical term that means "smoothly connected." This technique helps you sound like a professional on your instrument in almost all genres of music including blues, folk, rock, jazz, Hawai'ian, classical and much more. Use this particular exercise as a warmup before you play other music.

- **Don't let the left hand bridge collapse!** Keep the bridge shape when each left-hand finger frets (holds down) a string.
- **Position your thumb *behind the second finger*** of the ukulele so you can maneuver more accurately.
- **Play slowly, smoothly and accurately.**
- **Learn the exercise on all strings** after you have mastered the exercise on the A string.
- **Right hand fingerpicking:**
    - A string—pick with the ring finger
    - E string—pick with the middle finger
    - C string—pick with the index finger
    - G string—pick with the thumb
- **Counting:** Before playing, "count four for nothing" to set your tempo.

    Say "1, 2, 3, Play" or "1, 2, 3, 4."

    Continue counting out loud through the rest of the exercise.
- **Alternate counting out loud with:**
    - saying the fret numbers
    - singing the names of the notes

How to Read Tablature

Tablature, or **TAB**, is a form of graphical musical notation. It is commonly used for guitar, bass, and ukulele. In many books, TABs are offered on a second staff beneath the treble clef staff (see **page 47**). Some music books are written entirely in TAB. Instead of using a standard musical staff and notation symbols, TAB uses a system of horizontal lines to represent the strings of the instruments. Uke tab lines are set up with the high A string on top and G string on the bottom. Notes are represented by fret numbers on the strings:

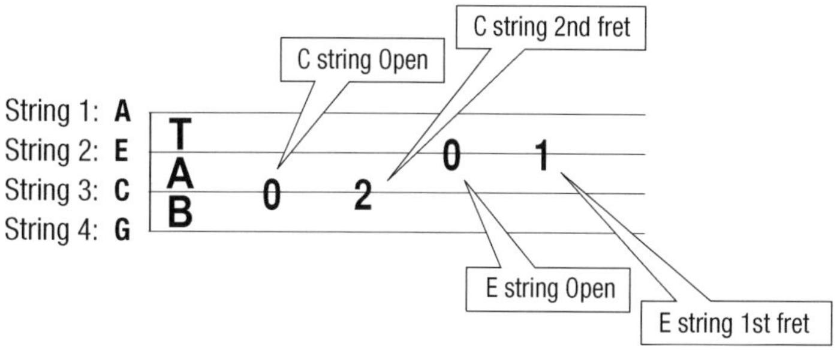

What are the drawbacks in reading Tablature?

1. In most cases, TAB does not give rhythmic markings. So, if you don't know what the music sounds like, you won't be able to "sight read" tabs like you can traditional musical notation.
2. TAB does not tell you which fingers fret the notes.
3. TAB usually does not give any fingerpicking or strumming notation.

Left hand fretting technique – learning to play legato, or smoothly connected

The following diagrams teach how to smoothly take fingers on and off frets so one note flows into another as you fingerpick with your right hand. Use the patterns below for all four strings.

Ascending Chromatic Scale Finger Pattern on the A String

As you play each ascending note (going up the fretboard toward the uke body), continue fretting each note hard, leaving your finger down on a fret after you play it.

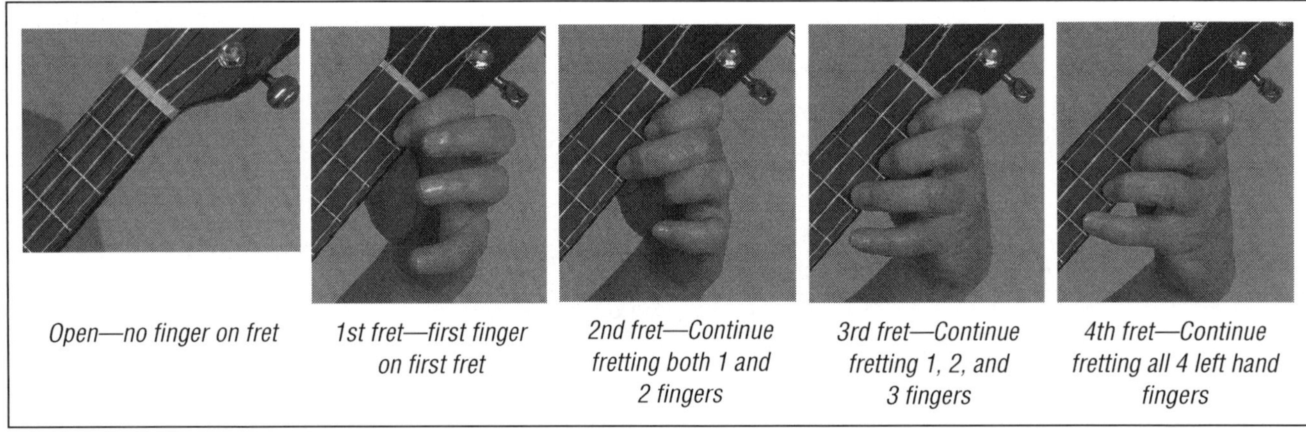

Open—no finger on fret | *1st fret—first finger on first fret* | *2nd fret—Continue fretting both 1 and 2 fingers* | *3rd fret—Continue fretting 1, 2, and 3 fingers* | *4th fret—Continue fretting all 4 left hand fingers*

Descending Chromatic Scale Finger Pattern on the A String

As the scale descends (going down the fretboard toward the uke head), lift each finger and let it hover closely to the fret it just played. Continue to strongly fret the remaining fingers.

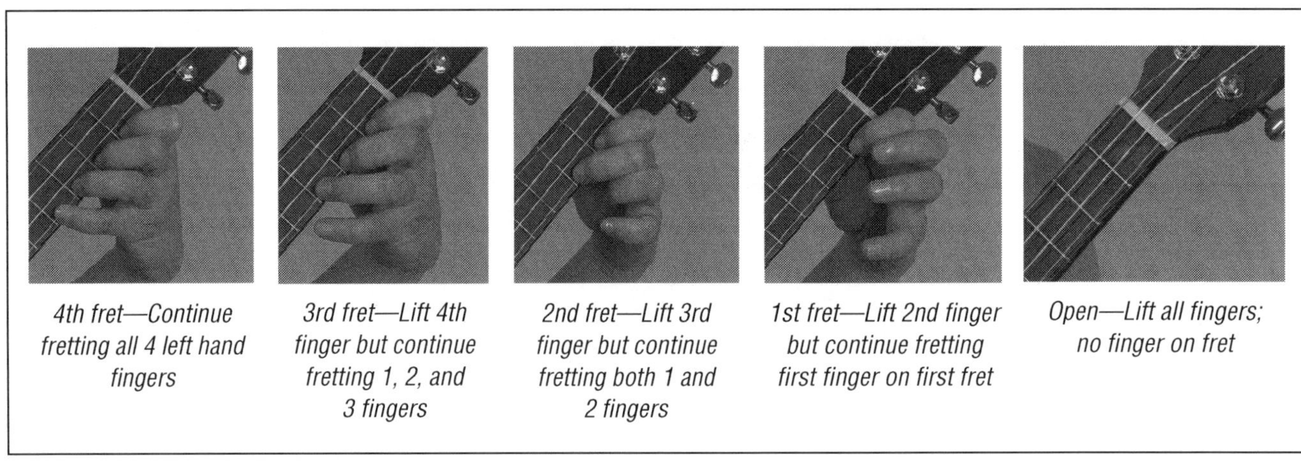

4th fret—Continue fretting all 4 left hand fingers | *3rd fret—Lift 4th finger but continue fretting 1, 2, and 3 fingers* | *2nd fret—Lift 3rd finger but continue fretting both 1 and 2 fingers* | *1st fret—Lift 2nd finger but continue fretting first finger on first fret* | *Open—Lift all fingers; no finger on fret*

1. 4-Fret Half-Step Chromatic Scale Exercise

TRACK 14

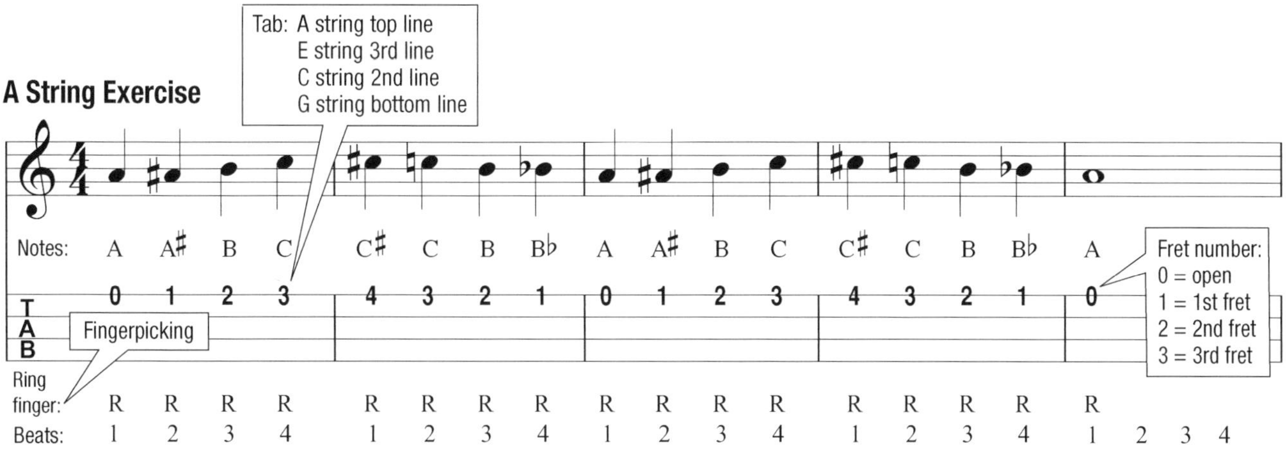

Tab: A string top line
E string 3rd line
C string 2nd line
G string bottom line

A String Exercise

Notes:	A	A♯	B	C	C♯	C	B	B♭	A	A♯	B	C	C♯	C	B	B♭	A			
TAB	0	1	2	3	4	3	2	1	0	1	2	3	4	3	2	1	0			
Ring finger:	R	R	R	R	R	R	R	R	R	R	R	R	R	R	R	R	R			
Beats:	1	2	3	4	1	2	3	4	1	2	3	4	1	2	3	4	1	2	3	4

Fingerpicking

Fret number:
0 = open
1 = 1st fret
2 = 2nd fret
3 = 3rd fret

E String Exercise

Notes:	E	F	F♯	G	G♯	G	G♭	F	E	F	F♯	G	G♯	G	G♭	F	E			
TAB	0	1	2	3	4	3	2	1	0	1	2	3	4	3	2	1	0			
Middle finger:	M	M	M	M	M	M	M	M	M	M	M	M	M	M	M	M	M			
Beats:	1	2	3	4	1	2	3	4	1	2	3	4	1	2	3	4	1	2	3	4

C String Exercise

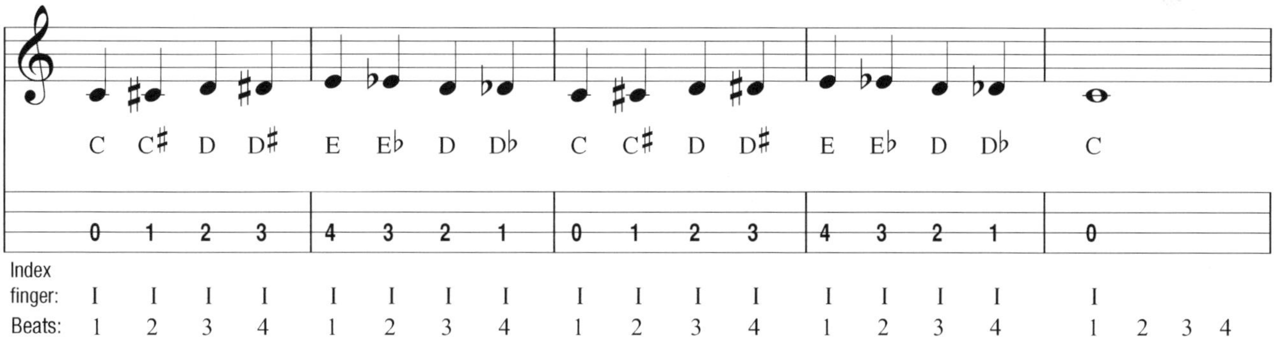

Notes:	C	C♯	D	D♯	E	E♭	D	D♭	C	C♯	D	D♯	E	E♭	D	D♭	C			
TAB	0	1	2	3	4	3	2	1	0	1	2	3	4	3	2	1	0			
Index finger:	I	I	I	I	I	I	I	I	I	I	I	I	I	I	I	I	I			
Beats:	1	2	3	4	1	2	3	4	1	2	3	4	1	2	3	4	1	2	3	4

G String Exercise

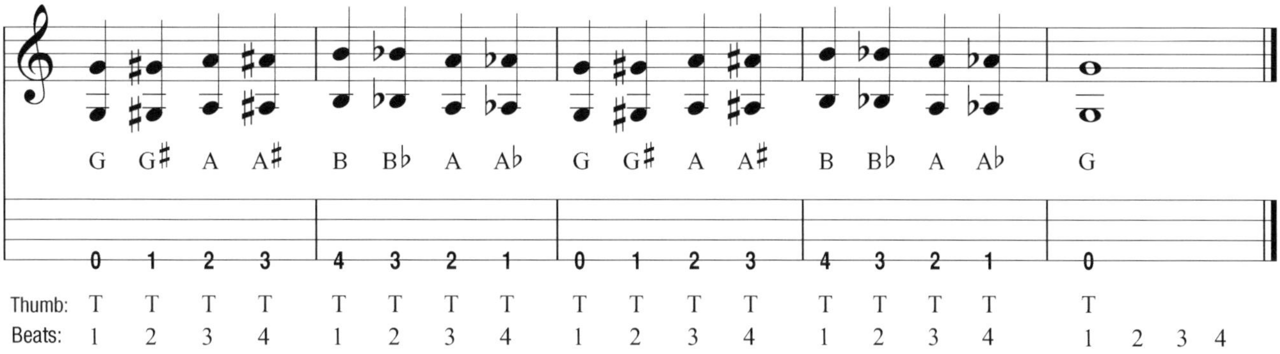

Notes:	G	G♯	A	A♯	B	B♭	A	A♭	G	G♯	A	A♯	B	B♭	A	A♭	G			
TAB	0	1	2	3	4	3	2	1	0	1	2	3	4	3	2	1	0			
Thumb:	T	T	T	T	T	T	T	T	T	T	T	T	T	T	T	T	T			
Beats:	1	2	3	4	1	2	3	4	1	2	3	4	1	2	3	4	1	2	3	4

Introducing the E, F, and G Notes

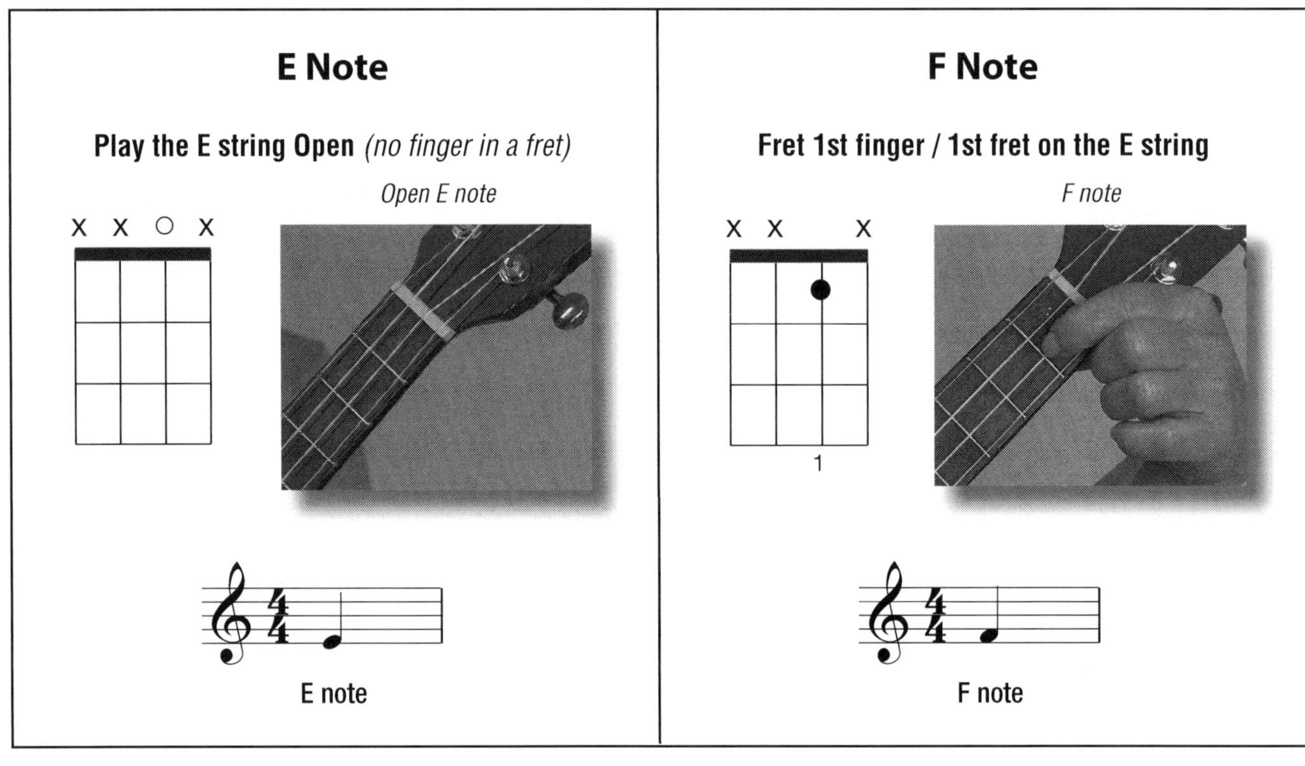

Right hand fingerpicking for E, F and G notes:

The E, F and G notes are plucked with the **Middle** finger notated as **M**.

Fingerpicking Tip: Rest your Thumb lightly on the G string and extend it toward the head of the uke to help keep your Middle finger in place.

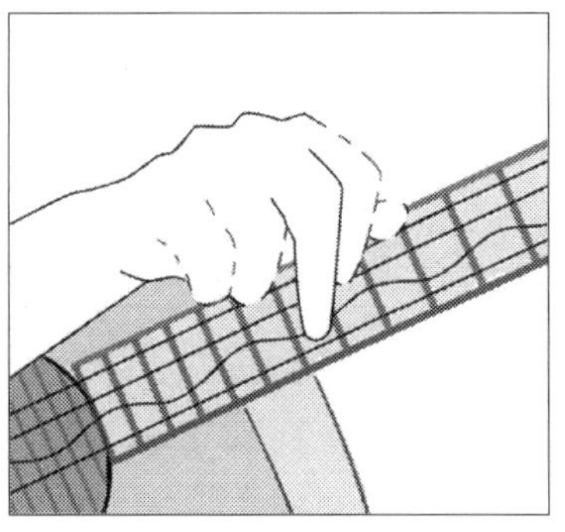

TRACK 15

2. E, F, and G Notes

- Before playing, count four for nothing: 1, 2, 3, Play or 1, 2, 3, 4.
- *Continue counting out loud through the rest of the piece.*

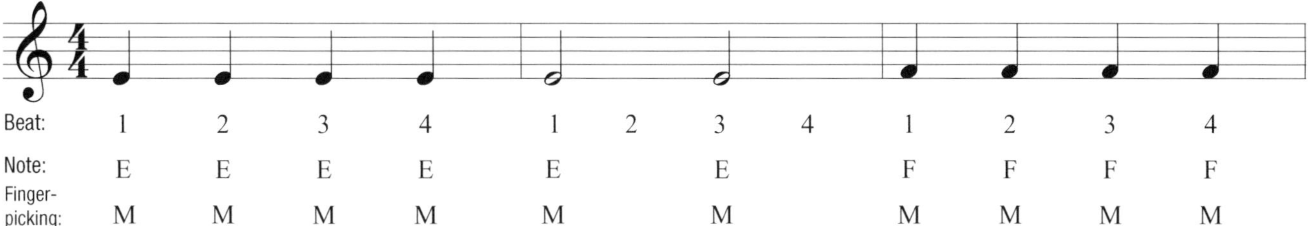

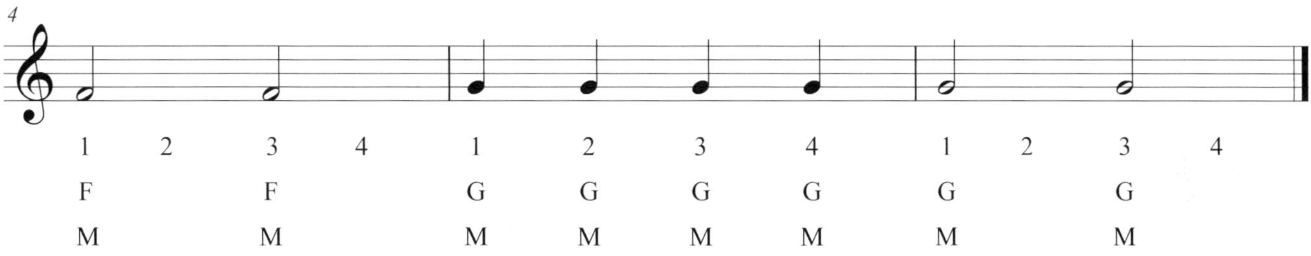

TRACK 16

3. E, F, and G Jumble

- Using pencil, write the names of the notes on the lines. Later you can erase and test yourself.
- Before playing, count four for nothing to set the tempo: 1, 2, 3, Play or 1, 2, 3, 4.
- *Continue counting out loud through the rest of the piece.*

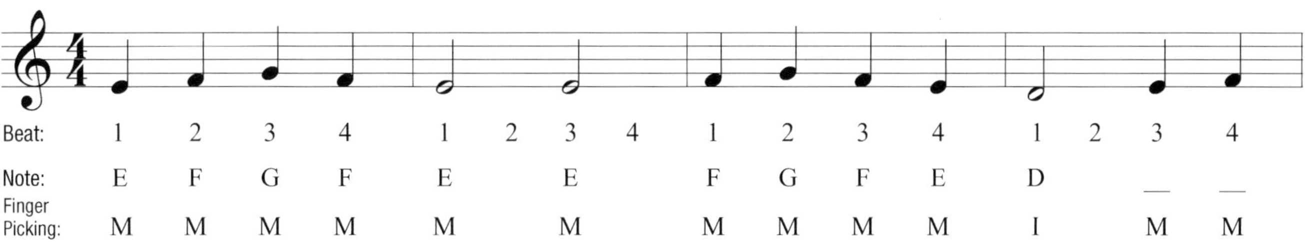

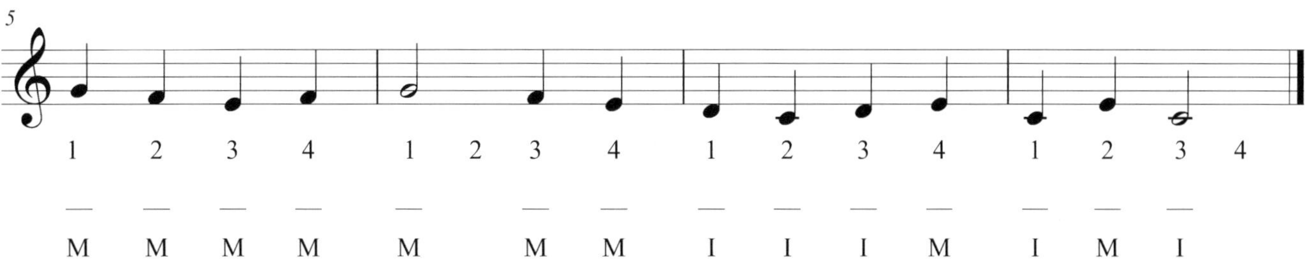

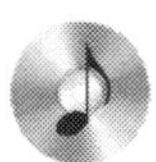

4. Five-Note Scale

- ***As you play each note, sing its letter name to help memorize the position and fingers you use to fret and pluck each string. Close your eyes as you sing and play the scale.***
- **Try *not* writing the letter names in the blank spaces. This will help train your eyes to recognize the notes.**
- Before playing, count four for nothing to set the tempo: 1, 2, 3, Play or 1, 2, 3, 4.
- *Practice counting out loud as you play the notes.*

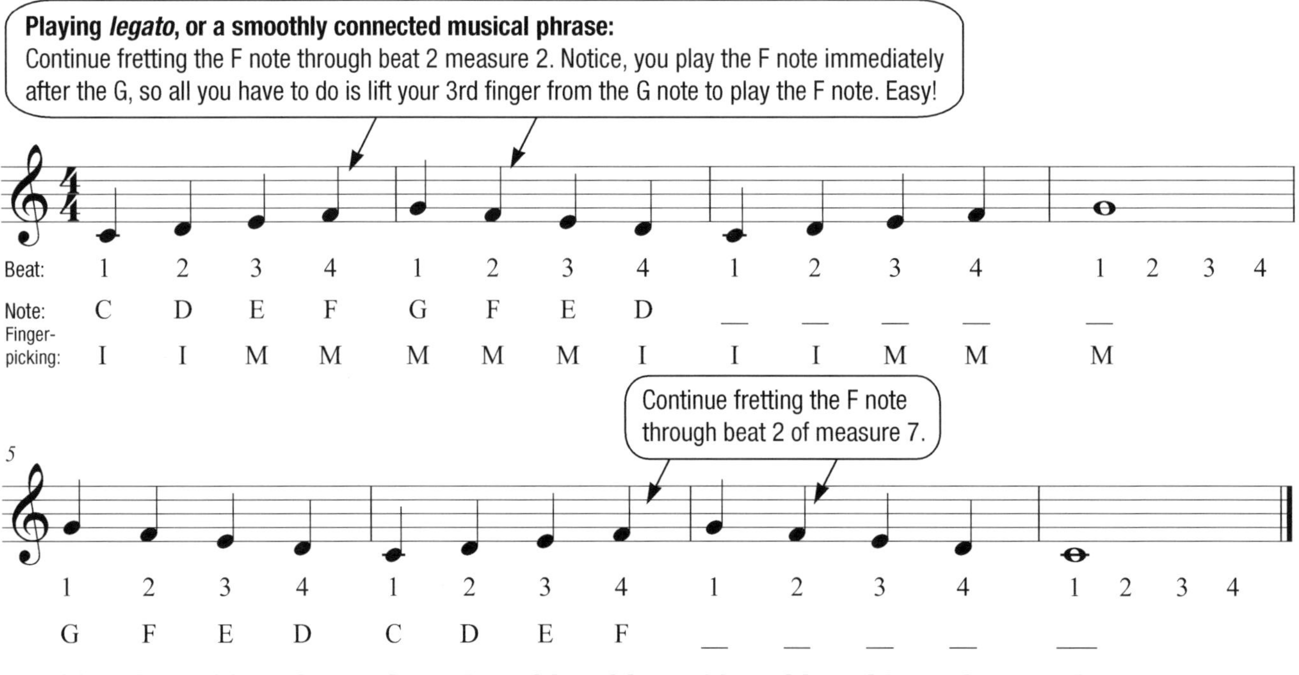

How to play legato on the E string when the music switches back and forth between the F and G notes

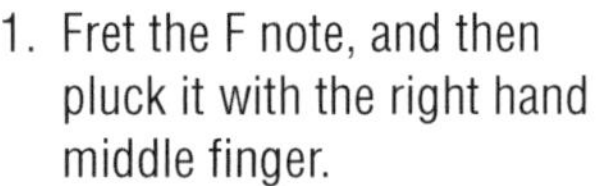
1. Fret the F note, and then pluck it with the right hand middle finger.

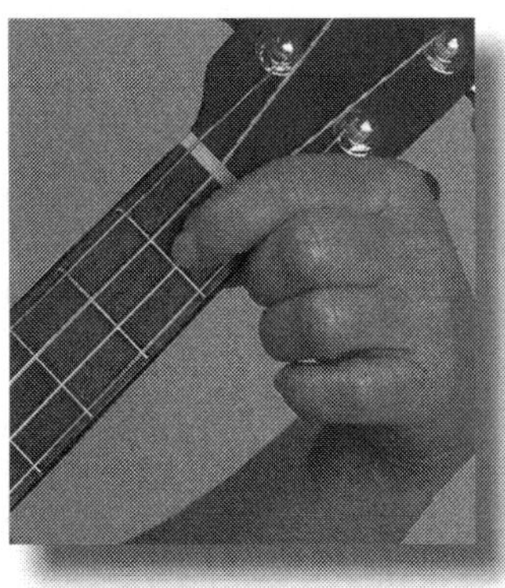

2. Firmly fret the F and G notes together with the 1 and 3 left hand fingers, and then pluck the G note with the right hand middle finger. When fretting the G note, continue to fret the F note because you are returning to it.

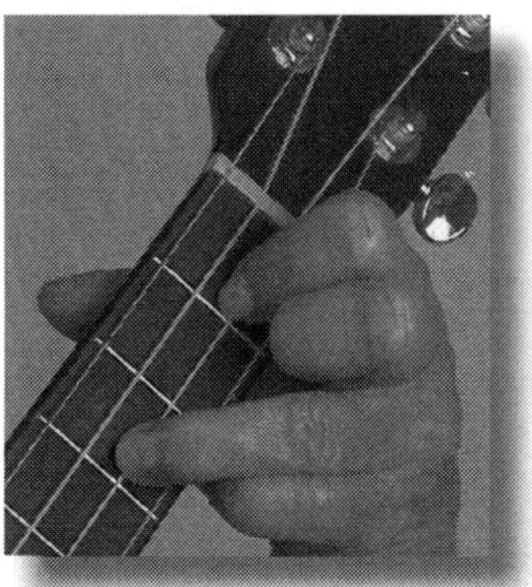

3. Lift the 3rd finger from the G note, and then pluck the F note with the right hand middle finger.

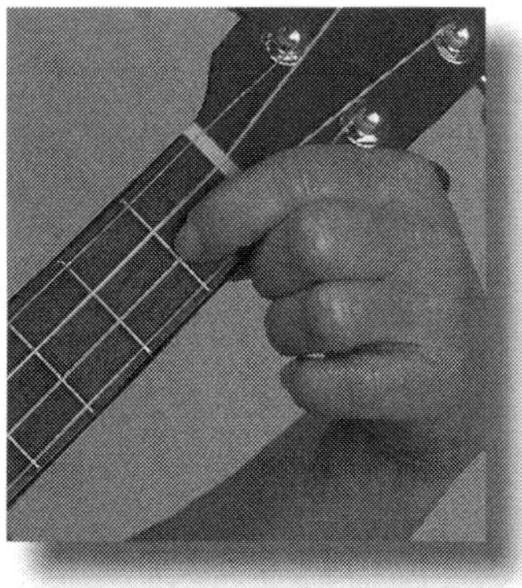

5. Five-Note Serenade

TRACK 18

- *Using pencil*, write the names of the notes on the lines. Later you can erase and test yourself.
- Before playing, count three for nothing to set the tempo: 1, 2, Play or 1, 2, 3.
- *Continue counting out loud through the rest of the piece.*

Let's Play Some Music!

Songs 6, 7 and 8 are easy three-note tunes that introduce the E note, while reviewing the notes C and D, and the chords C and G7. Before playing each song in:

- 4/4 time, count four for nothing: 1, 2, 3, Play or 1, 2, 3, 4.
- 3/4 time, count three for nothing: 1, 2, Play or 1, 2, 3.
- *Continue counting out loud through the rest of the piece.*

6. Hot Cross Buns

TRACK 19

This song is arranged to teach you to anticipate fretting a chord before you play it. The note directly before each chord is contained within the chord. ***Practice plucking the chords with all four fingers instead of strumming them.***

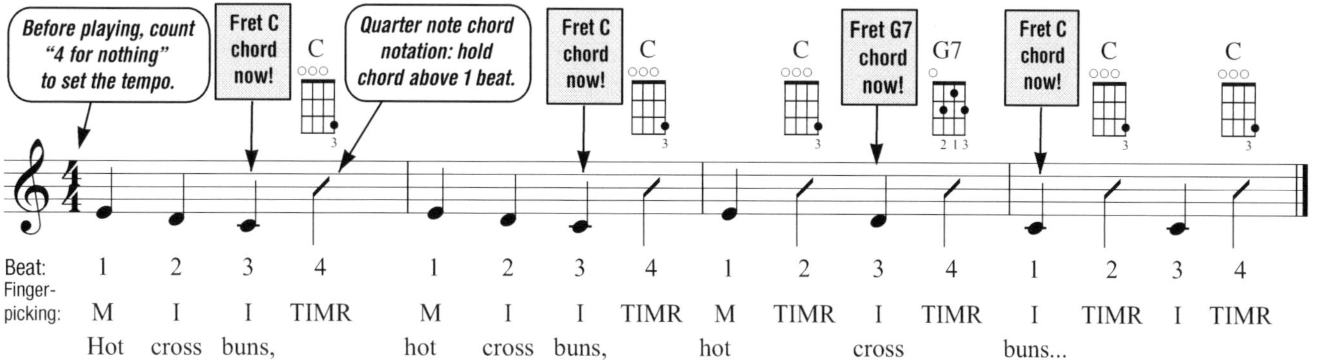

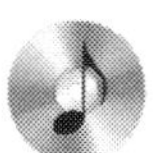

7. Merrily We Roll Along

TRACK 20

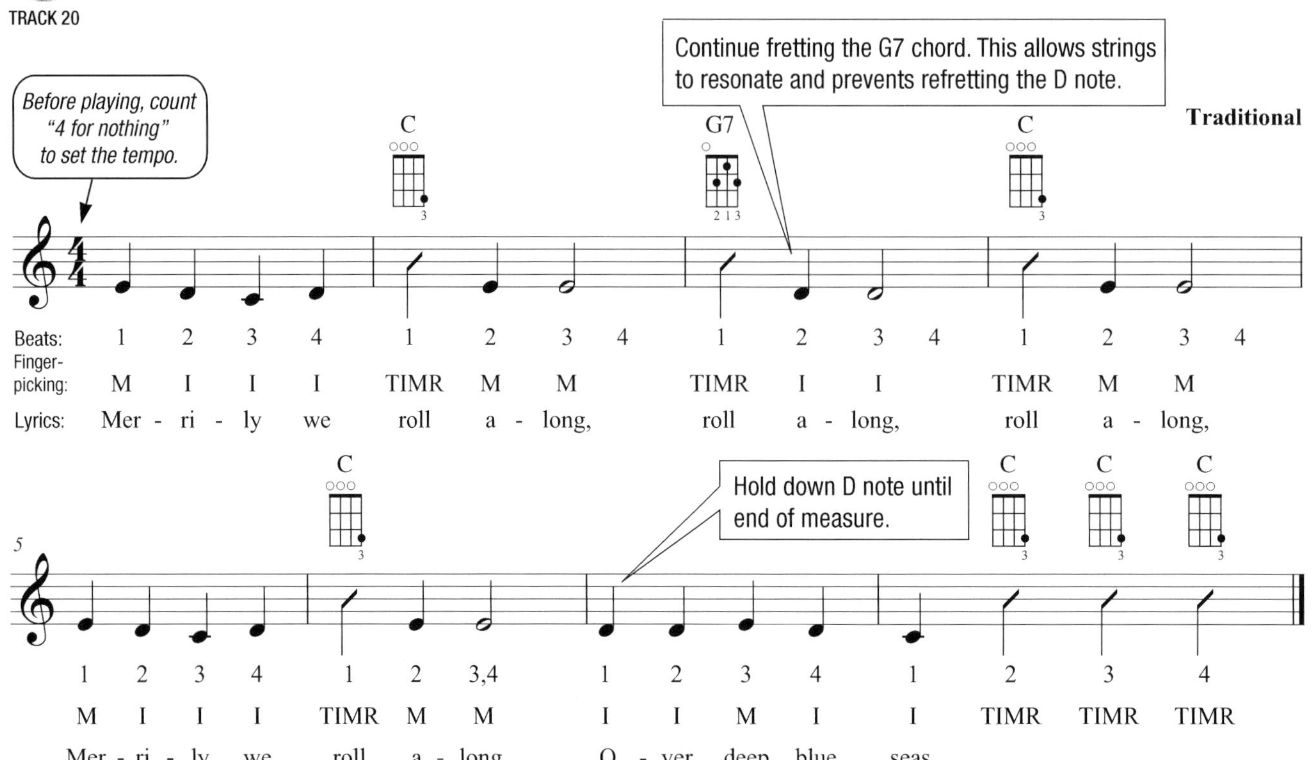

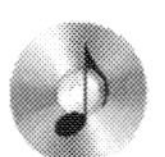

8. Au Clair De La Lune

TRACK 21

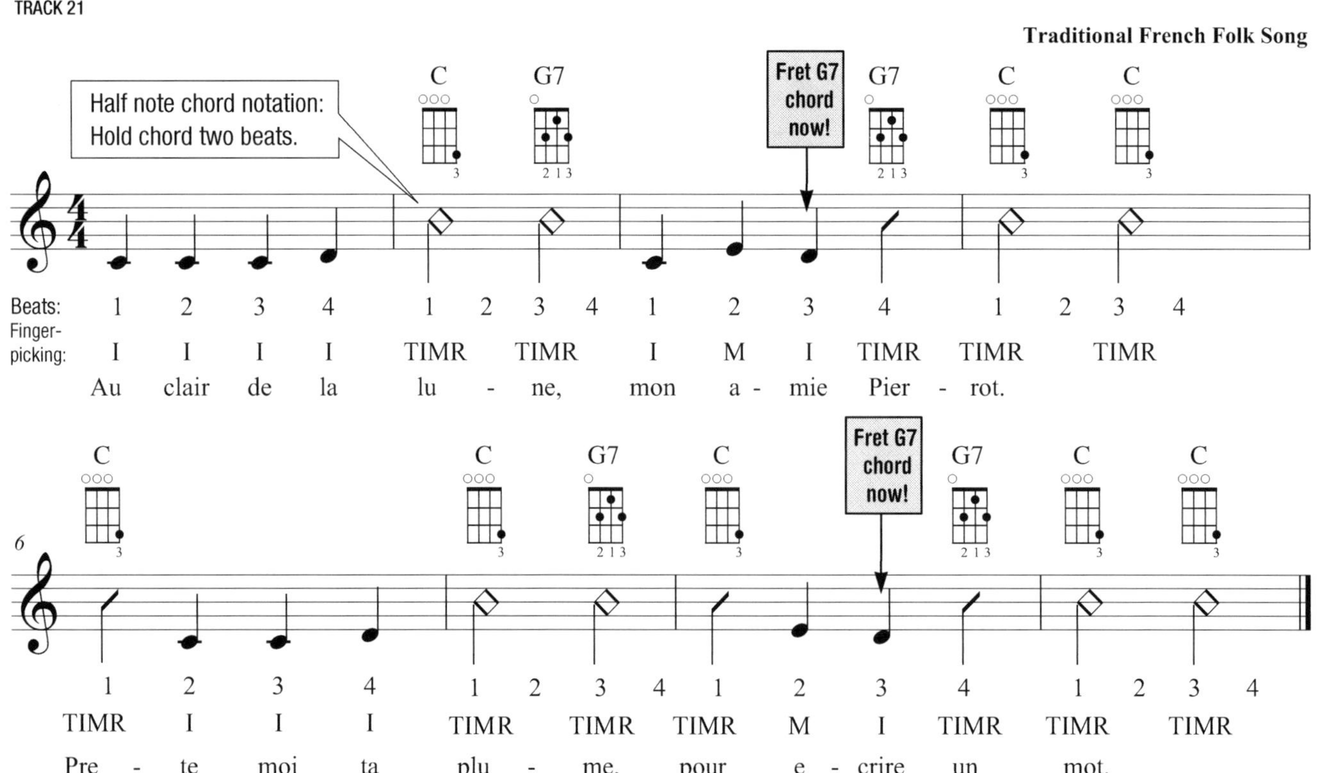

Translation: By the light of the moon, my friend Pierrot, give me your pen, to write a word.

Songs 9 and 10 add the F and G notes.

9. Love Somebody

TRACK 22

10. Austrian Waltz

TRACK 23

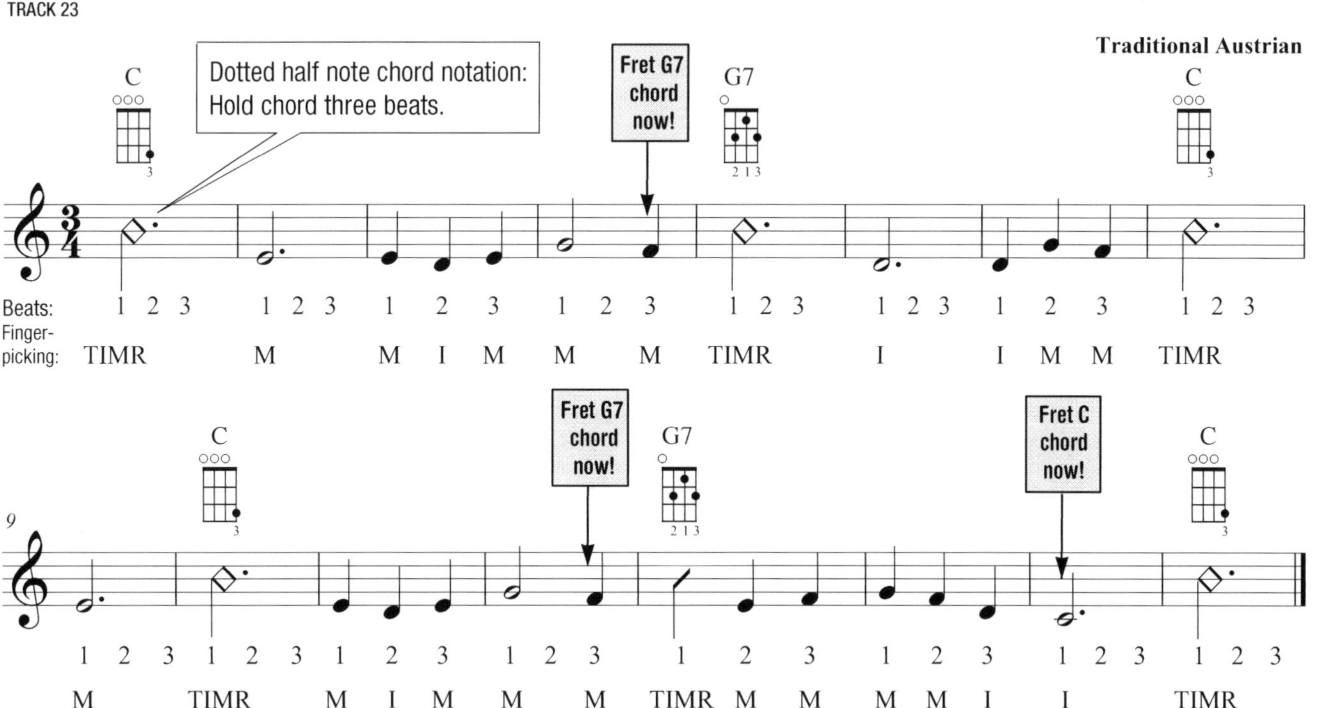

Introducing the F Chord

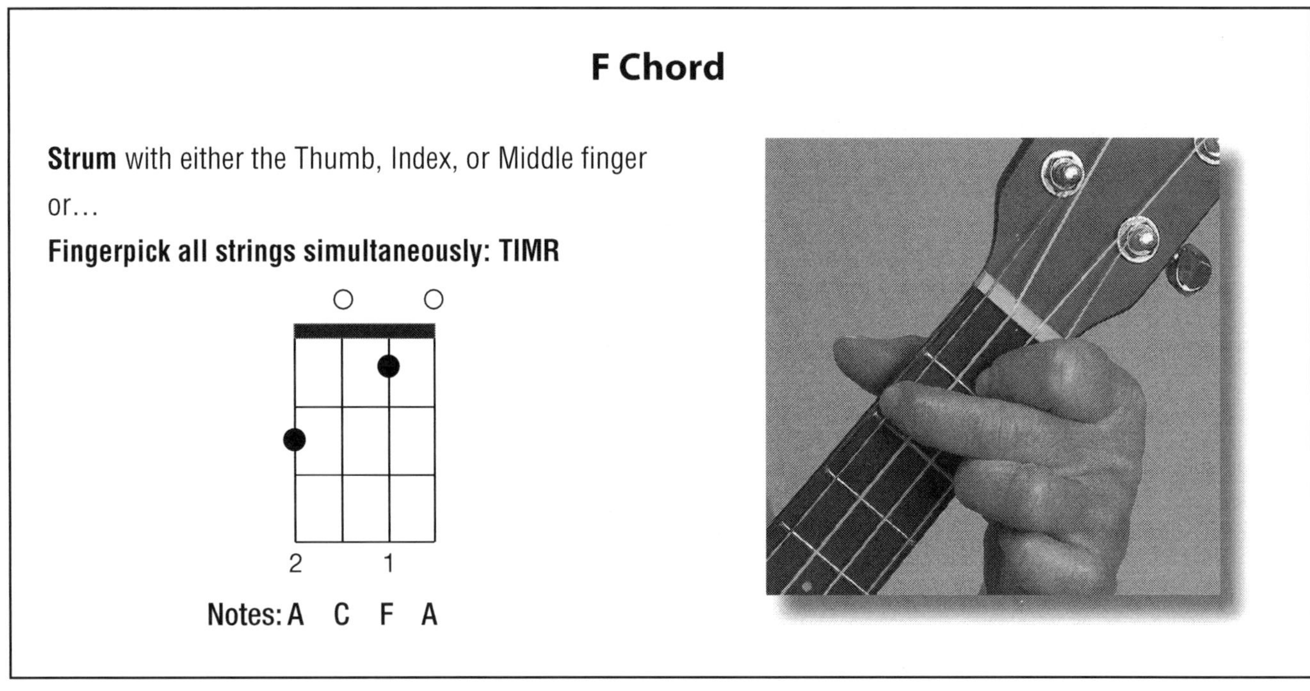

Road map for moving smoothly between F and G7 chords:

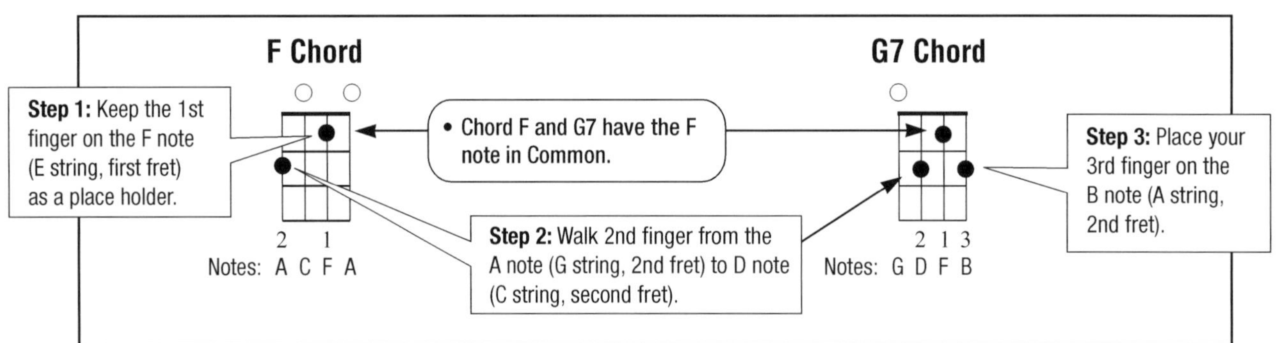

Road map for moving smoothly between F and C chords:

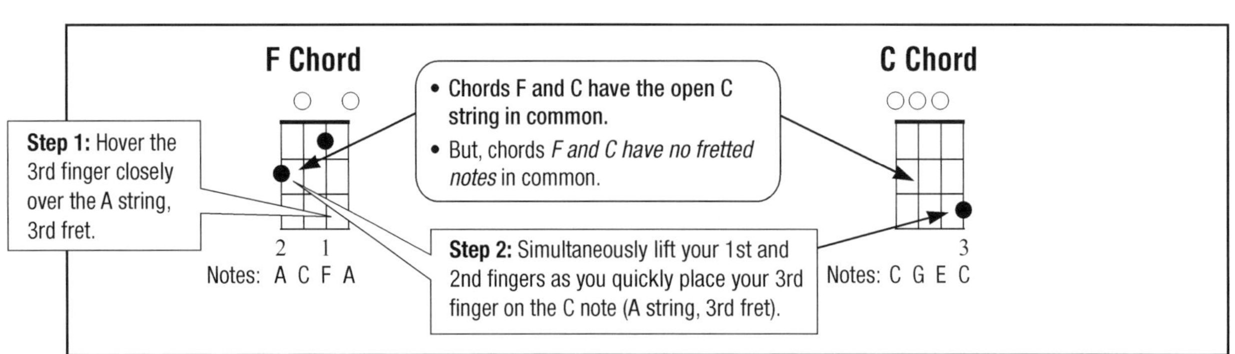

Combine the E, F, and G Notes with Chords

Exercises 11–13 train you to play melody notes with accompanying chords.

11. Make it Mine in 4/4 Time

TRACK 24

- At the top of each measure, fret your left hand fingers on the chord. Leave them there to play the note that follows each chord.
- Before playing, count four for nothing: 1, 2, 3, Play or 1, 2, 3, 4.
- *Continue counting out loud through the rest of the piece.*

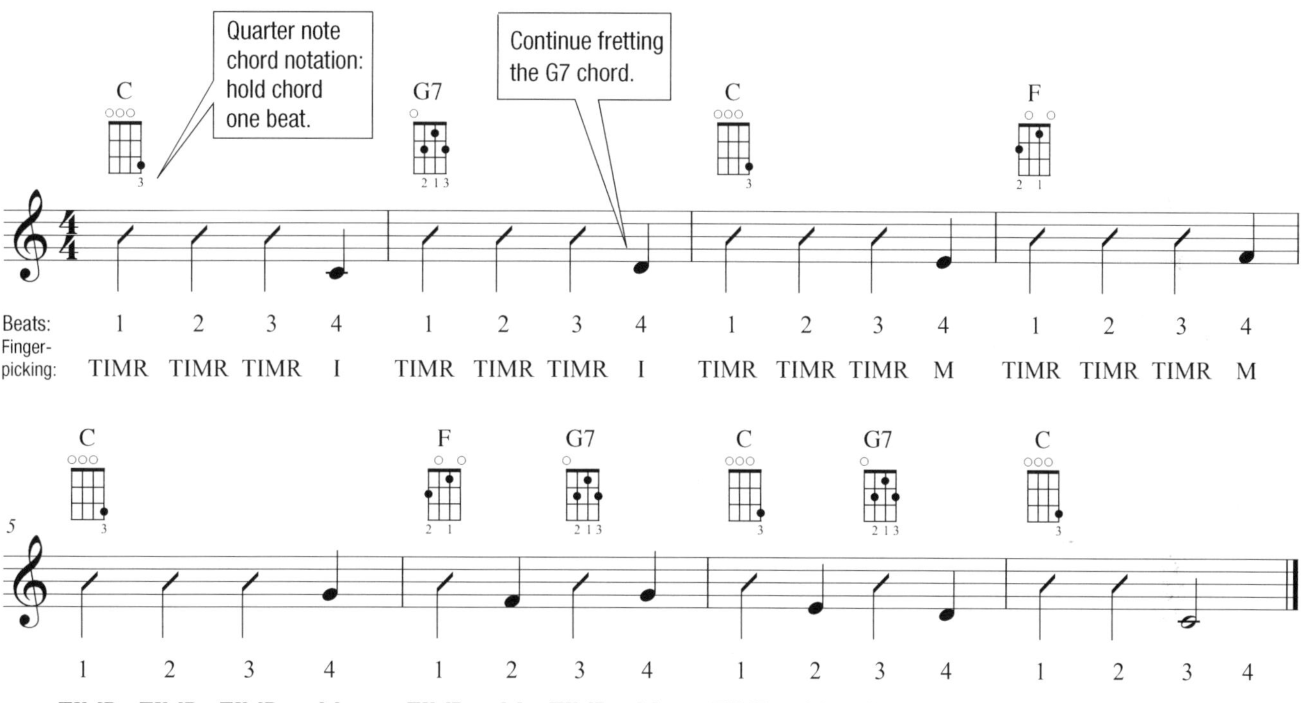

Note: For ukes strung with a high G string

When playing a G above middle C note on a uke strung with a high G string, you can either play the G note on the E string, or substitute playing an open high G string. It is the same note or pitch.

Both of the notes below are exactly the same "G above Middle C" pitches:

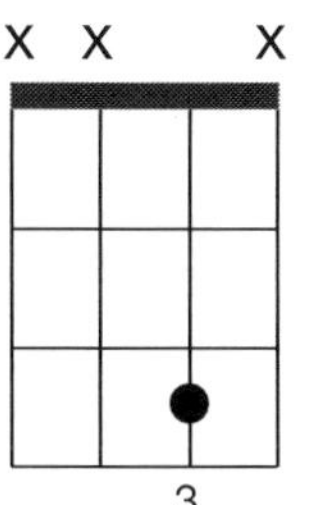

G note above Middle C on E string

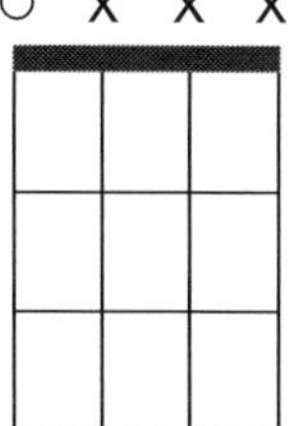

Same G note on High G string

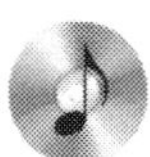

TRACK 25

12. Chords Follow Notes in 4/4 Time

This song is arranged to teach you to anticipate fretting a chord before you play it:

- In this exercise, all of the notes in each measure are contained in the chord that follows.
- Anticipate the chord by fretting it at the beginning of each measure, as you begin to play the notes.
- Before playing, count four for nothing: 1, 2, 3, Play or 1, 2, 3, 4.
- *Continue counting out loud through the rest of the piece.*

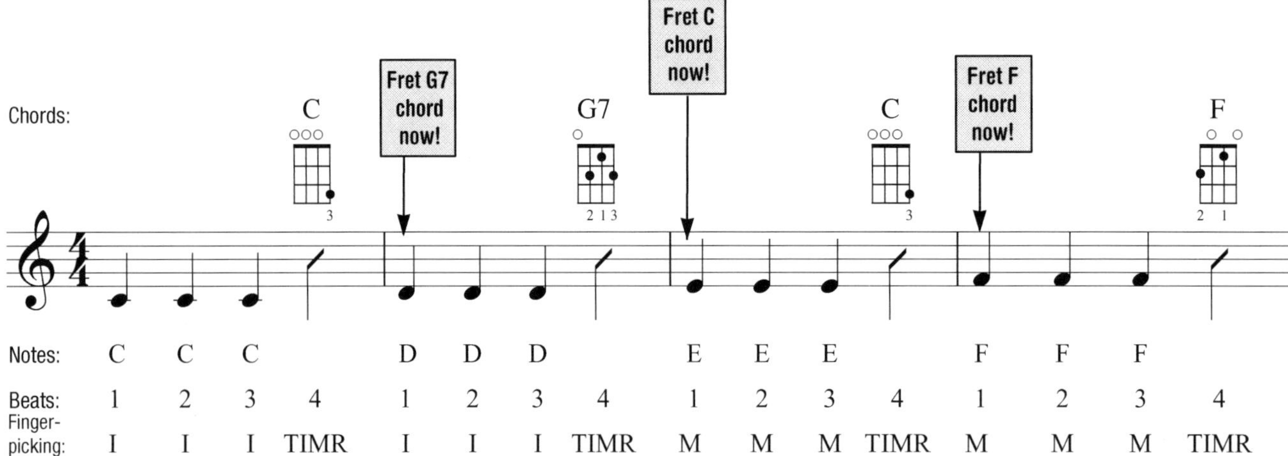

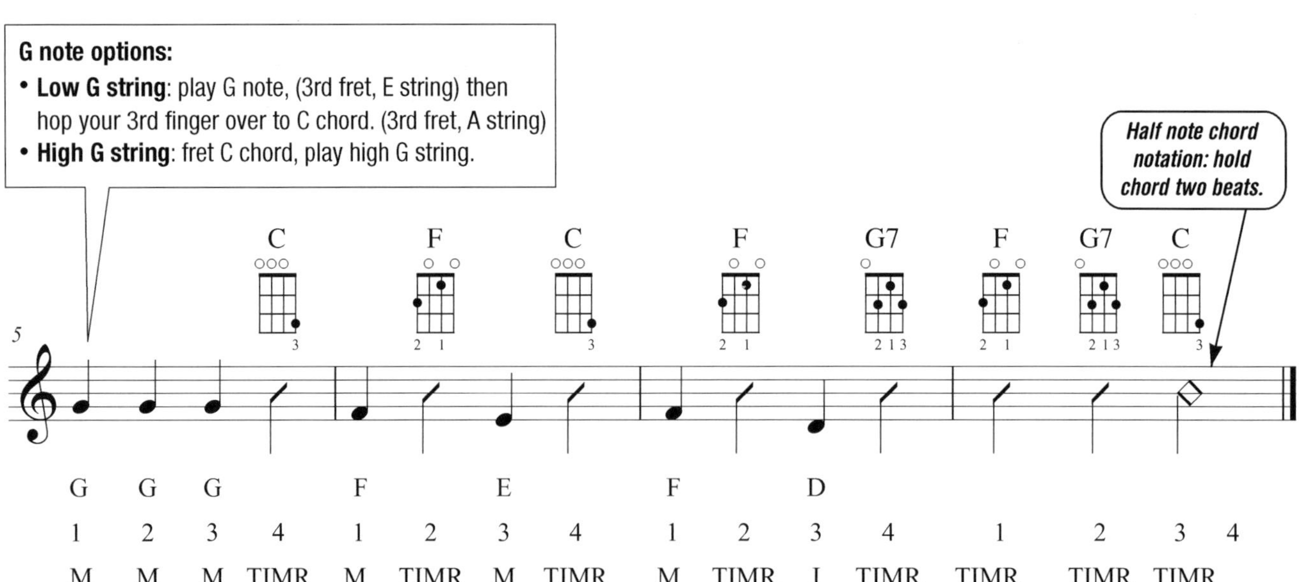

13. Notes and Chords in 3/4 Time

TRACK 26

This exercise trains you to look ahead in the music:

- If the notes being played are contained in the chord that follows, fret the chord as soon as the music allows.
- Before playing, count three for nothing: 1, 2, Play or 1, 2, 3.
- *Continue counting out loud through the rest of the piece.*

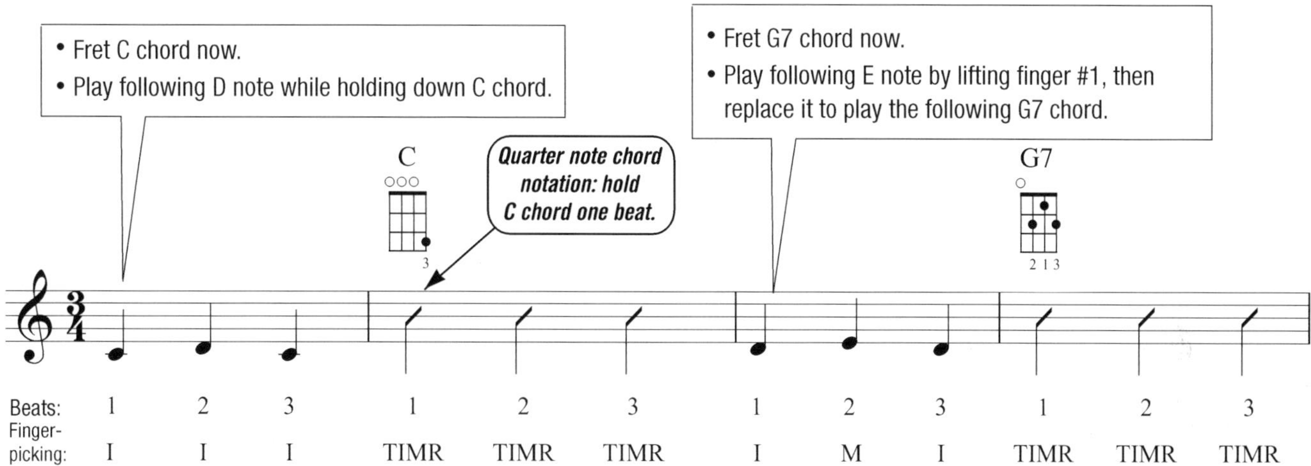

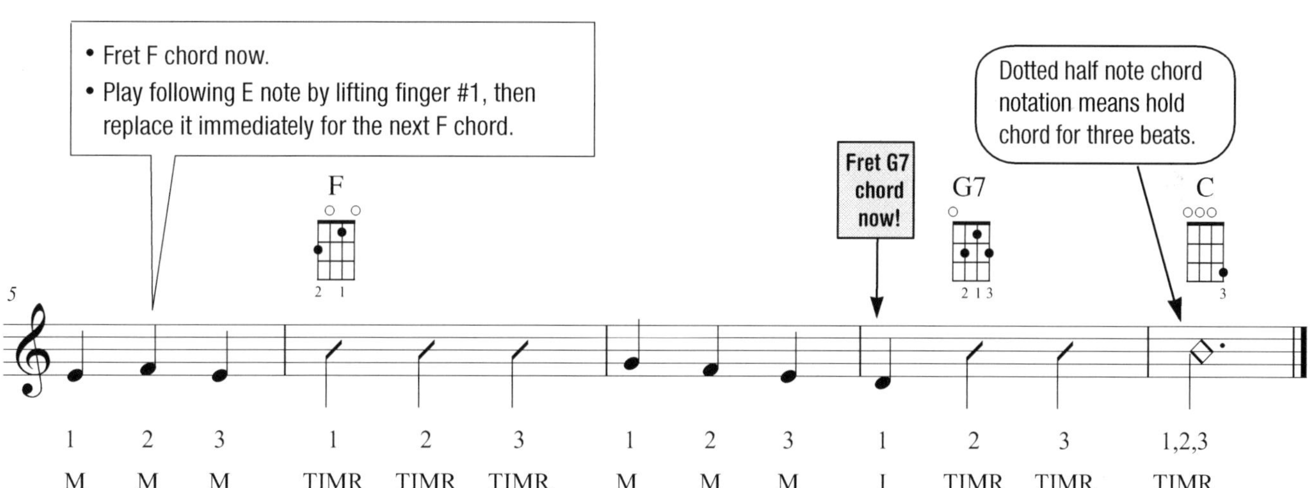

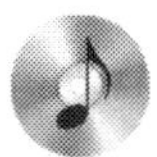

14. Jingle Bells

Playing options: Play melody and chords as an instrumental solo, then play chords to accompany singing.

Words and Music by
James Pierpont

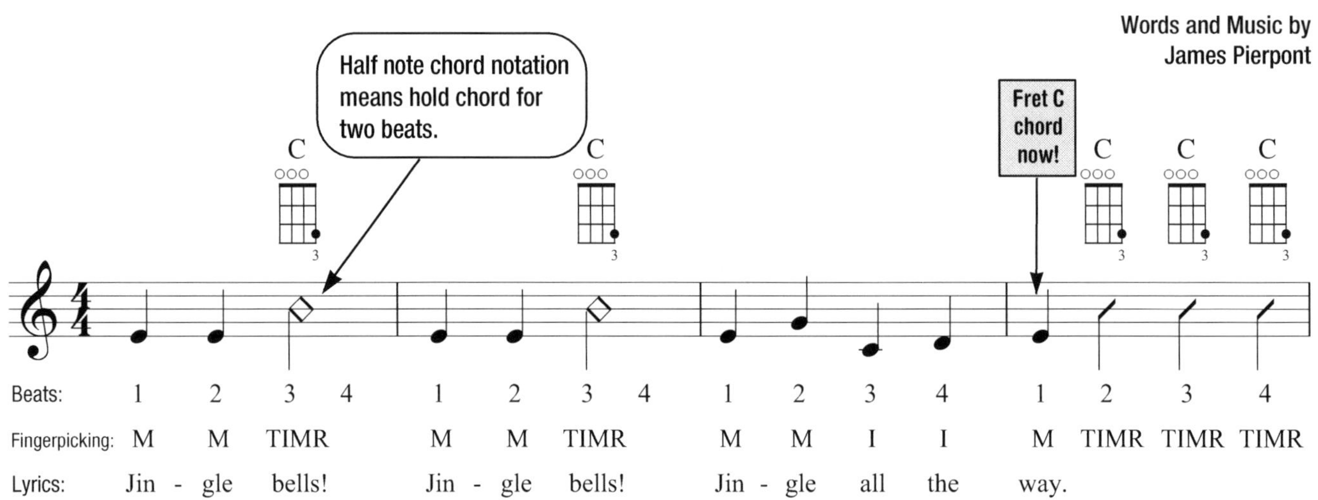

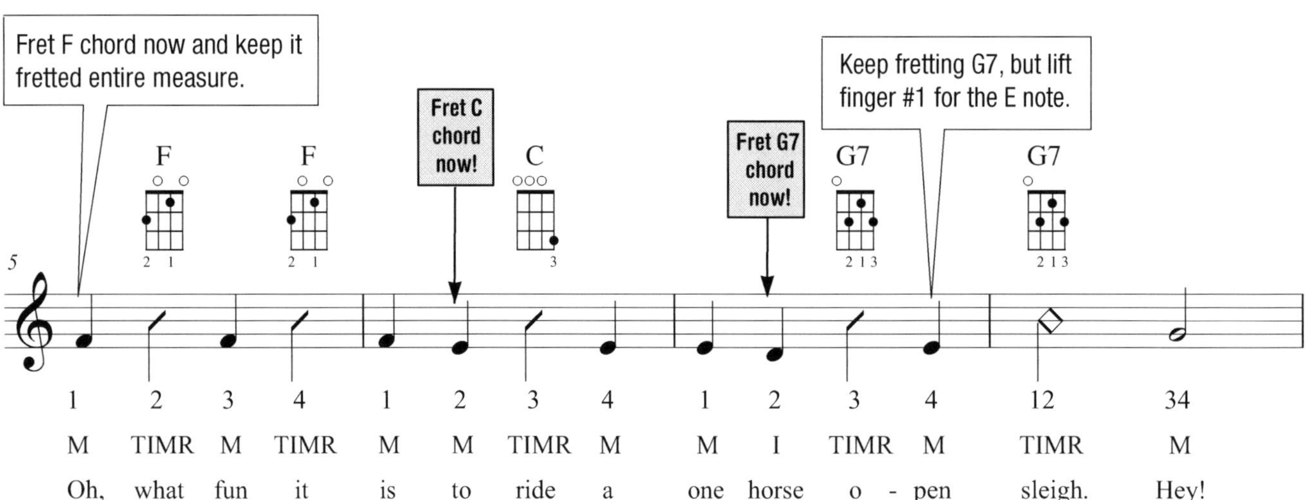

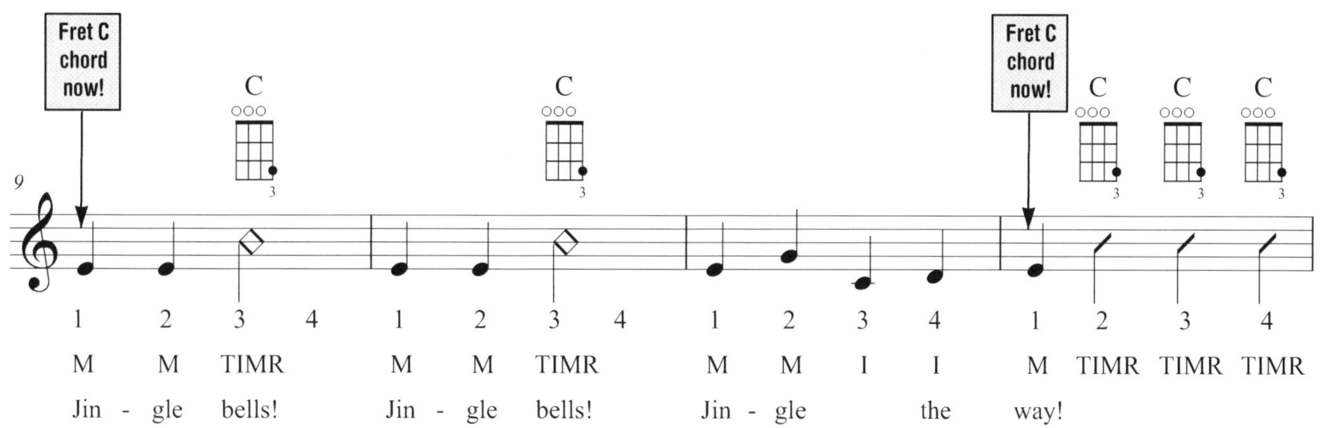

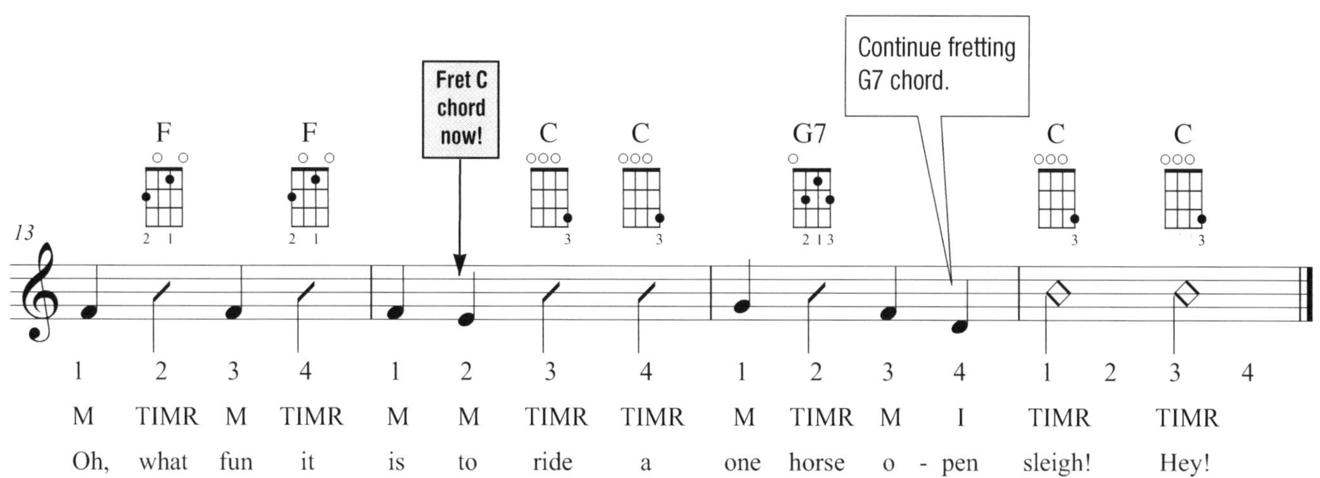

History: "Jingle Bells" was written by James Pierpont in 1857 for a Thanksgiving program at the Boston church where he taught Sunday school. His students performed it at Christmas time, and "Jingle Bells" became a Christmas favorite.

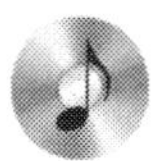

15. Beautiful Brown Eyes

TRACK 28

Accompany your singing with the chords, and then play an instrumental using my arrangement that combines melody and chords below.

Traditional

Fret C chord through measures 1–2.

Dotted half note chord notation means hold chord for three beats.

	C						F			F		
Beats:	1	2	3	1	2	3	1	2	3	1	2	3
Finger-picking:	TIMR	M	M	I	I	M	TIMR			TIMR		
Lyrics:	Beau -	ti -	ful,	beau -	ti -	ful	brown			eyes,		

Fret C chord through measures 5–6.

Fret G and F notes together on first beat for legato playing from G to F.

5

C						G7					
1	2	3	1	2	3	1	2	3	1	2	3
TIMR	M	M	I	I	M	TIMR			M		M
smil -	ing	right	in -	to	my	heart.			But		now

Fret C chord through measures 9–10.

Fret F chord for entire measure. Pick F note out of fretted chord.

9

C						F			F		
1	2	3	1	2	3	1	2	3	1	2	3
TIMR	M	M	I	I	M	TIMR			TIMR		M
where	are	those	beau -	ti -	ful	brown			eyes?		Why

Continue fretting G7 chord.

Keep fretting G7, but lift finger #1 for the E note.

13

G7			G7			C			C		
1	2	3	1	2	3	1	2	3	1	2	3
TIMR	I	M	TIMR	M	I	TIMR			TIMR		
must	we	be	so	far	a	part?					

How to Read and Play Lyric and Chord Charts

Following is an example of how songs are shared by many ukulele players. Instead of traditional music notation, you have lyrics and chords. So, you must know the melody to play the song. Simply play the chord indicated over a lyric and change chords when a new chord is specified. Sometimes this type of chart will indicate the strong beat with a strum slash.

Beautiful Brown Eyes

Chord indicator: Start playing the C chord on the word "Beautiful." Change to the F chord on the word "brown."

Strum Slash: Tells you to strum when you sing the word or syllable under the slash.

CHORUS

C   /   F   /
Beautiful, beautiful brown eyes,
C   /   G7
Shining right into my heart.
G7   C   /   F   /
But now where are those beautiful brown eyes?
     G7   /   C   /
Why must we be so far a-part?

VERSE 1

C   /   F   /
Molly my darling, I love you,
C   /   G7   /
Love you with all of my heart.
   C   /   F   /
To-morrow we were to be mar-ried,
     G7   /   C   /
But ramblin' has kept us a-part.

Sing Chorus

VERSE 2

C   /   F   /
Life's full of struggle and sor-row,
C   /   G7   /
Life's full of heartaches and woes.
C   /   F   /
I need the love of my wo-man,
   G7   /   C   /
To guide me where-ever I go.

Sing Chorus

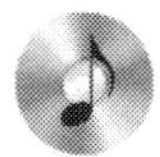

16. Ode to Joy

TRACK 29

Yes! You can play Beethoven on your uke with only 5 notes and 3 chords!

Ludwig von Beethoven (1770-1827)
Lyrics by Friedrich Schiller (1759-1805)

Hold down F note as you move to G note for a smooth legato sound.

For entire measure hold G7 chord and lift 1 finger off of F note to play E note.

Keep G7 chord fretted for entire measure.

	C				G7				C				G7		G7	
Beats:	1	2	3	4	1	2	3	4	1	2	3	4	1	2	3	4
Finger-picking:	TIMR	M	M	M	TIMR	M	M	I	TIMR	I	I	M	M	I	TIMR	
Lyrics:	Freu -	de	schö -	ne	Göt -	ter -	fun -	kin,	Toch -	ter	aus	El -	y -	si -	um,	

5

C				G7				C				G7		C	
1	2	3	4	1	2	3	4	1	2	3	4	1	2	3	4
TIMR	M	M	M	TIMR	M	M	I	TIMR	I	I	M	TIMR	I	TIMR	
Wir	be -	tre -	ten	Feu -	er -	trun -	ken	Him -	li -	she,	dein	Hei -	lig -	tum.	

9

Fret G7 chord now!

G7				G7				G7				F		G7	
1	2	3	4	1	2	3	4	1	2	3	4	1	2	3	4
TIMR	I	M	I	TIMR	M	M	I	TIMR	M	M	I	TIMR	I	TIMR	
Deine -	ne	Zau -	ber	bin -	den	wei -	der	Was	die	Mo -	de	streng	ge -	teilt	

13

C				G7				C				G7		C	
1	2	3	4	1	2	3	4	1	2	3	4	1	2	3	4
TIMR	M	M	M	TIMR	M	M	I	TIMR	I	I	M	TIMR	I	TIMR	
al -	le	Men -	schen	wer -	den	bru -	der	Wo	dein	san -	fter	Flü -	gle	weilt.	

"Ode to Joy" History: Ludwig van Beethoven was completely deaf in 1824 when he composed his final complete symphony *No. 9 in D minor.* Known as a choral symphony, it is the first example of a major composer using human voices in a symphony. The lyrics were taken from the "Ode to Joy," a poem written by Friedrich Schiller in 1785. The lyrics are sung during the fourth and final movement of the symphony by four vocal soloists backed by a chorus.

"Ode to Joy" lyric translation

The ukulele transcription on the previous page is the most famous excerpt from the full set of lyrics.

German original

Freude, schöner, Götterfunken
Tochter aus Elysium,
Wir betreten feuertrunken,
Himmlische, dein Heiligtum!
Deine Zauber binden wieder
Was die Mode streng geteilt;
Alle Menschen werden Brüder,
Wo dein sanfter Flügel weilt.

English translation

Joy, beautiful spark of the gods,
Daughter of Elysium,
We enter, drunk with fire,
Heavenly one, your sanctuary!
Your magic reunites
What custom strictly divided;
All men become brothers,
Where your gentle wing rests.

Optional Assignment: Research Beethoven's *Ninth Symphony* and the era in which it was written.

- What prompted Beethoven to make this a choral symphony?
- What elements make the main melody in the excerpt you are learning so memorable and adaptable to a variety of solo instruments?
- How was the poem relevant to the time it was written?
- Is the message in the poem relevant today? If so, why?

Ties, Slurs and Legato Playing

The **TIE** connects two of the same notes. It means hold the note.

Beat: 1 - 2 - 3 --- 1 - 2 - 3
Hold the A note for a total of 6 counts: 1 - 2 - 3 --- 4 - 5 - 6

LEGATO: Italian word for playing or singing notes smoothly and connected. In classical guitar music, you may see the Spanish term "ligado."

SLUR: a curved line over or under notes on different lines or spaces. If the notes are different, it's a *slur* and it means play legato.

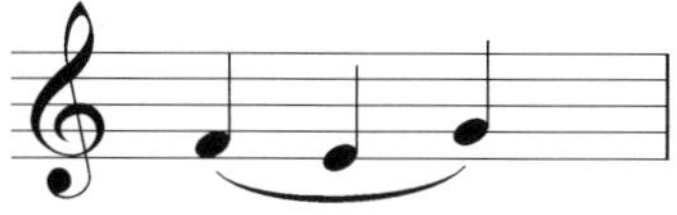

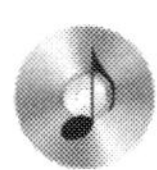

17. Barcarolle from "Tales of Hoffman"

TRACK 30

A ***barcarolle*** (from French; also Italian *barcarola, barcarole*) is a folk song sung by Venetian gondoliers, or a piece of music composed in that style. In classical music, one of the most famous barcarolles is this one by French composer, Jacques Offenbach, from his opera *The Tales of Hoffmann.* Offenbach is considered the "father of operetta." Operetta, which combines songs with dialogue, was the precursor of the 20th century American musical. Offenbach's most famous works, *Orphée aux Enfers* (Orpheus in the Underworld), 1858, and *Les Contes d'Hoffmann* (Tales of Hoffman), 1880, are still performed today in opera houses throughout the world.

Slur: indicates the E and D notes are to be sung and played "legato" (smoothly connected).
To sing legato: sing these two notes same syllable.
To play legato: After playing the E note, allow it to continue resonating as you play the D note.

Jaques Offenbach (1819–1880)

Chords:	C			F						G7					
Beats:	1	2	3	1	2	3	1	2	3	1	2	3	1	2	3
Finger-picking:	TIMR		M	TIMR		M	M	I	M	TIMR		M	M	I	M
Lyrics:	Joy	-	ous	night,		oh	night___		of	love,		your	mys	-	tic
	Bel	-	le	nuit,		Ô	nuit___		d'a -	mour,		Sou -	ris		á

6

G7			C			C			C			F		
1	2	3	1	2	3	1	2	3	1	2	3	1	2	3
TIMR		M	TIMR			TIMR			TIMR		M	TIMR		M
shad	-	ows	bless			us.			Star	-	ry	heav	-	ens
nos		i -	vres	-		ses.			Nuit		plus	dou	-	ce

11

			G7						G7			C		
1	2	3	1	2	3	1	2	3	1	2	3	1	2	3
M	I	M	TIMR		M	M	I	M	TIMR		M	TIMR		
high___		a -	bove,		oh ,	joy	-	ous	night		of	love.		
que___		le	jour,		Ô	bel	-	le	nuit		d'a -	mour.		

Rests and Their Rhythmic Values

Silence in music is indicated by a rest that corresponds to each type of note. Each rest has a specific "rhythmic value":

TYPES OF NOTES	Count the beats as you clap the note values in each rhythm below.
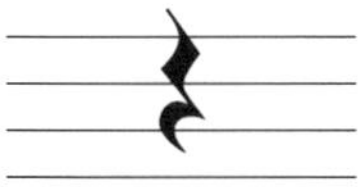 Quarter Note Rest = 1 beat (Silence for 1 beat.)	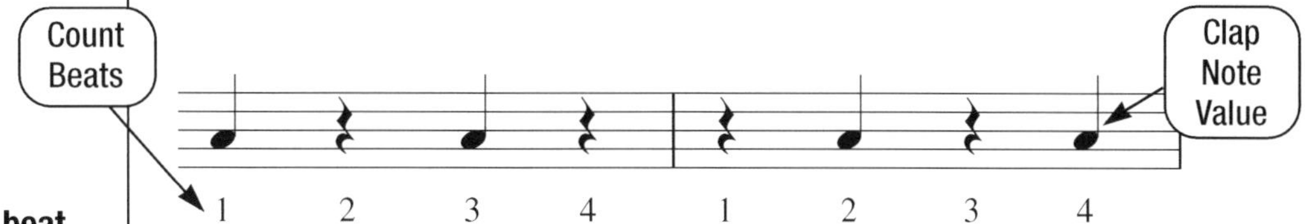 Count Beats / Clap Note Value 1 2 3 4 1 2 3 4 Clap the notes as you count beats aloud. Do not clap the quarter note rests.
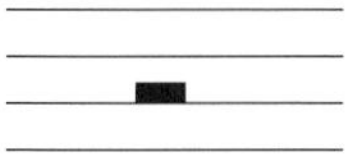 Half Note Rest = 2 beats (Silence for 2 beats.)	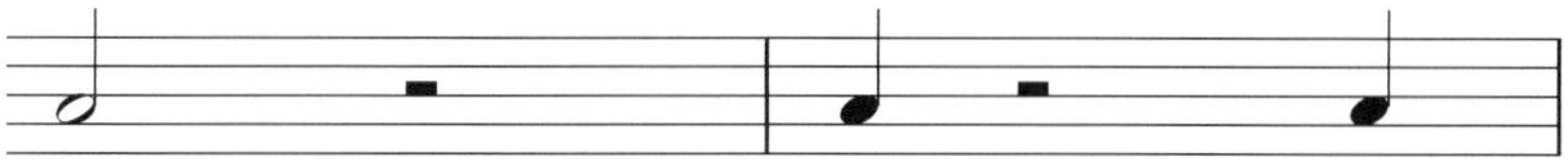 1 2 3 4 1 2 3 4 Clap the notes as you count beats aloud. Do not clap the half note rest.
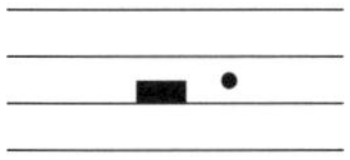 Dotted Half Note Rest = 3 beats (Silence for 3 beats.)	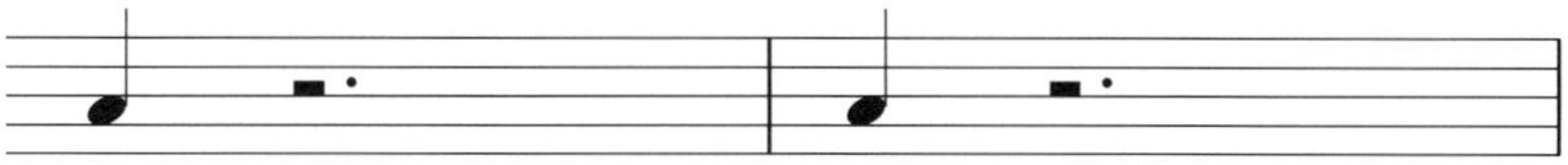 1 2 3 4 1 2 3 4 Clap the notes as you count beats aloud. Do not clap the dotted half note rest.
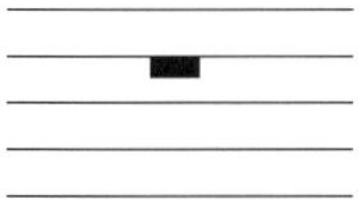 Whole Note Rest = 4 beats (Silence for 4 beats.)	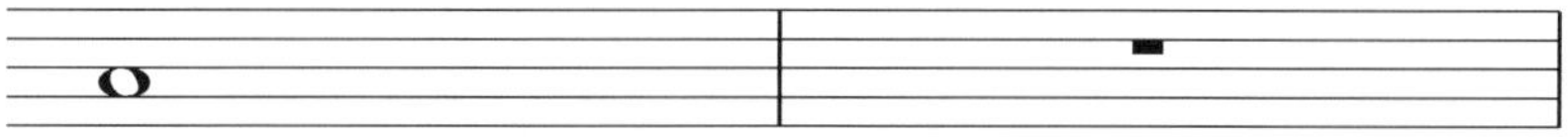 1 2 3 4 1 2 3 4 Clap the note as you count beats aloud. Do not clap the whole note rest.

Learning Tip: To remember the difference between half and whole note rests, think of the following visuals:

Learning to play by ear trains your auditory senses and helps you to memorize music!

Have you ever heard a song that you liked so much that the melody played over and over in your head? Have you ever picked the notes of that melody out on your ukulele? If so, that is known as "playing by ear," or hearing a tune and playing it on an instrument. To train yourself to play by ear, learn any melody in this book by looking at the notes. Play two to four measures while reading the music. Then, close the book, close your eyes, hear the melody, then play the music on your ukulele with your eyes closed. Learning music this way also helps you memorize entire pieces by training your ears and fingers!

Incomplete measures

Take a look at the first measure of the next two songs. You will notice that both songs do not start on the first beat. The "Kumbayah" melody starts on beat three of the first measure, while "When the Saints Go Marching In" starts on beat two of the first measure.

- **Music is mathematical. Everything has to add up**—These song melodies start on what is called an **"incomplete measure."** So in 4/4 time, if the first measure only has two beats as in "Kumbayah" (not counting the C chord two-beat intro), the last measure of the song has to "add up" with two beats. When the beats of the first and last measure are added together, they equal four beats.
- **Up-Beat/ Pick-up / Anacrusis**—The note (or sequence of notes) in an incomplete measure, which precedes the first downbeat *(the 1 beat)* of the next measure, is called any of the following: UP-BEAT, or PICK-UP, or ANACRUSIS.

18. Kumbayah

TRACK 31

In this arrangement, I have given you a melody mixed with chords. You can play it simply as an instrumental, an intro to the song, or between sung verses. For example, sing two verses then play an instrumental before you sing the last verse. Have fun and be creative!

Traditional

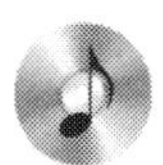

19. When the Saints Go Marching In

TRACK 32

American Gospel Hymn

Quarter note chord notation: Hold chord one beat.

Chords:					C	C	F	C					C	C	F
Beats:	2	3	4	1	2	3	4	1	2	3	4	1	2	3	4
Fingerpicking:	I	M	M	M	TIMR	TIMR	TIMR	TIMR	I	M	M	M	TIMR	TIMR	TIMR
	Oh,	when	the	Saints,					go	march -	ing	in,			

4

C					C		C		C		C		G7	G7	G7
1	2	3	4	1	2	3	4	1	2	3	4	1	2	3	4
TIMR	I	M	M	M	TIMR	M	TIMR	I	TIMR	M	TIMR		TIMR	TIMR	TIMR
	oh,	when	the	Saints		go		march	-	ing		in,			

8

G7					C	C			C					F	F
1	2	3	4	1	2	3	4	1	2	3	4	1	2	3	4
TIMR		M	I	I	TIMR	TIMR	I	M	TIMR	M	M	M	M	TIMR	TIMR
		oh,	I	want			to	be		in	that	num -	ber,		

13

F					C		C		G7		G7		C	F	F	C
1	2	3	4	1	2	3	4	1	2	3	4	1	2	3	4	1
TIMR		M	M	M	TIMR	M	TIMR	I	TIMR	I	TIMR	I	TIMR	TIMR	TIMR	TIMR
		when	the	Saints		go		march	-	ing,		in!				

When the Saints Go Marching In: Verses and Chords

I have arranged this traditional song so it can be played in a variety of ways. Try it as:

1. **An Instrumental** version with melody and chords.
2. **A Chord Accompaniment** for singing (this page).
3. **A Combination Accompaniment and Instrumental**. In this version try singing verse one and two, then play an instrumental before singing verse 3, 4 and 5.

Note: This song starts with the chorus. The chorus is also repeated after each verse. At the end of each verse are the chords C F F C, which is the introduction to the chorus. Starting after verse 1, do not play the initial C chord of the chorus.

CHORUS

```
C     /        /     C C F C    /          /  C C F C
   Oh, when the saints           go marching in,
   /      /    /  /   /     G7  / /
Oh, when the saints go mar-ching in,
       G7   C    /   / /      F       / /
Lord, how I want    to be in that number,
F          C     /  G7  /     C  C F F C
When the saints go mar-ching in!
```

VERSE 1

```
    C     /    C C F C      /     /    C    C F C
Oh, we are trav-            'ling in the foot-steps,
C  /   /       /   /  G7  / /
Of those who've gone be-fore,
G7        C  /   /  / F    / /
And we'll all   be re-u-nited,
F    C  /    G7  /  C     C F F C
On a new and sun-lit shore.
```

Chorus

VERSE 2

```
    C        /  C C F C     /      /      C C F C
And when the sun            re-fuse to shine,
     C        /   /   /   /  G7     / /
And when the sun re-fuse to shine,
      G7  C     /    / /      F        / /
Lord, how I want    to be in that number,
F          C   /  G7      C     C F F C
When the sun re-fuse to shine.
```

Chorus

VERSE 3

```
    C        /     C C F C        /        /    C C F C
And when the moon            turns red with blood,
    C        /     /    /  /   G7    / /
And when the moon turns red with blood,
      G7  C     /   /  /     F       / /
Lord, how I want    to be in that number,
F         C     /    G7 /    C     C F F C
When the moon turns red with blood.
```

Chorus

VERSE 4

```
    C        /    C C F C     /           /    C C F C
Oh, when the trum-            pet sounds its call,
    C        C    /   /       /  G7  / /
Oh, when the trum-pet sounds its call,
      G7  C     /   /  /     F       / /
Lord, how I want    to be in that number,
F         C    /   G7     /  C     C F F C
When the trum-pet sounds its call.
```

Chorus

VERSE 5

```
     /      /      C C F C      /        /    C C F C
Some say this world            of trouble is,
C  /  /  /   /   G7   / /
the on-ly one we need,
G7     C    /    /  /    F          / /
But I'm wait-  ing for that morning,
F          C    /    G7  /  C      C F F C
When the new world is    re-vealed.
```

Chorus

Song Notes: "When the Saints Go Marching In" is a traditional gospel hymn from Louisiana. Though it originated as a spiritual, it is often played as jazz. Known as the signature tune of New Orleans, the tune is traditionally played as a funeral march there, where funerals are often called "jazz funerals." While accompanying the coffin to the cemetery, a band plays the tune as a dirge. On the way back, it switches to the "Dixieland" jazz style as mourners follow in a joyous parade to celebrate the life of the person they loved.

WRITTEN EXERCISE 1:
Get Spaced!

Instructions: Use pencil.

1. If there is a line below a note, write its letter name.
2. If there is a space above a letter name, write in a quarter note.
3. **Remember:** Notes above the B line get a downwards stem to the left. Notes below the B line get an upwards stem to the right. Stems are 3 spaces long.

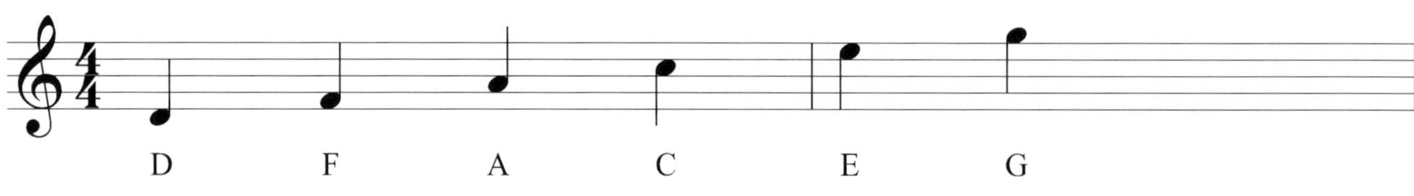

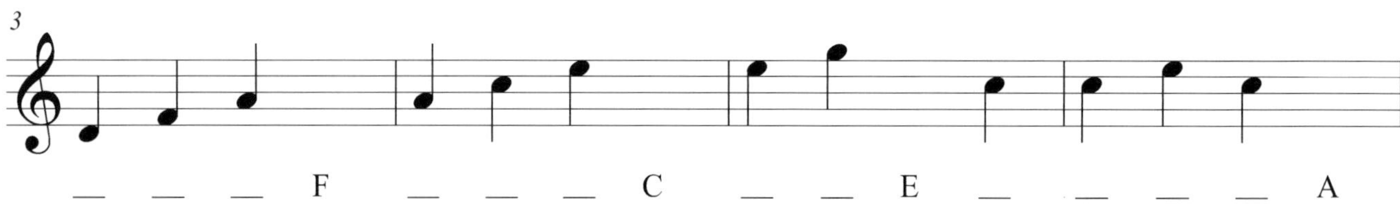

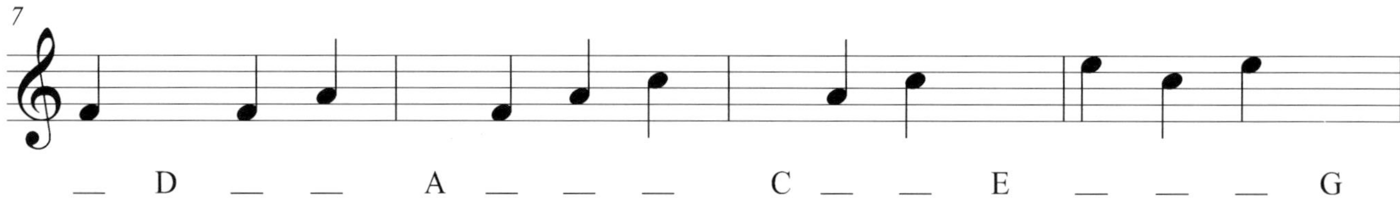

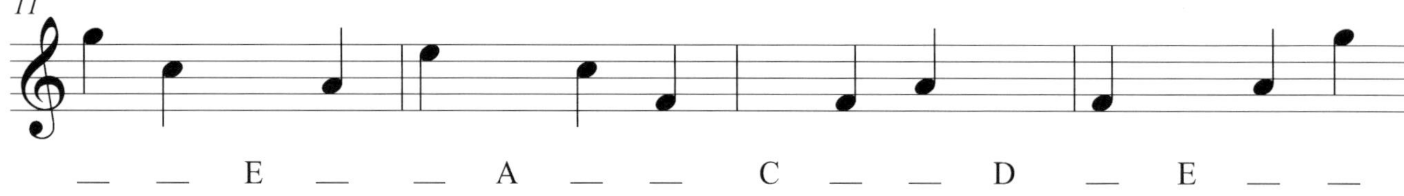

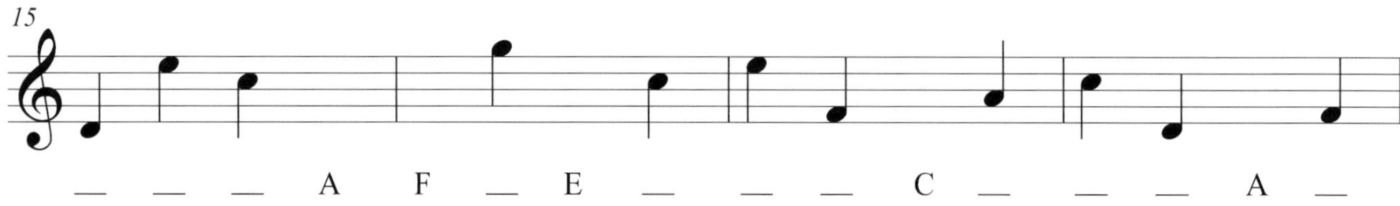

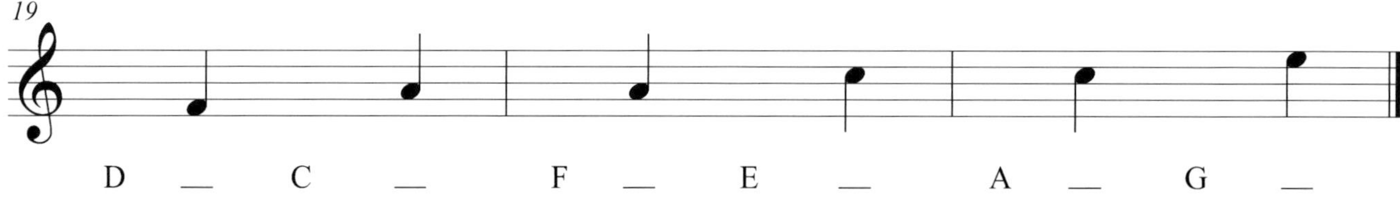

WRITTEN EXERCISE 2:
Note Writing Middle C, D, E, F, G

Instructions: Use pencil.

1. First write the G Clef at the beginning of each staff below.
2. Next write a 4/4 time signature on the first staff only.
3. Write a quarter or half note above the letter name indicated below the staff. Half notes rhythms are notated with a comma between beats.
4. Be sure to make the stem of each note 3 spaces long.
5. Add the beat number under each note.

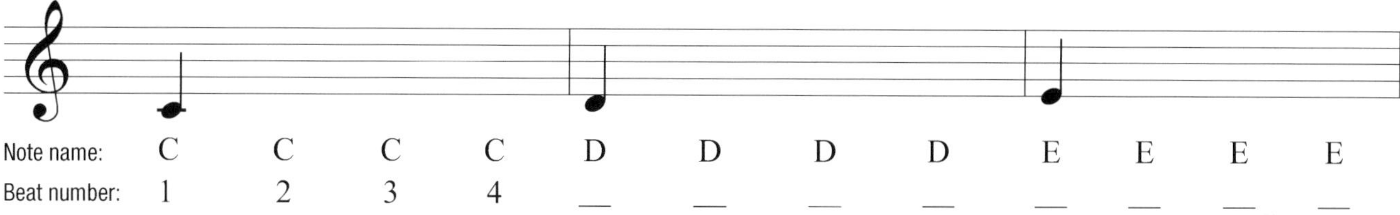

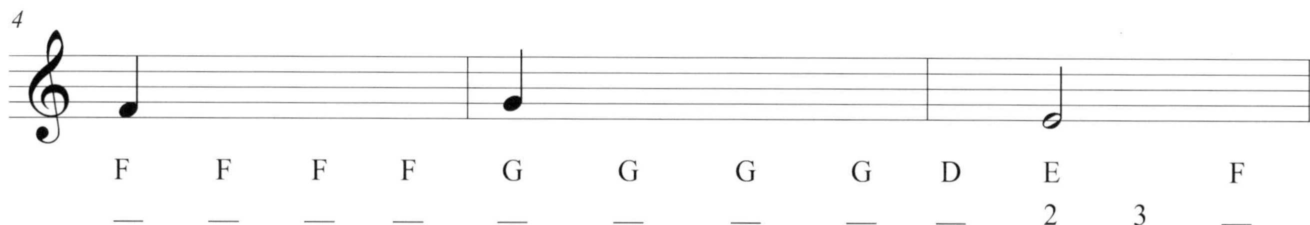

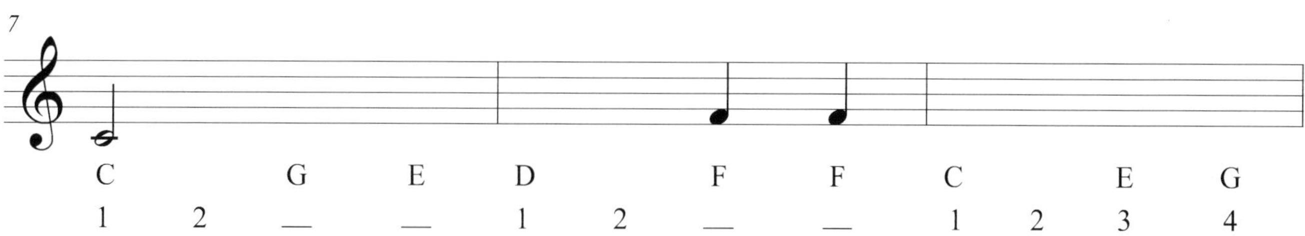

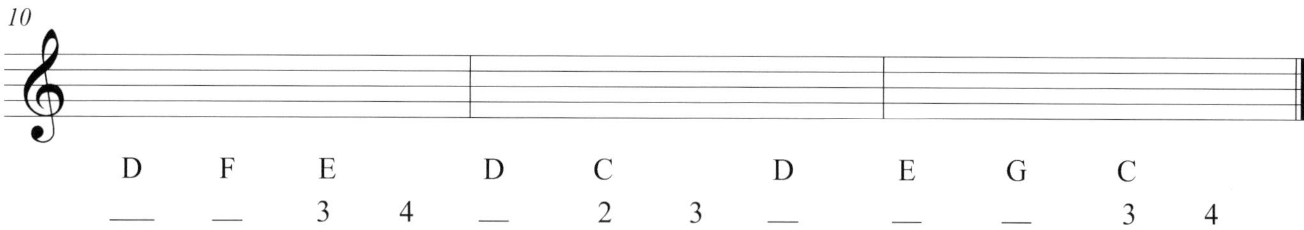

WRITTEN EXERCISE 3:
Know Your Rests

Instructions: Use pencil.

1. In the staff above each note letter and rest, write in the appropriate note and rest notation.
2. To figure out the duration of each note and rest, pay attention to the beat numbers below each measure.
3. **NOTES**: Use quarter, half, dotted half and whole notes.
4. **RESTS**: Use quarter and half note rests. (Refer to **"Rests and Their Rhythmic Values" on page 65**.)
5. **Play** the melody when you have completed the exercise. Count aloud as you play.

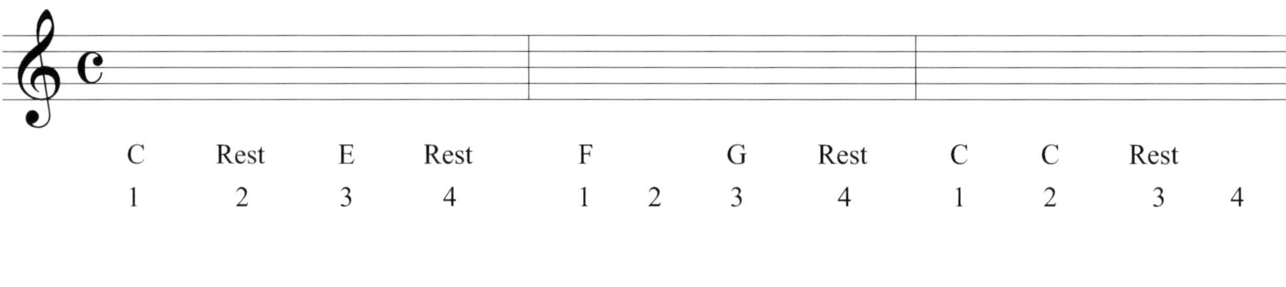

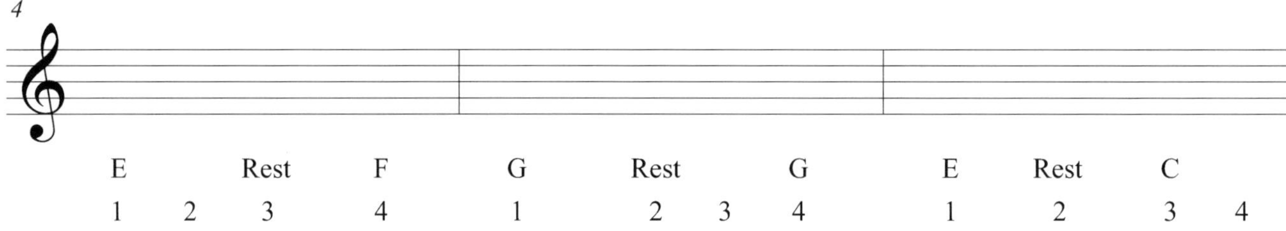

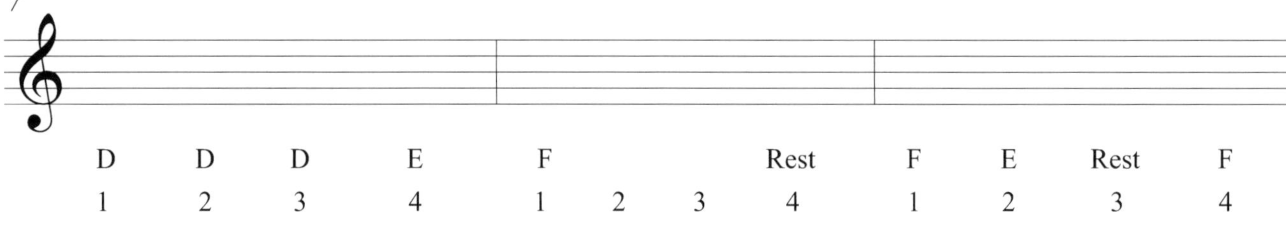

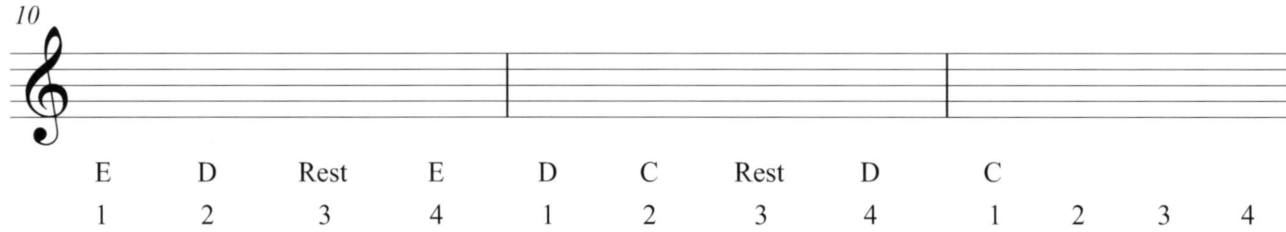

WRITTEN EXERCISE 1:
Answer Key For Get Spaced!

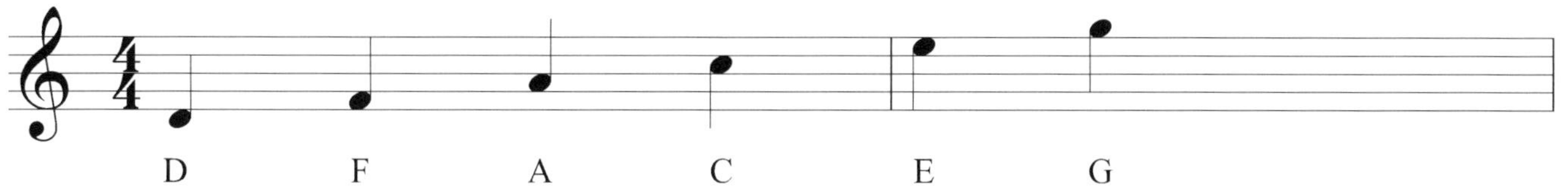

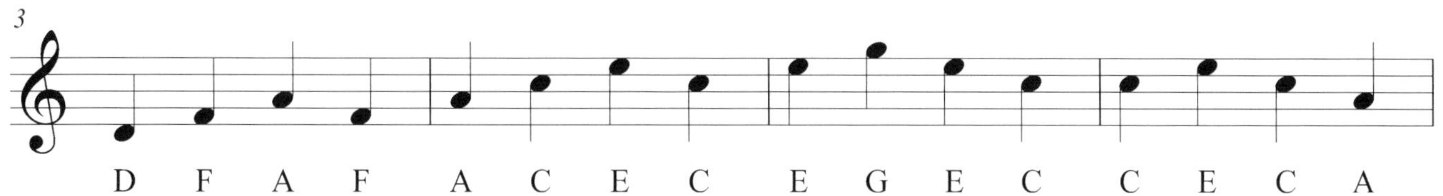

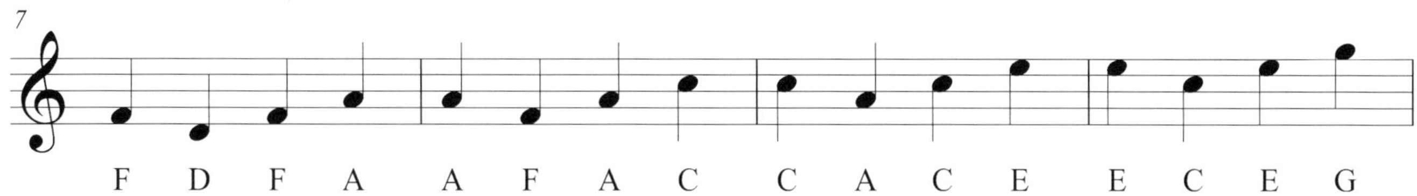

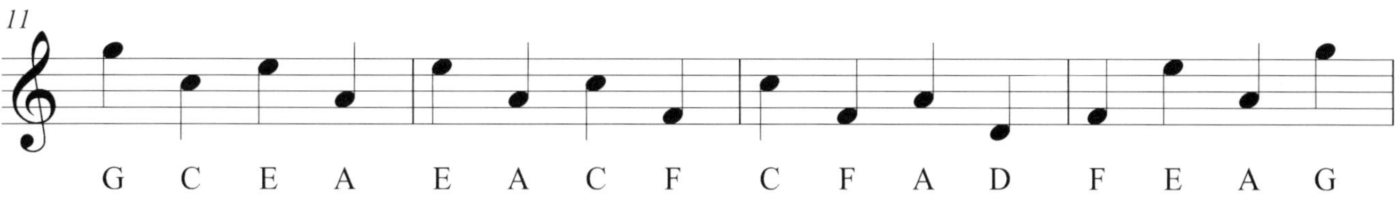

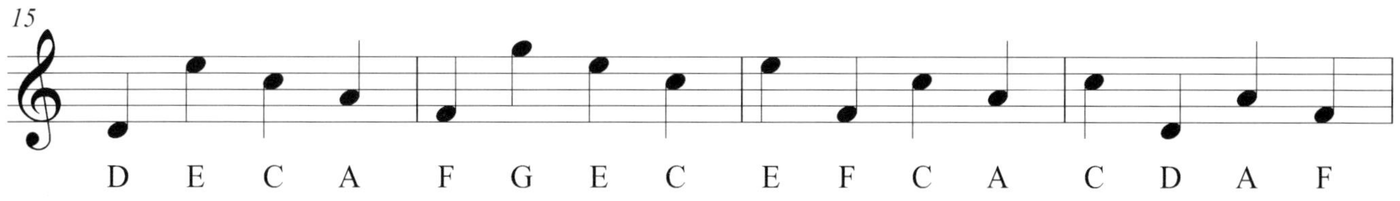

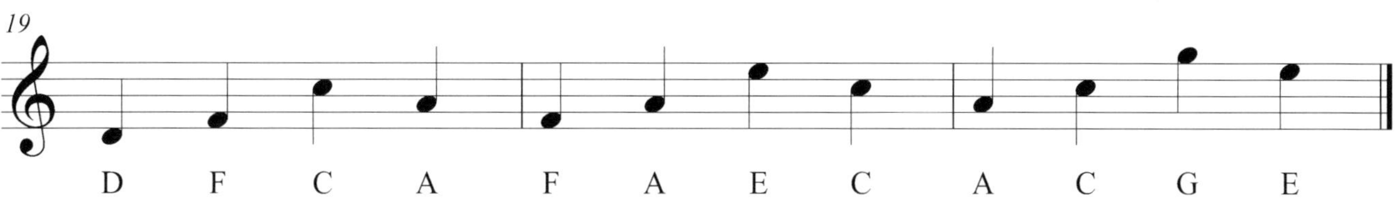

WRITTEN EXERCISE 2:
Answer Key For Note Writing Middle C, D, E, F, G Notes

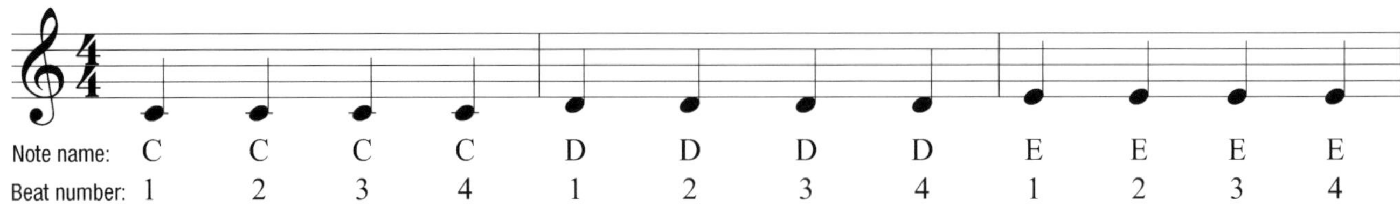

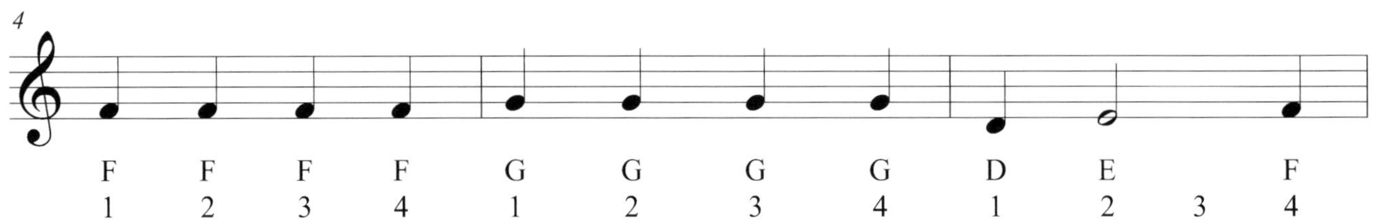

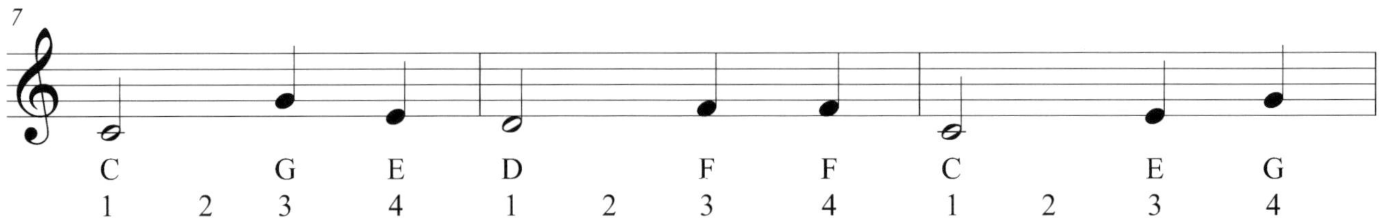

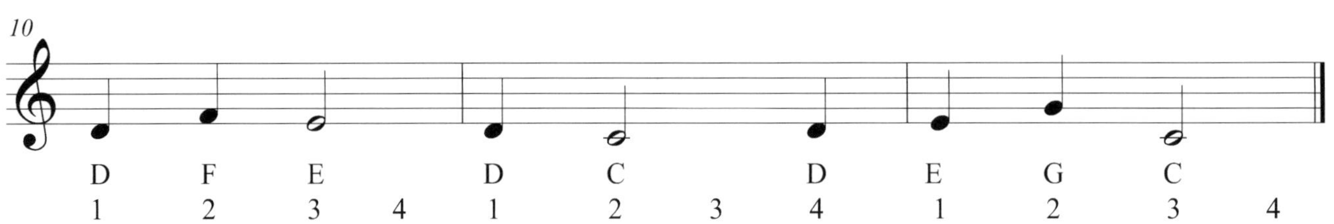

WRITTEN EXERCISE 3:
Answer Key For Know Your Rests

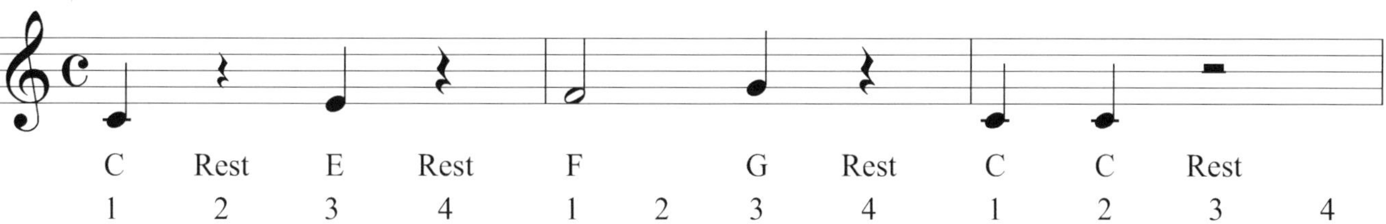

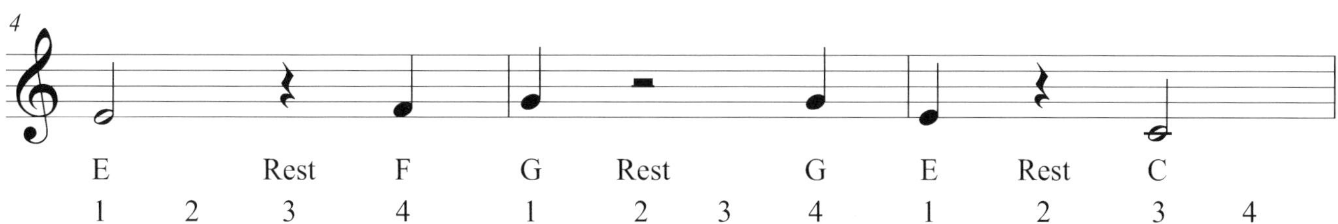

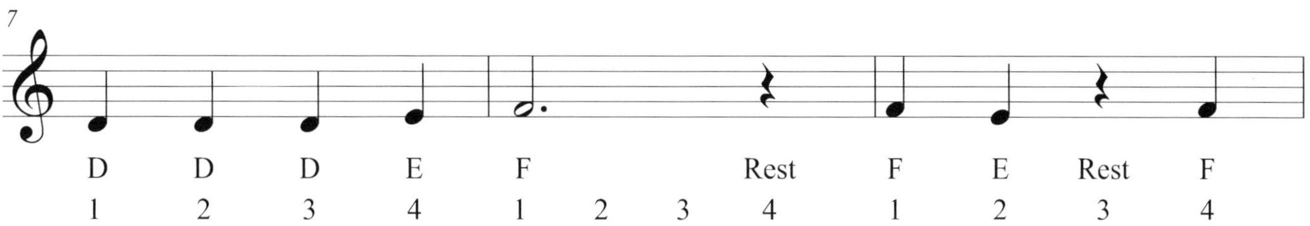

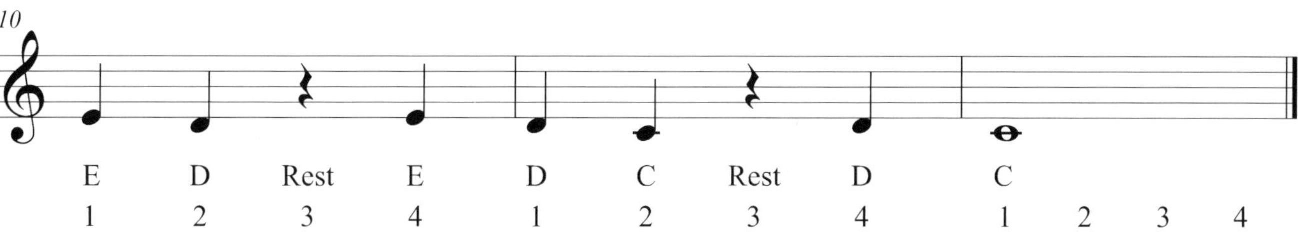

Lesson 3

Assignment

1. **Warm-up:** Each time you sit down to practice, play the following in this order...

   A. **4-Fret Half-Step Chromatic Scale Exercise** (**page 47**)

   B. **C Scale:** Practice the C scale using legato playing techniques. As you play, sing the note names forwards and backwards.

   C – D – E – F – G – A – B – **C** – B – A – G – F – E – D – C

   Do not look at your left hand as it frets the notes. Practice playing while looking at the music, then with your eyes closed (**page 81**)

2. **Review:** Play through your favorite music and songs in *Lesson 1* and *2* as a refresher and for reinforcement. Work on anything challenging that you still need to master… a chord change, a musical passage, whatever. Practice while reading the music. Then close your eyes and play short passages to train your memory, ears and fingers.

3. **Learn:** Each time you sit down to practice, play the following in this order...

   A. **A, B, and C notes** on the A string (**pages 78-79**)

   B. **G major chord** (**page 83**)
   Practice the G major chord by learning the following chord progressions:

   1) G to F to C to G
   2) G to C to F to G
   3) G to G7 to C to F to G to C
   4) G to C to F to G to C

   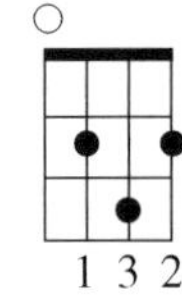

   C. **Combine chords and notes** (**pages 84-85**)

   D. **Music and songs—*Don't try to learn everything in the entire lesson at once*.** Be patient and take your time to learn the music and internalize the techniques:

   1) **Select 1–3 songs and practice them until they are mastered.** When you learn those well enough to play them slowly and in rhythm, learn a couple more until you learn them all. Songs start on **page 86**.
   2) **If you can say it, you can play it!** Play each piece you are learning 3 ways:
      a) First count the beats in each measure while reading music.
      b) Second, say the note names while reading the music.
      c) Third, say the right hand finger names while plucking the strings.

4. **Written Exercises:** *(Please use a pencil for the following exercises)*

   A. Fill in the "Lines and Spaces" exercise (**page 96**)

   B. Note Writing—The C Scale (**page 97**)

Introducing Notes on the A String: A, B and C Note

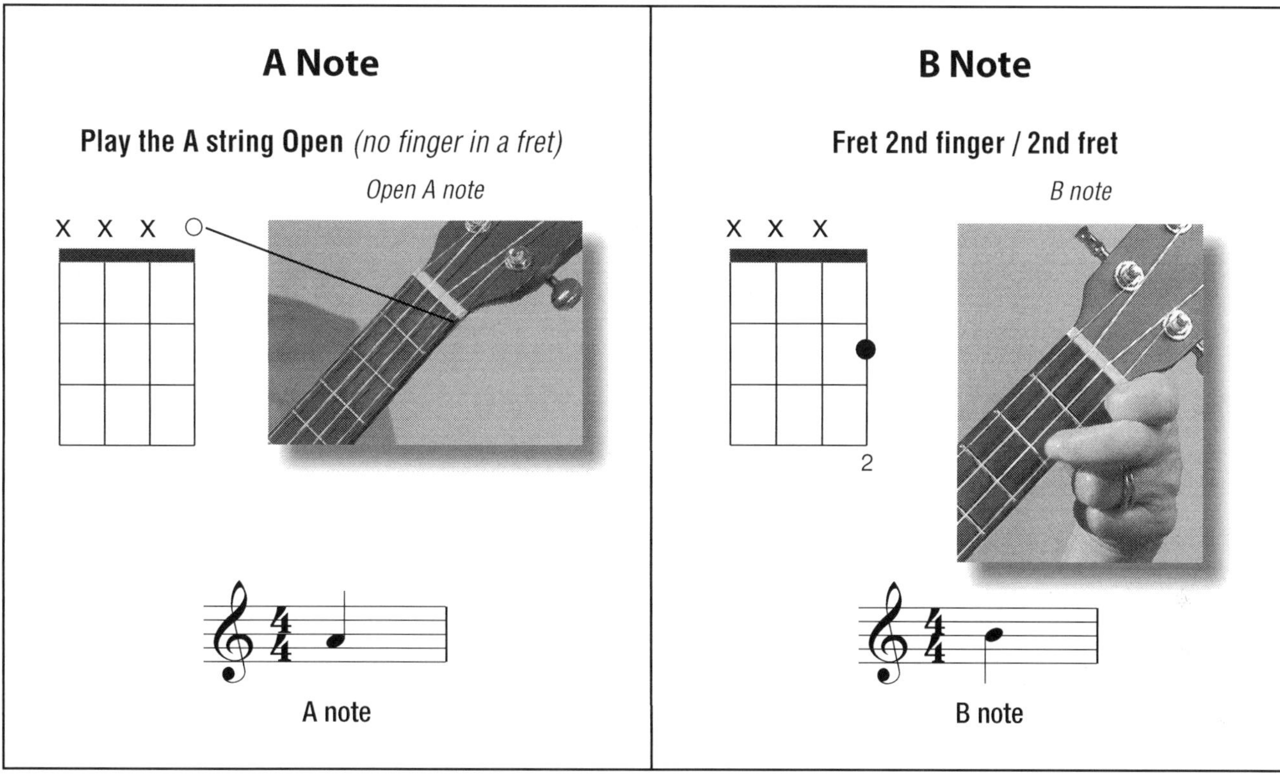

Right hand fingerpicking for A, B and C notes:

The A, B and C notes are plucked with the **Ring** finger notated as **R**.

Fingerpicking Tip: Rest your Thumb lightly on the A string and extend it toward the head of the uke to help keep your Ring finger in place.

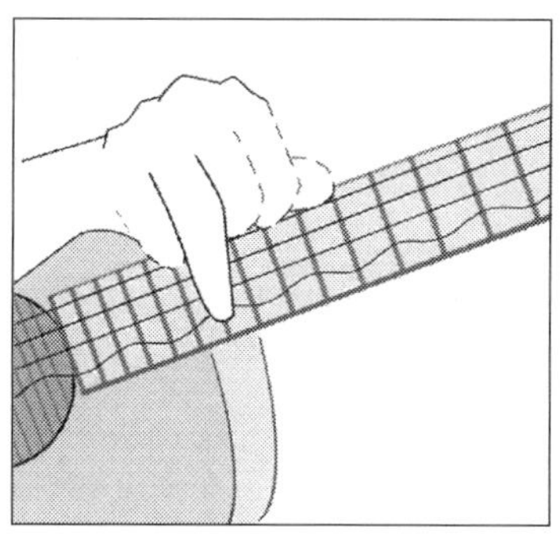

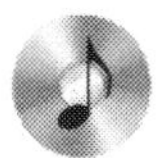

1. Learn Your A, B, Cs

TRACK 33

- Before playing, count four for nothing: 1, 2, 3, Play or 1, 2, 3, 4.
- *Continue counting out loud through the rest of the piece.*

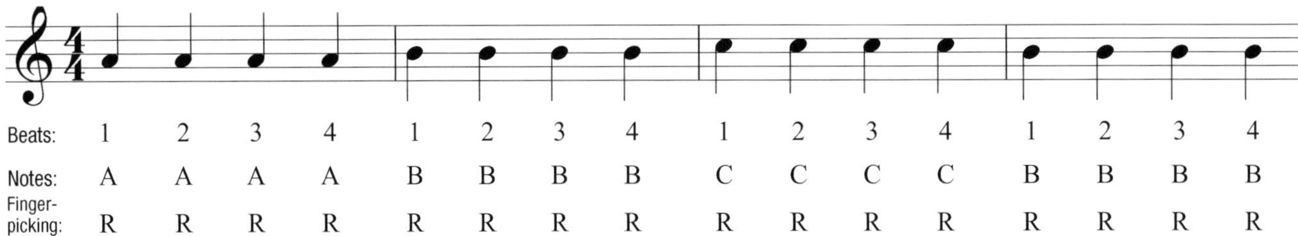

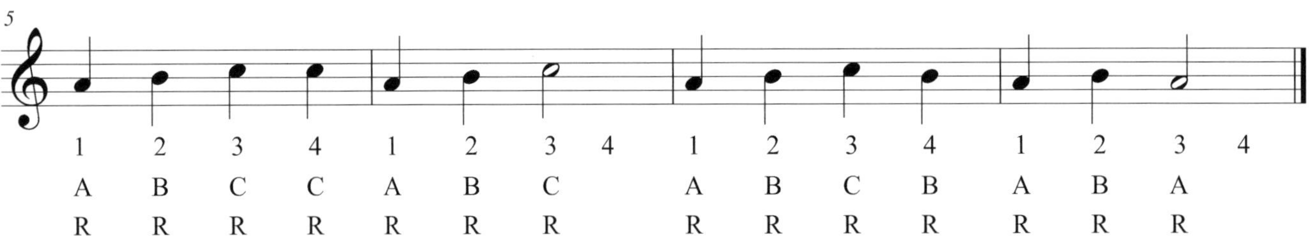

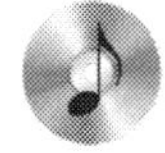

2. A, B, C Warm Up in 3/4 Time

TRACK 34

- Before playing, count three for nothing: 1, 2, Play or 1, 2, 3.
- *Continue counting out loud through the rest of the piece.*

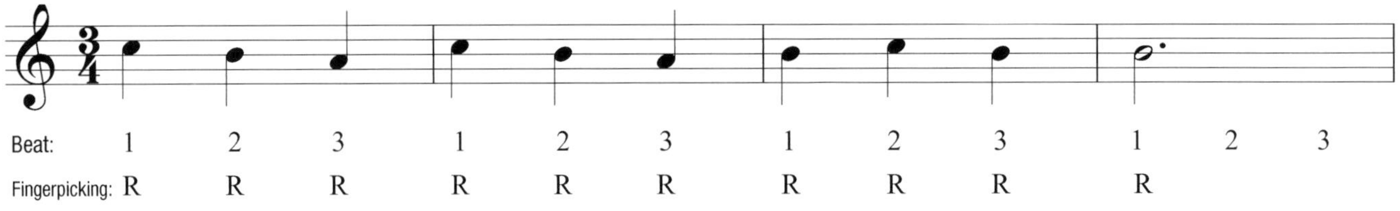

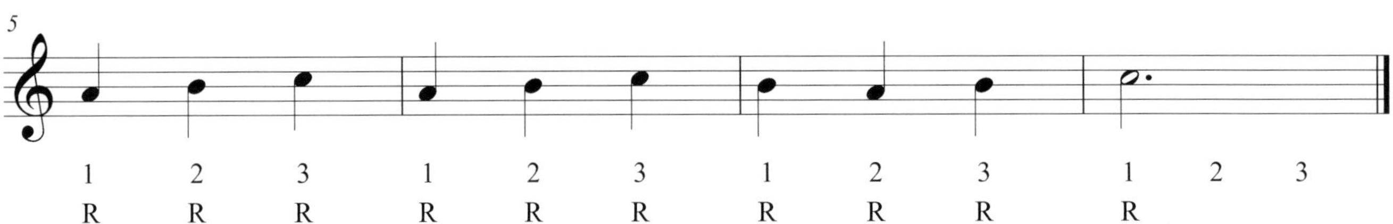

3. More A, B, Cs

TRACK 35

- Before playing, count four for nothing: 1, 2, 3, Play or 1, 2, 3, 4.
- *Continue counting out loud through the rest of the piece.*

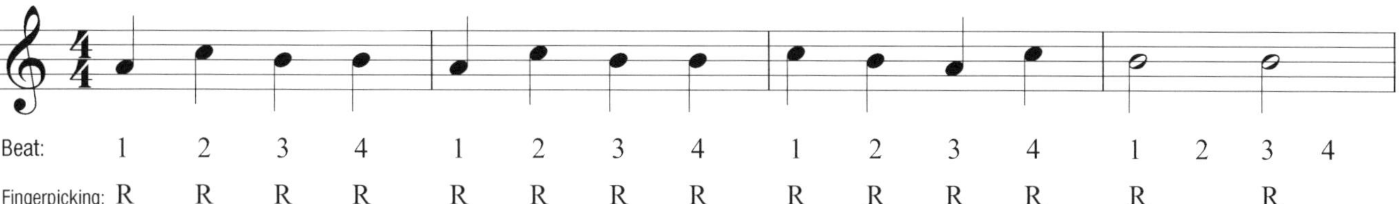

Congratulations! You now know the C Scale!

The A, B, and C notes that you just learned complete the C major scale. This scale of eight notes is also known as an octave which starts on middle C and ends on the C above middle C. Below is a diagram of a piano keyboard that shows how the C scale on your ukulele relates to the C scale on the piano keyboard. The pitches or notes on both instruments are exactly the same.

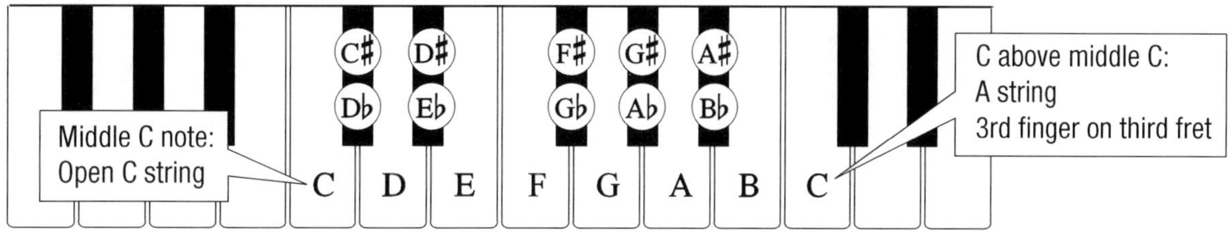

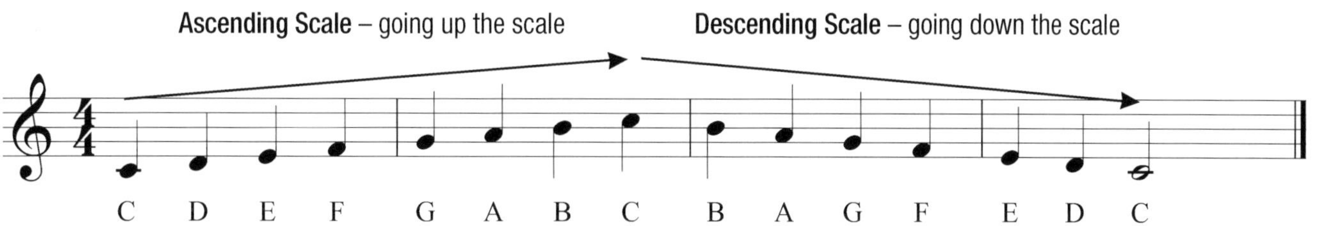

How to Play the C Major Scale Legato

The following techniques will enable you to play legato or smoothly connected; one note flowing into the next. Make the left hand finger patterns and exercise one of your daily warmups. Over time, it will make your playing sound very professional.

Technique:

Fretting an ascending scale—going up the scale from middle C (C string, 2nd string played open) to C (A string, 3rd fret):

- When fretting an ascending note followed by a note on an open string, continue fretting the first note firmly until the next note is played on the open string. Then lift the finger fretting the first note.

  For example, when playing the fretted D note to the open E note, continue fretting the D note firmly so it continues to resonate while you play the E string. Then lift your second finger off of the D note just as you fret the F note (the next scale note after the E note).

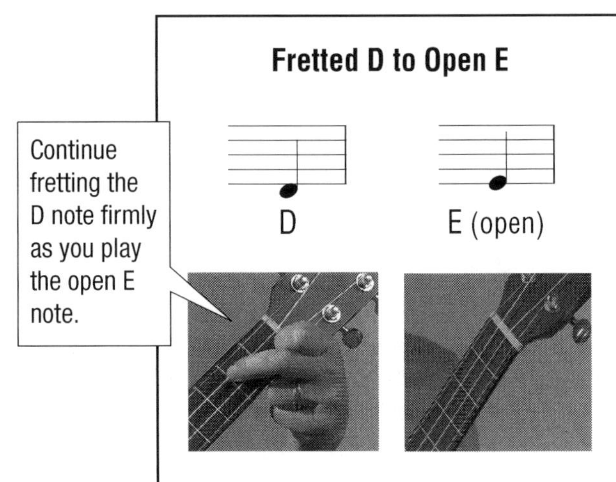

- **When fretting ascending notes on the same string**, continue fretting the first note firmly after you play it while you fret the next note.

  For example, when playing the F then G notes on the E string, fret the F note firmly with your first finger and leave it there after playing as you place your third finger on the G note. Use the same technique when playing the B to C notes on the A string. See examples below.

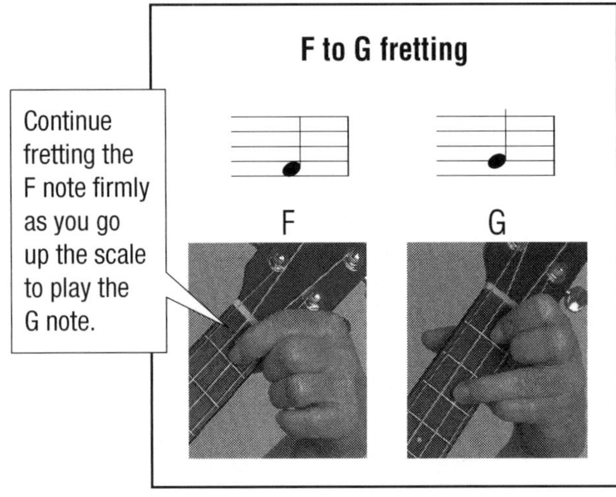

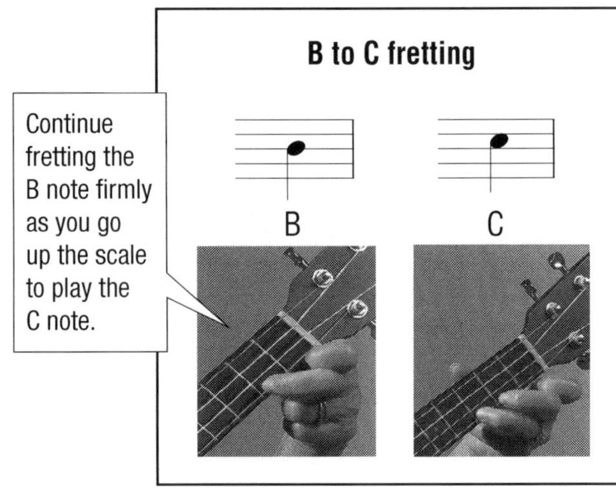

Fretting a descending scale—going down the scale from C (A string, 3rd fret) to middle C (C string, played open):

- Fret all the fingers on a string with hard pressure simultaneously. Then lift each finger until all the notes are played. For example, before playing the descending C-B-A scale on the A string, simultaneously fret your second and third fingers firmly on the C and B notes. Lift each finger after you play the note it is holding down. Use the same technique of the G-F-E scale on the E string. Simultaneously fret the third finger on the G note and the first finger on the F note firmly before playing the notes.

Left Hand C Scale Fretting Exercise:

Do not play these notes with your right hand; fret with the left hand only. Do not look at your left hand.

With your eyes closed, practice simultaneously fretting all the notes firmly on each string as you move from the A string to the C string. Make sure your fingers are next to the fret bars and not on top of them. Then practice the reverse, by fretting notes from the C string to the A string.

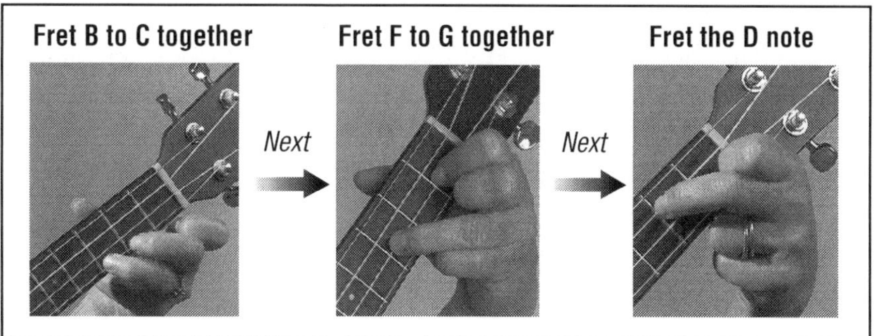

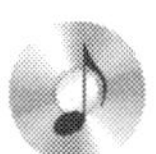

4. C Scale Exercise

TRACK 36

Practice reading both the notation and the tablature. Sing or say the note name as you play. Then, live dangerously! Close your eyes; play and sing the note names. If it sounds incorrect, take a peek, readjust your left hand fingers, then continue practicing without looking.

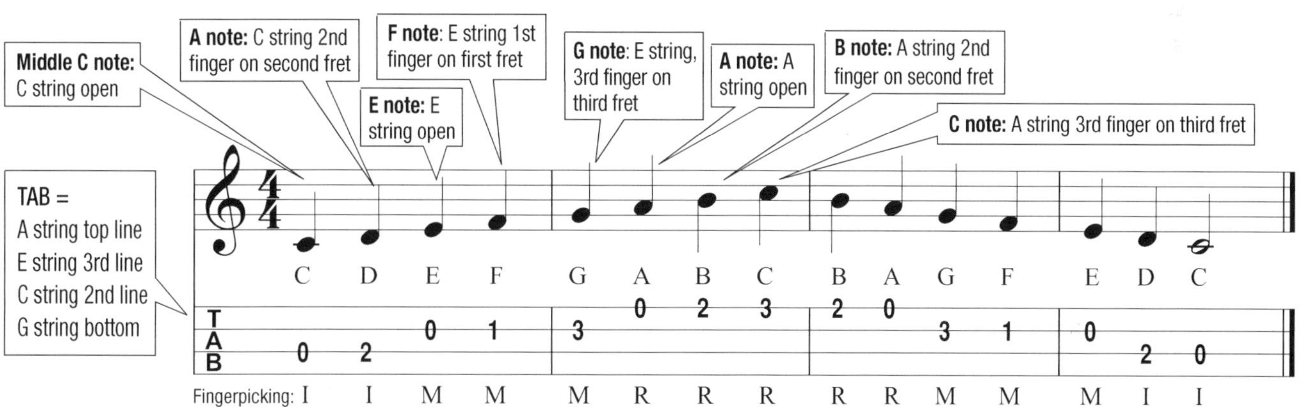

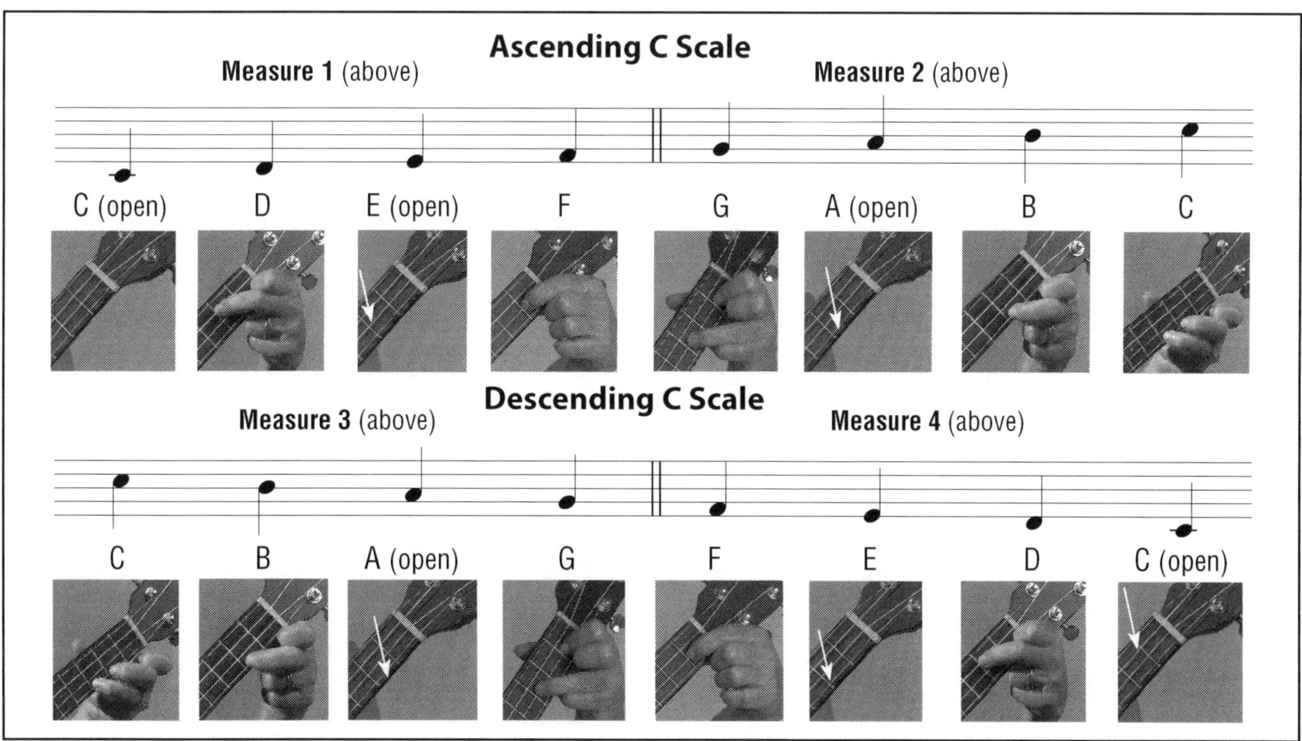

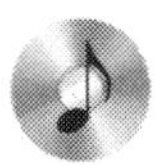

5. A Tisket, A Tasket

TRACK 37

This song introduces the A note within a familiar melody. Notice that this song starts on an incomplete measure. In the first measure of the song, the melody starts on beat 4 (the up-beat), while in the last measure, the song ends on beat 3. (Review **"Incomplete measures" on page 66**.)

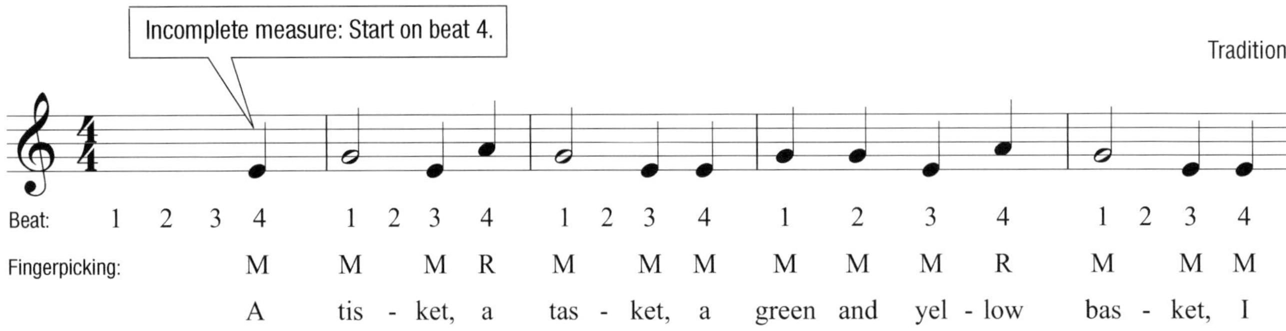

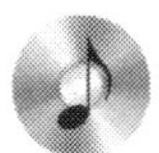

6. Reuben, Reuben

TRACK 38

This familiar song mixes up your new A, B and C notes in a way that will help you learn their fretting positions.

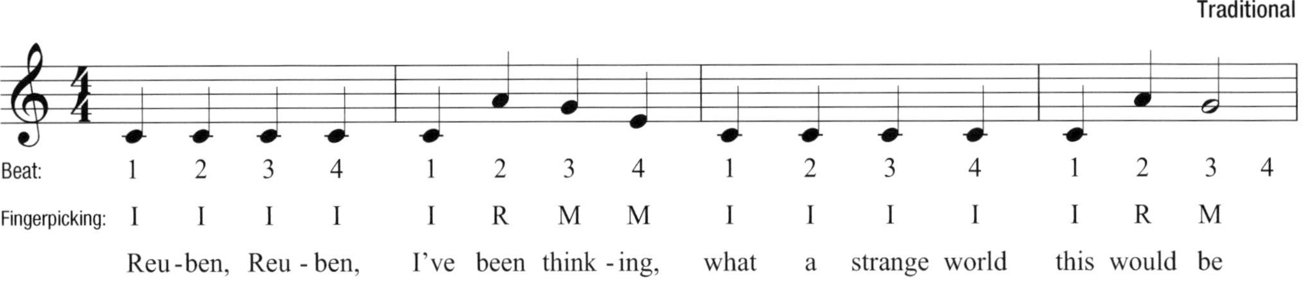

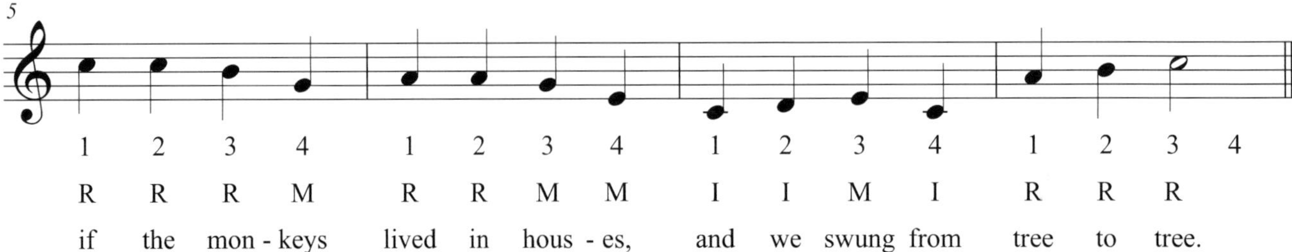

Introducing the G Major Chord

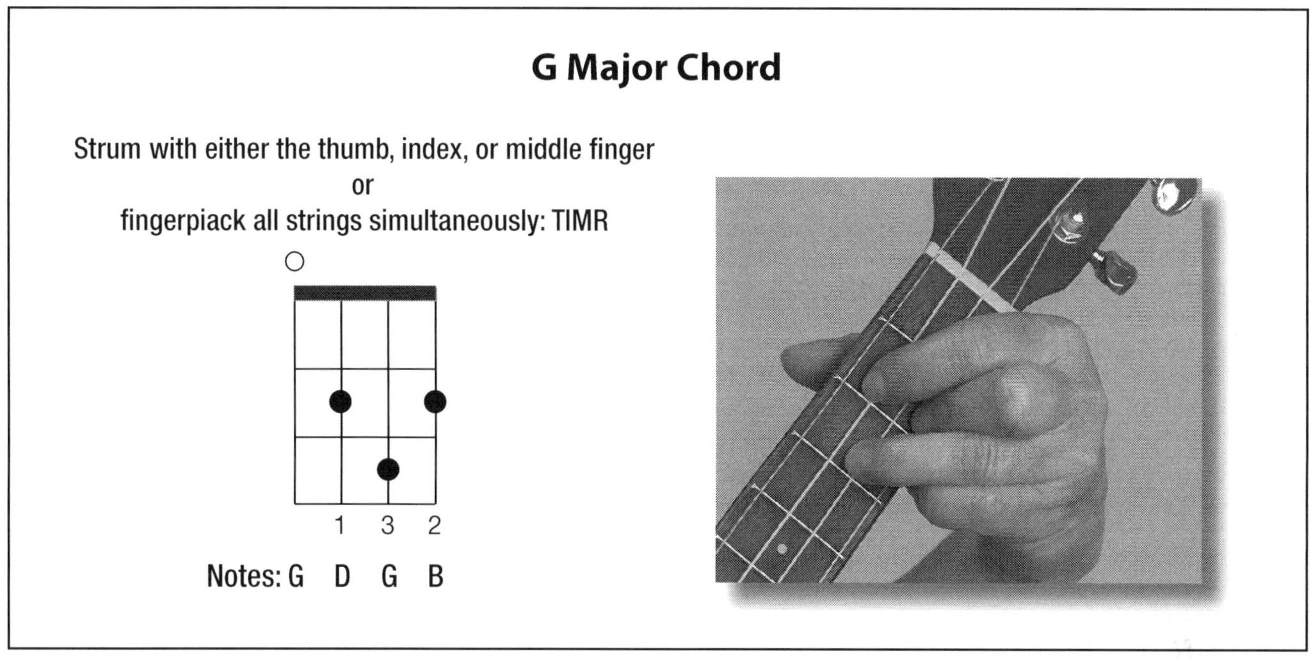

Roadmap for Moving Smoothly between the G, C and F Chords:

These chords have no fretted notes in common.

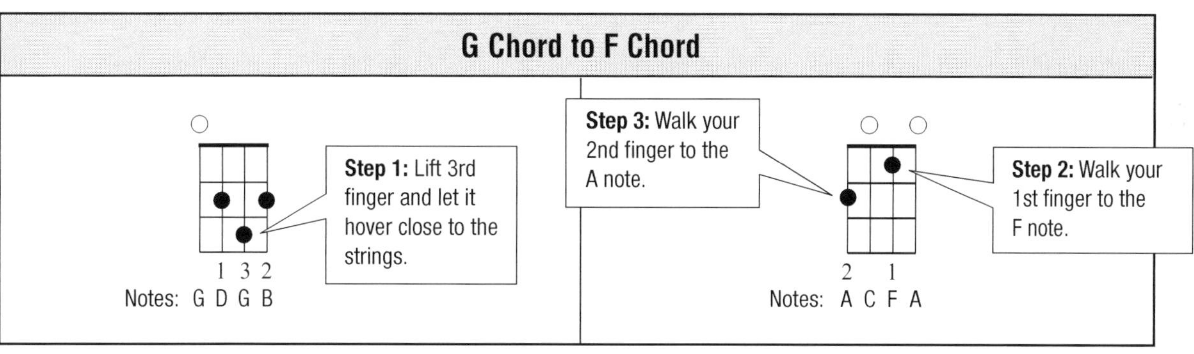

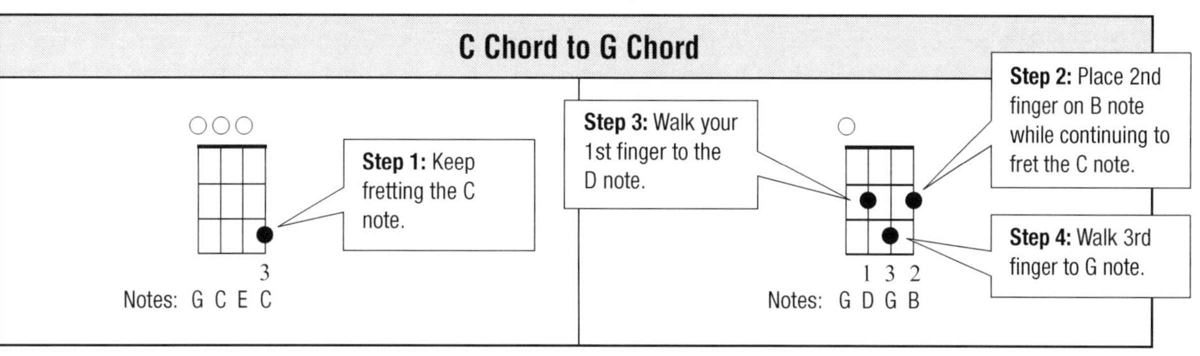

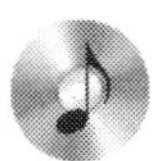

7. Combine C Scale Notes with Chords

TRACK 39

- In this exercise, fret your left hand fingers on the chord and leave them there to play the notes that follow each chord.
- Under each chord "T I M R" (**T**humb **I**ndex **M**iddle **R**ing) indicates that the four strings of the chord should be plucked simultaneously with individual fingers instead of strummed.
- Before playing, count four for nothing: 1, 2, 3, Play or 1, 2, 3, 4.

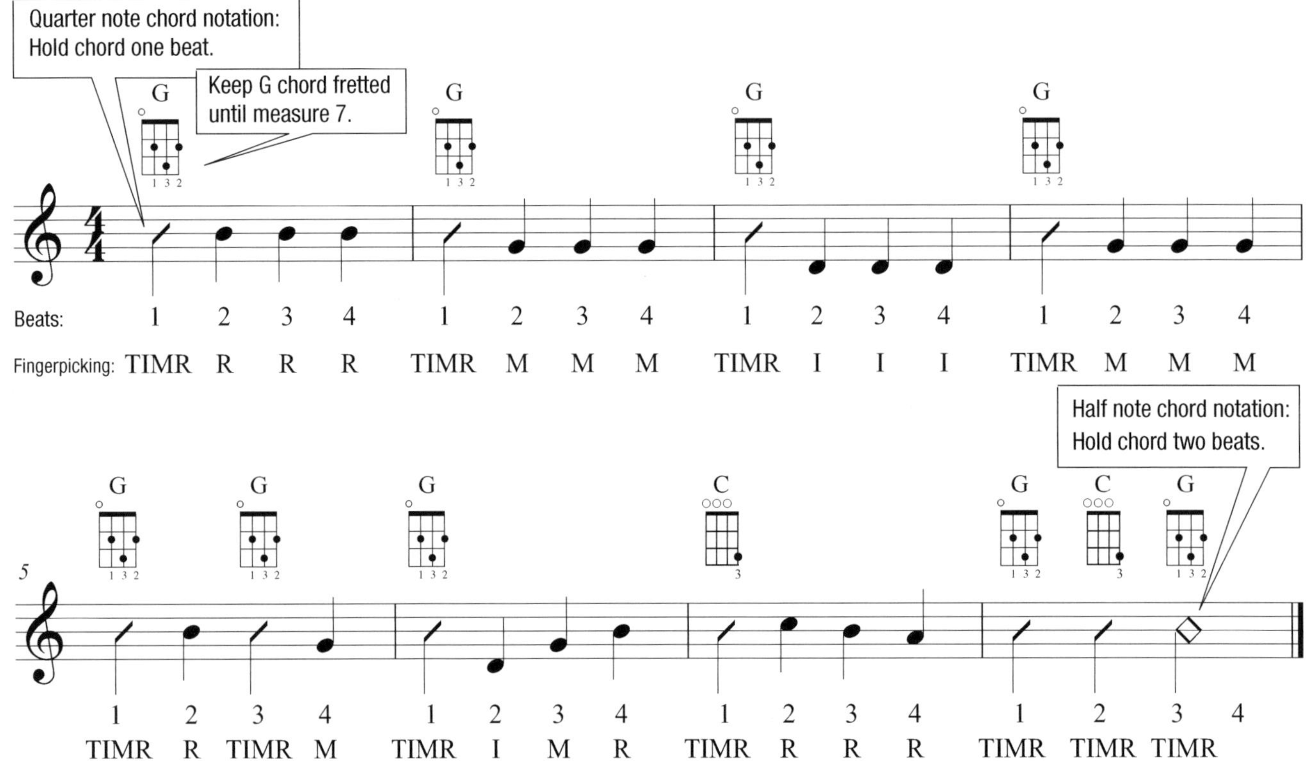

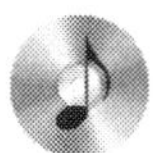

8. Your A-B-Cs in 4/4 Time

TRACK 40

- In this exercise, fret your left hand fingers on the chord and leave them there to play the notes that follow each chord.
- Under each chord "T I M R" (**T**humb **I**ndex **M**iddle **R**ing) indicates that the four strings of the chord should be plucked simultaneously with individual fingers instead of strummed.
- Before playing, count four for nothing: 1, 2, 3, Play or 1, 2, 3, 4.
- *Continue counting out loud through the rest of the piece.*

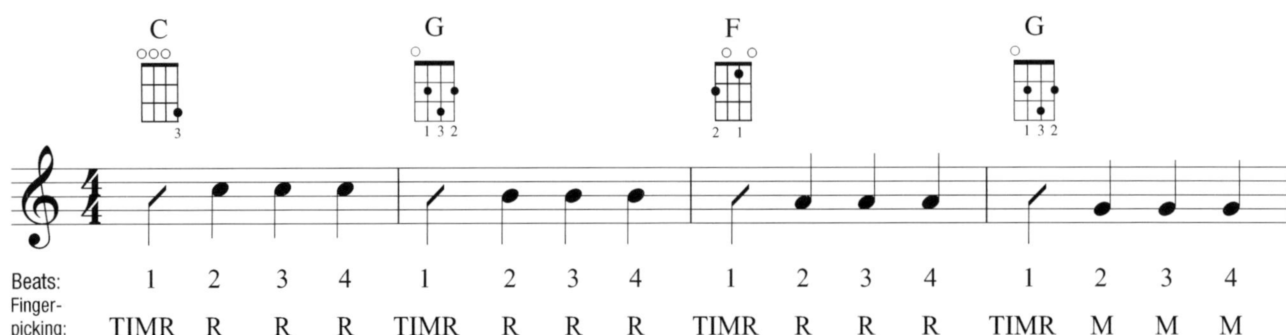

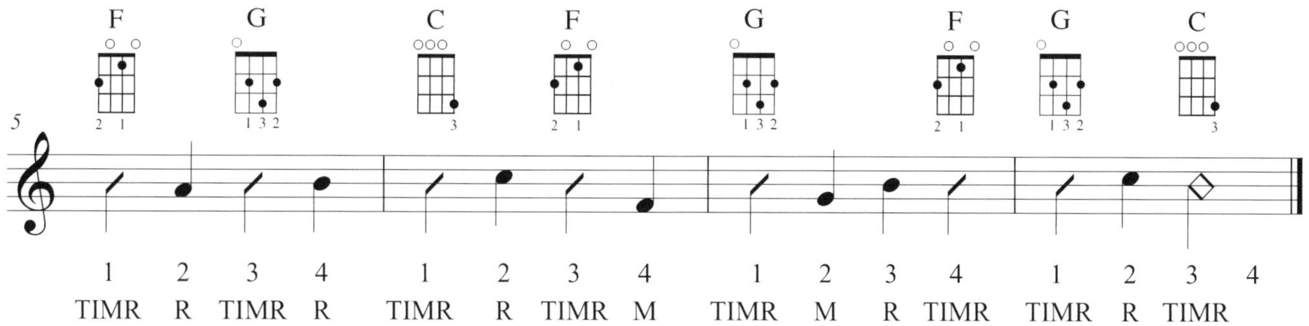

Intro to the Arpeggio

"Arpeggio" in Italian literally means "like a harp." In musical terms, it means the notes of a chord are played individually, one after the other in rapid succession, instead of being simultaneously strummed or plucked. The following exercise trains you to play an "arpeggiated" chord followed by a full or "block" chord.

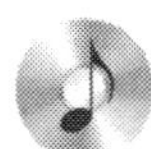

9. A Little Arpeggio, Please

TRACK 41

- In this exercise, all of the notes are contained in the chord that follows at the end of each measure. Anticipate the chord by fretting it at the beginning of each measure as you play each note.
- Under each chord "T I M R" (**T**humb **I**ndex **M**iddle **R**ing) indicates that the four strings of the chord should be plucked simultaneously with individual fingers instead of strummed.
- Before playing, count four for nothing: 1, 2, 3, Play or 1, 2, 3, 4.
- *Continue counting out loud through the rest of the piece.*

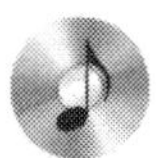

10. For He's a Jolly Good Fellow

TRACK 42

Play this traditional song 3 ways:

1. **As an Instrumental**—Play the arrangement below that combines melody and chords.
2. **As a Song**—Play the chords to accompany your singing.
3. **As a Combination**—Sing the song through while accompanying yourself with chords, then play an instrumental version… or vice versa.

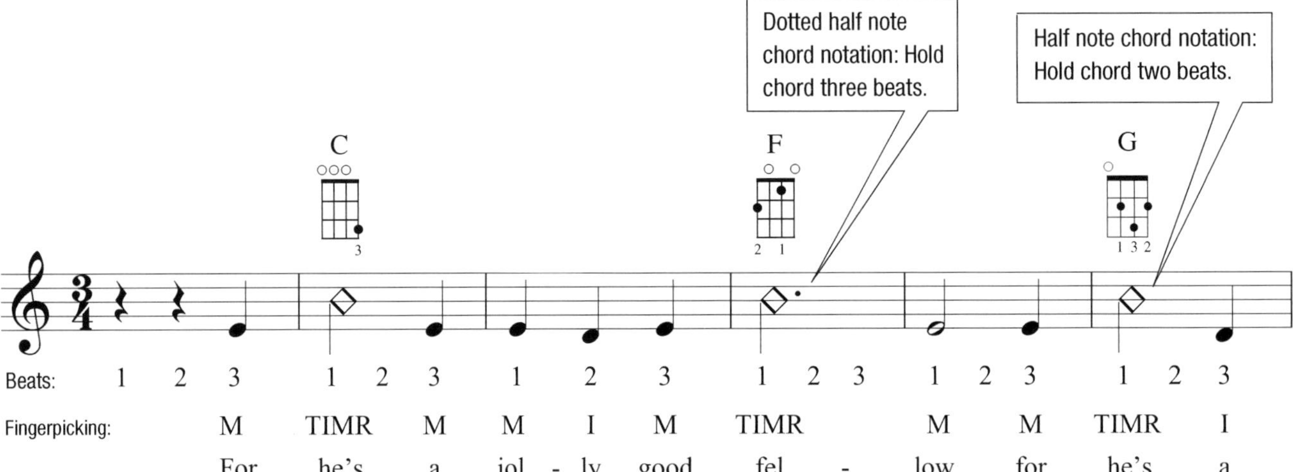

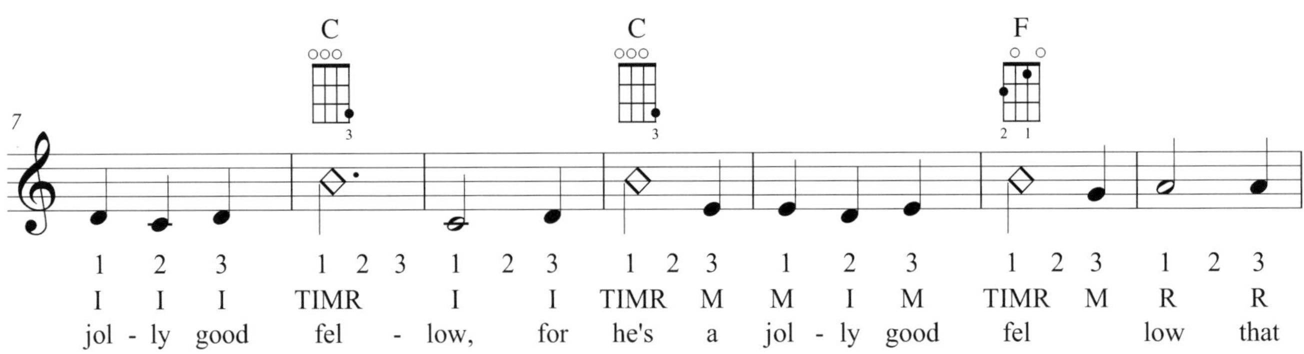

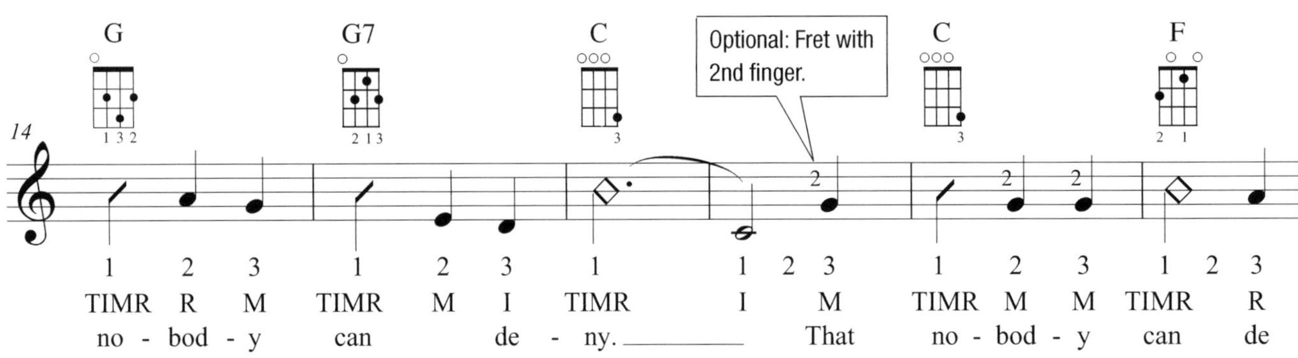

Playing technique: Fingering a G melody note within a C chord

In music for fretted instruments (ukulele, guitar, mandolin, banjo), you will often see small numbers near notes. These notations indicate fretting fingers of the left hand.

Take a look at measures 16–18 on the previous page. In measure 16 you play a C chord and let it resonate for 3 beats. In measures 17–18 melody notes are combined with a C chord. *The small number 2 next to the G note means fret that note with your second left hand finger.* In order to keep the strings of the C chord resonating, while you play melody notes, you continue fretting the C chord while you simultaneously fret the G note with your second finger.

Deciphering small numbers next to notes:
The small number 2 next to the G note in measures 17-18 means fret the G note with the 2nd finger (left hand). This enables you to continue fretting the C note as part of an accompanying C chord that you played in measure 16.

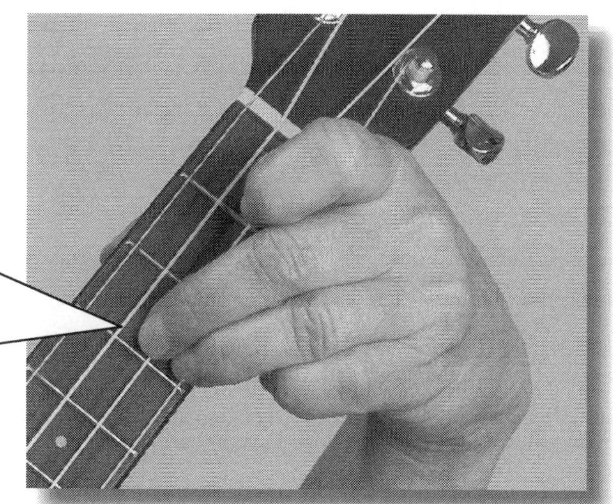

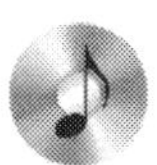

11. Twinkle, Twinkle Little Star

TRACK 43

When you perform this, tell your friends you are playing "Ode to a Star." They will have a good chuckle when they figure out the true name of this song!

Play this traditional song 3 ways:

1. **As an Instrumental**—Play the arrangement below that combines melody and chords.
2. **As a Song**—Play the chords to accompany your singing.
3. **As a Combination**—Sing the song through while accompanying yourself with chords, then play an instrumental version… or vice versa.

Optional: The number "2" next to the G note refers to left-hand fretting. It means fret the note with the 2nd finger (left hand). Normally you fret the G note with the 3rd finger, but in this case, fretting the G note with the 2nd finger allows you to continue fretting the C chord during the 4th beat of the measure. This provides a chord accompaniment (harmony) as you play the G note, which is part of the melody. See bottom of page 87 for a visual.

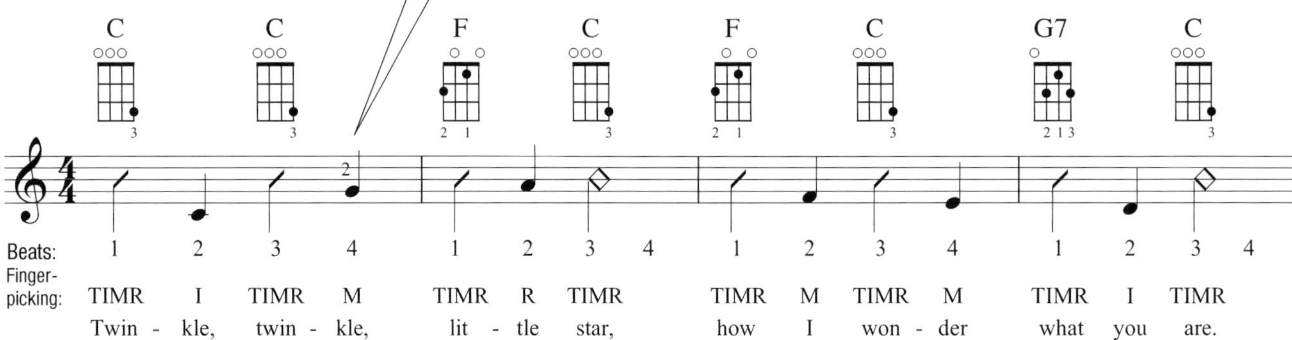

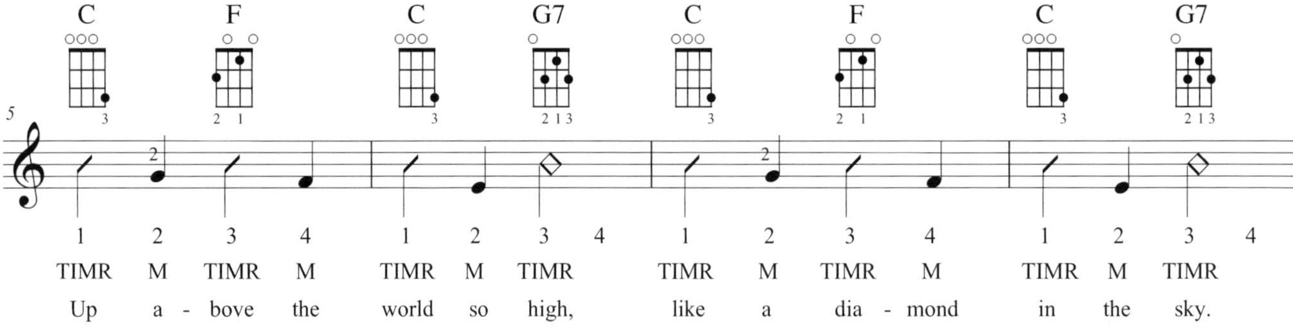

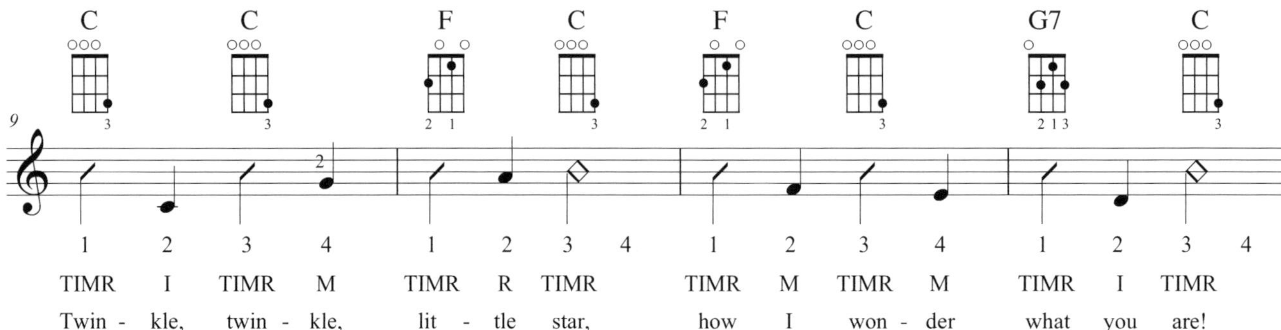

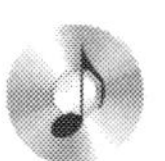

12. Theme from Carmen

TRACK 44

This piece of music contains all the notes and chords you have learned so far. Mastering it will help you fluently read and remember them.

History: *Carmen* is an opera written and sung in French by composer Georges Bizet. It is the story of the beautiful and hot-tempered Carmen, a Spanish gypsy responsible for the downfall of many men. For a year after its premiere at the Opéra Comique of Paris on March 3, 1875, it was considered a failure, denounced by critics as "immoral" and "superficial." Today, it is one of the world's most beloved and popular operas.

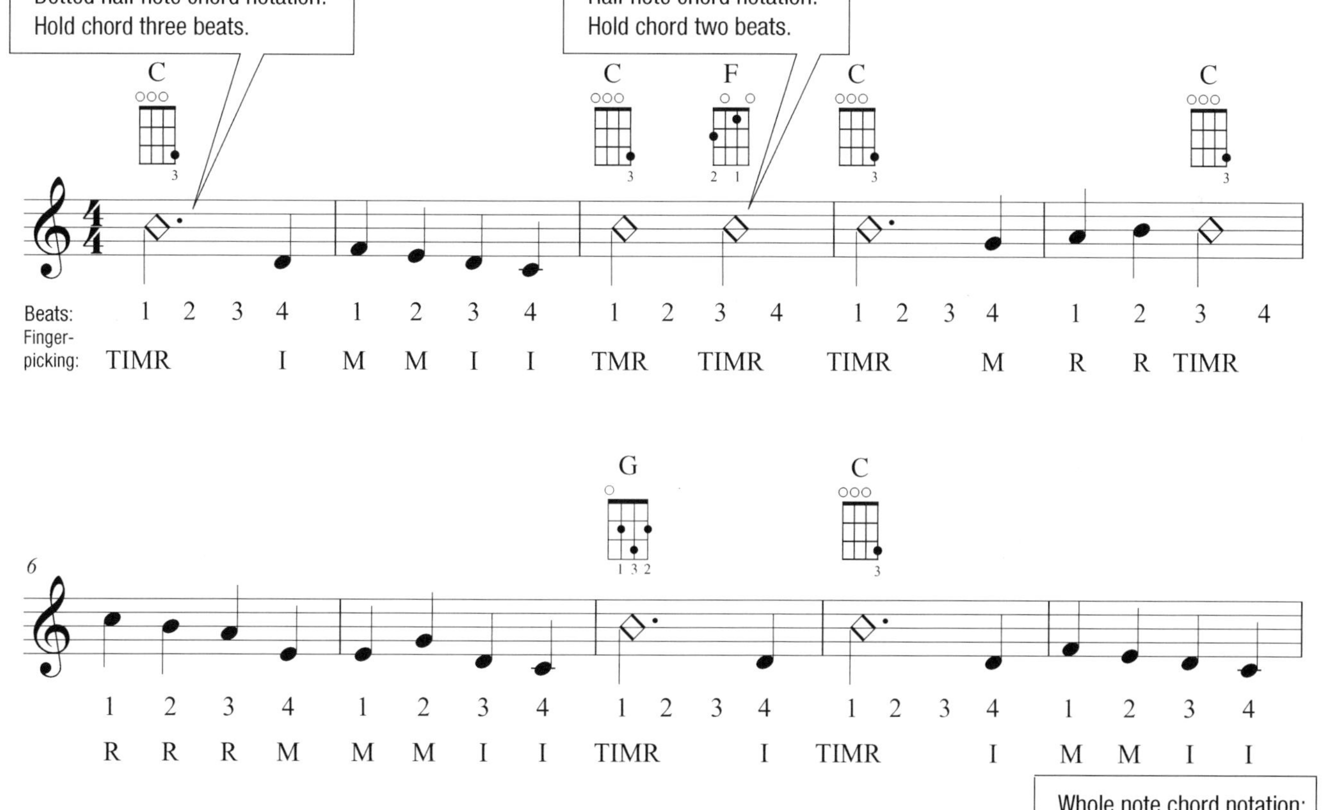

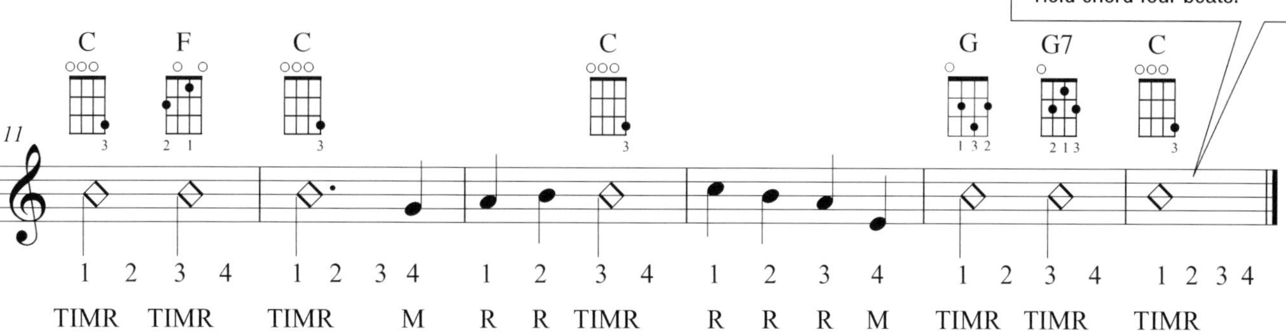

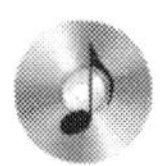

13. Sweet Betsy from Pike

TRACK 45

History: This bittersweet comic folk song, first popular in the American gold rush era of 1849-59, describes the hardships and frustrations experienced by pioneer women as they moved west with their families along the immigrant trails in covered wagons.

C C C G7

Beats: 1 2 3 1 2 3 1 2 3 1 2 3
Finger-picking: TIMR TIMR I TIMR M M M M I TIMR I I
Oh, don't you re - mem - ber sweet Bet - sy from

5 C C G G

1 2 3 1 2 3 1 2 3 1 2 3 1 2 3
TIMR I I M M TIMR R R TIMR M M TIMR R
Pike, who crossed the wide prai - rie with her lov - er Ike? With

10 C G F C

Hold down F chord firmly throughout measure. Fret G note with 4th finger.

1 2 3 1 2 3 1 2 3 1 2 3
TIMR R R TIMR M M TIMR M R TIMR M
two yoke of ox - en a big yel - low dog, a

14 Fret G chord now! G Fret G7 chord now! G7 C

1 2 3 1 2 3 1 2 3 1 2 3
I M M TIMR M I TIMR I I TIMR
tall spot - ted roost - er and one spot - ted hog.

Sweet Betsy from Pike: Lyrics and Chord Chart

Play this song 3 ways:

1. **As an Instrumental**—Play my arrangement that combines melody and chords.
2. **As a Song**—Play the chords below to accompany your singing.
3. **As a Combination**—Sing a couple verses while accompanying yourself with chords. Add an instrumental between verses.

VERSE 1

```
     C        /               G7         C
Oh, don't you remember Sweet Betsy from Pike?
      C               /             G7         /
Who crossed the wide mountains with her lover, Ike.
      C          G      F         C
With two yoke of oxen, a big yellow dog,
   C          G           G7         C
A tall spotted rooster and one spotted hog.
```

VERSE 2

```
     C            /         G7            C
One evening quite early they camped on the Platte.
      C          /         G7          /
'Twas nearby the road on a green, shady flat.
C           G         F       C
Betsy, sore-footed, lay down to repose,
   C          G           G7          C
In wonder Ike gazed on his Pike country rose.
```

VERSE 3

```
     C            /         G7         C
The Indians came down in a wild yelling horde,
     C     /                    G7         /
And Betsy got scared they would scalp her a-dored.
C          G           F        C
Under the wagon wheel Betsy did crawl,
     C              G           G7          C
She fought off them Indians with musket and ball.
```

VERSE 4

```
C          /          G7          C
Out on the prairie one bright starry night,
      C           /           G7       /
They broke out the whiskey and Betsy got tight.
     C            G           F             C
She sang and she shouted, she danced on the plain.
     C           G            G7           C
She made a great show for that whole wagon train.
```

VERSE 5

```
     C            /          G7     C
The Shanghai ran off and the cattle all died.
     C          /          G7          /
The last piece of bacon that morning was fried.
C          G            F        C
Ike got dis-couraged and Betsy got mad,
     C              G             G7          C
The dog wagged his tail and looked wondrously sad.
```

VERSE 6

```
      C                 /           G7         C
They soon reached the desert where Betsy gave out,
     C          /            G7    /
And down in the sand she lay rolling about.
C          G            F         C
Ike in great terror looked on in sur-prise
        C        G            G7          C
Saying, Betsy get up, you'll get sand in your eyes.
```

VERSE 7

```
       C        /       G7          C
Sweet Betsy got up in a great deal of pain.
     C             /            G7      /
De–clared she'd go back to Pike County again.
C          G               F          C
Ike, he just sighed, and they fondly em-braced,
        C         G             G7            C
And she traveled a-long with her arm round his waist.
```

14. Blow the Man Down

TRACK 46

On sailing ships throughout the 1400–1800's, "Blow the Man Down" meant "knock the man down."

Play this traditional song 3 ways:

1. **As an Instrumental**—Play the arrangement below that combines melody and chords.
2. **As a Song**—Play the chords to accompany your singing.
3. **As a Combination**—Sing the song through while accompanying yourself with chords, then play an instrumental version… or vice versa.

Traditional Sea Shanty

Beats:	1	2	3	1	2	3	1	2	3	1	2	3	1	2	3
Finger-picking:	M	R	M	TIMR	I	M	M	R	M	TIMR			M		
Lyrics:	Blow	the	man	down,	bul	lies,	blow	the	man	down.			Way!		

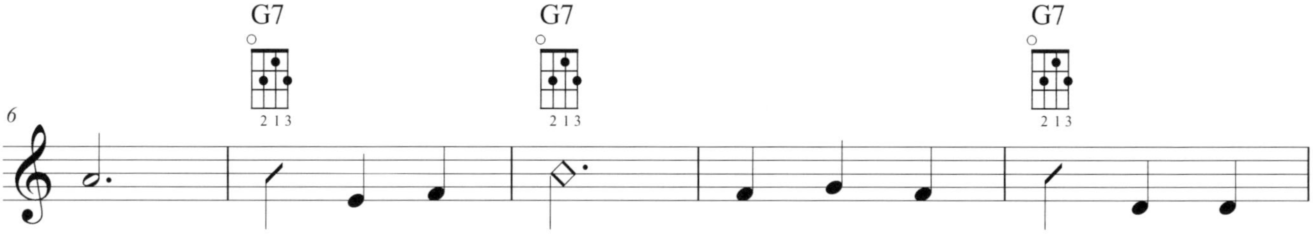

1	1	2	3	1	2	3	1	2	3	1	2	3		
R	TIMR	M	M	TIMR			M	M	M	TIMR	I	I		
Hey,	blow	the	man	down.			Blow	the	man	down,	bul	lies,		

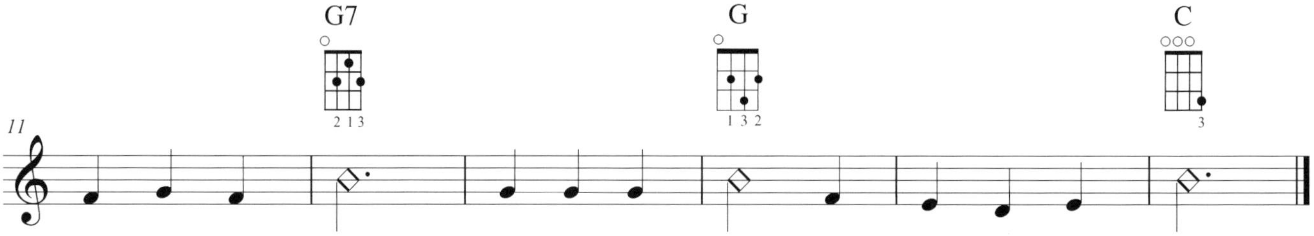

1	2	3	1	1	2	3	1	2	3	1	2	3	1	2	3
M	M	M	TIMR	M	M	M	TIMR		M	M	I	M	TIMR		
blow	him	right	down.	Give	us	the	time		to	blow	the	man	down.		

Blow the Man Down: Lyrics and Chord Charts

VERSE 1

```
C              /              /              /
Blow the man down, bullies, blow the man down!
C    /    G7              /
Way! Hey! Blow the man down!
G7             /              /              /
Blow the man down, bullies, blow him right down.
G7          /     G            C
Give us the time to blow the man down.
```

VERSE 2

```
        C          /          /          /
Come all ye young fellers that follow th' sea.
C    /    G7              /
Way! Hey, Blow the man down!
   G7        /           /     /
I'll sing ye a song if ye'll listen t' me.
G7          /     G            C
Give us the time to blow th' man down!
```

VERSE 3

```
        C          /      /             /
'Twas in a Black Baller I first served my time.
C    /    G7              /
Way! Hey! Blow the man down!
    G7         /      /          /
And in a Black Baller I wasted my prime.
G7          /     G            C
Give us the time to blow th' man down!
```

VERSE 4

```
   C                /           /           /
But when the Black Baller gets clear o' the land.
C    /    G7              /
Way! Hey! Blow th' man down!
   G7            /              /             /
It's then as ye'll hear the sharp word o' com-mand,
G7          /     G            C
Give us the time to blow th' man down!
```

VERSE 5

```
    C              /           /              /
Wi' soldiers an' tailors an' Dutchmen an' all.
C    /    G7              /
Way! Hey! Blow the man down!
   G7                 /          /               /
As ships for prime seamen a-board the Black Ball,
G7          /     G            C
Give us the time to blow the man down!
```

History: Sea shanties were shipboard working songs. The singular, "shanty," also spelled "chantey," comes from the French word "chanter" or "to sing." Shanties flourished from the 1400s when sailors sang them on square-rigged sailing ships, through the days of steam ships in the first half of the 20th century. Most surviving shanties date from the 19th and, less commonly, 18th centuries.

In the days when human muscles were the only power source available aboard ship, sea shanties helped make hard work tolerable. As the sailors sang, the rhythm of sea shanties helped relieve the boredom of repetitive tasks like raising and lowering sails or swabbing (mopping) the deck.

Most sea shanties are "call and response" songs. A lead voice (the shantyman) would sing a phrase. Then a chorus of sailors would bellow a response. For example, in "Blow the Man Down," you would hear the following:

Shantyman:	*Come all ye young fellers that follow the sea.*
Sailors' Chorus:	*Way! Hey! Blow the man down!*

15. Bohemian Folk Song

TRACK 47

History: Bohemia is an historic country of central Europe. Since 1993 it has formed much of the Czech Republic.

Traditional

G G F G7 C C

Beats: 1 2 3 4 | 1 2 3 4 | 1 2 3 4 | 1 2 3 4

Finger-picking: R R TIMR M | R R TIMR M | TIMR R TIMR R | TIMR TIMR

5

G G F G7 C

1 2 3 4 | 1 2 3 4 | 1 2 3 4 | 1 2 3 4

R R TIMR M | R R TIMR M | R TIMR R TIMR | R TIMR

9

C G7 C G7

1 2 3 4 | 1 2 3 4 | 1 2 3 4 | 1 2 3 4

R M TIMR M | TIMR M I | TIMR M M M | TIMR M I

13

C G C G F G7 C C

1 2 3 4 | 1 2 3 4 | 1 2 3 4 | 1 2 3 4

TIMR R TIMR M | TIMR R TIMR M | TIMR R TIMR R | TIMR TIMR

16. The Can-Can

TRACK 48

Mastering this piece of music will help you fluently read and remember all the notes you have learned so far.

Jacques Offenbach (1819–1880)

C C G7

Beats: 1 2 3 4 1 2 3 4 1 2 3 4 1 2 3 4 1 2 3 4

Finger-picking: I TIMR I M M I M TIMR M R M M I TIMR

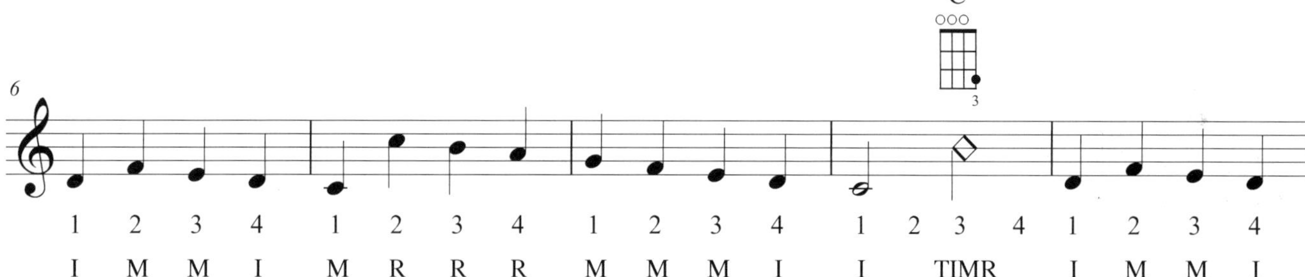

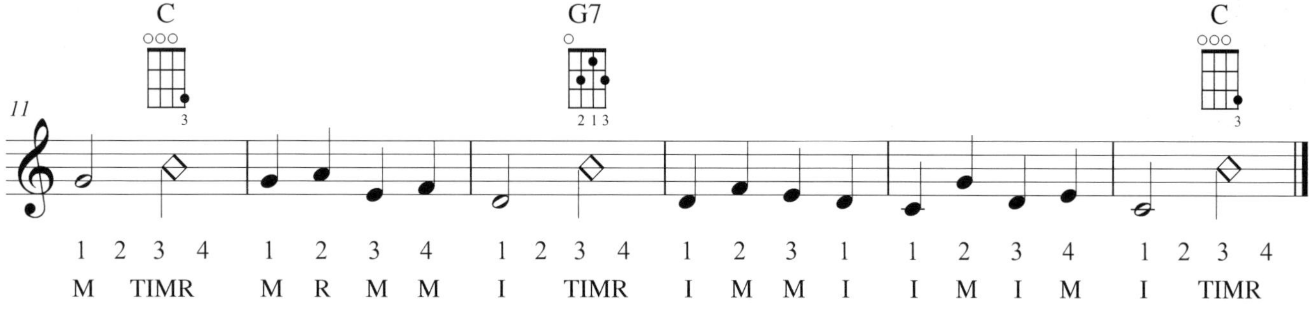

History: The Can-Can first appeared in the working-class ballrooms of Montparnasse in Paris around 1830. It was originally a dance for couples that involved high kicks, the "grand écart" (jump splits), and other wild gestures with arms and legs. By the 1880s it evolved into a chorus-line dance featured in French dance halls. *Cancan* meant "scandal," or "edge," since the dancers usually danced on the edge of the stage. The Can-Can is said to be the start of public nudity, because when dancers lifted their long skirts, they displayed bare legs between their stockings tops and frilly panties, which at the time was very indecent. In the 1890s the Moulin Rouge in Paris was world famous for its Can-Can reviews and for talented, highly paid star performers such as La Goulue and Jane Avril, both immortalized by Toulouse Lautrec in his paintings of the Moulin Rouge. The Can-Can was done to March and later Ragtime music. This galop from Jacques Offenbach's *Orpheus in the Underworld* is the tune most associated with the Can-Can.

Toulouse Lautrec's painting of the Moulin Rouge Can-Can line

WRITTEN EXERCISE 1:
Lines and Spaces

Instructions: Use pencil.

1. Write the name of the note on the lines below. C above middle C is noted HC (High C). All notes above High C are also noted with an H to differentiate them: HD, HE, HF, HG, HA.
2. Where there is a letter name, draw a corresponding quarter note.

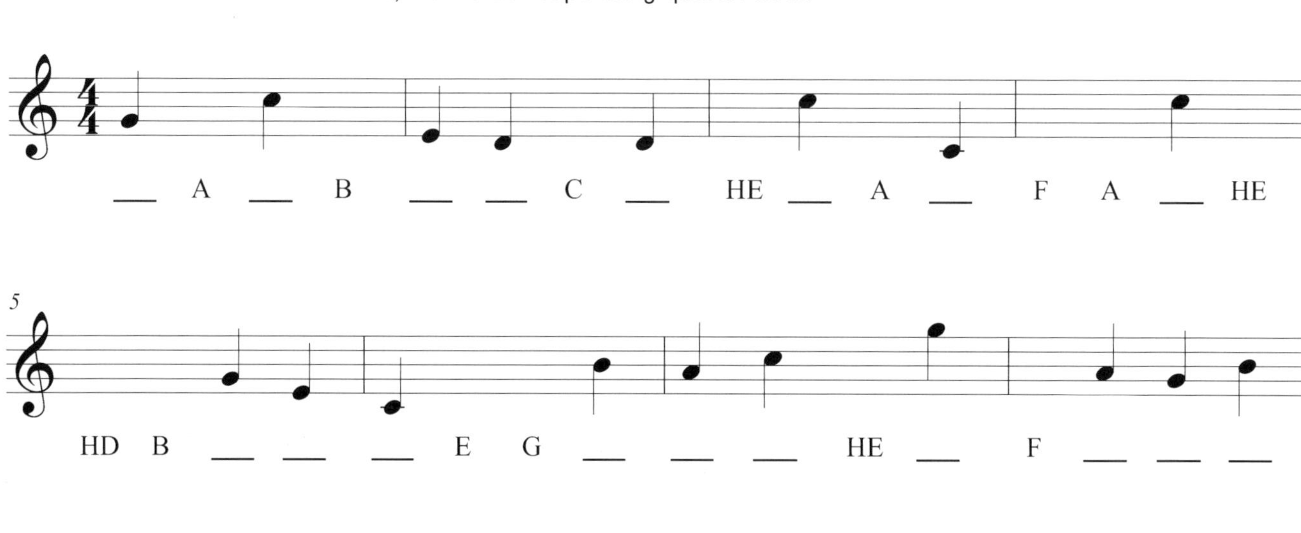

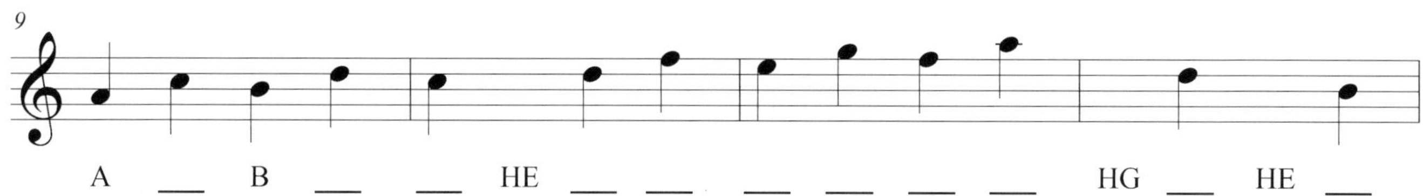

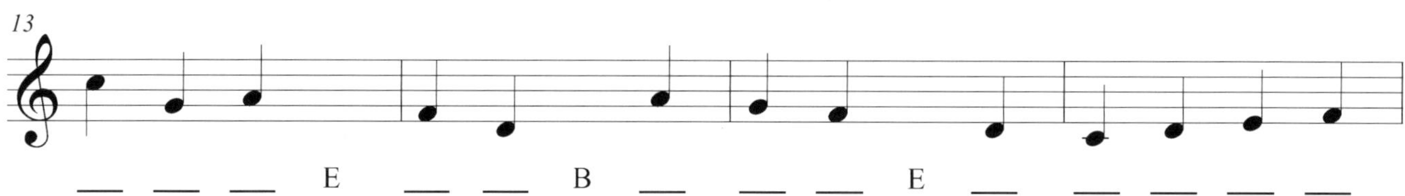

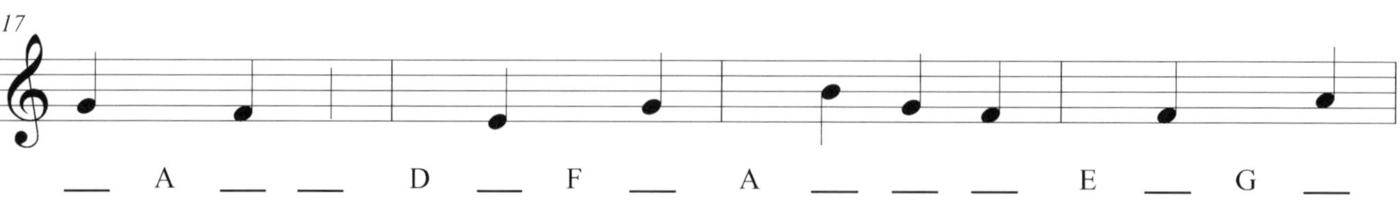

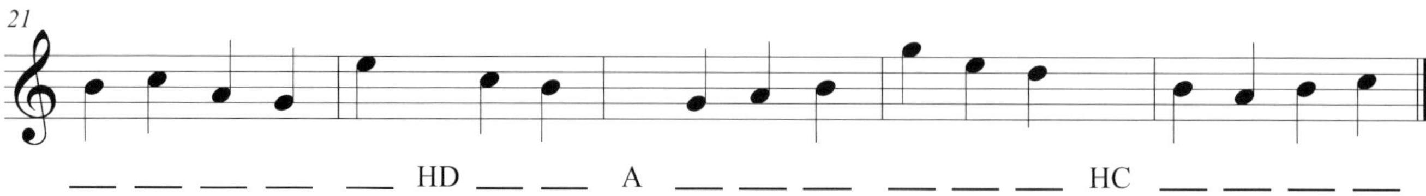

WRITTEN EXERCISE 2:
Note Writing—The C Scale

1. First write the G Clef at the beginning of each staff below.
2. Next write a 4/4 time signature on the first staff only.
3. Write a quarter or half note above the letter name indicated below the staff. Half notes rhythms are indicated by two-beat numbers under a note letter. C above middle C is notated as HC.
4. Be sure to make the stem of each note 3 spaces long.
5. Add the beat number under each note.

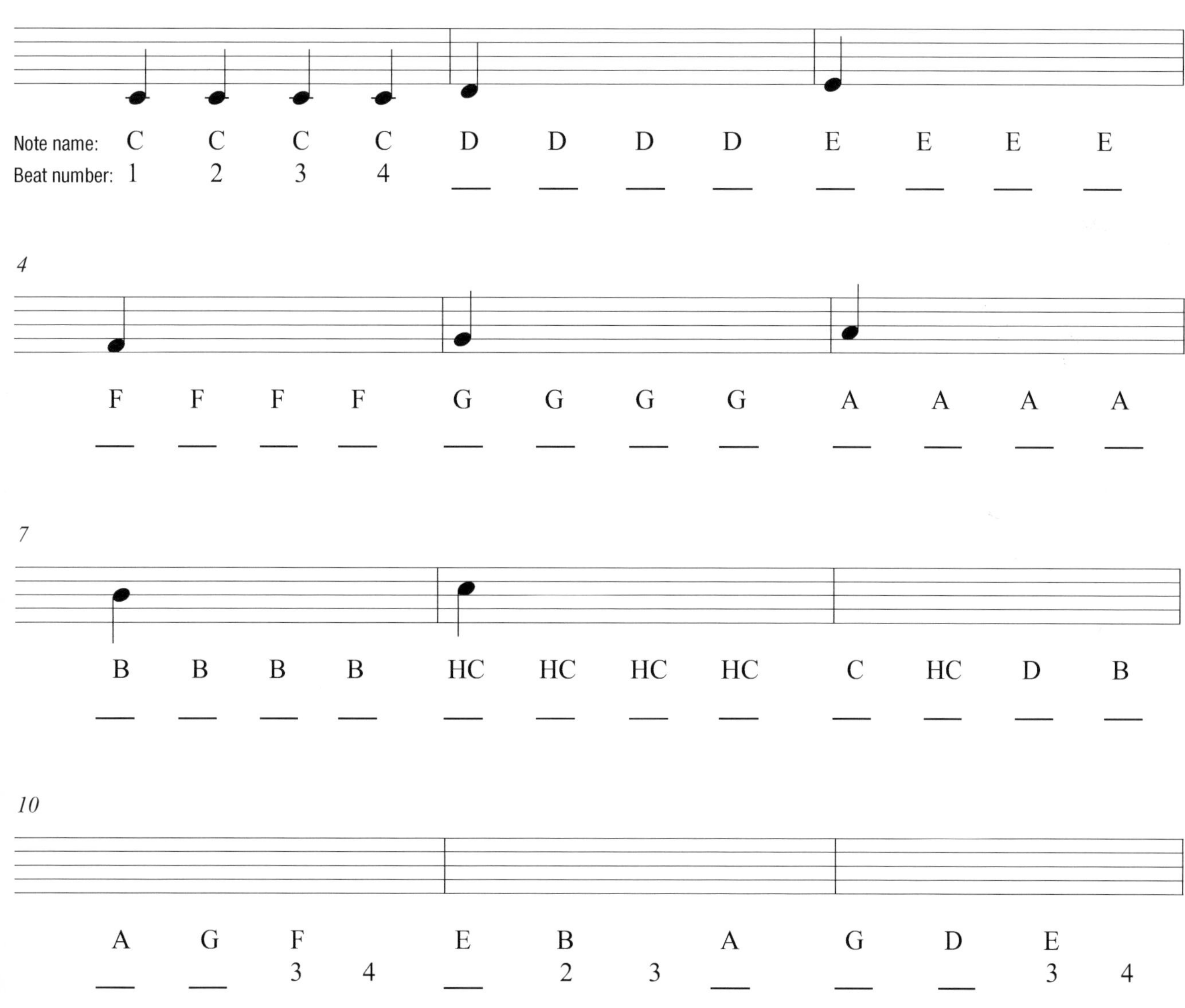

WRITTEN EXERCISE 1:
Answer Key For Lines and Spaces

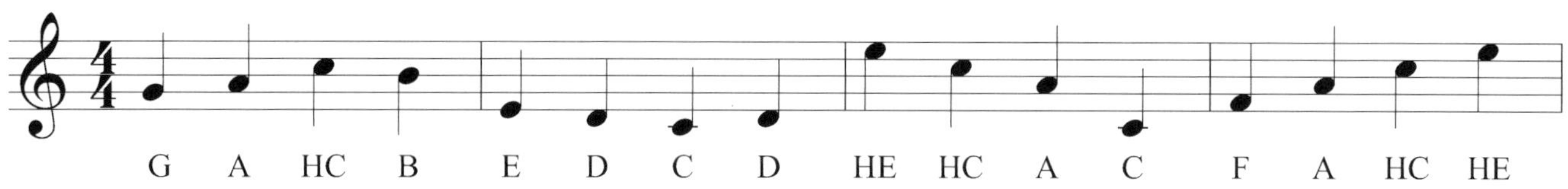

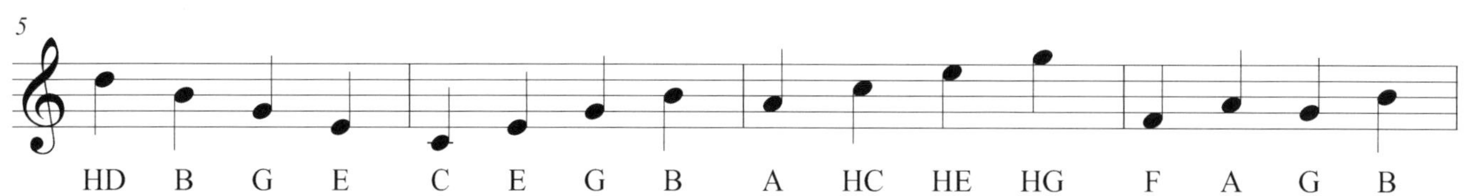

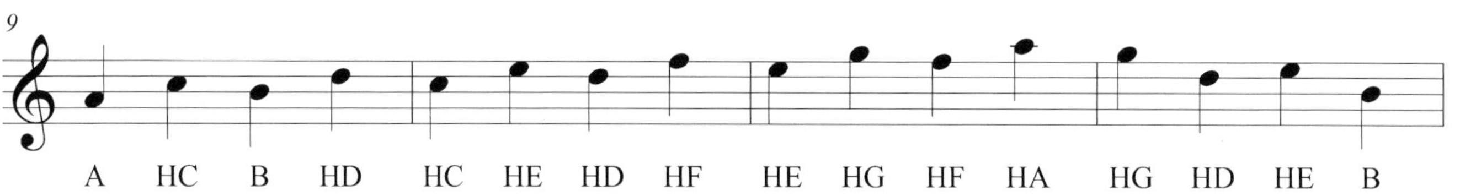

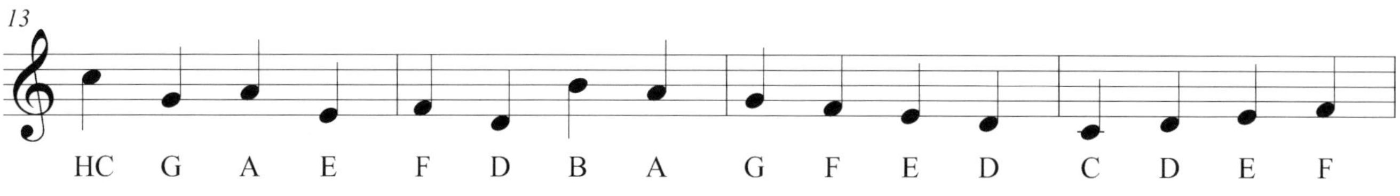

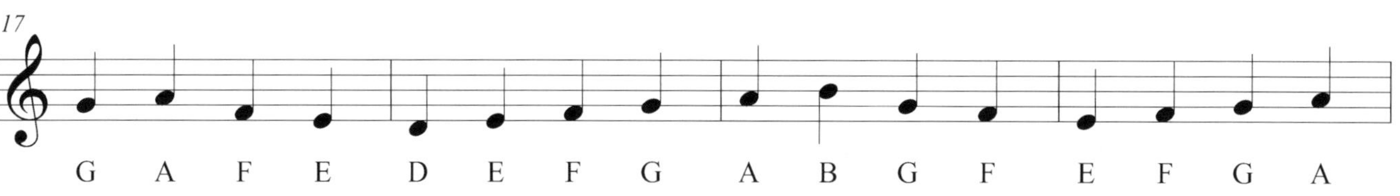

WRITTEN EXERCISE 2:
Answer Key For Note Writing—C Scale

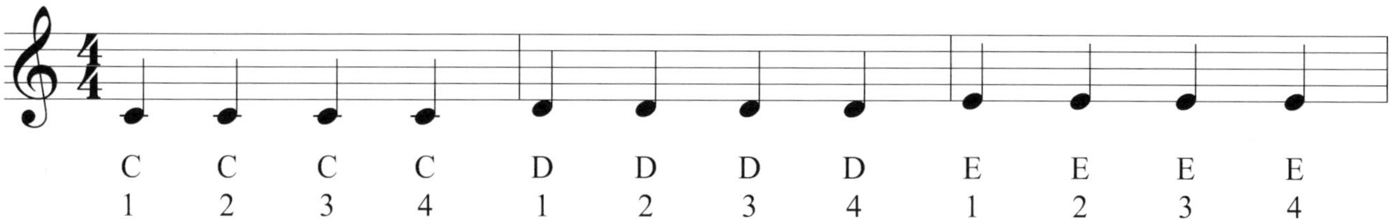

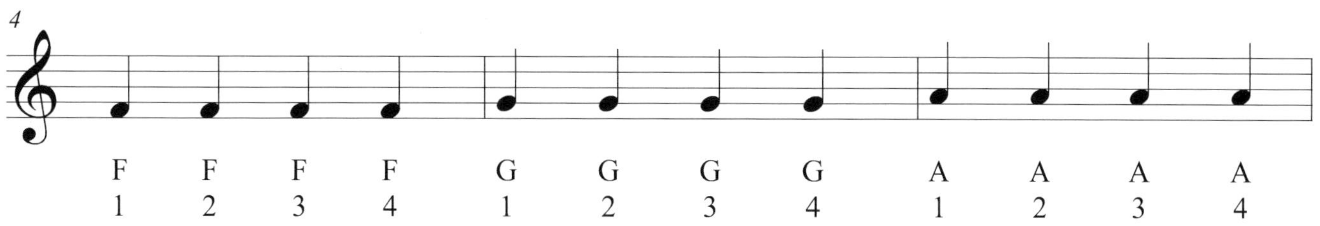

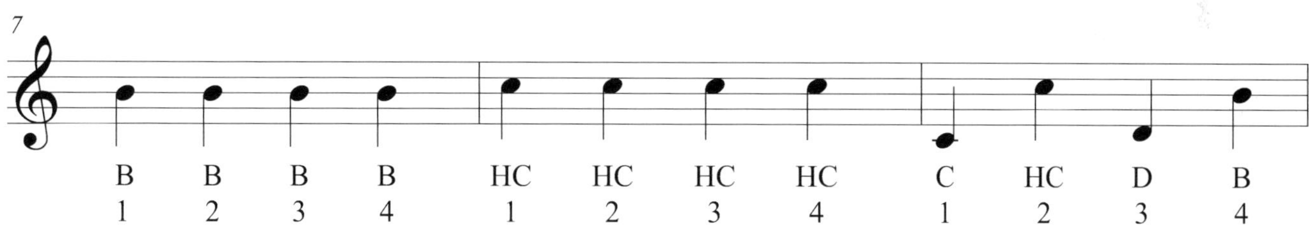

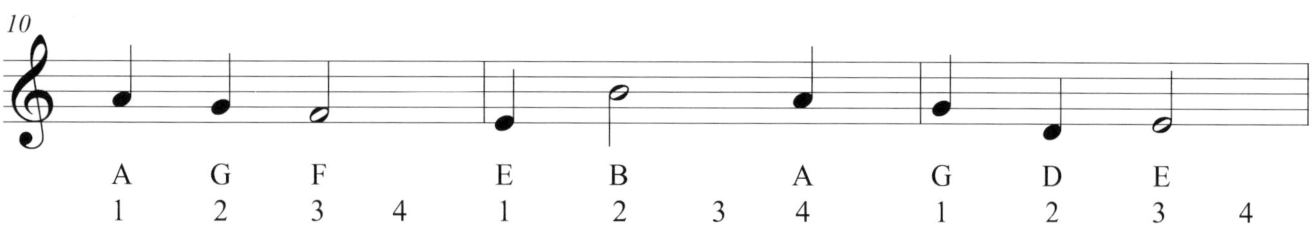

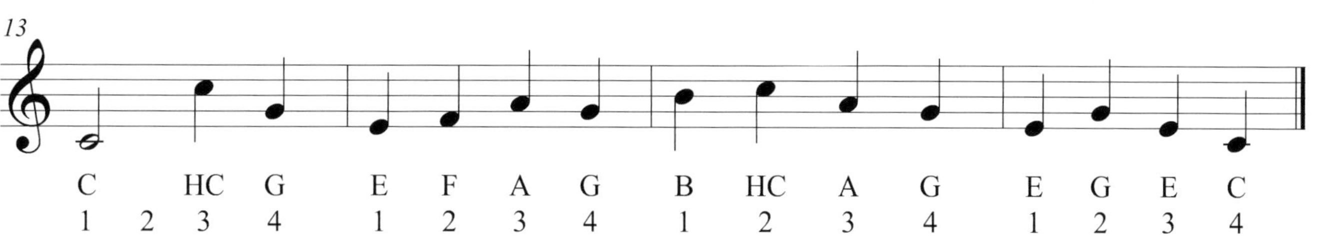

Lesson 4

Assignment

1. **Warm-up:** Each time you sit down to practice, play the following in this order...

   A. **4-Fret Half-Step Chromatic Scale Exercise** (**page 47**)

   B. **C Scale:** Practice the C scale using legato playing techniques. As you play, sing the note names forwards and backwards.

   C – D – E – F – G – A – B – **C** – B – A – G – F – E – D – C

   Do not look at your left hand as it frets the notes. Practice playing while looking at the music, then with your eyes closed (**page 81**).

2. **Review:** Play through your favorite music and songs in *Lesson 2* and *3* as a refresher and for reinforcement. Work on anything challenging that you still need to master... a chord change, a musical passage, whatever. Practice while reading the music. Then close your eyes and play short passages to train your memory, ears and fingers.

3. **Learn:** Each time you sit down to practice, play the following in this order...

   A. **Low G, A and B notes** on the G string (**page 101**)

   B. **Minor Chords: Am, Dm and Em** (**page 108**)
   Practice the **Am, Dm** and **Em chords** by learning the following chord progressions

   1) C to Am to Dm to G7

   2) Am to Em to Dm to G

   3) Am to F to Dm to Em

   4) C to Em to Dm to F

   5) F to Em to Am to C

   C. **Music and songs—*Don't try to learn everything in the entire lesson at once.*** Be patient and take your time to learn the music and internalize the techniques.

   1) Select 1–3 songs and practice them until they are mastered. When you learn those well enough to play them slowly and in rhythm, learn a couple more until you learn them all. Songs start on **page 104**.

   2) If you **can say it, you can play it!** Play each piece you are learning 3 ways:

      a) First, count the beats in each measure while reading music.

      b) Second, say the note names while reading the music.

      c) Third, say the right hand finger names while plucking the strings.

4. **Written Exercise:** *(Please use a pencil for the following exercise)*

   A. **How Low Can You Go?** (**page 122**)

Introducing Notes on the G String: G, A, and B Notes

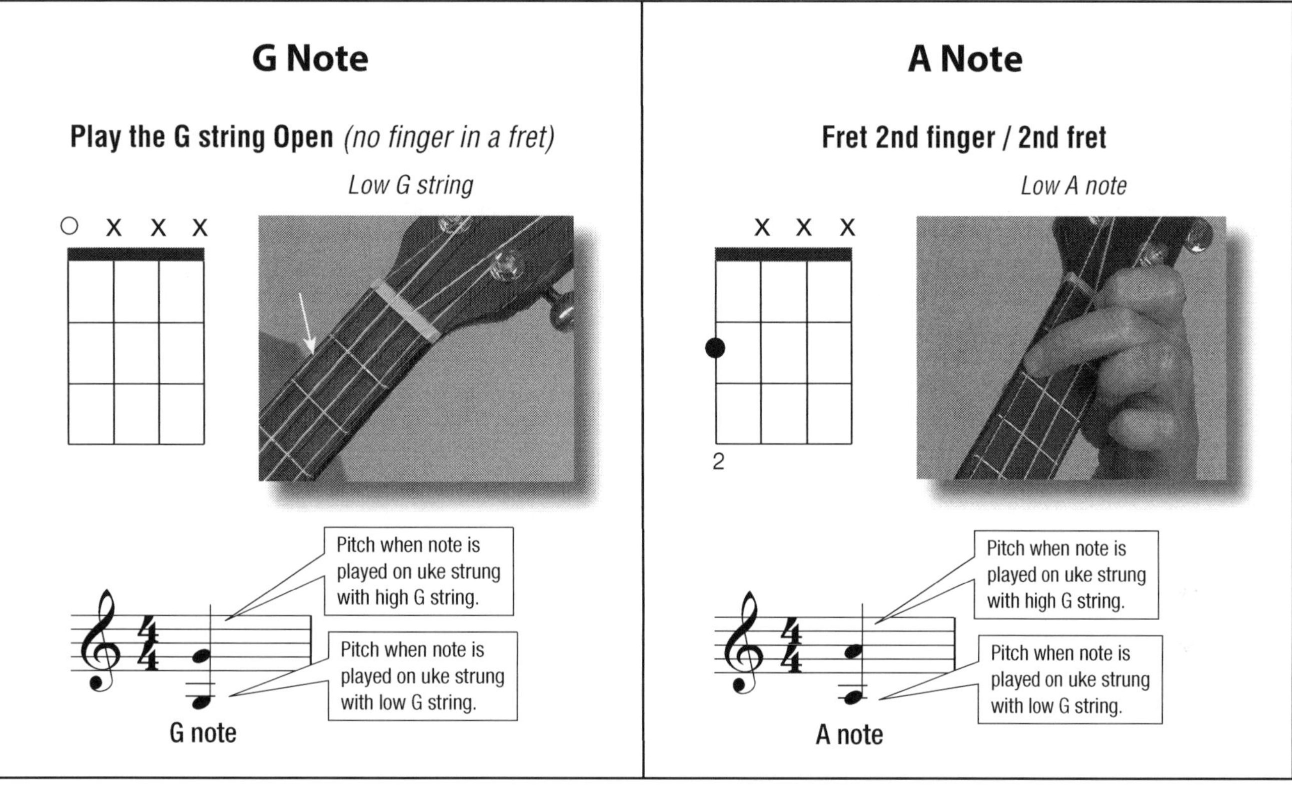

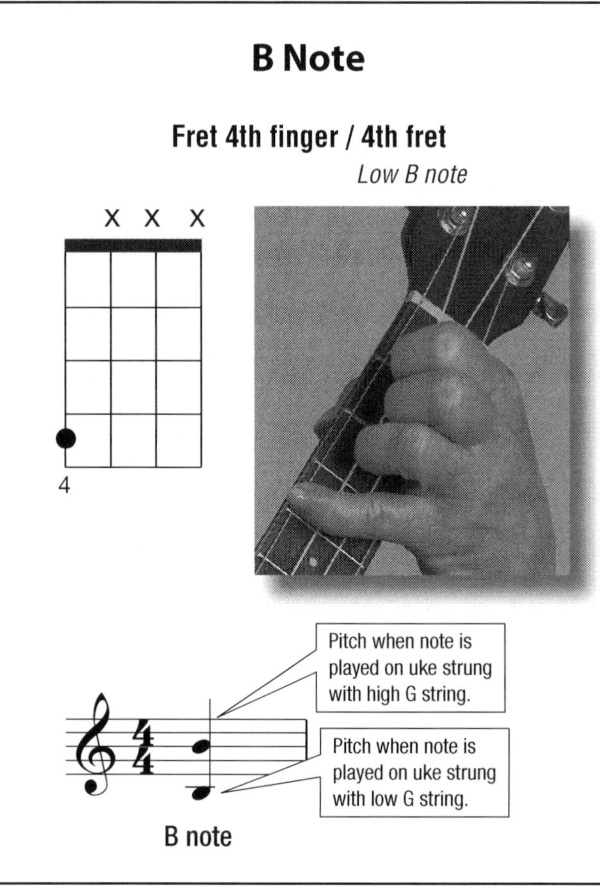

Right hand fingerpicking:

The G, A, and B notes on the G string are plucked with the **thumb**, notated **T**.

Fingerpicking Tip: Lightly rest your index finger on the C string, middle finger on the E string, and ring finger on the A string. The tip of the thumb continues to point toward the head of the uke. Keep the thumb straight and move it in a down, around and up arc from the joint above the knuckle.

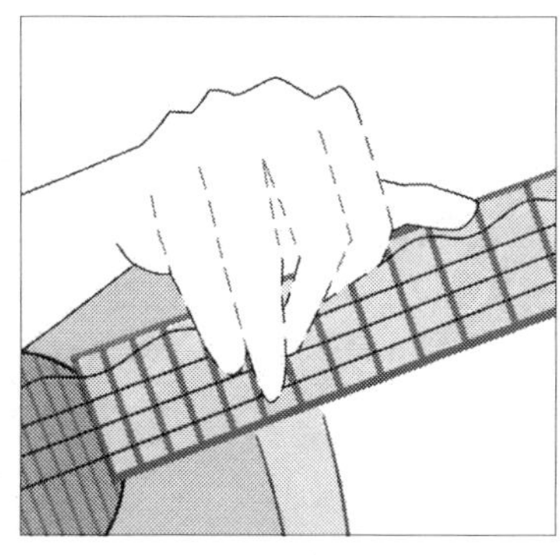

Ukes Strung with a High G String:

- The High G string is an octave (8 notes) higher than a Low G string, so the notes you play on the High G actually are the same pitch as the following notes.
- Notes on both strings can be substituted for each other.

When played on high G, both pitches are the same		When played on high G, both pitches are the same		When played on high G, both pitches are the same	
G note Open string O X X X G	G note 3nd finger/3rd fret X X X 3 G	A note 2nd finger/2nd fret X X X 2 A	A note Open string X X X O A	B note 4th finger/4th fret X X X 4 B	B note 2nd finger/2nd fret X X X 2 B
G note	G note	A note	A note	B note	B note

 1. Low G, A, and B

TRACK 49

Learning Tip: The note-name blanks under the notes are there to train your eye. To help you memorize the note positions as you play, say the names of the notes and pay attention to their placement. Is the note below two lines? On a line? Below one line?

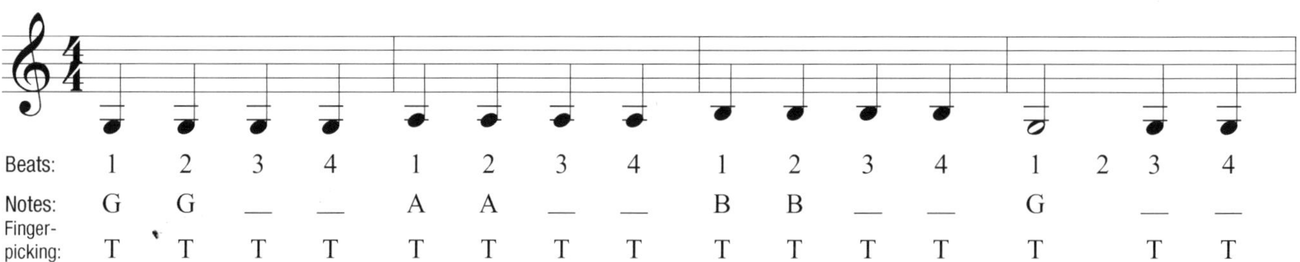

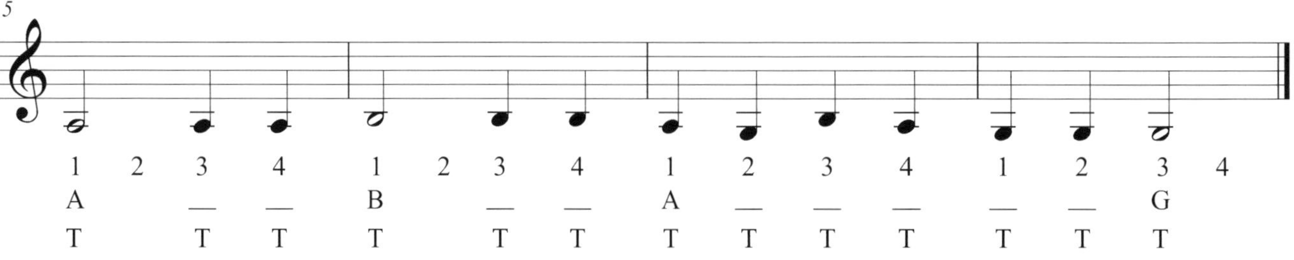

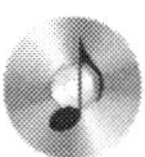

2. Work It Now in 3/4 Time

TRACK 50

Beats:	1	2	3	1	2	3	1	2	3	1	2	3
Notes:	G	A	B	__	__	G	__	__	__	A	__	__
Fingerpicking:	T	T	T	T	T	T	T	T	T	T	T	T

1	2	3	1	2	3	1	2	3	1	2	3
B	__	__	__	__	__	__	__	__	__		G
T	T	I	T	T	T	T	T	T	T		T

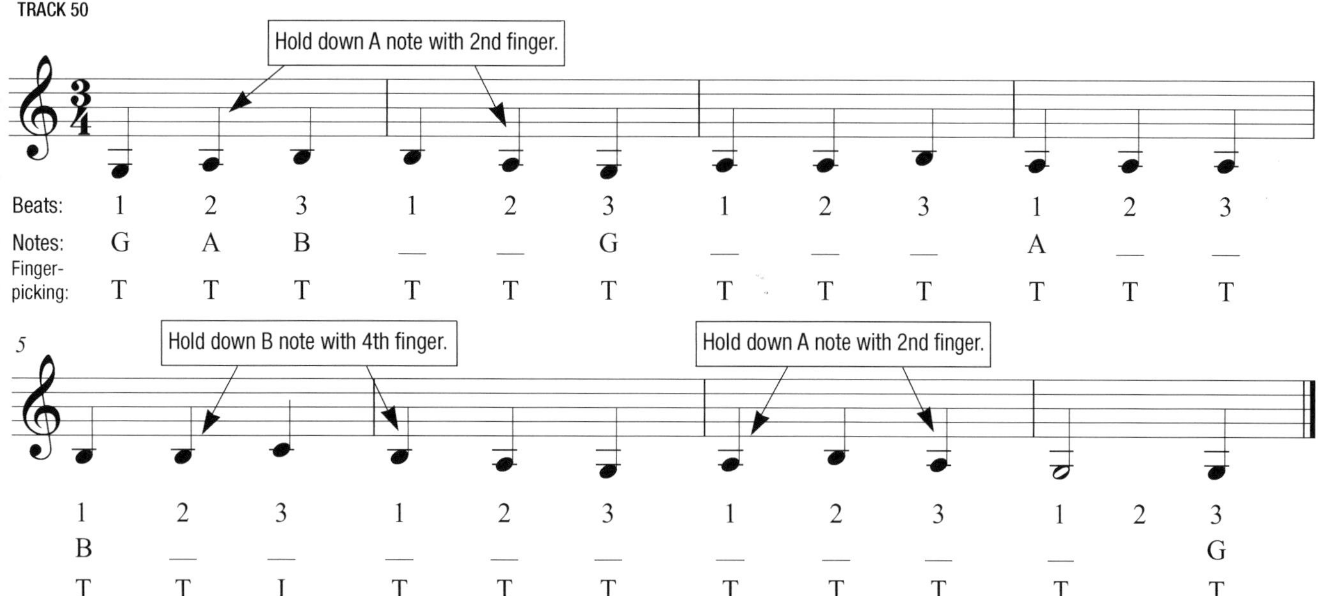

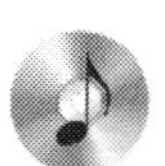

3. Note Your Naturals in C

TRACK 51

Use this exercise as a warm up to practice all the natural notes in the first 4 frets of your ukulele. While reading the music, sing or say the name of each note as you play it. Then close your eyes while playing and singing the note names.

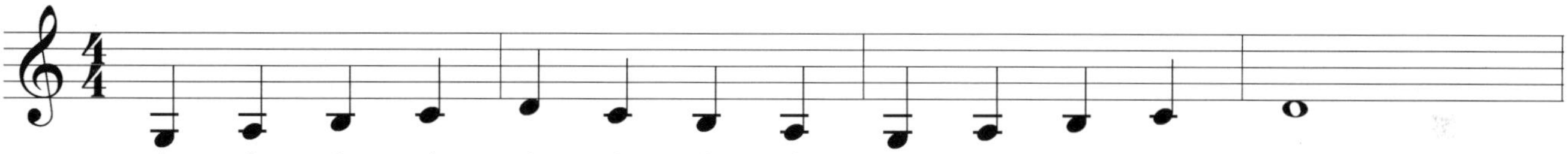

Beats:	1	2	3	4	1	2	3	4	1	2	3	4	1	2	3	4
Notes:	G	A	B	C	D	__	__	__	__	__	__	__	________			
Fingerpicking:	T	T	T	I	I	I	T	T	T	T	T	I	I			

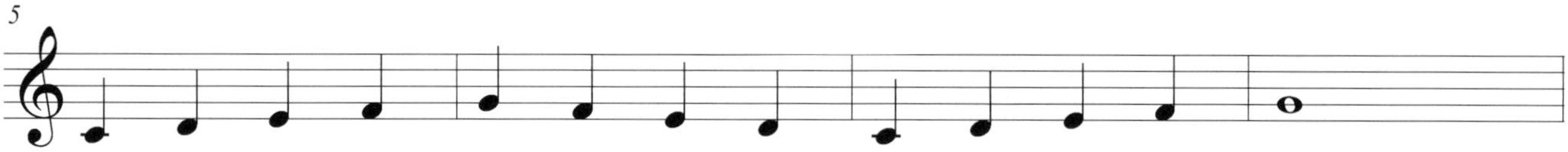

1	2	3	4	1	2	3	4	1	2	3	4	1	2	3	4
C	D	E	F	G	__	__	__	__	__	__	__	________			
I	I	M	M	M	M	M	I	I	I	M	M	M			

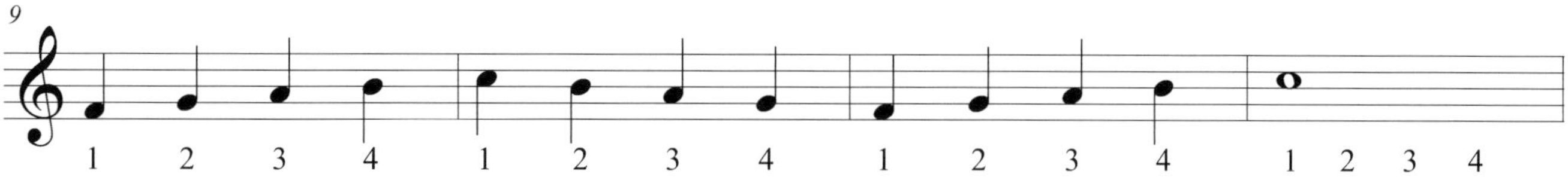

1	2	3	4	1	2	3	4	1	2	3	4	1	2	3	4
F	G	A	B	C	__	__	__	__	__	__	__	________			
M	M	R	R	R	R	R	M	M	M	R	R	R			

1	2	3	4	1	2	3	4	1	2	3	4	1	2	3	4
__	__	__	__	__	__	__	__	__	__	__	__	________			
R	R	R	M	M	M	I	I	T	T	T	I	I			

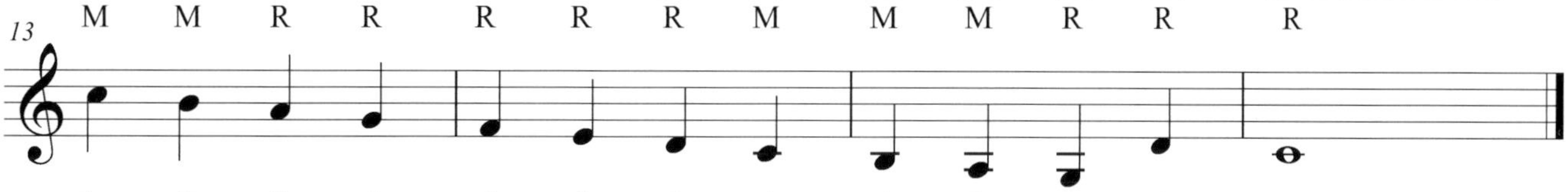

TRACK 52

4. A-B-C Blues

Learning Tip: In this basic blues piece there is a lot of repetition, making it easy to learn. Measures 1–2 and 2–4 are exactly the same, while measures 9–12 are the same as 1–4. In addition, measures 5–6 are the same as 7–8. Pay attention to the stationary, "hold down" fingers indicated with the dotted arrows above staves 1–3. This technique gives you economy of motion for accurate and faster playing.

Holly Rudin-Braschi

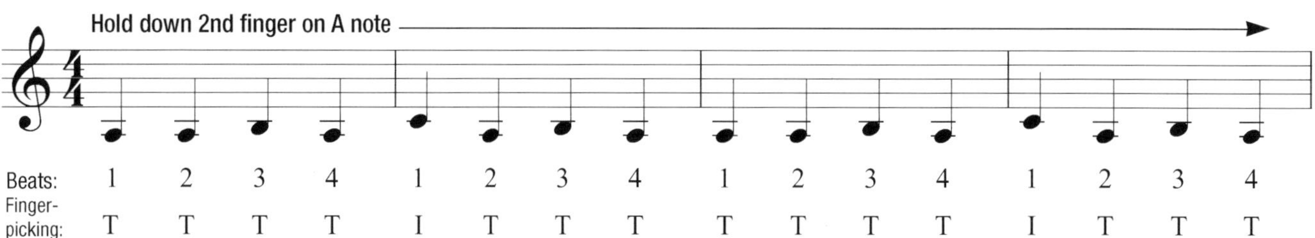

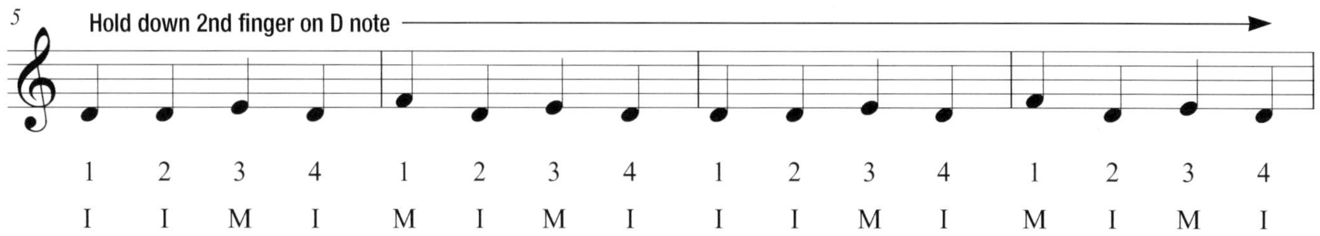

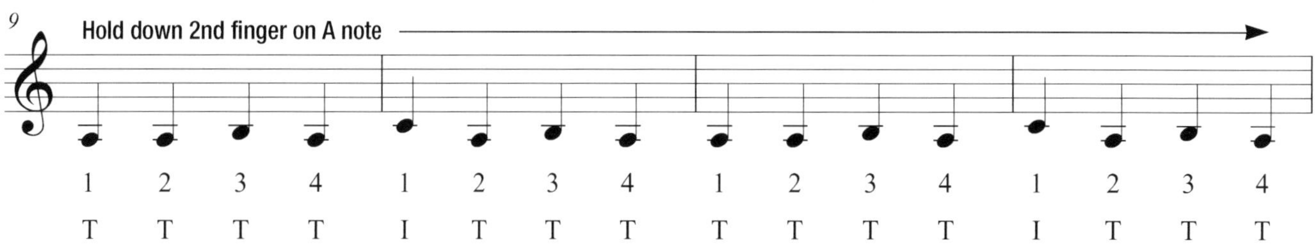

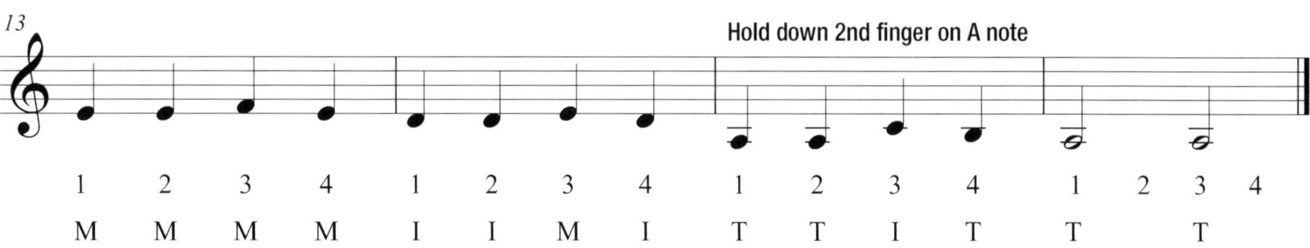

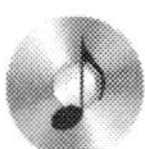

5. Peter Gray

TRACK 53

Traditional American Folk Tune

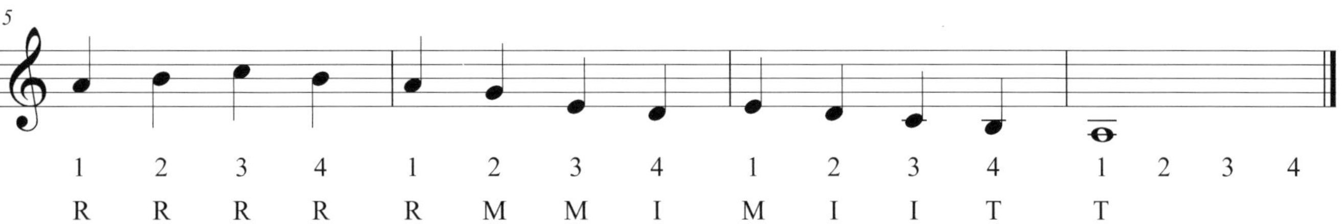

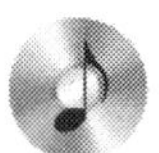

6. Minor Serenade

TRACK 54

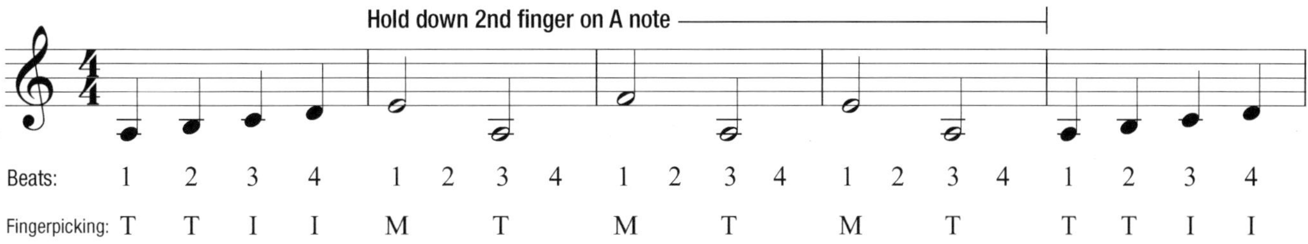

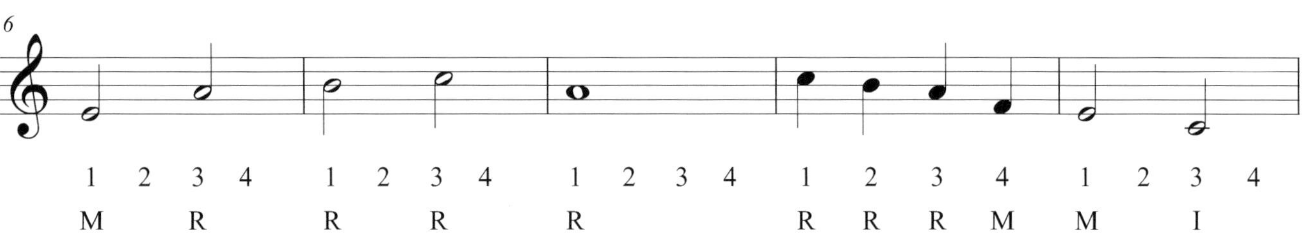

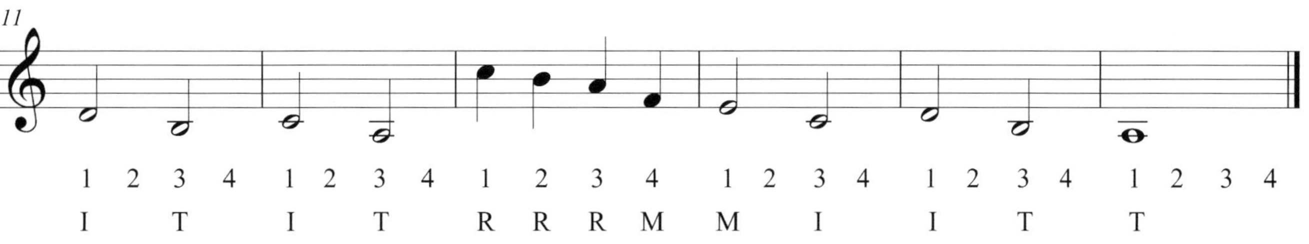

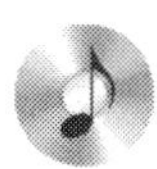
TRACK 55

7. Daisy Bell A.K.A "A Bicycle Built for Two"

Play this song 3 ways:

1. **As an Instrumental**—Play the arrangement below that combines melody and chords.
2. **As a Song**—Play the chords to accompany your singing.
3. **As a Combination**—Sing the song through while accompanying yourself with chords, then play an instrumental version… or vice versa.

Composed in 1892
by Harry Dacre (1860–1922)

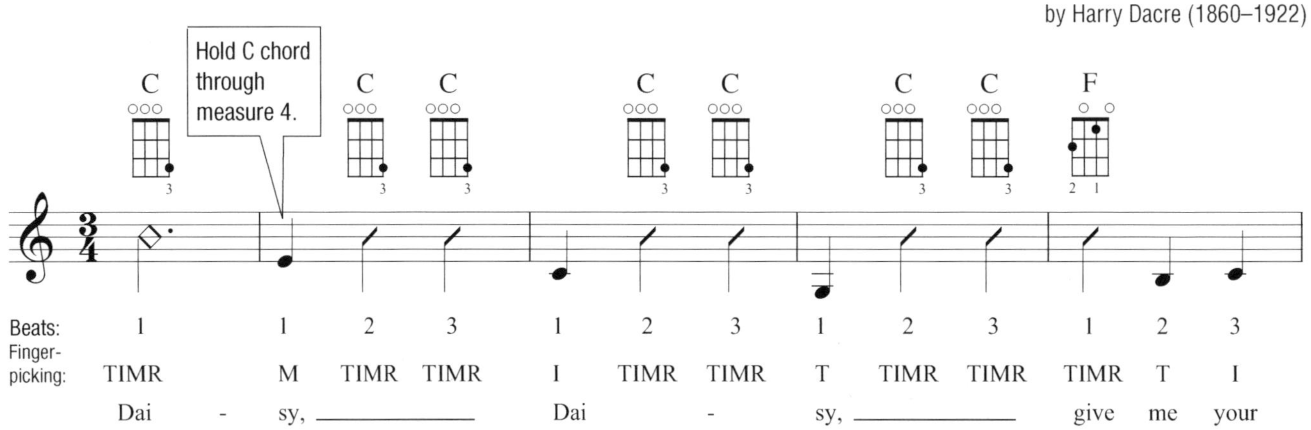

Hold C chord through measure 4.

C C C C C C C F

Beats: 1 | 1 2 3 | 1 2 3 | 1 2 3 | 1 2 3

Finger-picking: TIMR | M TIMR TIMR | I TIMR TIMR | T TIMR TIMR | TIMR T I

Dai - sy, _____ Dai - sy, _____ give me your

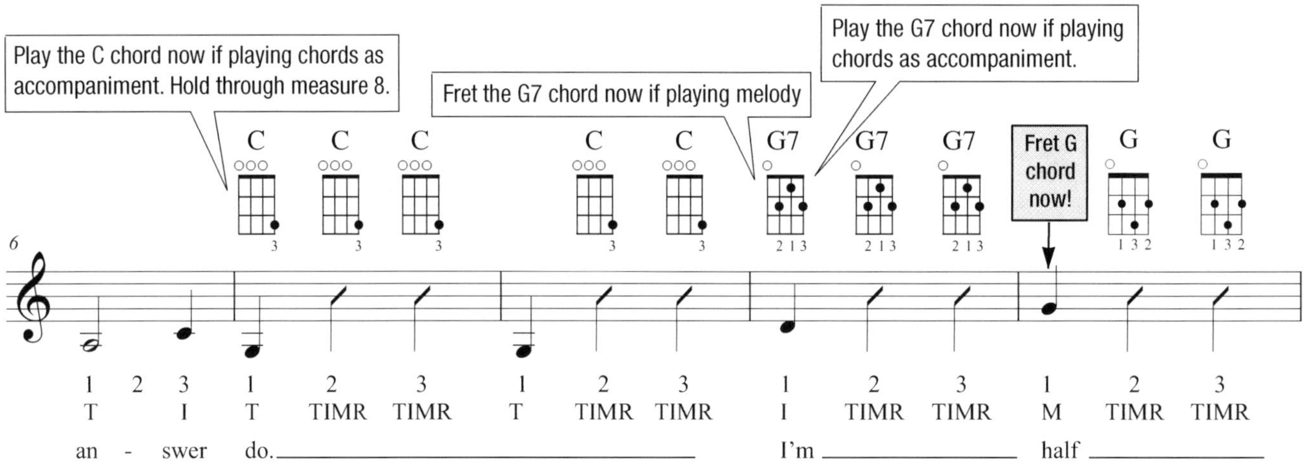

Play the C chord now if playing chords as accompaniment. Hold through measure 8.

Fret the G7 chord now if playing melody

Play the G7 chord now if playing chords as accompaniment.

Fret G chord now!

C C C C C G7 G7 G7 G G

6

1 2 3 | 1 2 3 | 1 2 3 | 1 2 3 | 1 2 3

T I | T TIMR TIMR | T TIMR TIMR | I TIMR TIMR | M TIMR TIMR

an - swer do. _____ I'm _____ half _____

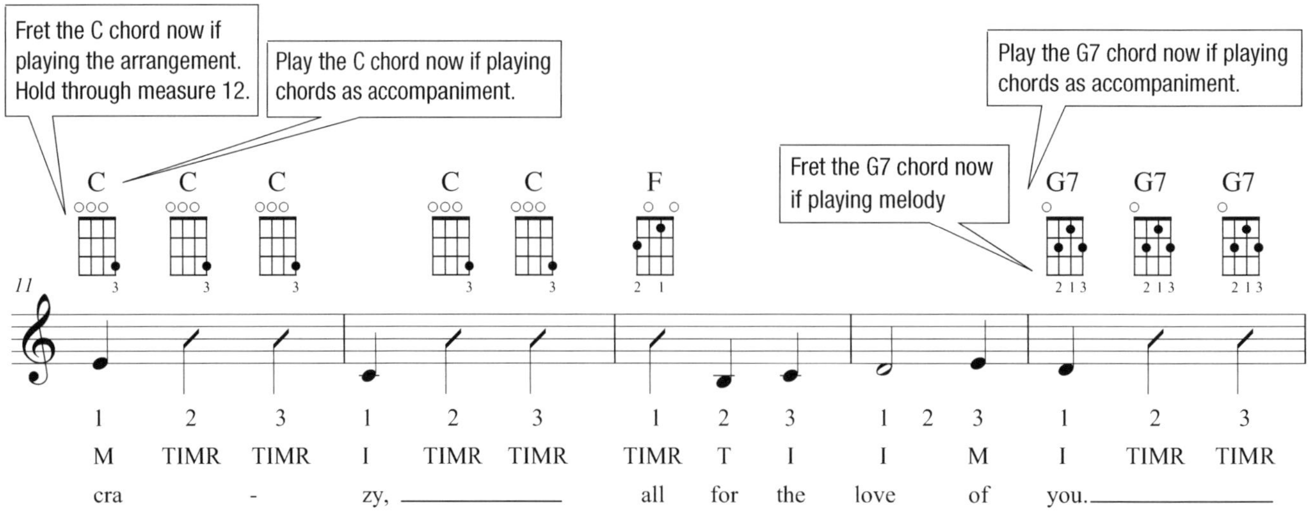

Fret the C chord now if playing the arrangement. Hold through measure 12.

Play the C chord now if playing chords as accompaniment.

Fret the G7 chord now if playing melody

Play the G7 chord now if playing chords as accompaniment.

C C C C C F G7 G7 G7

11

1 2 3 | 1 2 3 | 1 2 3 | 1 2 3 | 1 2 3

M TIMR TIMR | I TIMR TIMR | TIMR T I | I M | I TIMR TIMR

cra - zy, _____ all for the love of you. _____

16

G7 C C

1 2 3 1 2 3 1 2 3 1 2 3 1 2 3

T TIMR M M M I M M TIMR I T TIMR I

It won't be a styl - ish mar - riage; I

21

Play the C chord now if playing chords as accompaniment.

F C G C G7

1 2 3 1 2 3 1 2 3 1 2 3 1 2 3 1 2 3

M I TIMR I T T TIMR T TIMR M TIMR T

can't af - ford a car - riage. But you'd look sweet, up -

27

C G7 C G7 C C C

1 2 3 1 2 3 1 2 3 1 2 3 1 2 3 1 2 3

TIMR M TIMR M M TIMR M I TIMR T TIMR I TIMR TIMR

on a seat of a bi - cy - cle built for two!

History: David Ewen writes in *American Popular Songs*[1]: "When Harry Dacre, a popular English composer, first came to the United States, he brought a bicycle with him, and was charged duty. His friend, the songwriter William Jerome, remarked lightly, 'It's lucky you didn't bring a bicycle built for two, otherwise you'd have to pay double duty.' Dacre was so taken with the phrase 'bicycle built for two' that he decided to use it in a song, which he titled "Daisy Bell." The real Daisy, who inspired the song, was the Countess of Warwick, Frances Brooke. Nicknamed Daisy, she was one of the most desirable and wealthiest women of her time. A spirited woman unafraid of scandal, Daisy was, for a time, the mistress of the Prince of Wales, subsequently Edward VII, King of England (1901–1910). She was also a vegetarian, championed women's education and stood as a labor (leftist/socialist) candidate. She eventually married John Boyd Dunlop, the founder of the Dunlop Pneumatic Tyre Co. Ltd.

Countess of Warwick, Frances Brooke (a.k.a. Daisy)

[1] Ewen, David (1966). *American Popular Songs*. Random House.

Introducing the Minor Chords: Am, Dm and Em

To play all chords below: Strum down with the thumb, index, or middle finger, or, **fingerpick** all strings simultaneously with the **T**humb, **I**ndex, **M**iddle and **R**ing fingers—T I M R

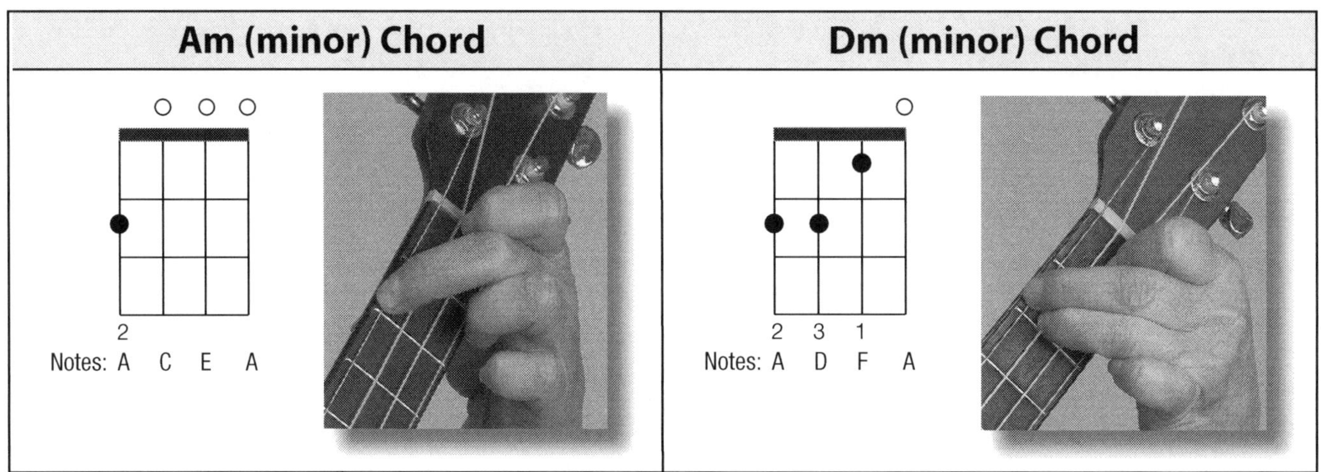

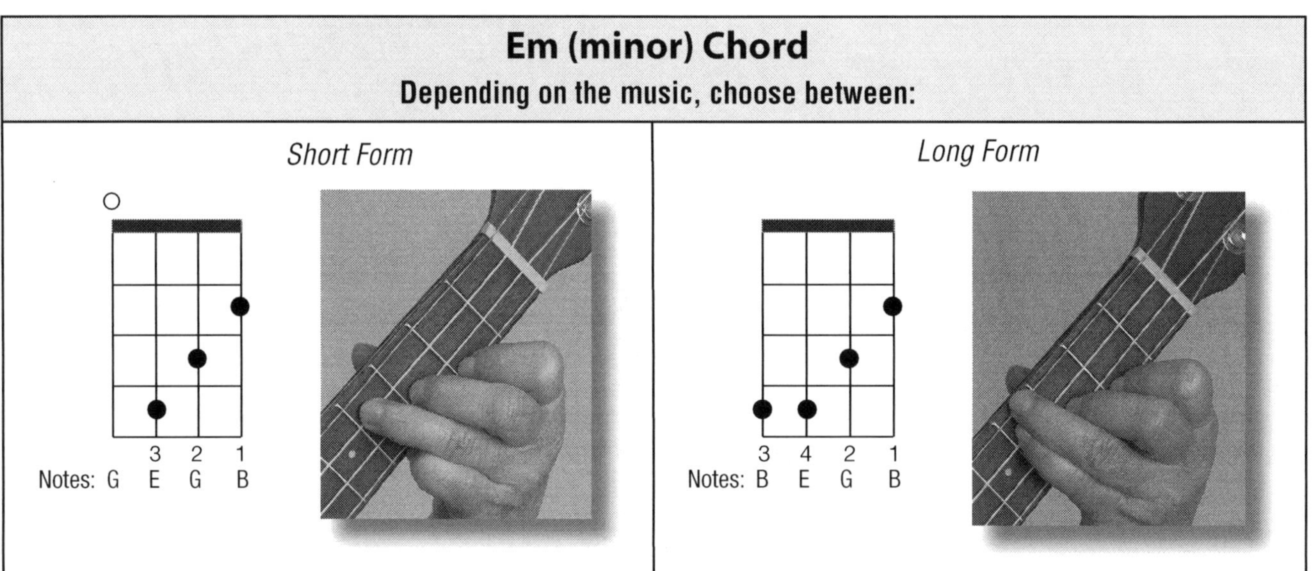

Roadmap for Moving Smoothly Between Am, F and Dm

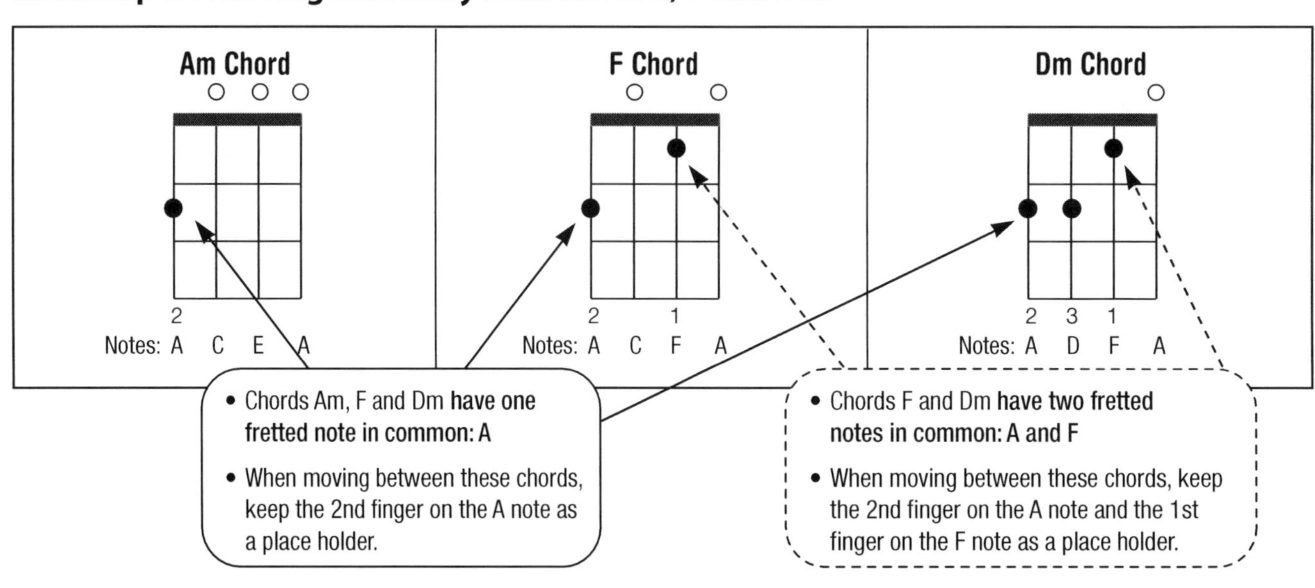

Roadmap for Moving Smoothly Between Em, and C Chords

Since these chords have NO Notes in Common, you "walk" your fingers into place.

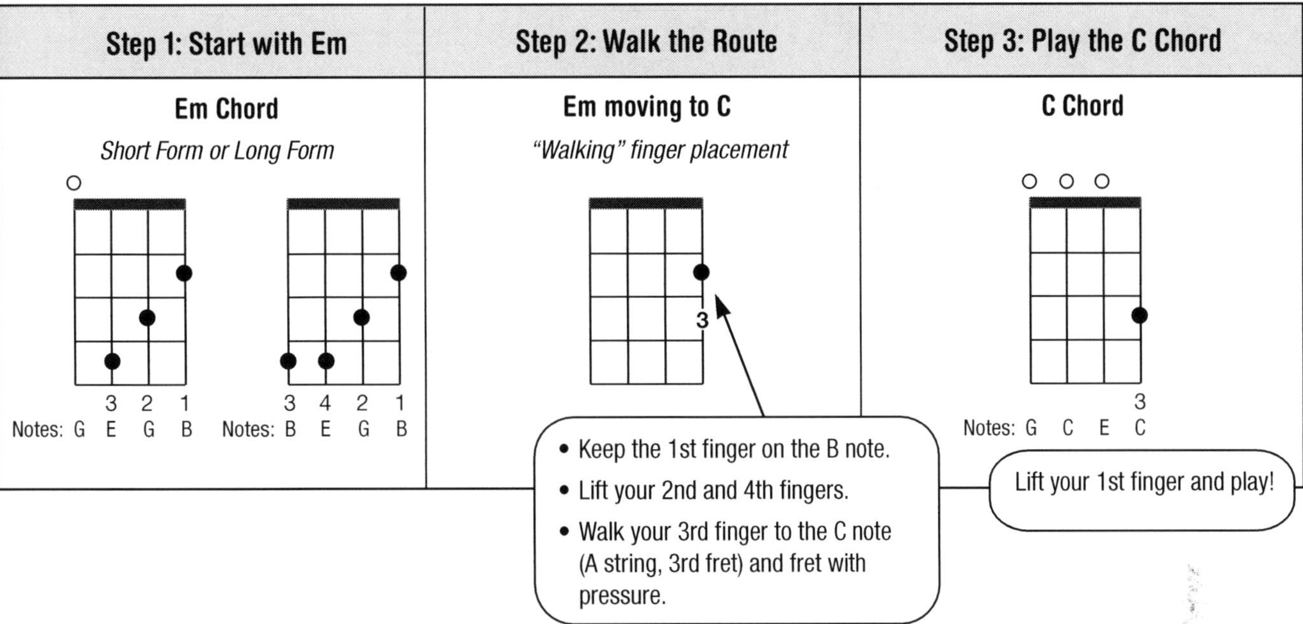

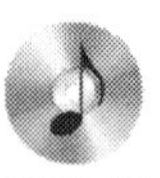

8. Chords with New Notes

TRACK 56

The alternate fingering designated below makes it easier to play the chord progression: Am – Dm – Em.

9. Minor Melody Exercise

TRACK 57

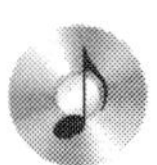

10. Volga Boatmen

TRACK 58

Learning Tip: Throughout the song, keep the 2nd finger fretted on the low A note (G string, 2nd fret).

Traditional Russian

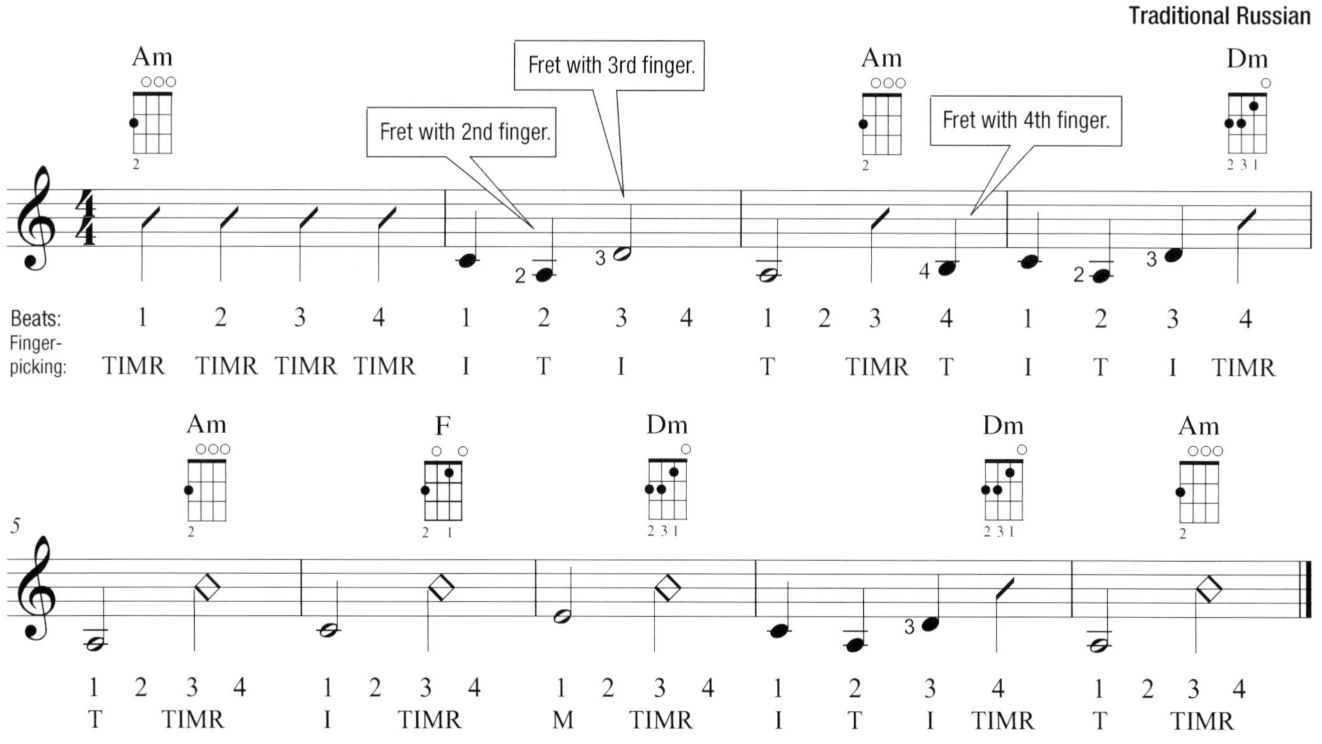

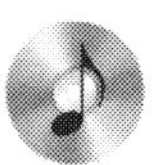

11. Amazing Grace

TRACK 59

Play this traditional song 3 ways:

1. **As an Instrumental**—Play the arrangement below that combines melody and chords.
2. **As a Song**—Play the chords to accompany your singing.
3. **As a Combination**—Sing the song through while accompanying yourself with chords, then play an instrumental version… or vice versa.

Lyrics written circa 1772 by John Newton

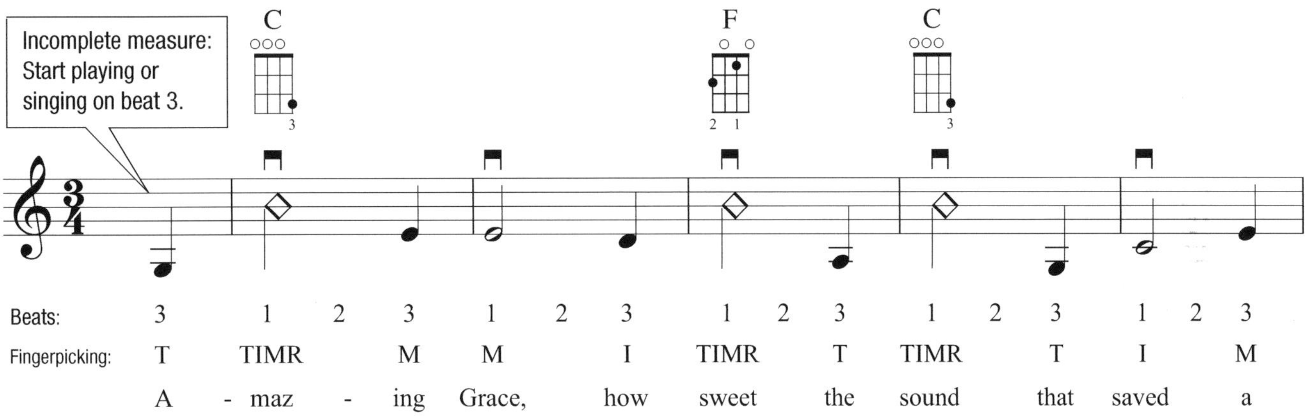

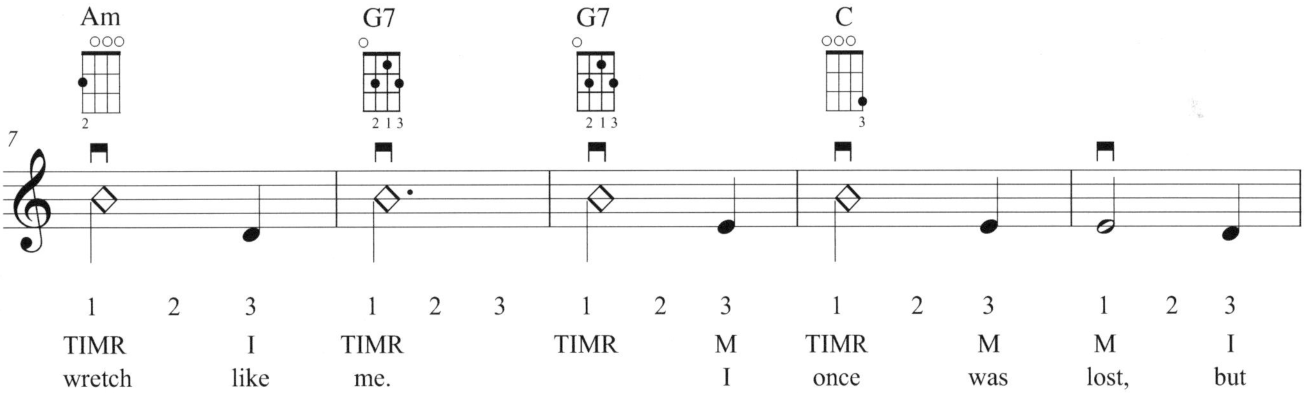

Incomplete measure: Start playing or singing on beat 3.

Chords:		C						F		C				
Beats:	3	1	2	3	1	2	3	1	2	3	1	2	3	1
Fingerpicking:	T	TIMR		M	M		I	TIMR		T	TIMR		T	I
	A	- maz	-	ing	Grace,		how	sweet		the	sound		that	saved

(continued: beats 2 3; fingerpicking M; lyric: a)

Am			G7			G7			C					
1	2	3	1	2	3	1	2	3	1	2	3	1	2	3
TIMR		I	TIMR			TIMR		M	TIMR		M	M		I
wretch		like	me.					I	once		was	lost,		but

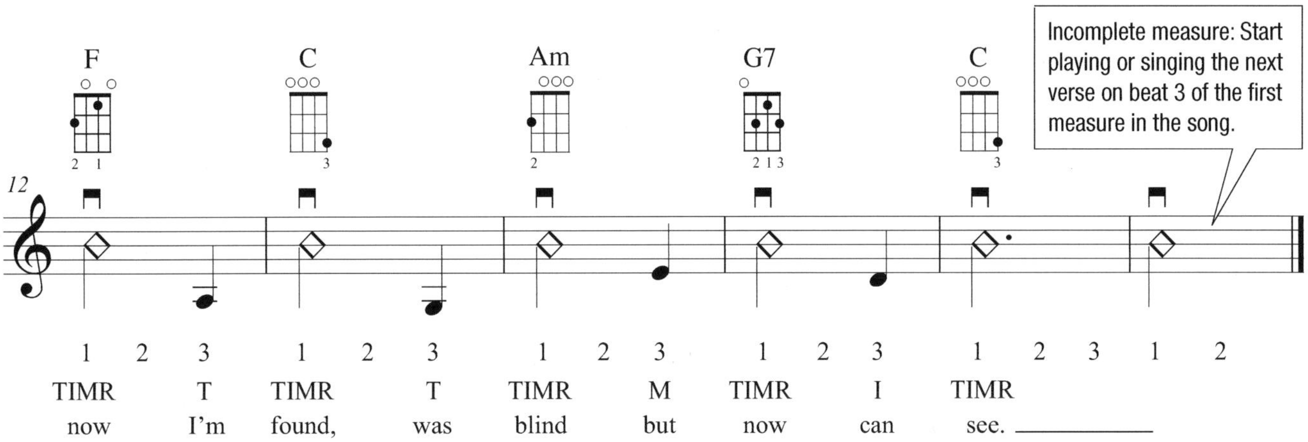

Incomplete measure: Start playing or singing the next verse on beat 3 of the first measure in the song.

F			C			Am			G7			C				
1	2	3	1	2	3	1	2	3	1	2	3	1	2	3	1	2
TIMR		T	TIMR		T	TIMR		M	TIMR		I	TIMR				
now		I'm	found,		was	blind		but	now		can	see. ______				

Amazing Grace: Lyrics and Chord Charts

VERSE 1

```
 C        /          F        C
A-mazing Grace, how sweet the sound,
    C        Am         G7  /
That saved a wretch like me.
 C        /       F      C
I once was lost but now I'm found,
     Am       G7       C  F  C
Was blind but now can see.
```

VERSE 2

```
     C           /          F       C
'Twas Grace that taught my heart to fear,
     C          Am     G7    /
And Grace my fears re-lieved;
     C      /      F        C
How precious did that Grace ap-pear,
     Am    G7     C    F C
The hour I first be-lieved!
```

VERSE 3

```
         C    /       F       C
Through many dangers, toils and snares,
     C      Am   G7      /
We have al-ready come;
     C          /          F       C
'Tis Grace hath brought me safe thus far,
      Am        G7      C     F  C
And Grace will lead me home.
```

VERSE 4

```
    C          /          F       C
The Lord hast promised good to me,
    C          Am        G7     /
His word my hope se-cures;
   C        /            F      C
He will my shield and portion be,
    Am      G7     C     F  C
As long as life en-dures.
```

VERSE 5

```
    C          /          F          C
Yea, when this heart and flesh shall fail,
     C      Am       G7    /
And mortal life shall cease;
 C         /          F     C
I shall pos-sess with-in the veil,
  Am   G7      C     F C
A life of joy and peace.
```

VERSE 6

```
    C           /        F          C
The earth shall soon dis-solve like snow,
    C       Am       G7    /
The sun for-bear to shine;
    C          /         F        C
But God, who called me here be-low,
     Am     G7  C    F  C
Will be for-ever mine.
```

Amazing Grace

John Newton (1725-1807)

History: On May 10, 1748, Englishman John Newton (1725–1807) was on board one of his slave ships returning home during a violent storm. Praying for survival, he experienced an epiphany that converted him to Christianity. Many years later, he left the slave trade, eventually became a minister in the United Kingdom, and was prominent in Britain's anti-slavery movement. The familiar, traditional melody most often used for this hymn was not original nor was Newton a composer. As with other hymns of this period, the words were sung to a number of tunes before it became linked to the current tune that appeared in American hymnals of the 1830s.

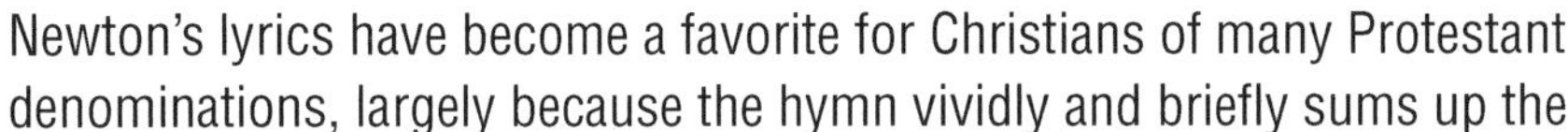

Newton's lyrics have become a favorite for Christians of many Protestant denominations, largely because the hymn vividly and briefly sums up the Protestant doctrine of divine grace. The lyrics are based on I Chronicles 17:16, where King David marvels at God's choosing him and his house. Newton apparently wrote this for use in a sermon he preached on New Year's Day, 1773. It has also become known as a favorite with supporters of freedom and human rights, both Christian and non-Christian, in part because many assume that it is testimony of his past as a slave trader. However there is nothing in the hymn or related sermon notes about slavery, and Newton did not actively speak against the slave trade until several years after the hymn was written.

In 1838, when the Cherokee Nation was forced to relocate from what is now Georgia to the Western United States on the "Trail of Tears," over 4,000 Indians perished along the way. They were not able to give their dead a full burial; instead, they sang "Amazing Grace." Since then, "Amazing Grace" is often considered the Cherokee National Anthem. The hymn was also popular with both Union and Confederacy troops during the American Civil War.

Largo from the New World Symphony, "Goin' Home"

Antonin Dvořák (1841–1904)

History: The Symphony No. 9, "Aus der Neuen Welt" (Op. 95), popularly known as the "New World Symphony," by Czeck composer Antonín Dvořák, was written in 1893 during his visit to the United States from 1892 to 1895. One of the more popular symphonies in the modern repertory, this theme is from the second movement.

The lyrics for this song were written by Nino Rota (December 3, 1911–April 10, 1979), an Italian composer best known for his film scores, notably for the films of Federico Fellini and Luchino Visconti. He also composed the music for two of Franco Zeffirelli's Shakespeare films, and for the first two films of Francis Ford Coppola's *Godfather* trilogy, receiving the Academy Award for Best Original Score for *The Godfather Part II* (1974). To learn more about Rota, visit: **www.ninorota.com**

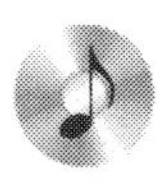

12. Largo from the New World Symphony, "Goin' Home"

TRACK 60

Antonin Dvořák

"Fret with 2nd finger."

"Strum down" sign. Use to accompany your singing with chords.

C C G Dm Dm G7

Beats: 1 2 3 | 1 2 3 | 1 2 3 4 | 1 2 3

Finger-picking: TIMR M M | TIMR I I | TIMR M M M | TIMR TIMR TIMR

Go - in' home, go - in' home, I'm a go - in' home.

C Am Dm C C

5

1 2 3 4 | 1 2 3 4 | 1 2 3 4 | 1 2 3

TIMR M M | TIMR I I | TIMR M I I | TIMR I TIMR

Qui - et, like some still day, I'm a go - in' home.

F Am Am F F

9

1 2 3 4 | 1 2 3 4 | 1 2 3 4 | 1 2 3 4

T I TIMR | T T TIMR | T I T T | T TIMR TIMR TIMR

It's not far, just close by through an op - en door.

F F Am F G7

13

1 2 3 4 | 1 2 3 4 | 1 2 3 4 | 1 2 3 4

T I TIMR | T T TIMR | T I T T | T TIMR TIMR TIMR

Work all done, care laid by, goin' to fear no more.

Goin' Home: Lyrics and Chord Chart

These lyrics are sung to the "Largo" melody from Dvořák's *New World Symphony.* The chords here designed for singing differ slightly from the arrangement on the previous page.

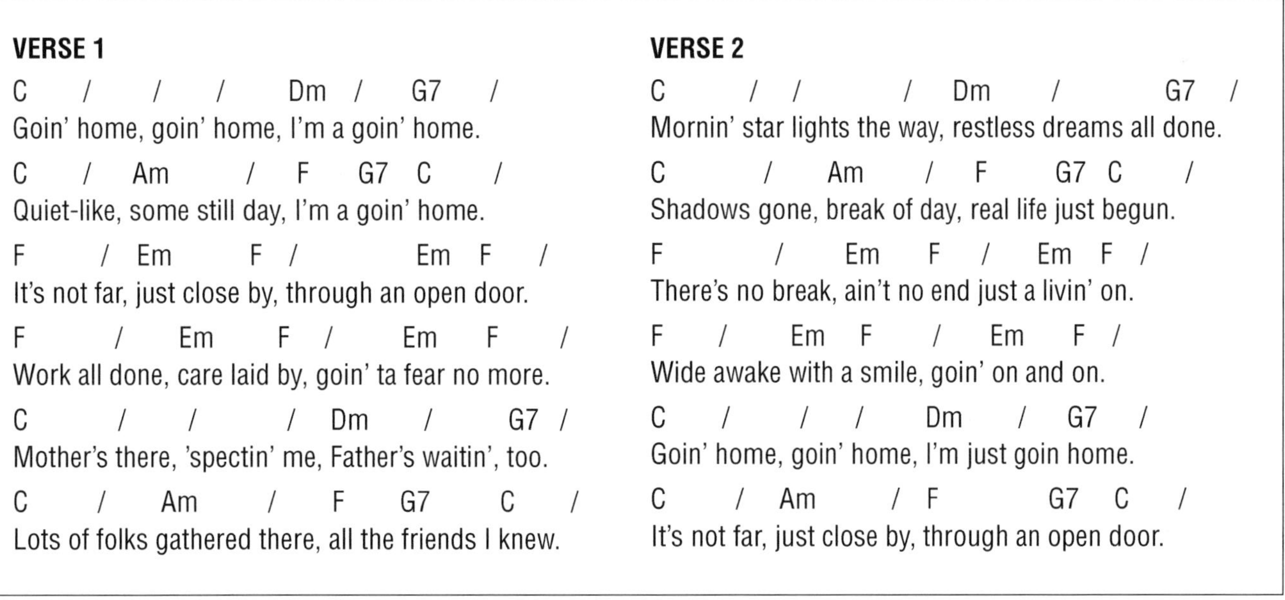

VERSE 1

C / / / Dm / G7 /
Goin' home, goin' home, I'm a goin' home.

C / Am / F G7 C /
Quiet-like, some still day, I'm a goin' home.

F / Em F / Em F /
It's not far, just close by, through an open door.

F / Em F / Em F /
Work all done, care laid by, goin' ta fear no more.

C / / / Dm / G7 /
Mother's there, 'spectin' me, Father's waitin', too.

C / Am / F G7 C /
Lots of folks gathered there, all the friends I knew.

VERSE 2

C / / / Dm / G7 /
Mornin' star lights the way, restless dreams all done.

C / Am / F G7 C /
Shadows gone, break of day, real life just begun.

F / Em F / Em F /
There's no break, ain't no end just a livin' on.

F / Em F / Em F /
Wide awake with a smile, goin' on and on.

C / / / Dm / G7 /
Goin' home, goin' home, I'm just goin home.

C / Am / F G7 C /
It's not far, just close by, through an open door.

13. Kilgarra Mountain

TRACK 61

Learning Tip: Play the notes to learn this melody. Then accompany yourself with chords as you sing it.

Traditional Irish

C Am Am

Beats: 4 | 1 2 3 4 | 1 2 3 4 | 1 2 3 4 | 1 2 3 4

Fingerpicking: M | M M R | M M M M | R R R | R M M

As I was a - go - in' o - ver Kil - gar - ra Moun - tain, I

6

F C

1 2 3 4 | 1 2 3 4 | 1 2 3 4 | 1 2 3 4 | 1 2 3 4

R R R | R R R R | M M R R | R M | M M M R

spied colo - nel Far - rell and his mo - ney he was coun - tin'. First I drew me

11

Am F

1 2 3 4 | 1 2 3 4 | 1 2 3 4 | 1 2 3 4 | 1 2 3 4

M M M | R R R R | R M M M | R R R | R R R R

pis - tol, and then I drew me ra - pier, say - in' "Stand and de - liv - er for I

16

C CHORUS G7 C

1 2 3 4 | 1 2 3 4 | 1 2 3 4 | 1 2 3 4 | 1 2 3 4

M M R R | R M M M | I I I I | I | M M I

am your bold de - ceiv - er!" Mush a ring - um du - ram - da, Whack fol the

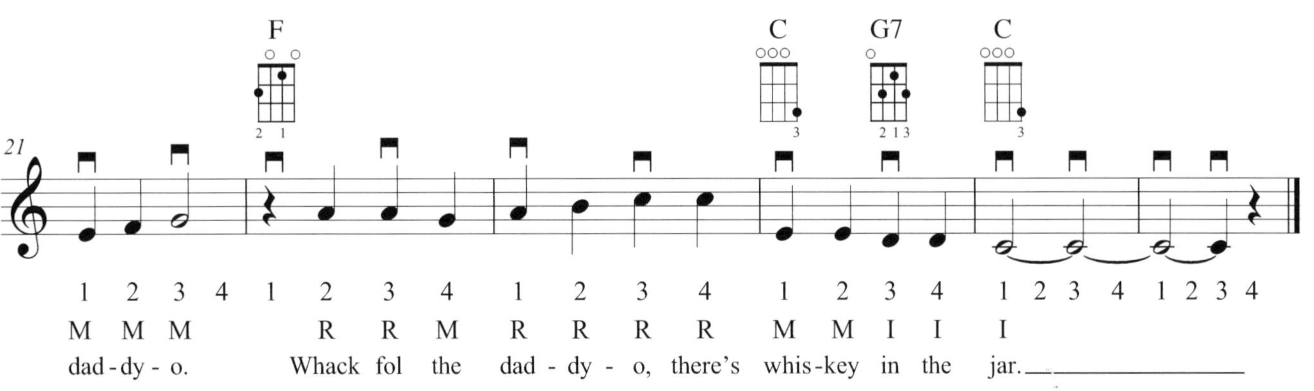

VERSE 2

C / / / Am / / /
He counted out his money and it made a pretty penny,
F / / / C / / /
I put it in me pocket to take home to darlin' Jenny.
C / / / / Am / Am /
She sighed and swore she loved me and never would de-ceive me.
F / / / C / /
But the devil take the women for they always lie so easy.
Chorus

VERSE 3

C / / / Am / / /
I went into me chamber all for to take a slumber,
F / / / C / / /
To dream of gold and girls and of course it was no wonder.
C / / / Am / / /
Me Jenny took me charges and she filled them up with water,
F / / / C / /
Then called on Colonel Farrell to get ready for the slaughter.
Chorus

VERSE 4

C / / / Am / / /
Next morning early be-fore I rose to travel,
F / / / C / / /
A-came a band of foot-men and likewise Colonel Farrell.
C / / / Am / / /
I goes to draw me pistol for she'd stole away me rapier,
F / / / C / /
But a prisoner I was ta-ken I couldn't shoot the water.
Chorus

VERSE 5

C / / / Am / / /
They put me into jail with a judge all a writin',
F / / / C / / /
For robbing Colonel Farrell on Kil-garra Mountain.
C / / / Am / / /
But they didn't take me fists so I knocked the jailer down,
F / / / C / /
And bid a fare-well to this tight fisted town.
Chorus

VERSE 6

C / / / Am / / /
I'd like to find me brother the one that's in the army,
F / / / C / / /
I don't know where he's sta-tioned in Cork or in Kil-larney
C / / / Am / / /
To-gether we'd go roving o'er the mountains of Kill-kenney,
F / / / C / C
And I swear he'd treat me fairer than me darlin' sportin' Jenny.
Chorus

VERSE 7

C / / / Am / / /
There's some takes delight in the car-ria-ges and rollin',
F / / / C / / /
Some takes de-light in the hurley or the bowlin'.
C / / / Am / / /
But I takes de-light in the juice of the barley,
F / / / C / /
Courtin' pretty maids in the morning oh so early.
Chorus

History: Also known as, "Whiskey in the Jar," the song's lyrics date to the late 18th century because the highwayman threatens his victim with a rapier (some versions, a saber), a weapon used by rapparees or Irish irregular soldiers and bandits of the 17th and 18th centuries. In 17th century Ireland, highwaymen were regarded as national patriots because they robbed English landlords and either kept the money for themselves, or shared it Robin Hood-style.

TRACK 62

14. Michael Row the Boat Ashore

Incomplete measure: Count 1, 2, then start playing on 3rd beat.

Fret the G note with your 2nd finger to make it easy to transition to the Em chord in the next measure.

C F G7 C

Beats: 3 4 1 2 3 4 1 2 3 4 1 2 3 4 1 2 3 4

Fingerpicking: I M M M M R M M M TIMR TIMR TIMR M M

Mi - chael row the boat a - shore, al - le - lu - ia! Mi-chael,

Em Dm F G7 C

6

1 2 3 4 1 2 3 4 1 2 3 1 2

TIMR M M M TIMR I I TIMR TIMR TIMR

row the boat a - shore, al - le - lu - u - ia!

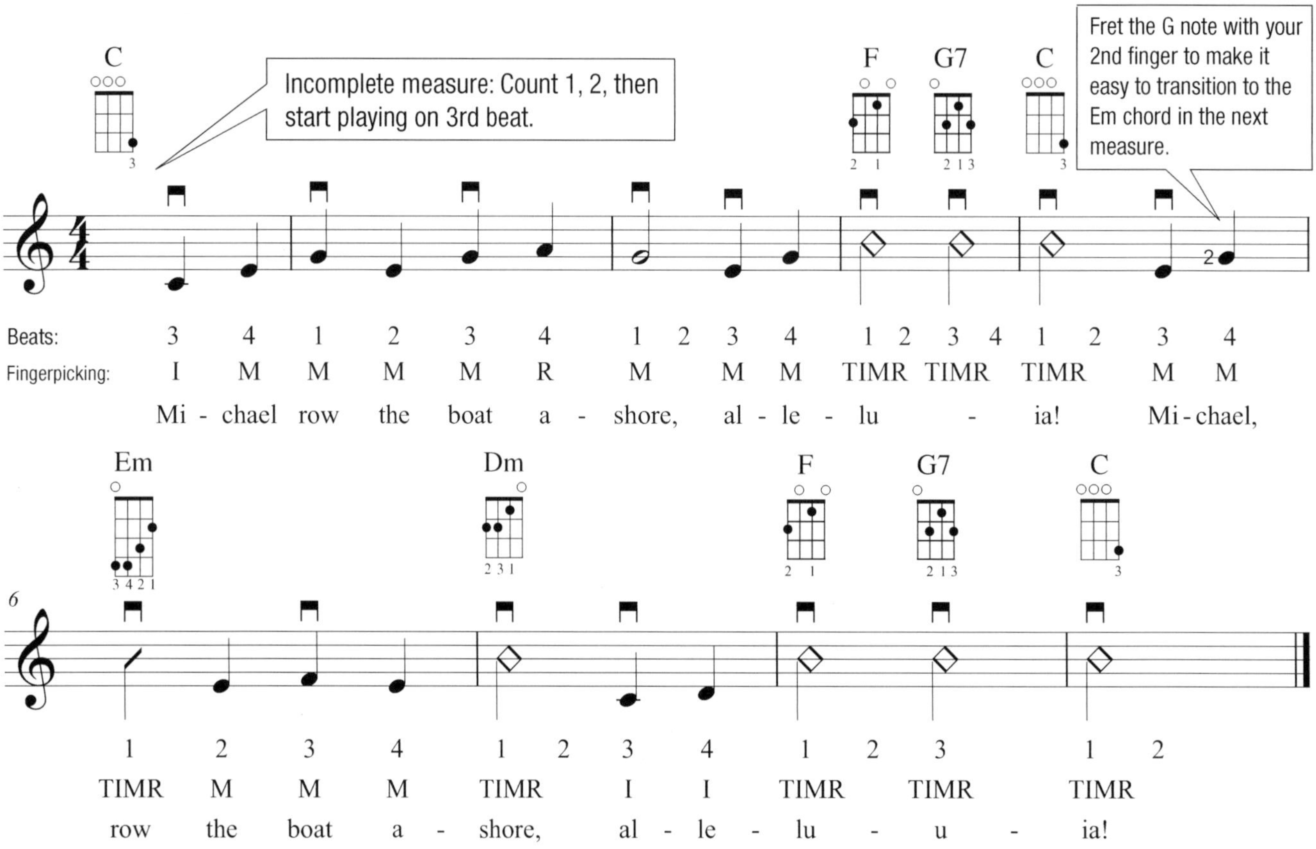

VERSE 2

C / / / / F G7 C
Michael's boat is a music boat, Alle-lu- u- ia
C Em / Dm / F G7 C
Michael's boat is a music boat, Alle-lu- u- ia

VERSE 3

C / / / / F G7 C
Sister, help to trim the sail, Alle-lu- u- ia
C Em / Dm / F G7 C
Sister, help to trim the sail, Alle-lu- u- ia

VERSE 4

C / / / / F G7 C
Jordan River is chilly and cold, Alle-lu- u- ia
C Em / Dm / F G7 C
Chills the body, but not the soul, Alle-lu- u- ia

VERSE 5

C / / / / F G7 C
The river is deep and the river is wide, Alle-lu- u- ia
C Em / Dm / F G7 C
Milk and honey on the other side, Alle-lu- u- ia

History: First published in *Slave Songs of the United States,* by William Francis Allen, in 1867[2], "Michael, Row the Boat Ashore" (or "Michael, Row Your Boat Ashore") is an African-American spiritual from the Sea Islands of Georgia. The only transportation around these islands was by small boats manned by strong-armed slaves. The River Jordan is often used as a metaphor for death. According to *Slave Songs of the United States,* the "Michael" referred to in the song is the Archangel Michael. In Christian tradition, Michael is often considered a conductor of the souls of the dead.

[2] William Francis Allen, Charles Pickard Ware, and Lucy McKim Garrison, *Slave Songs of the United States,* http://docsouth.unc.edu/church/allen/allen.html

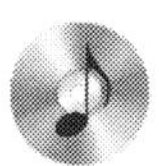

TRACK 63

15. Shenandoah—3 Ways

I offer this song in three versions to help you learn:

- **Version 1:** Melody with chords to strum (below)—will teach you to both play and sing the melody
- **Version 2:** Arrangement (**page 120**)—will teach you to simultaneously play melody and chords
- **Version 3:** Lyrics and chords (**page 121**)—will teach you the verses while playing the chords

Shenandoah Version 1: Melody

Learning Tip: Pay attention to the slurs and the ties in this song. In singing, ties indicate holding a single note for an extended period, while slurs indicate singing a single syllable (on a vowel) on two different notes.

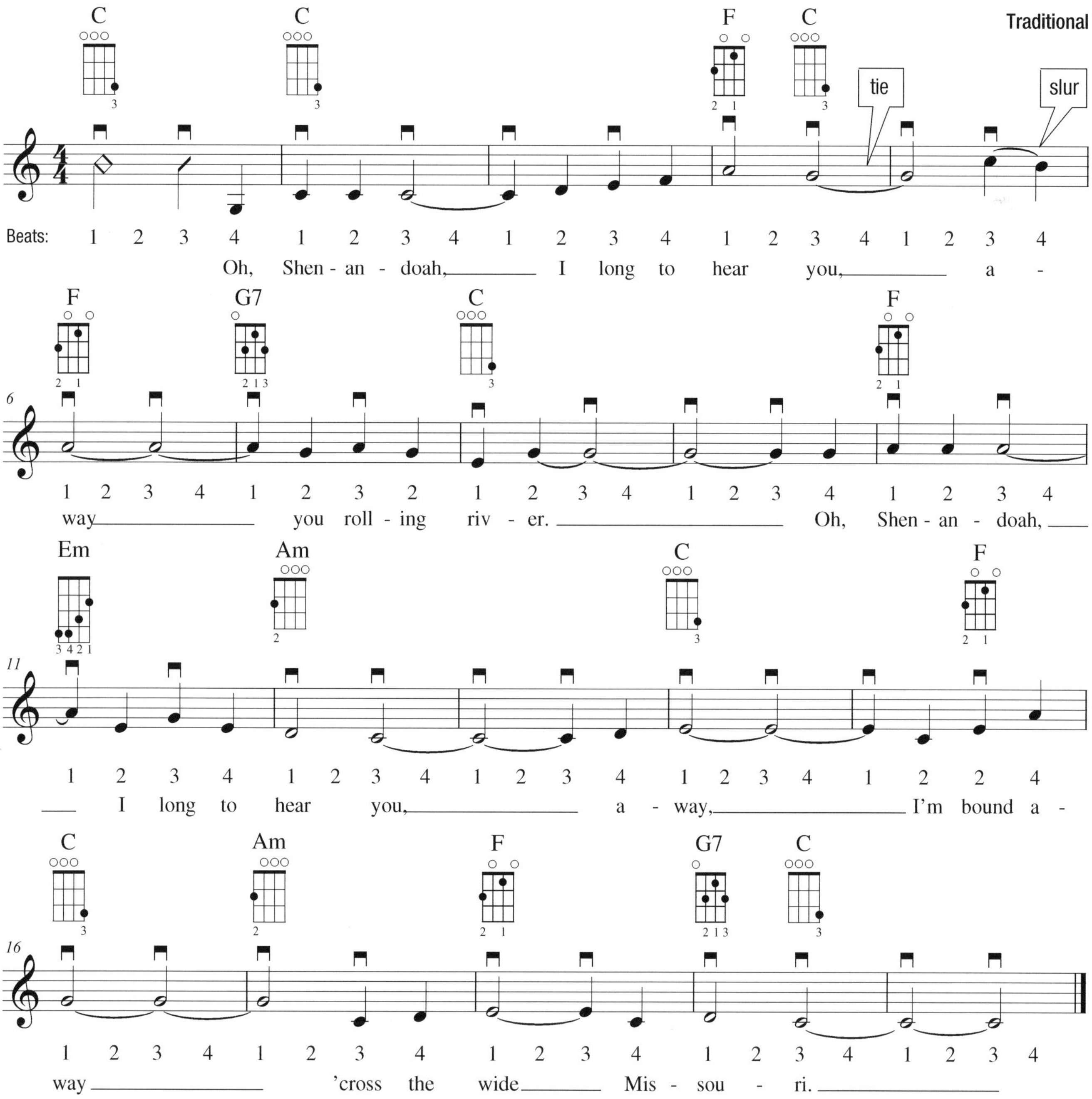

Traditional

C C F C

tie

slur

Beats: 1 2 3 4 1 2 3 4 1 2 3 4 1 2 3 4 1 2 3 4

Oh, Shen - an - doah, I long to hear you, a -

F G7 C F

1 2 3 4 1 2 3 2 1 2 3 4 1 2 3 4 1 2 3 4

way you roll - ing riv - er. Oh, Shen - an - doah,

Em Am C F

1 2 3 4 1 2 3 4 1 2 3 4 1 2 3 4 1 2 2 4

I long to hear you, a - way, I'm bound a -

C Am F G7 C

1 2 3 4 1 2 3 4 1 2 3 4 1 2 3 4 1 2 3 4

way 'cross the wide Mis - sou - ri.

16. Shenandoah Version 2: Arrangement

TRACK 64

Learning Tip: Fret each chord firmly as long as possible to allow all the accompanying strings to resonate as you play the melody notes.

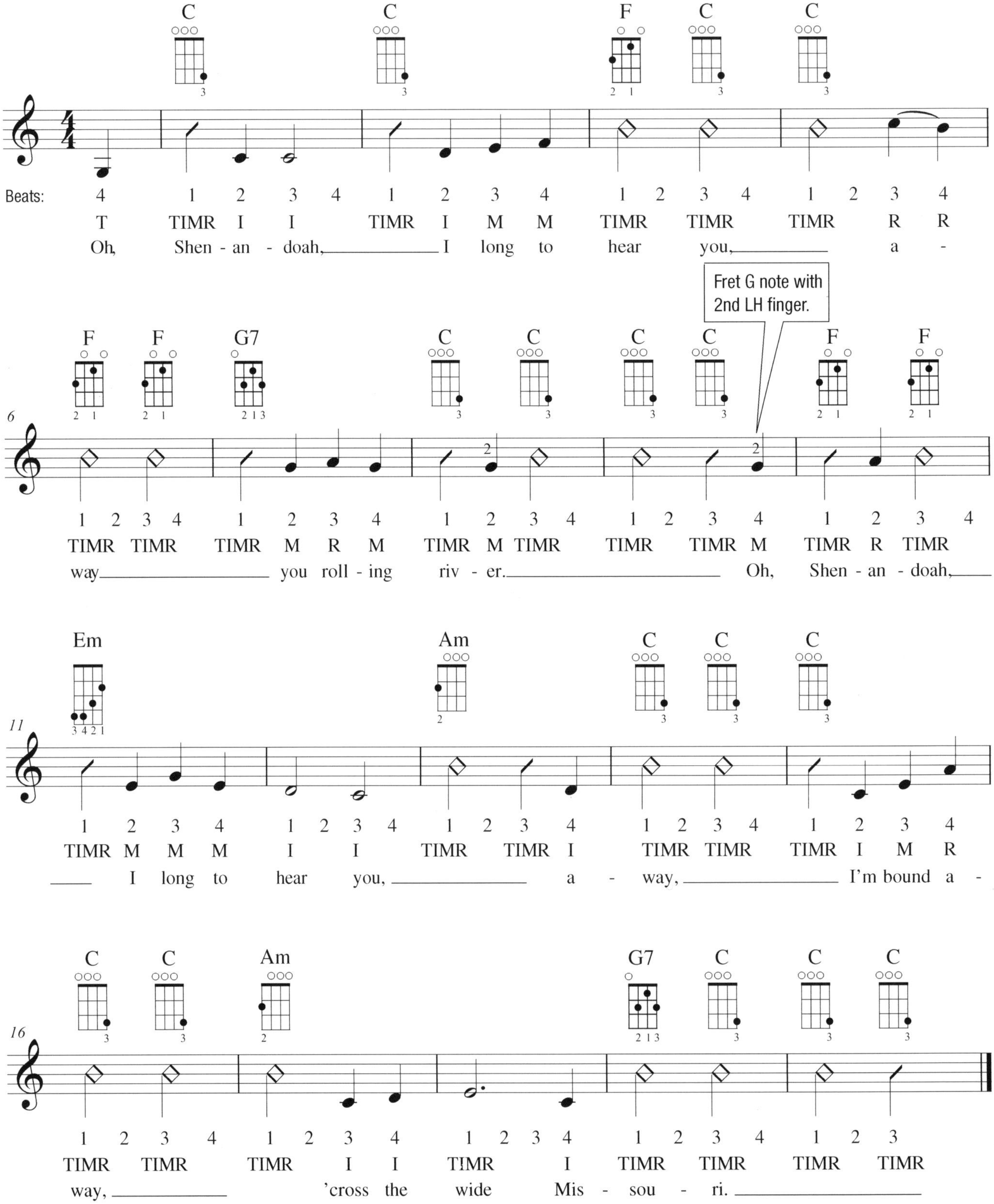

Shenandoah Version 3: Lyrics and Chord Chart

VERSE 1

```
   C        /    / /      F    C   /
Oh, Shenan-doah,  I long to hear you.
C F   / G7       /      C     / / /
A-way,        you rolling river!
    F        /    Em    /      Am   /   / /
Oh, Shenan-doah,     I long to hear you.
  C  //     F         C   / Am /          F      /      G7 C / /
A-way,   I'm bound a-way,         'cross the wide  Mis-sou-ri.
```

VERSE 2

```
   C        /    / /          F     C   /
Oh, Shenan-doah,  I love your daugh-ter.
C   F  / G7      /      C     / / /
A-way,        you rolling river!
    F        /      Em       /      Am     / / /
For her, I'd cross       the rolling water.
  C  //     F         C   / Am /          F      /      G7 C / /
A-way,   I'm bound a-way,         'cross the wide  Mis-sou-ri.
```

VERSE 3

```
   C        /    /    /        F    C    /
Oh, Shenan-doah,  I'm bound to leave you.
C F   / G7       /      C     / / /
A-way,        you rolling river!
    F        /      Em      /      Am     / / /
Oh, Shenan-doah,       I'll not de-ceive you.
  C  //     F         C   / Am /          F      /      G7 C / /
A-way,   I'm bound a-way,         'cross the wide  Mis-sou-ri.
```

History: The Shenandoah River, a tributary of the Potomac River, meanders along the base of the Blue Ridge Mountains in the heart of Virginia's historic Shenandoah Valley. This song is the story of a trader who fell in love with the daughter of the Indian Chief Shenandoah. It originated in the early 19th century as a land ballad in the areas of the Mississippi and Missouri Rivers. Adopted by sailors plying the rivers in keel and Mackinaw boats, they brought it down the Mississippi to the open ocean where it became a popular sea chantey for deep sea sailors. It first reached popularity in the early 1840s, the beginning of the fast clipper ship era, and a time of great American expansion.

An aerial view of the Shenandoah River in Virginia.
http://www.learnnc.org/lp/media/uploads/2007/12/shenandoah.jpg

WRITTEN EXERCISE:
How Low Can You Go?

Directions: Write the name of each note on the line below it. Use the following abbreviations:

MC = Middle C　**HC** = High C　**HD** = High D　**HE** = High E
HF = High F　**LG** = Low G　**LA** = Low A　**LB** = Low B

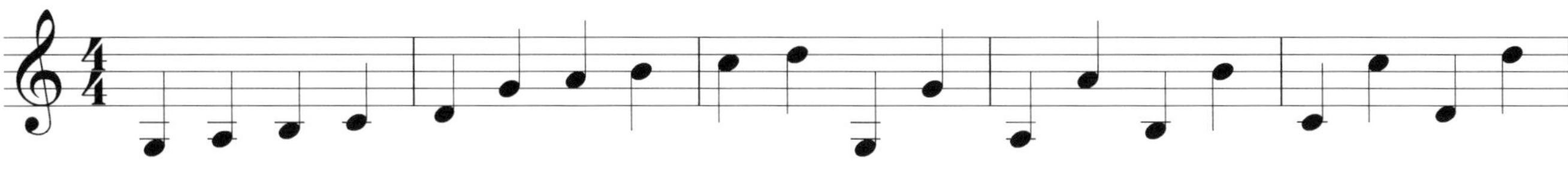

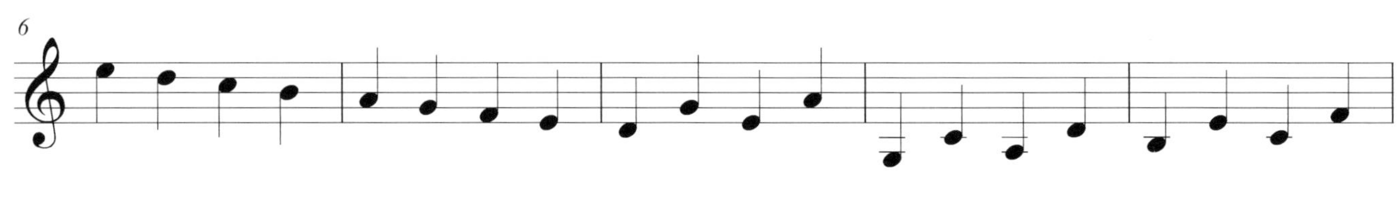

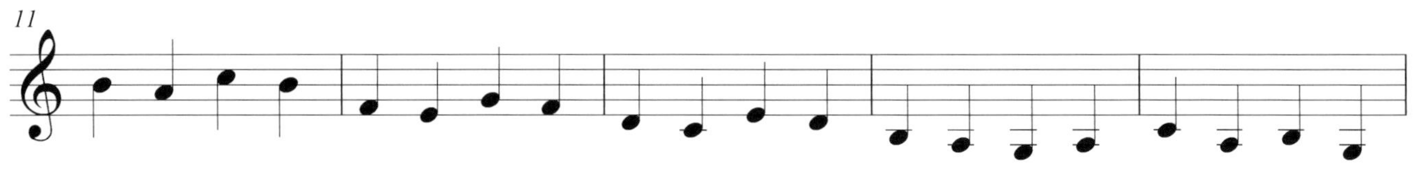

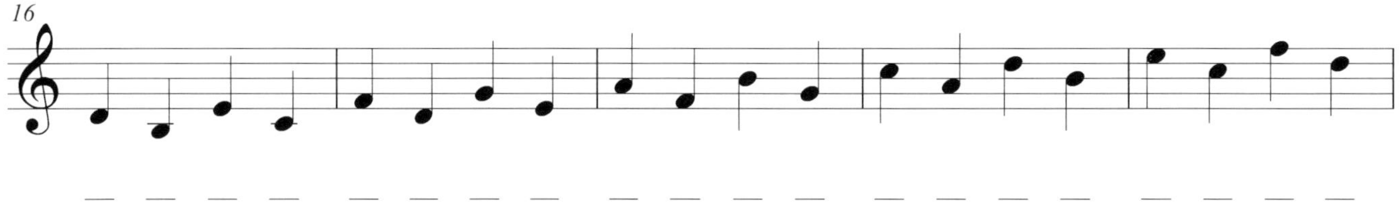

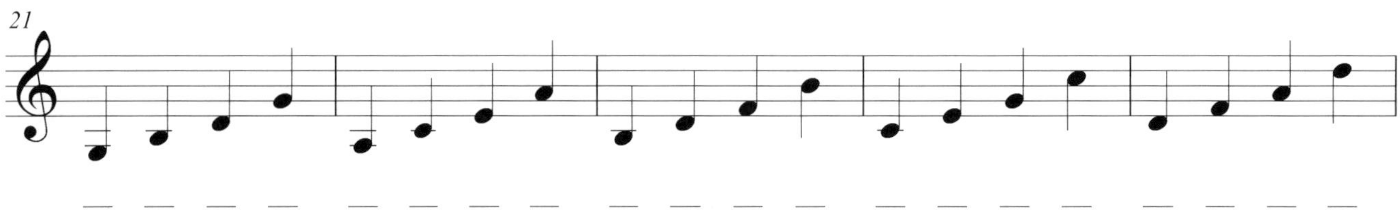

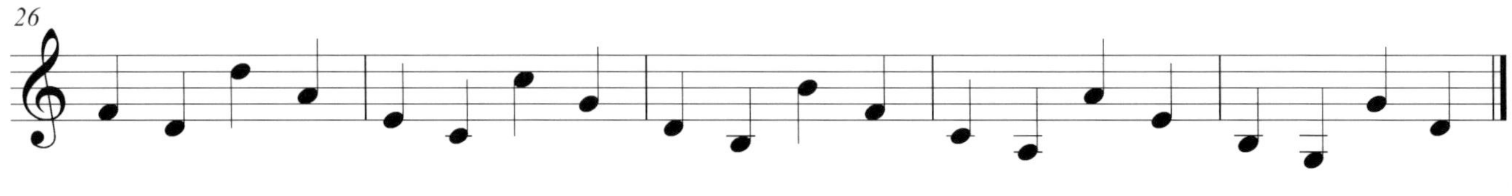

WRITTEN EXERCISE:
Answer Key For How Low Can You Go?

MC = Middle C **HC** = High C **HD** = High D **HE** = High E
HF = High F **LG** = Low G **LA** = Low A **LB** = Low B

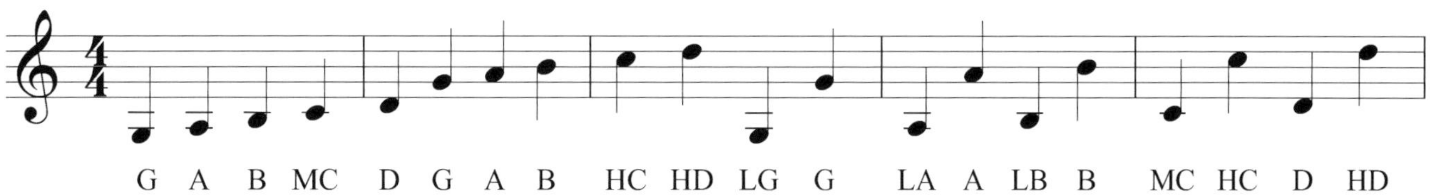

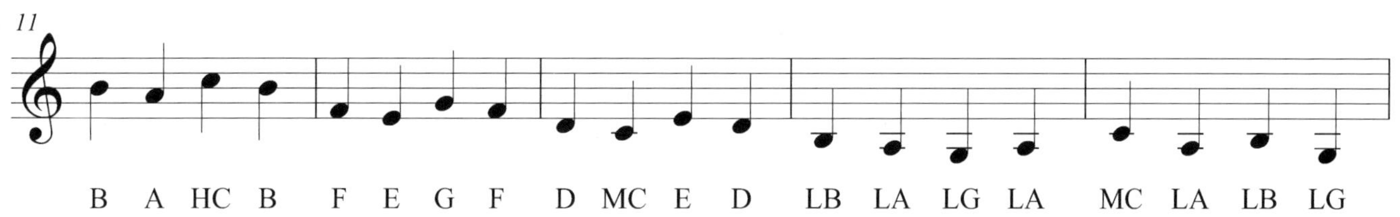

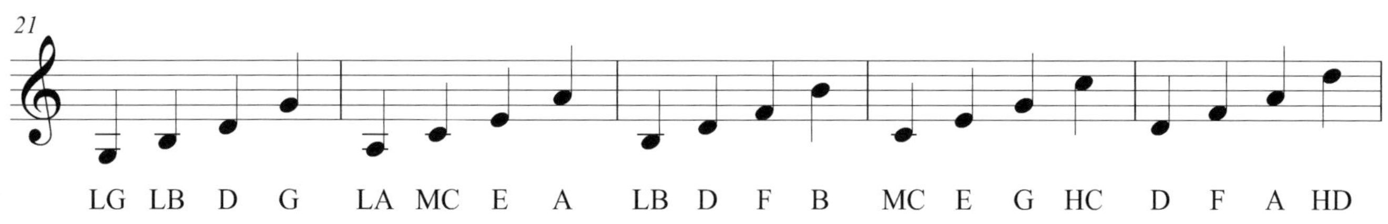

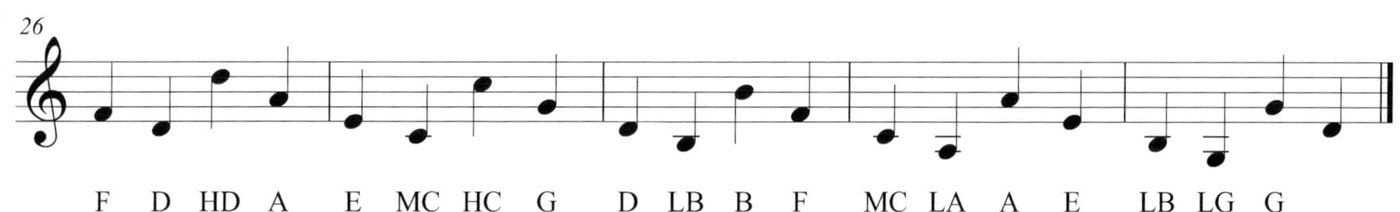

Lesson 5

Assignment

1. **Warm-up:** Each time you sit down to practice, play the following in this order...

   A. **4-Fret Half-Step Chromatic Scale Exercise** (**page 47**)

   B. **C Scale** (**page 81**)

   C. **Note Your Naturals in C** (**page 103**)

2. **Review:** Play through your favorite music and songs in *Lesson 3* and *4* as a refresher and for reinforcement. Work on anything challenging that you still need to master... a chord change, a musical passage, whatever. Practice while reading the music. Then close your eyes and play short passages to train your memory, ears and fingers.

3. **Learn:** Each time you sit down to practice, play the following in this order...

   A. **Chords: C7, D7, A7** (**page 125**)
   Practice the **C7, D7** and **A7 chords** by learning the following chord progressions

   1) G7 to A7 to Dm to D7 to G7
   (Practice the D7 in this progression by fretting with the 2 and 3 finger option, **page 125**)

   2) Dm to D7 to C to C7 *(Practice the D7 barre, long form option in this progression,* **page 125**)

   3) G to C7 to F to A7

   4) A7 to F to C7 to F

   B. **Music and songs:** ***Don't try to learn everything in the entire lesson at once***—Be patient and take your time to learn the music and internalize the techniques.

   1) **Select one fingerpicking pattern from page 128 and one pattern from page 130.** Practice them using the **"4. Down in the Valley: Fingerpicking Practice Guide" on page 132** until you can sing and play simultaneously. If you don't like to sing, play along with the Track 68 recording to get the timing right. When you learn your first two choices well enough to play slowly and in rhythm, apply them to the remaining songs in this lesson, as well as to other 3/4 time songs in *Lessons 1-4*. When you have mastered the first two patterns, learn two more patterns the same way until you learn them all.

   2) **As you practice, don't forget to:**

      a) Start counting with **"one measure for nothing."**

      b) **Continue counting** to make sure you are on the correct beat that correlates with the right hand fingers in the pattern you are learning.

Introducing the C7, D7 and A7 Chords

To play all chords below: **Strum** down with the Thumb, Index, or Middle finger, or, **fingerpick** all strings simultaneously with the Thumb, Index, Middle and Ring fingers, TIMR.

C7 Chord

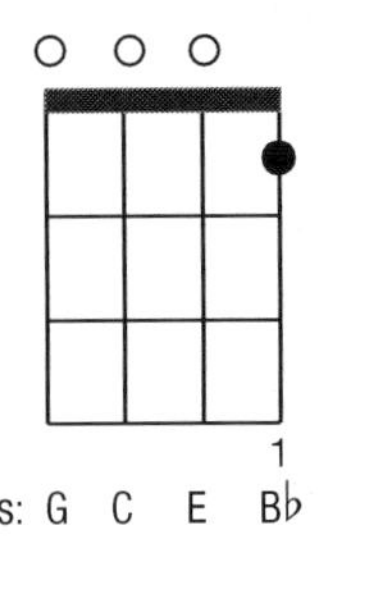

- **C7 chord has a B♭ (B flat) note**: Flats lower a note one half step in pitch. The C7 chord is spelled C-E-G-B♭. The B♭ (A string, first fret) note is one fret lower in pitch, or a half step lower than a B note (A string, second fret).
- **When used**: In the key of C, when the C7 chord is substituted for a C chord, it is usually preceded or followed by an F chord, or a D minor chord.

D7 Chord

Both D7 chords are interchangeable –

Choose the form and fingering that suits your hand size and the music you are playing.

Depending on the music, choose between:

Short Form—can be fretted two ways depending on the following chord

When moving to:

- G major or
- D major

1 3

Notes: A C F♯ A

When moving to:

- G7 or
- E7

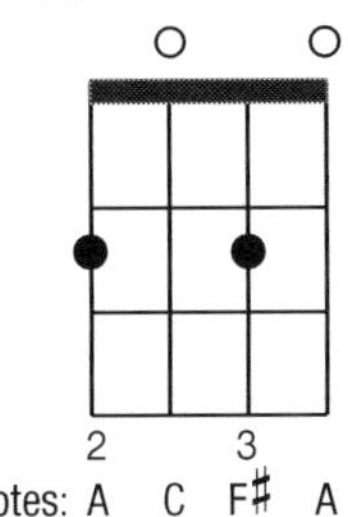

Long Form—Note optional fretting below:

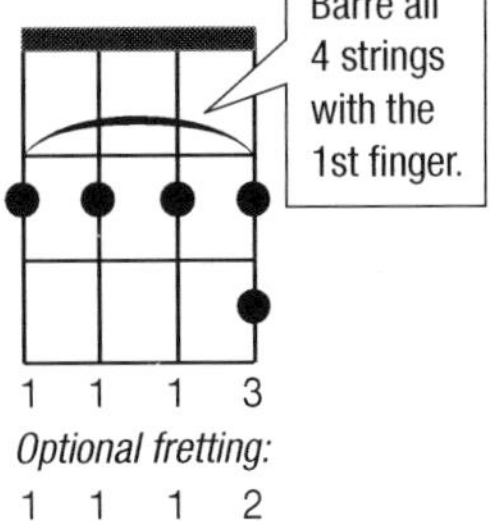

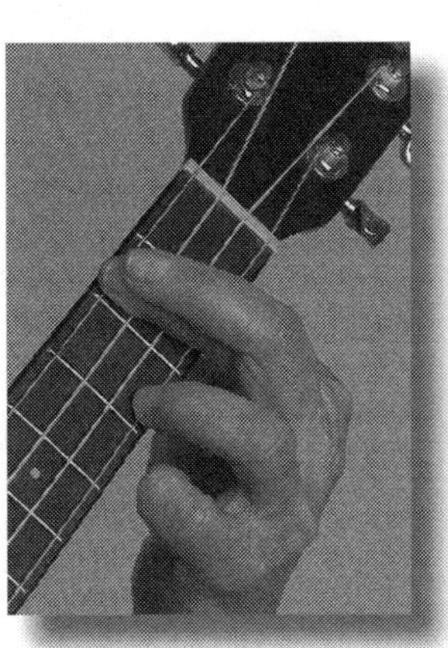

- **Which version to use:** The short version D7 and D7 barred chord above may be played interchangeably. The barred D7 chord is best for players with large fingertips.
- **When used:** In the key of C, the D7 chord is often substituted for a D minor chord. You will commonly find this substitution in Hawai'ian music, particularly in the Hawai'ian vamp progression: D7-G7-C.
- **Difference between the short version D7 and the D7 barred chord:**
  - The short version chord does not contain a D note, a.k.a. the root of the chord. The ear hears the D note even though it isn't being played.
  - The barred version contains all four notes of the chord—D, F♯, A, C.

A7 Chord

Notes: G C♯ E A

- A7 Chord has a C♯ (C sharp) note: Sharps raise a note one half step in pitch. The A7 chord is spelled A-C♯-E-G. The C♯ (C string, first fret) note is one fret higher in pitch, or a half step higher, than a C note (C string, Open).

1. C7, D7 and A7 Chord Workout

TRACK 65

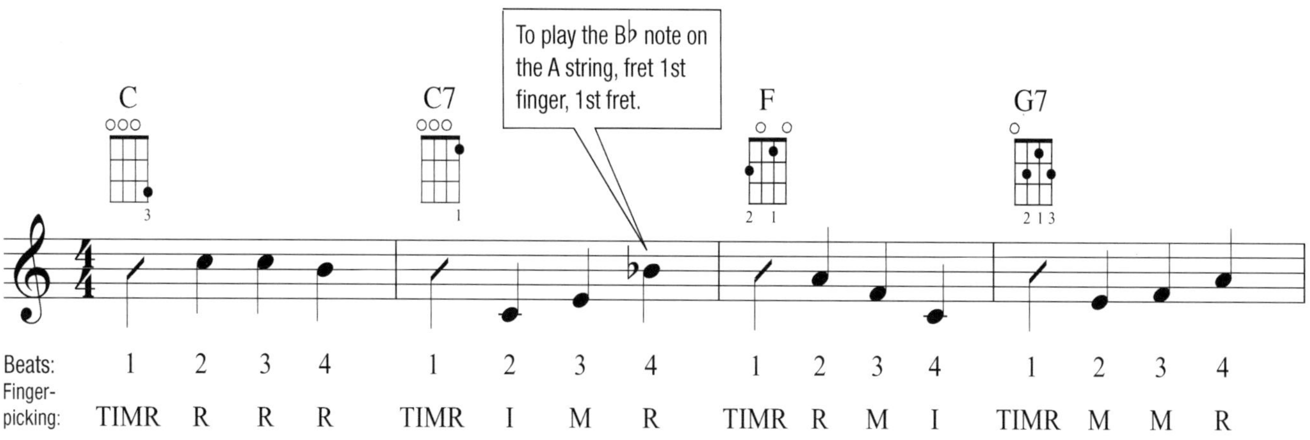

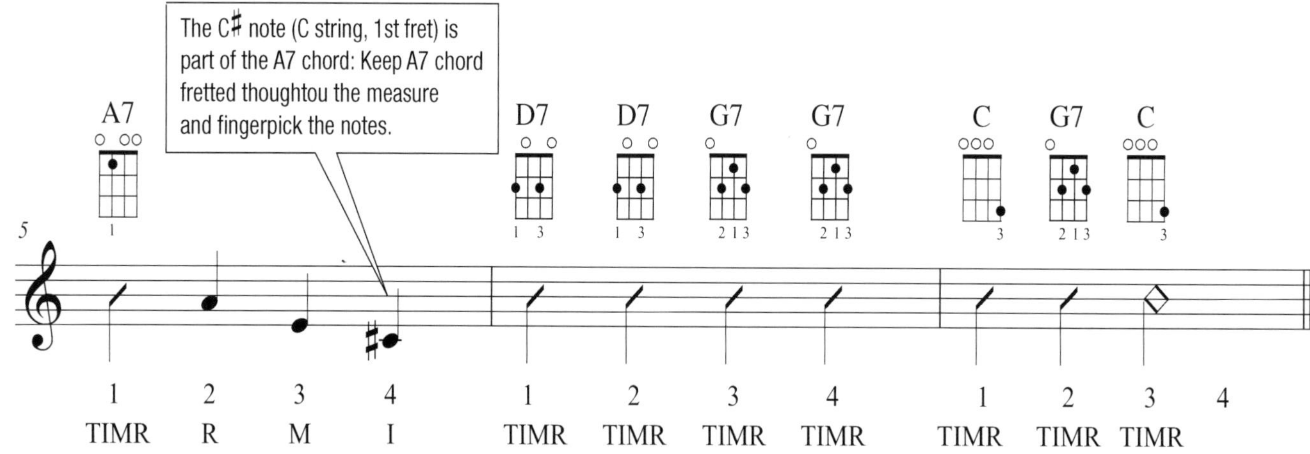

The Difference Between Block and Arpeggiated Chords

Block Chords: Up to this point, you have been playing chords by either strumming all the strings simultaneously with your **T**humb, **I**ndex, or **M**iddle finger, or plucking all four strings with individual fingers (T I M R). ***Whenever you play two or more strings simultaneously, you are playing a block chord.***

Arpeggiated Chords: "Arpeggio" literally means in Italian, "like a harp." ***An arpeggiated chord is a chord that is played broken***, or ***each note of the chord is played individually in a pattern***. To train your fingers to do this, we have been playing melody notes with one finger per string.

Triple Time Fingerpicking Patterns

On the following pages, these six fingerpicking patterns combine arpeggios and block chords.

- **Patterns A, B, and C:** Combine fingerpicking and block chords. Pattern C can also be considered as an arpeggiated pattern.
- **Patterns D, E and F:** Combine fingerpicking and strumming.
- **Rhythm Ukulele:** All of the patterns teach you to play rhythm ukulele. That means your right hand:
    - Acts like a metronome, keeping the rhythm steady as it fingerpicks and/or strums
    - Plays the harmonies in rhythm to accompany a voice or solo instrument as it sings or plays the melody

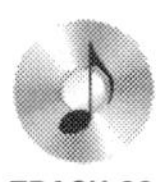

2. Triple Time Fingerpicking Patterns for Songs in 3/4 Time

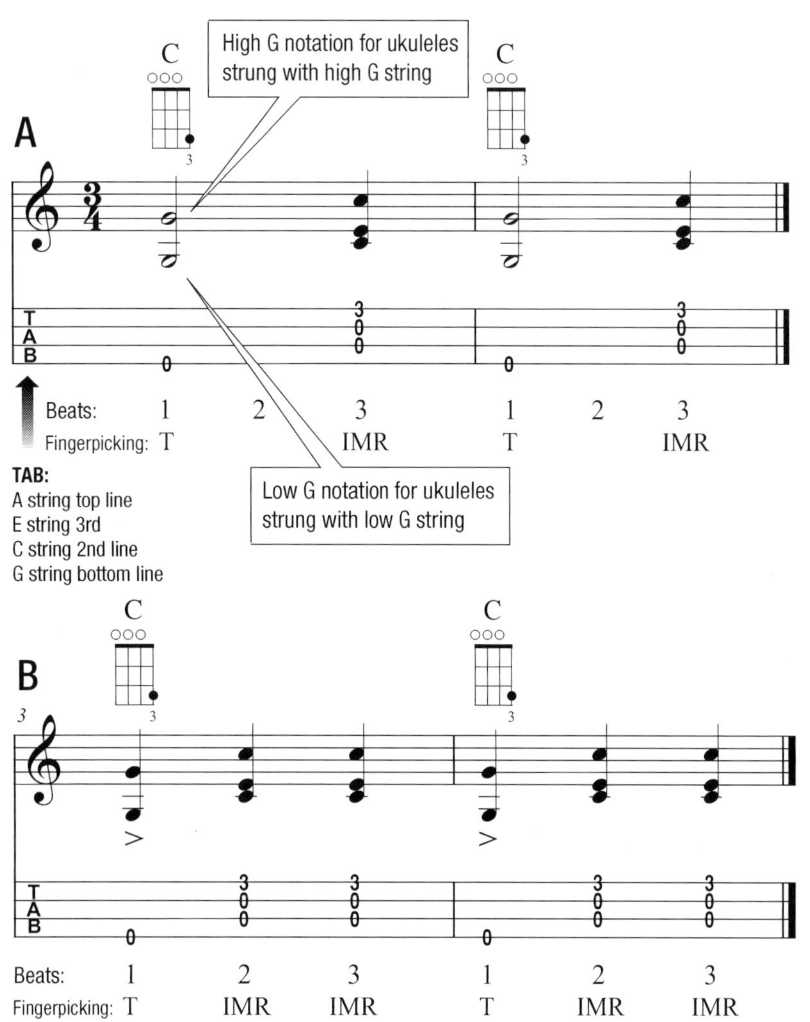

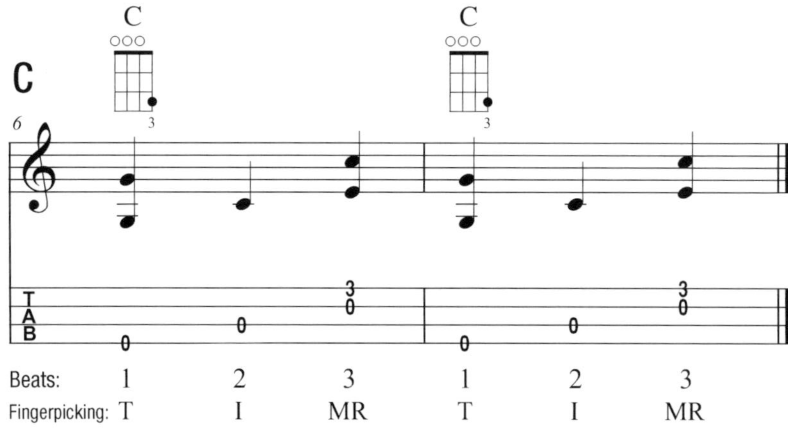

Triple Time Songs That Match These Patterns

Traditional:

- Amazing Grace
- Bicycle Built for Two
- Blow the Man Down
- Clementine
- Down in the Valley
- Drink to Me Only With Thine Eyes
- Greensleeves
- Irene, Good Night
- Man on the Flying Trapeze
- Mollie Malone
- My Bonnie Lies Over the Ocean
- On Top of Old Smoky
- Take Me Out to the Ball Game
- Tumbalalaika

Cowboy Songs:

- Home on the Range
- Streets of Laredo
- Spanish Is the Loving Tongue
- Whoopie, Ti, Yi, Yo

Spanish Songs:

- De Colores
- Cielito Lindo

Christmas Songs:

- Silent Night
- We Wish You a Merry Christmas

Movie Songs:

- Around the World in 80 Days
- My Favorite Things (*Sound of Music*)
- Moon River *(Breakfast at Tiffany's)*

Triple Time Fingerpicking Patterns for Songs in 3/4 Time

VISUALS FOR PAGE 128

PATTERN A

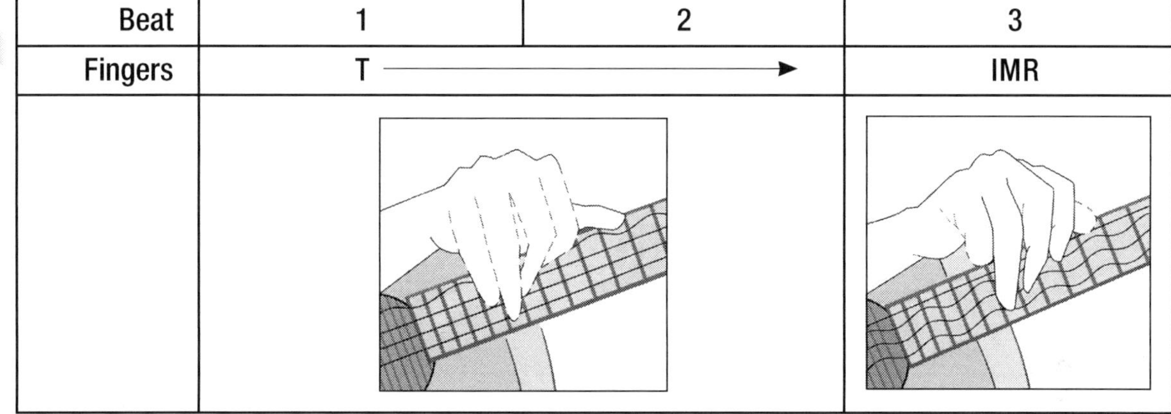

Beat	1	2	3
Fingers	T ——————→		IMR

PATTERN B

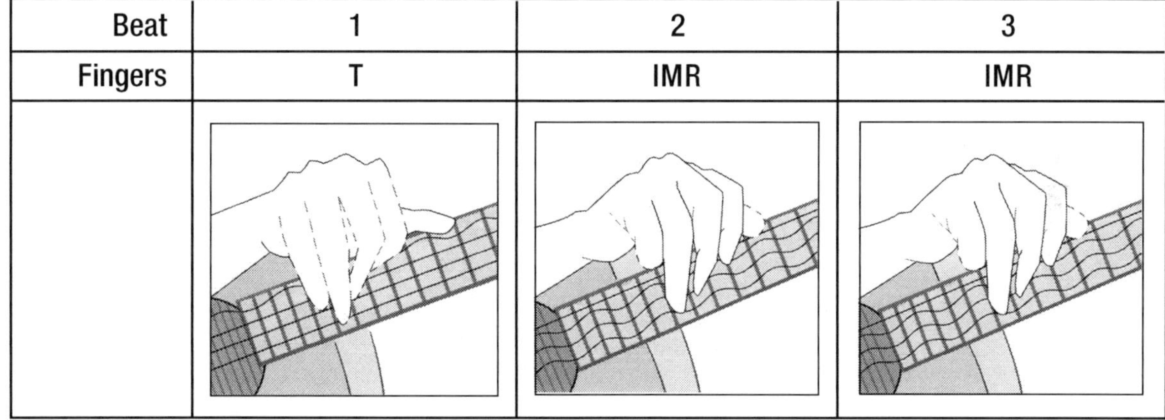

Beat	1	2	3
Fingers	T	IMR	IMR

PATTERN C

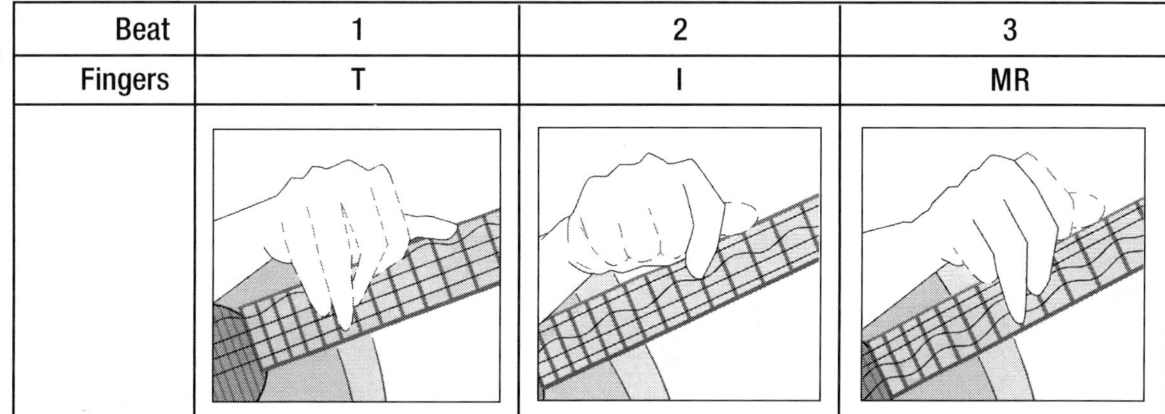

Beat	1	2	3
Fingers	T	I	MR

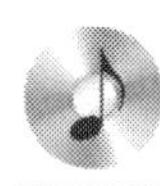

3. Triple Time Fingerpicking and Brush Patterns for Songs in 3/4 Time

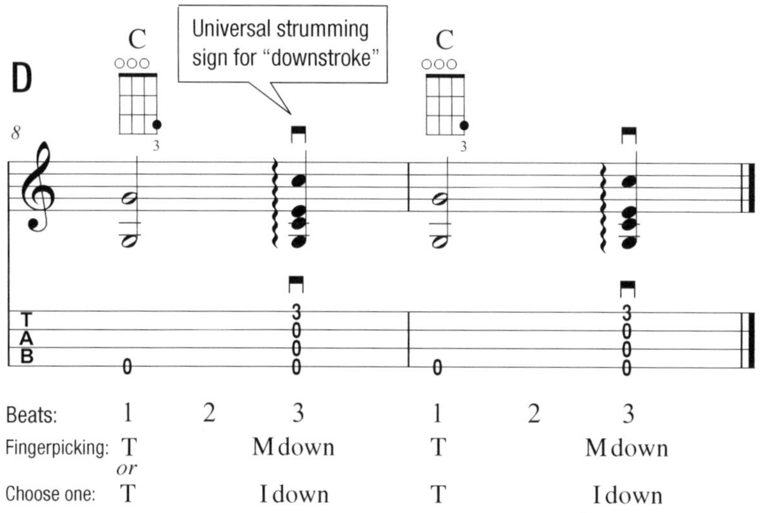

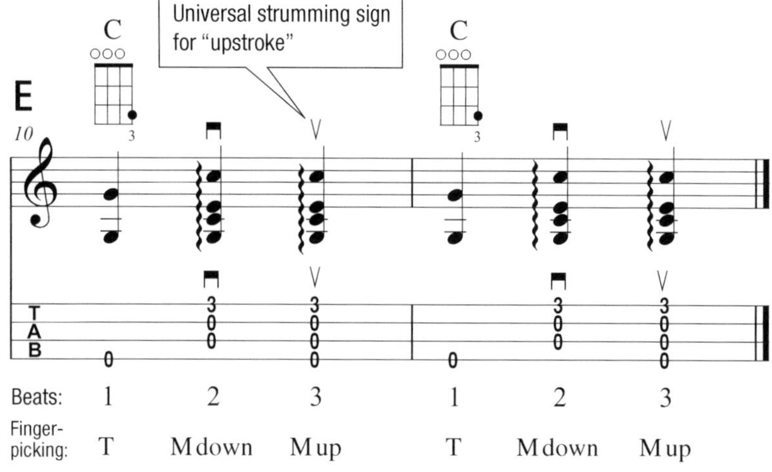

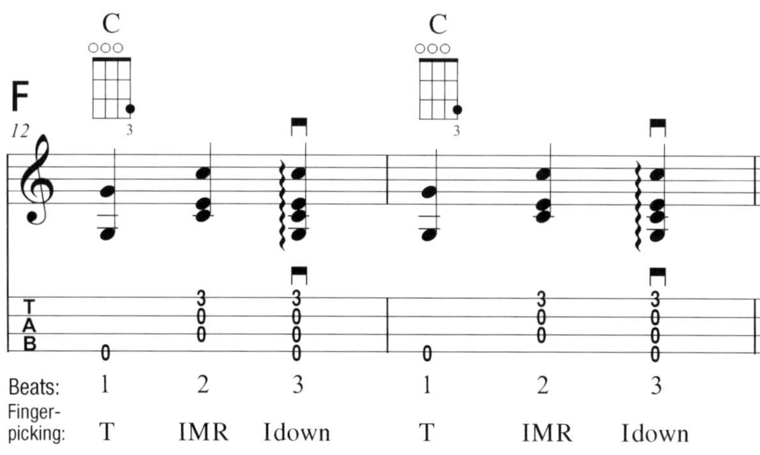

Fingerpicking and Finger Brush:

All of the patterns on this page combine fingerpicking with finger brushes.

- **M**down = Brush down with the middle finger
- **I**down = Brush down with the index finger

Options: For any of these patterns, you can choose to brush with either your Middle or Index finger.

Down Brushes:

Use the top of the fingernail.

Up Brushes:

Use the underside of the fingernail.

Triple Time Fingerpicking and Brush Patterns for Songs in 3/4 Time

VISUALS FOR PAGE 128

PATTERN D

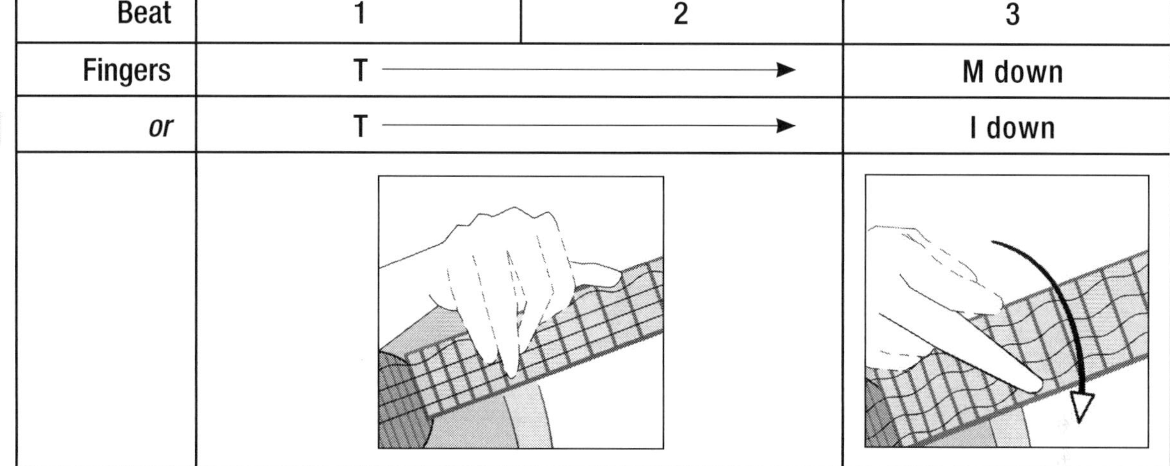

Beat	1	2	3
Fingers	T ——————→		M down
or	T ——————→		I down

PATTERN E

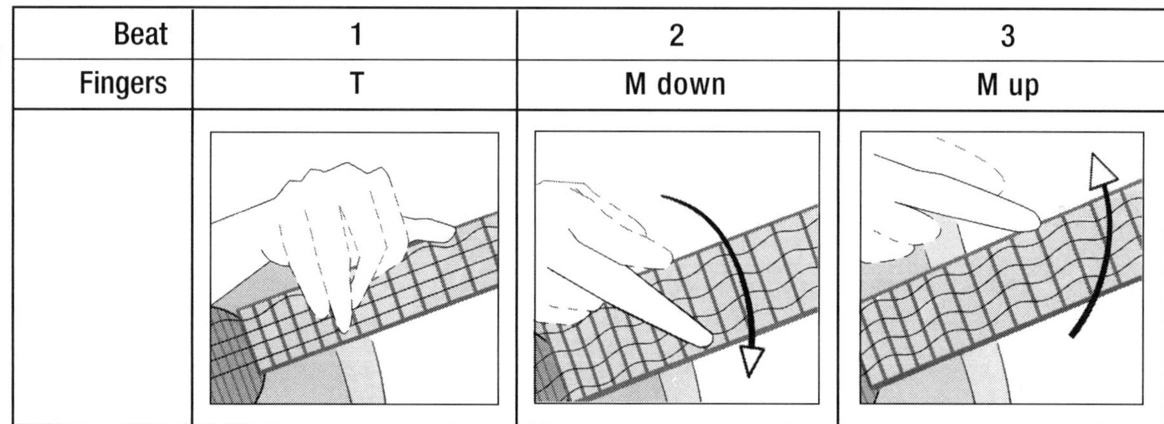

Beat	1	2	3
Fingers	T	M down	M up

PATTERN F

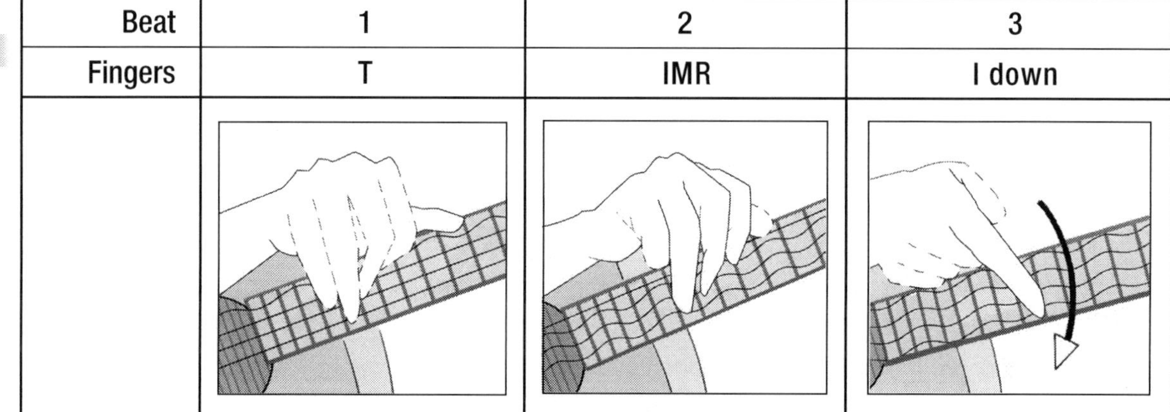

Beat	1	2	3
Fingers	T	IMR	I down

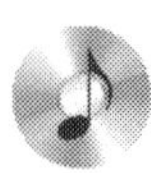

4. Down in the Valley: Fingerpicking Practice Guide

TRACK 68

This shortened version of "Down in the Valley" lays out all six new fingerpicking patterns and strums for easy practice.

Learning Tip: Practice playing each strum three ways:

1. **Count** each measure as you practice each right-hand pattern. As you count the beats make sure that the thumb is always played on the 1 beat of each measure and that you change chords accurately.
2. **Say** the strum pattern as you play it, e.g., Pattern A: Thumb–2 (for beat place holder)—IMR.
3. **Sing** the song as you practice each right-hand pattern.

C (3)

Beats:	1	2	3	1	2	3	1	2	3	1	2	3
Lyrics:	Down	in	the	val	-		ley,___					
Fingerpicking Patterns:												
Pattern A:	T	—	IMR	T	—	IMR	T	—	IMR	T	—	IMR
Pattern B:	T	IMR	IMR	T	IMR	IMR	T	IMR	IMR	T	IMR	IMR
Pattern C:	T	I	MR	T	I	MR	T	I	MR	T	I	MR
Fingerpicking + Finger Brush Patterns:												
Pattern D:	T	—	M(Down)	T	—	M(D)	T	—	M(D)	T	—	M(D)
Pattern E:	T	M(Down)	M(Up)	T	M(D)	M(U)	T	M(D)	M(U)	T	M(D)	M(U)
Pattern F:	T	IMR	I(Down)	T	IMR	I(D)	T	IMR	I(D)	T	IMR	I(D)

5

G7 (2 1 3)

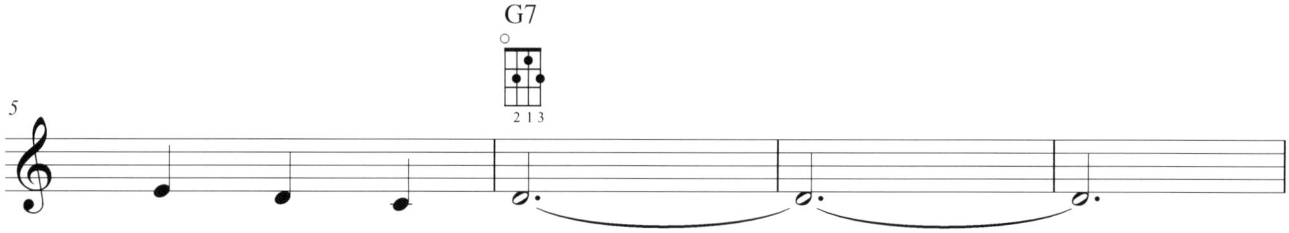

	1	2	3	1	2	3	1	2	3	1	2	3
	val -	ley	so	low,___								
Fingerpicking Patterns:												
Pattern A:	T	—	IMR	T	—	IMR	T	—	IMR	T	—	IMR
Pattern B:	T	IMR	IMR	T	IMR	IMR	T	IMR	IMR	T	IMR	IMR
Pattern C:	T	I	MR	T	I	MR	T	I	MR	T	I	MR
Fingerpicking + Finger Brush Patterns:												
Pattern D:	T	—	M(Down)	T	—	M(D)	T	—	M(D)	T	—	M(D)
Pattern E:	T	M(Down)	M(Up)	T	M(D)	M(U)	T	M(D)	M(U)	T	M(D)	M(U)
Pattern F:	T	IMR	I(Down)	T	IMR	I(D)	T	IMR	I(D)	T	IMR	I(D)

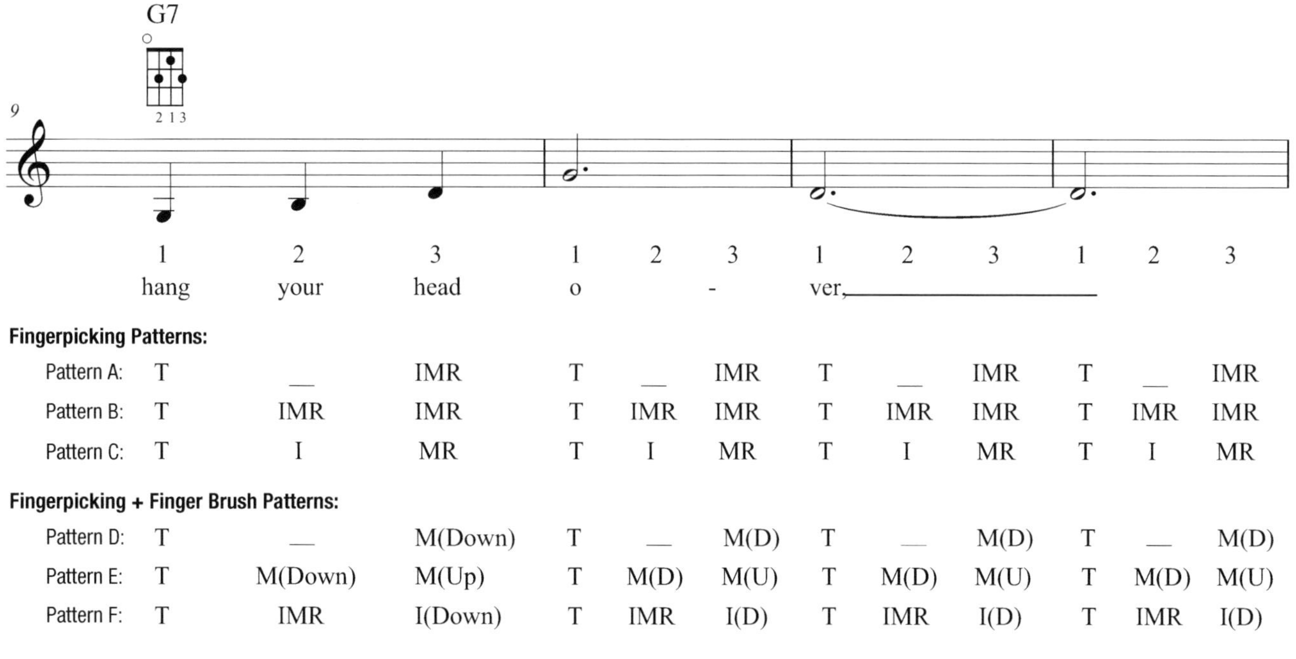

Fingerpicking Patterns:

Pattern A:	T	__	IMR	T	__	IMR	T	__	IMR	T	__	IMR
Pattern B:	T	IMR	IMR	T	IMR	IMR	T	IMR	IMR	T	IMR	IMR
Pattern C:	T	I	MR	T	I	MR	T	I	MR	T	I	MR

Fingerpicking + Finger Brush Patterns:

Pattern D:	T	__	M(Down)	T	__	M(D)	T	__	M(D)	T	__	M(D)
Pattern E:	T	M(Down)	M(Up)	T	M(D)	M(U)	T	M(D)	M(U)	T	M(D)	M(U)
Pattern F:	T	IMR	I(Down)	T	IMR	I(D)	T	IMR	I(D)	T	IMR	I(D)

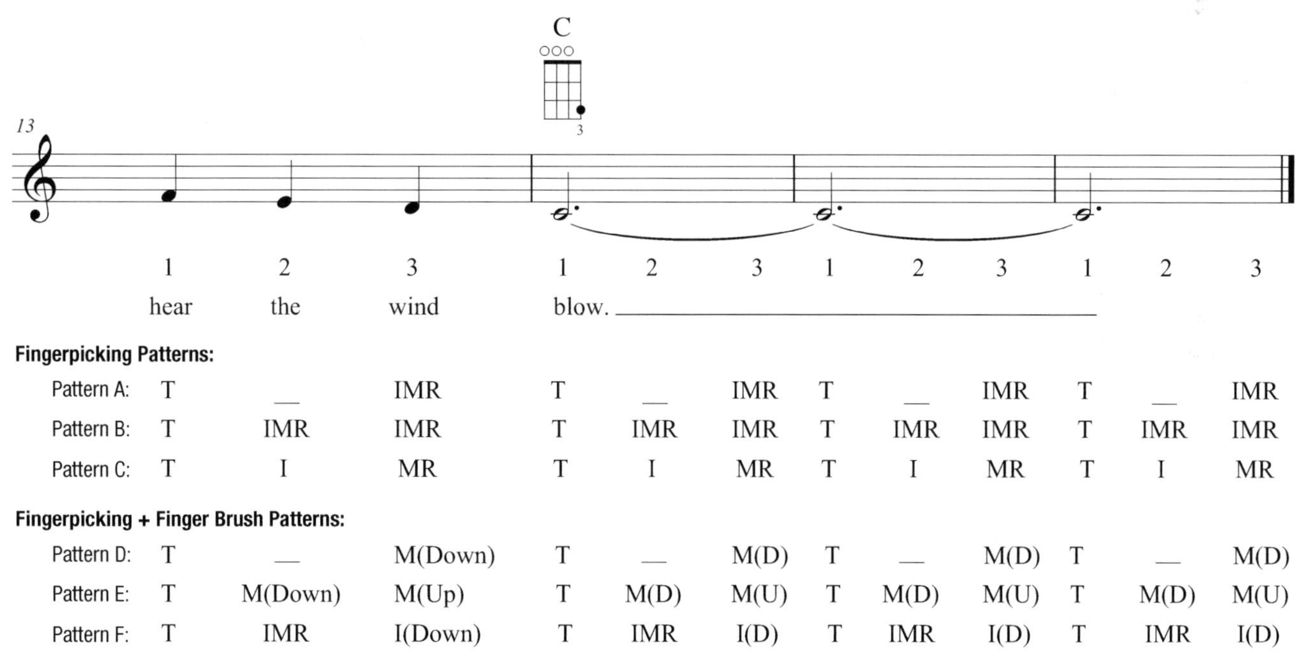

Fingerpicking Patterns:

Pattern A:	T	__	IMR	T	__	IMR	T	__	IMR	T	__	IMR
Pattern B:	T	IMR	IMR	T	IMR	IMR	T	IMR	IMR	T	IMR	IMR
Pattern C:	T	I	MR	T	I	MR	T	I	MR	T	I	MR

Fingerpicking + Finger Brush Patterns:

Pattern D:	T	__	M(Down)	T	__	M(D)	T	__	M(D)	T	__	M(D)
Pattern E:	T	M(Down)	M(Up)	T	M(D)	M(U)	T	M(D)	M(U)	T	M(D)	M(U)
Pattern F:	T	IMR	I(Down)	T	IMR	I(D)	T	IMR	I(D)	T	IMR	I(D)

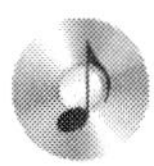

5. Down in the Valley (Version 2)

TRACK 69

Learning Tip: The following full version of "Down in the Valley" offers musical interest with the addition of two chords, G7 and F. Notice that the additional chords require quick left hand fretting changes on the 1 beat of the measure in the music between the sung phrases. See measures 6–8, 14–16, 22–24, and 30–32.

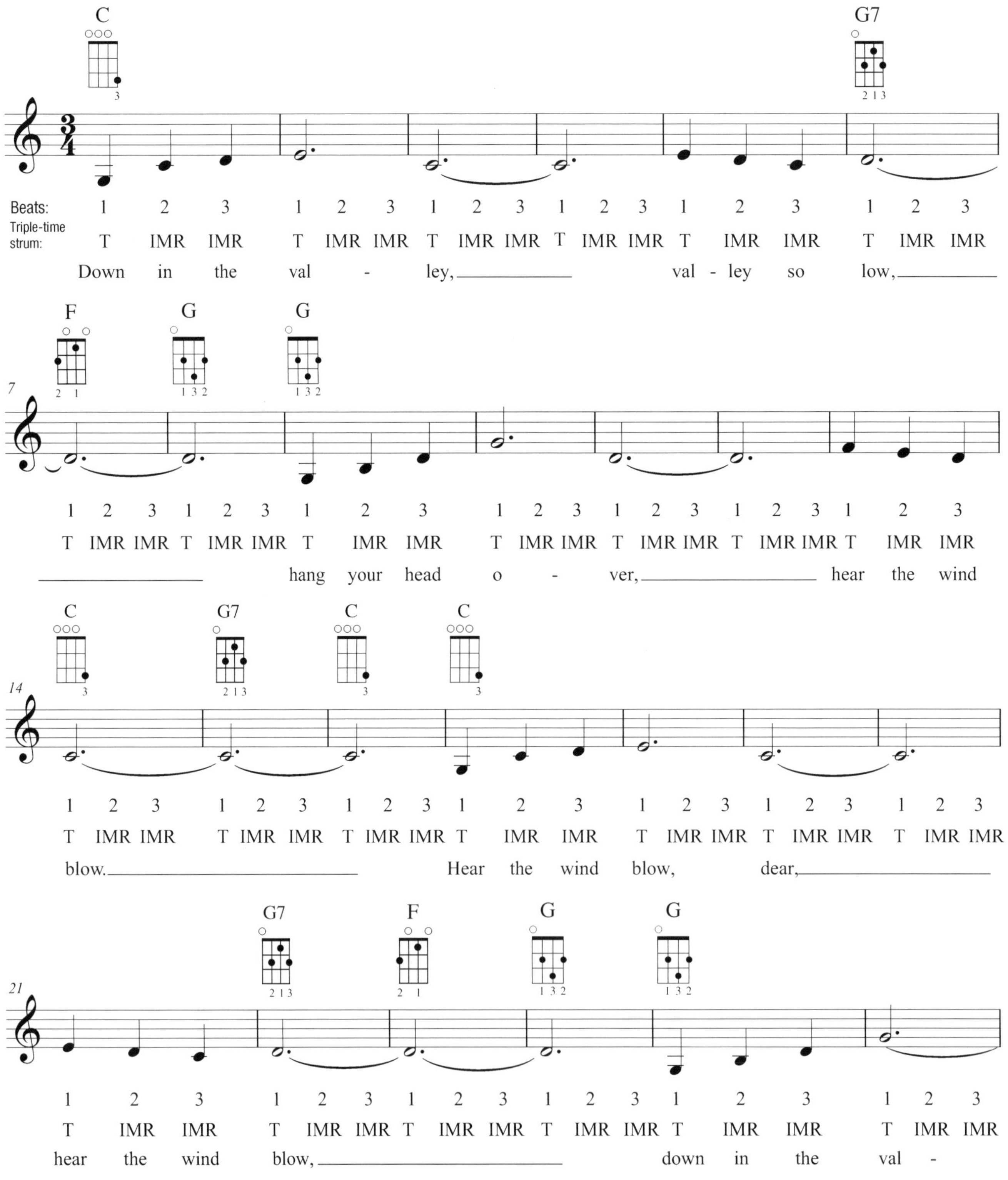

C G7

Beats: 1 2 3 1 2 3 1 2 3 1 2 3 1 2 3 1 2 3
Triple-time strum: T IMR IMR T IMR IMR T IMR IMR T IMR IMR T IMR IMR T IMR IMR
Down in the val - ley,____ val - ley so low,____

7

F G G

1 2 3 1 2 3 1 2 3 1 2 3 1 2 3 1 2 3 1 2 3
T IMR IMR T IMR IMR T IMR IMR T IMR IMR T IMR IMR T IMR IMR T IMR IMR
____ hang your head o - ver,____ hear the wind

14

C G7 C C

1 2 3 1 2 3 1 2 3 1 2 3 1 2 3 1 2 3 1 2 3
T IMR IMR T IMR IMR T IMR IMR T IMR IMR T IMR IMR T IMR IMR T IMR IMR
blow.____ Hear the wind blow, dear,____

21

G7 F G G

1 2 3 1 2 3 1 2 3 1 2 3 1 2 3 1 2 3
T IMR IMR T IMR IMR T IMR IMR T IMR IMR T IMR IMR T IMR IMR
hear the wind blow,____ down in the val -

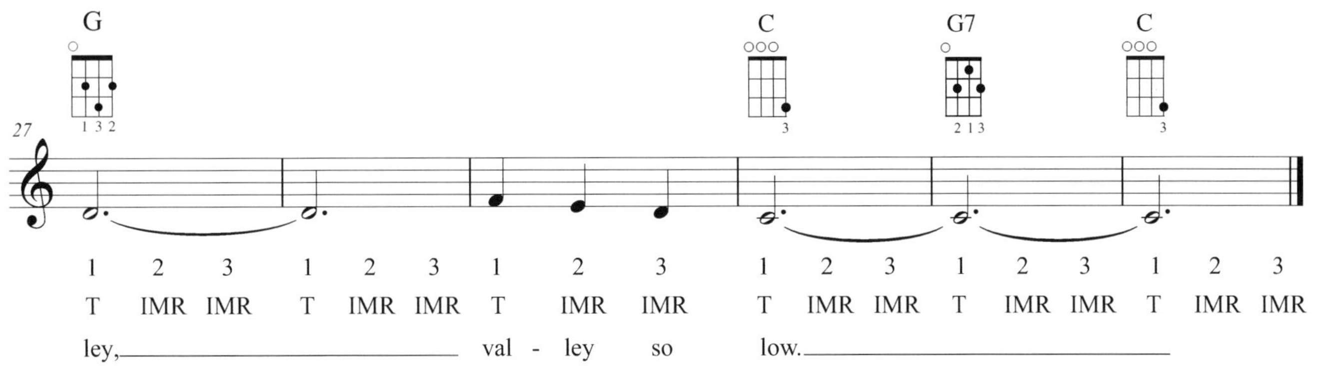

Down in the Valley (Version 2): Lyrics and Chord Chart

Playing Tip: Each Chord indication and Slash mark below represent the 1 beat of each measure.

VERSE 2

C / / / / G7 F G
If you don't love me, love whom you please,
G / / / / C G7 C
throw your arms round me, give my heart ease,
C / / / / G7 F G
Give my heart ease, love, give my heart ease.
G / / / / C G7 C
Throw your arms round me, give my heart ease.

VERSE 3

C / / / / G7 F G
Writing the let-ter, con-taining three lines.
G / / / / C G7 C
Answer my ques-tion: Will you be mine?
C / / / / G7 F G
Will you be mine, dear, will you be mine?
G / / / / C G7 C
Answer my ques-tion, will you be mine?

VERSE 4

C / / / / G7 F G
Roses love sun-shine, violets love dew;
G / / / / C G7 C
angels in heav-en, know I love you.
C / / / / G7 F G
Know I love you, dear, know I love you;
G / / / / C G7 C
Angels in heav-en, know I love you.

VERSE 5

C / / / / G7 F G
Build me a cas-tle forty feet high,
G / / / / C G7 C
so I can see him as he rides by.
C / / / / G7 F G
As he rides by, love, as he rides by,
G / / / / C G7 C
So I can see him, as he rides by.

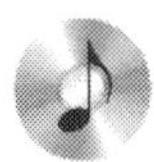

6. On Top of Old Smokey

TRACK 70

Play this traditional song 3 ways:

1. **As an Instrumental**—Play the melody below.
2. **As a Song**—Play the chords to accompany your singing. Instead of right hand fingering to pick the melody, I have given you a Triple Time strum pattern for the chords to accompany yourself while singing. The thumb plucks on the 1 beat of each measure.
3. **As a Combination**—Sing the song through while accompanying yourself with chords, then play an instrumental version… or vice versa.

C C C C

Beats: 1 2 3 1 2 3 1 2 3 1 2 3

Triple-time strum: T IMR IMR T IMR IMR T IMR IMR T IMR IMR

On top of Old

F C

1 2 3 1 2 3 1 2 3 1 2 3 1 2 3

T IMR IMR T IMR IMR T IMR IMR T IMR IMR T IMR IMR

Smok - ey, ______ all cov - ered with snow, ______

G7

1 2 3 1 2 3 1 2 3 1 2 3 1 2 3

T IMR IMR T IMR IMR T IMR IMR T IMR IMR T IMR IMR

______ I lost my poor sweet - heart, ______

C G7 C

1 2 3 1 2 3 1 2 3 1 2 3 1 2 3

T IMR IMR T IMR IMR T IMR IMR T IMR IMR T IMR IMR

______ from court - ing too slow. ______

On Top of Old Smokey: Lyrics and Chord Chart

VERSE 1

```
   C        F   /  /  /          C   / /
On top of old Smo-ky!  all covered with snow,
 C           G7   /     /    /          C   G7  C
I lost my poor sweet-heart,  from courting too slow.
```

VERSE 2

```
     C          F   /   /   /        C    G7  C
Well, courting's a plea-sure,  and parting is grief.
     C           G7 /  /   /          C   G7  C
But a false-hearted lov-er   is worse than a thief.
```

VERSE 3

```
  C         F  /   /   /         C   / /
A thief he will rob you,  and take all you have,
     C           G7 / /     /              C    G7  C
But a false-hearted lov-er,  will send you to your grave.
```

VERSE 4

```
       C          F  /  /    /         C   / /
And the grave will de-cay you,  and turn you to dust.
    C         G7    /   /  /         C   G7  C
And where is the young man,   a poor girl can trust.
```

History: This traditional American folk song takes place on "Old Smoky," which may be Clingmans Dome, a high mountain in the Ozarks or the central Appalachians. The melody has characteristics of those sung by the Scottish and Irish people who settled the region whose name for Clingmans Dome was "Smoky Dome."

Clingmans Dome, a.k.a. "Smoky Dome" in the Great Smoky Mountains of Tennessee and North Carolina is covered by a spruce-fir forest. At an elevation of 6,643 feet (2,025 m), it is the highest mountain in the Smokies, the highest point in the state of Tennessee, and the highest point along the 2,174-mile (3,499 km) Appalachian Trail.

Clingmans Dome (Smoky Dome) in the Great Smoky Mountains of Tennessee and North Carolina

TRACK 71

7. Take Me Out to the Ballgame

Playing Tip: Instead of right hand fingering to pick the melody, I have given you a Triple Time strum pattern for the chords to accompany yourself while singing. The thumb plucks on the 1 beat of each measure.

Jack Norworth

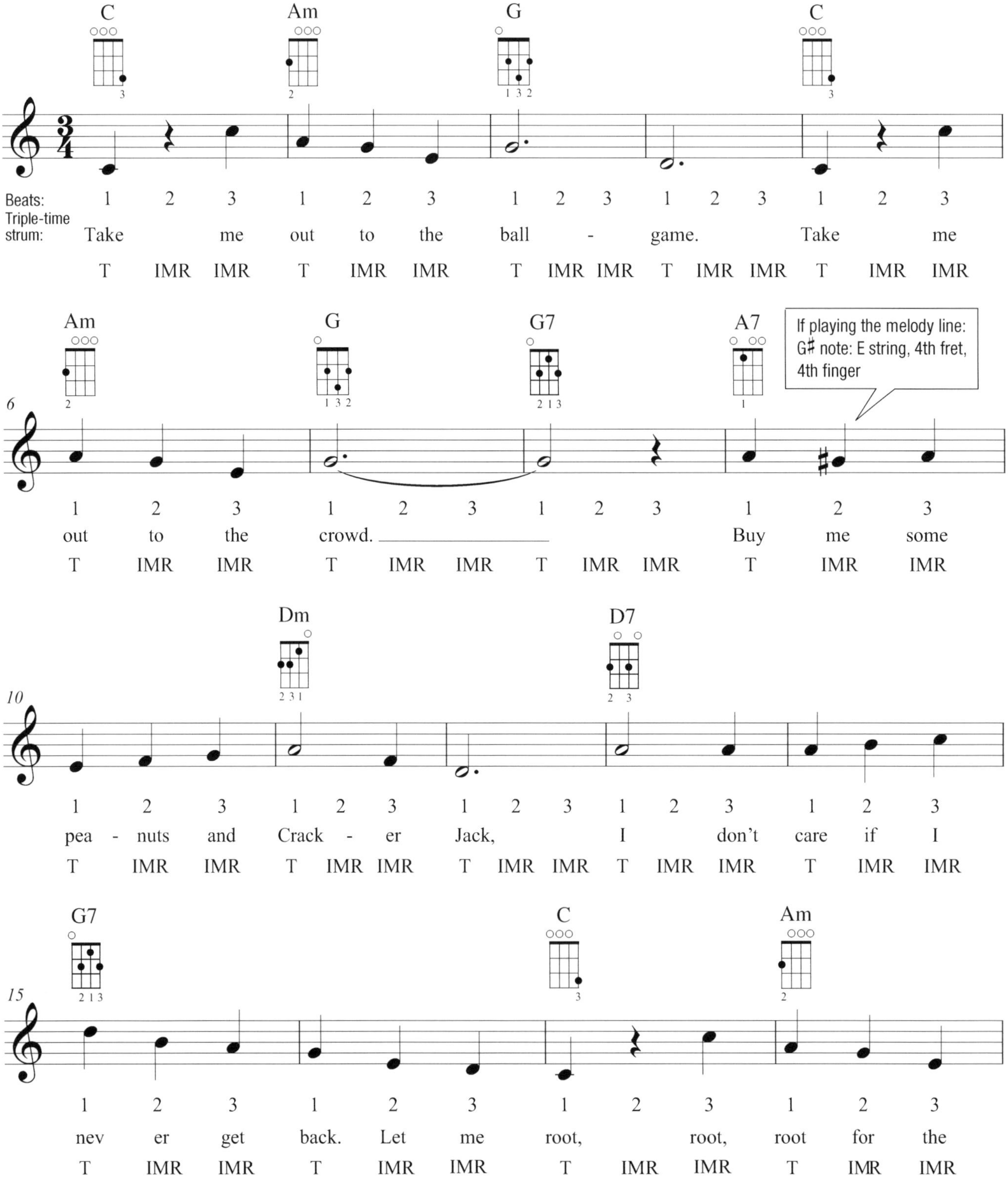

Chords: C (3) | Am (2) | G (1 3 2) | | C (3)

Beats:	1	2	3	1	2	3	1	2	3	1	2	3	1	2	3
	Take		me	out	to	the	ball	-		game.			Take		me
Triple-time strum:	T	IMR	IMR	T	IMR	IMR	T	IMR	IMR	T	IMR	IMR	T	IMR	IMR

6

Chords: Am (2) | G (1 3 2) | G7 (2 1 3) | A7 (1)

If playing the melody line: G♯ note: E string, 4th fret, 4th finger

1	2	3	1	2	3	1	2	3	1	2	3
out	to	the	crowd. ___						Buy	me	some
T	IMR	IMR	T	IMR	IMR	T	IMR	IMR	T	IMR	IMR

10

Chords: | Dm (2 3 1) | | D7 (2 3) |

1	2	3	1	2	3	1	2	3	1	2	3	1	2	3
pea -	nuts	and	Crack	-	er	Jack,			I		don't	care	if	I
T	IMR	IMR	T	IMR	IMR	T	IMR	IMR	T	IMR	IMR	T	IMR	IMR

15

Chords: G7 (2 1 3) | | C (3) | Am (2)

1	2	3	1	2	3	1	2	3	1	2	3
nev	er	get	back.	Let	me	root,		root,	root	for	the
T	IMR	IMR	T	IMR	IMR	T	IMR	IMR	T	IMR	IMR

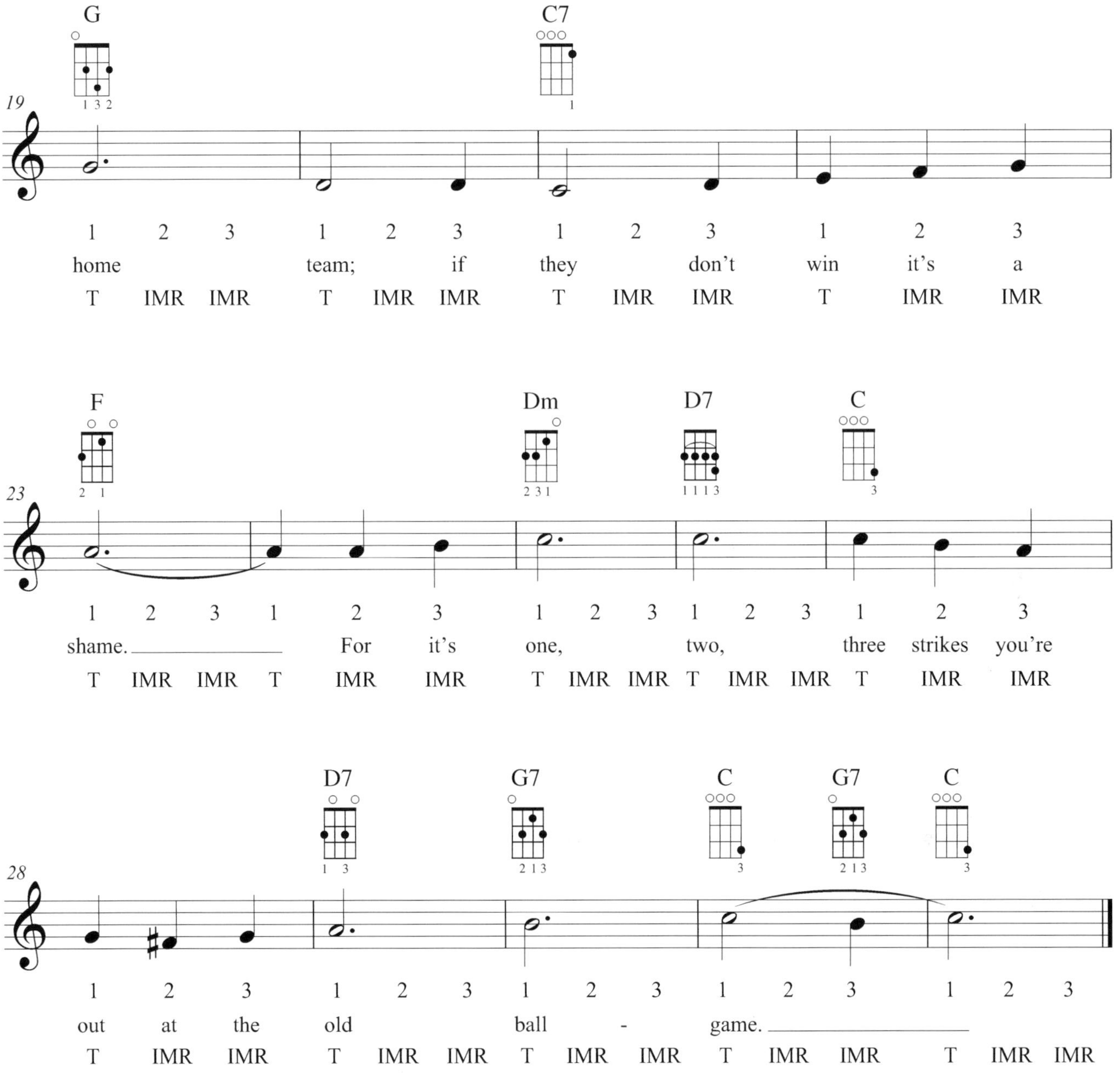

19

G						C7					
1	2	3	1	2	3	1	2	3	1	2	3
home			team;		if	they		don't	win	it's	a
T	IMR	IMR	T	IMR	IMR	T	IMR	IMR	T	IMR	IMR

23

F						Dm			D7			C		
1	2	3	1	2	3	1	2	3	1	2	3	1	2	3
shame.___				For	it's	one,			two,			three	strikes	you're
T	IMR	IMR	T	IMR	IMR	T	IMR	IMR	T	IMR	IMR	T	IMR	IMR

28

			D7			G7			C		G7	C		
1	2	3	1	2	3	1	2	3	1	2	3	1	2	3
out	at	the	old			ball		-	game.___					
T	IMR	IMR	T	IMR	IMR	T	IMR	IMR	T	IMR	IMR	T	IMR	IMR

History: Jack Norworth, a successful vaudeville entertainer/songwriter, wrote this classic baseball song in fifteen minutes on scrap paper while riding a train to Manhattan, New York in 1908. Norworth gave the scrap paper lyrics to Albert Von Tilzer to compose music, which was published by the York Music Company. By the end of 1908, a hit song was born and is sung to this day during the seventh inning stretch at all major league baseball games.

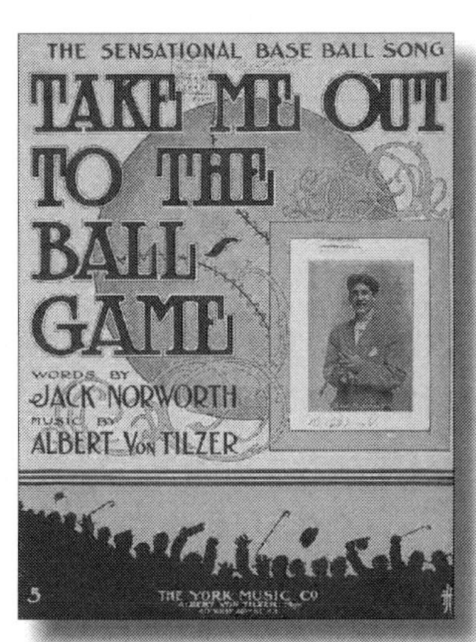

Copy of the original sheet music for Take Me Out To The Ballgame

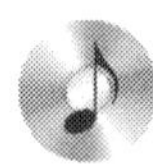

8. The Cowboy's Lament A.K.A. Streets of Laredo

TRACK 72

Play this song 3 ways:

1. **As an Instrumental**—Play the arrangement below that combines melody and chords.
2. **As a Song**—Play the chords to accompany your singing with any fingerpicking pattern in **pages 128-131**.
3. **As a Combination**—Sing the song through while accompanying yourself with chords, then play the instrumental version... or vice versa.

Francis Henry Maynard

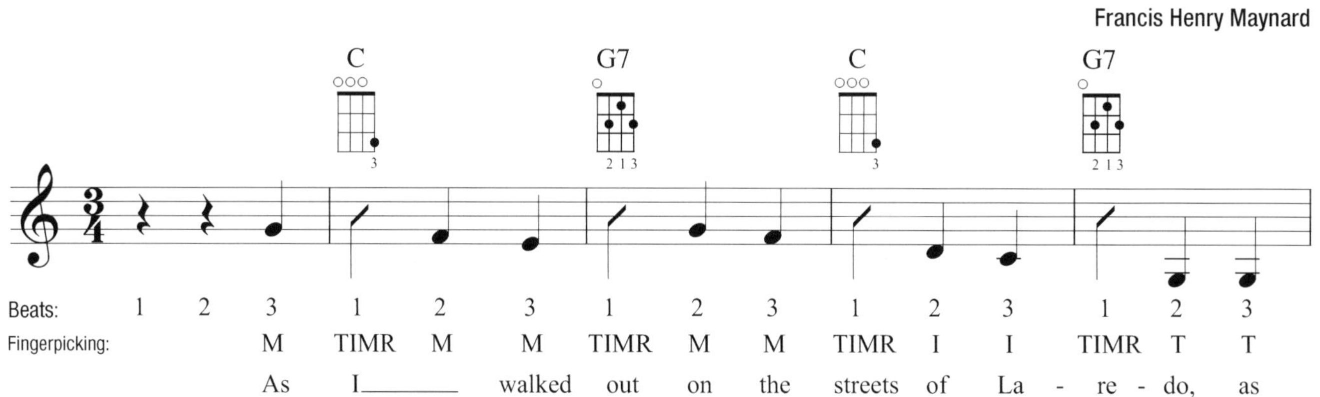

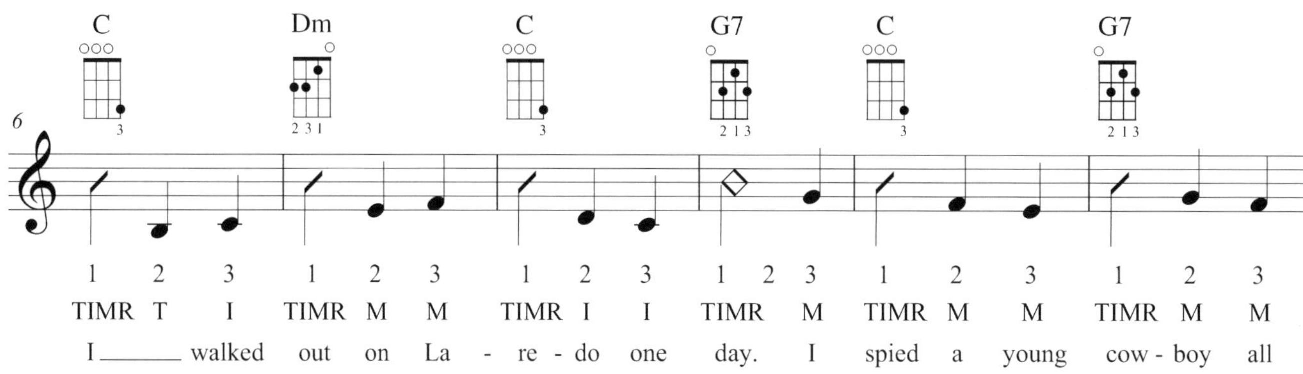

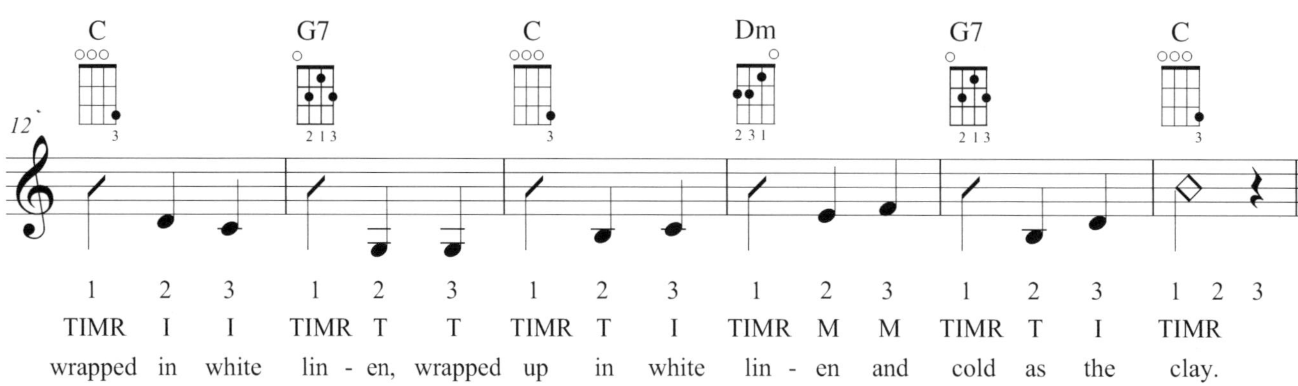

The Cowboy's Lament: Lyrics and Chord Chart

VERSE 1

```
    C        G7         C            G7
As I walked out on the streets of La-redo,
   C        Dm         C         G7
As I walked out on La-redo one day,
 C               G7          C                 G7
I spied a young cowboy all wrapped in white linen;
C                 Dm         G7          C
Wrapped in white linen and cold as the clay.
```

VERSE 2

```
   C              G7         C             G7
O' beat the drum slowly and play the fife lowly,
C              Dm            C            G7
Play the Dead March as you carry me a-long.
         C            G7         C           G7
Take me to the green valley and lay the sod o'er me,
    C            Dm             G7              C
For I'm a young cowboy and I know I've done wrong.
```

VERSE 3

```
  C            G7         C         G7
I see by your outfit that you are a cowboy,
       C             Dm      C               G7
These words he did say as I boldly stepped by.
       C            G7           C             G7
Come sit down be-side me and hear my sad story,
    C           Dm           G7           C
I'm shot in the breast and I know I must die.
```

VERSE 4

```
       C           G7       C          G7
It was once in the saddle I used to go dashing,
       C           Dm       C          G7
It was once in the saddle I used to go gay;
C           G7                C            G7
First to the dram house and then to the card house,
     C           Dm            G7      C
Got shot in the breast and I'm dying today.
```

VERSE 5

```
     C       G7          C         G7
Get six jolly cowboys to carry my coffin,
     C         Dm          C           G7
Get six pretty maidens to bear up my pall,
    C            G7        C       G7
Put bunches of roses all over my coffin,
     C       Dm          G7             C
Put roses to deaden the clods as they fall.
```

VERSE 6

```
    C        G7           C                G7
Go gather a-round you a group of young cowboys,
     C             Dm      C            G7
And tell them the story of this my sad fate.
     C           G7        C            G7
Tell one and the other, be-fore they go further
   C               Dm        G7          C
To stop their wild roving be-fore it's too late.
```

VERSE 7

```
     C           G7     C         G7
"Go bring me a cup, a cup of cold water
   C                 Dm        C                 G7
To cool my parched lips," the young cowboy said.
    C        G7          C         G7
Be-fore I re-turned, the spirit had left him
     C           Dm          G7           C
And gone to it's Maker, the cowboy was dead.
```

VERSE 8

```
    C             G7          C              G7
We beat the drum slowly and played the fife lowly,
     C       Dm          C         G7
And bitterly wept as we bore him along.
        C            G7            C
For we all loved our comrade, so brave, young, and
     G7
     handsome.
     C            Dm          G7                 C
We all loved our comrade al-though he'd done wrong.
```

History: Like many other cowboy songs, "Streets of Laredo" was written in 3/4 time to mimic the popular waltzes of the era. Composed in 1876 in a Dodge City, Kansas barroom, this song was sung by cowboys on the trail. When they finally rode into town after months in the saddle, they danced this waltz in saloons.

Teacher Note: Have students research and learn other cowboy songs in waltz tempo (3/4 time).

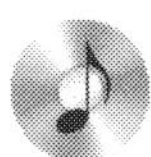

9. Whoopee Ti-Yi-Yo, Git Along Little Doggies

TRACK 73

Play this song 3 ways:

1. **As an Instrumental**—Play the arrangement below that combines melody and chord fingerpicking.
2. **As a Song**—Play the chords to accompany your singing with any fingerpicking pattern in **pages 128-131**.
3. **As a Combination**—Sing the song through while accompanying yourself with chords, then play an instrumental version... or vice versa.

History: This trail song was published in 1910 by John Lomax. He first heard it sung by a Gypsy woman who was camped in a grove of trees near the cattle pens on the Fort Worth, Texas stockyards.

Traditional

Verse

C F G C

Beats:	3	1	2	3	1	2	3	1	2	3	1	2	3
Fingerpicking:	I	TIMR	M	M	TIMR	M	M	TIMR	M	M	TIMR	I	I
	As	I	was	out	walk -	ing	one	morn -	ing	for	pleas -	ure,	I

6

C F G C C

1	2	3	1	2	3	1	2	3	1	2	3	1	2	3
TIMR	M	M	TIMR	M	M	TIMR	M	M	TIMR		I	TIMR	M	M
spied	a	young	cow -	boy	a	rid -	in'	a	long.		His	hat	was	pulled

11

F G C C F

1	2	3	1	2	3	1	2	3	1	2	3	1	2	3
TIMR	M	M	TIMR	M	M	TIMR	I	I	TIMR	M	M	TIMR	M	M
back	and	his	spurs	were	a	jing -	lin',	and	as	he	ap -	proached	he	was

16

G C Chorus G7 C C

1	2	3	1	2	3	1	2	3	1	2	3	1	2	3	1	2	3
TIMR	M	M	TIMR	I	I	TIMR		I	I	I	I	TIMR	M	I	TIMR	T	I
sing -	in'	this	song:	Whoo -	pee	ti		- yi	- yo,	git	a -	long	lit -	tle	dog -	gies.	It's

Whoopee Ti-Yi-Yo, Git Along Little Doggies: Lyrics and Chord Chart

VERSE 1

```
  C        F           G            C
As I was out walking one morning for pleasure,
  C          F          G      C
I spied a cow-puncher a-ridin' a-long.
    C                F              G                C
His hat was throwed back and his spurs were a-jinglin'
    C   F                      G            C
And as he approached he was singin' this song:
```

CHORUS

```
C          G7  /         C          /
Whoopee ti-yi-yo, git a-long little doggies,
   G7       /            C          /
It's your mis-fortune and none of my own.
             C   F       G7        C
Whoopee ti-yi-yo, git a-long little doggies,
     C               F         G7            C
You know that Wy-oming will be your new home.
```

VERSE 2

```
C    F                G              C
Early in springtime we round up the doggies,
C             F              G            C
Mark 'em and brand 'em, and bob off their tail;
C              F            G           C
Round up the horses, load up the chuck wagon,
       C               F             G           C
Then throw the little doggies out on the long trail.
```

Chorus

VERSE 3

```
C             F          G                C
Night comes on and we hold 'em on the bed ground,
     C           F            G          C
The same little doggies that rolled on so slow.
     C           F        G          C
We roll up the herd and cut out the stray ones,
      C                 F          G       C
Then roll the little doggies like never be-fore.
```

Chorus

VERSE 4

```
      C         F           G       C
Some boys go up the long trail for pleasure,
     C                  F          G      C
But that's where they get it most awfully wrong.
     C          F          G           C
For you'll never know the trouble they give us,
    C     F            G           C
As we go driving the doggies a-long.
```

Chorus

10. De Colores

TRACK 74

Learning Tip: To learn the melody, play the notes. Then use the triple-time strum below to accompany your singing.

Traditional Mexican Children's Song

C

Beats: De co - lo - res, De co - lo - res se

Triple-time strum: 1 2 3 1 2 3 1 2 3 1 2 3 1 2 3

T IMR IMR T IMR IMR T IMR IMR T IMR IMR T IMR IMR

G7

6

vis - ten los cam - pos en la pri - ma - ve - ra.

1 2 3 1 2 3 1 2 3 1 2 3 1 2 3

T IMR IMR T IMR IMR T IMR IMR T IMR IMR T IMR IMR

G7

11

De co - lo - res, de co - lo - res son los pa - ja -

1 2 3 1 2 3 1 2 3 1 2 3 1 2 3 1 2 3

T IMR IMR T IMR IMR T IMR IMR T IMR IMR T IMR IMR T IMR IMR

C C

17

ri - tos que vie - nen de_a - fue - ra. De co -

1 2 3 1 2 3 1 2 3 1 2 3 1 2 3 1 2 3

T IMR IMR T IMR IMR T IMR IMR T IMR IMR T IMR IMR T IMR IMR

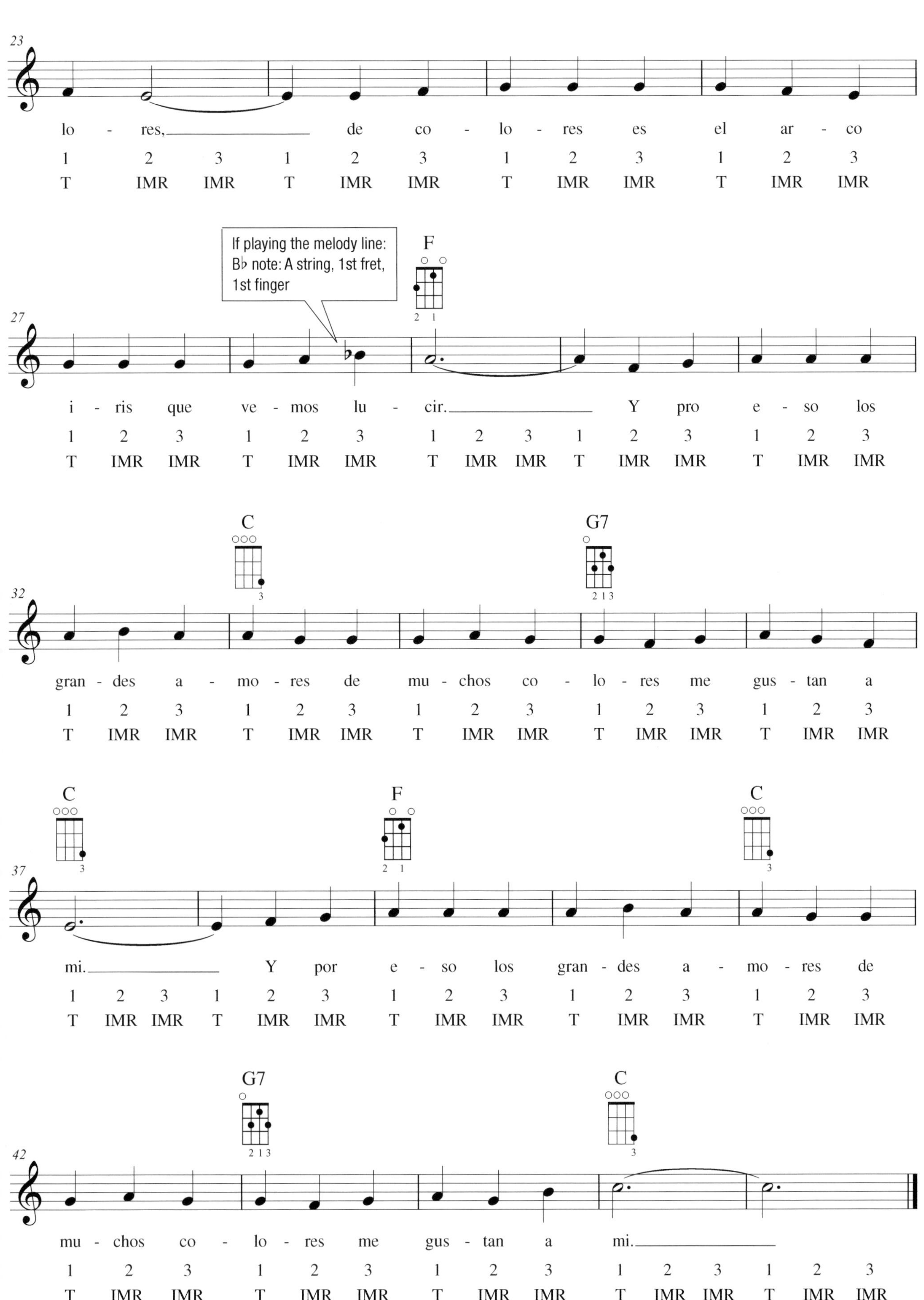
23
lo - res, de co - lo - res es el ar - co
1 2 3 1 2 3 1 2 3 1 2 3
T IMR IMR T IMR IMR T IMR IMR T IMR IMR
If playing the melody line: B♭ note: A string, 1st fret, 1st finger
F
27
i - ris que ve - mos lu - cir. Y pro e - so los
1 2 3 1 2 3 1 2 3 1 2 3 1 2 3
T IMR IMR T IMR IMR T IMR IMR T IMR IMR T IMR IMR
C
G7
32
gran - des a - mo - res de mu - chos co - lo - res me gus - tan a
1 2 3 1 2 3 1 2 3 1 2 3 1 2 3
T IMR IMR T IMR IMR T IMR IMR T IMR IMR T IMR IMR
C
F
C
37
mi. Y por e - so los gran - des a - mo - res de
1 2 3 1 2 3 1 2 3 1 2 3 1 2 3
T IMR IMR T IMR IMR T IMR IMR T IMR IMR T IMR IMR
G7
C
42
mu - chos co - lo - res me gus - tan a mi.
1 2 3 1 2 3 1 2 3 1 2 3 1 2 3
T IMR IMR T IMR IMR T IMR IMR T IMR IMR T IMR IMR

De Colores of the Colors: Lyrics and Chord Chart

Lyrics	Translation
Verse 1 C / / / / / / / G7 / De co-lores, de co-lores se visten los campos en la prima-vera. G7 / / / / / / / C / De co-lores, de co-lores son los paja-ritos que vienen de a-fuera. C / / / / / / / F / De co-lores, de co-lores es el arco iris que vemos lucir.	**Verse 1** Of colors that dress the fields in springtime. Of colors, are the birds that are out doors. Of colors, is the rainbow that we see shining.
Chorus F / / C / G7 / C / Y por eso los grandes a-mores de muchos co-lores me gustan a mí. F / / C / G7 / C / Y por eso los grandes a-mores de muchos co-lores me gustan a mí.	**Chorus** And because of that grand love, many colors appeal to me.
Verse 2 C / / / / / / / G7 / Can - ta el gallo, canta el gallo con el kiri, kiri, ki-ri, kiri, kiri. G7 / / / / / / / C / La gal-lina, la gal-lina con el cara, cara, ca-ra, ca-ra, C / / / / / / / F / Los pol-litos, los pol-litos con el pío, pío, pí-o, pío, pí.	**Verse 2** Sings the rooster with his kiri-kiri, kiri, kiri-kiri. The hen with her kara-kara, kara, kara-kara, The chicks with their pio-pio, pio, pio-pi.
Chorus F / / C / G7 / C / Y por eso los grandes a-mores de muchos co-lores me gustan a mí. F / / C / G7 / C / Y por eso los grandes a-mores de muchos co-lores me gustan a mí.	**Chorus** And because of that grand love, many colors appeal to me.

History: "De Colores" is a Mariachi tune—a style of folk music from Mexico. The name also refers to the musicians and the band or orchestra that plays it. Mariachi music often includes European musical styles like polkas and waltzes. These musical forms came from the German settlers who started colonizing in Mexico as early at the 1830s and the French who occupied the country in the 1860s. "De Colores" is in waltz tempo, or 3/4 time.

Lesson 6

Assignment

1. **Warm-up:** Each time you sit down to practice, play the following in this order...

   A. **4-Fret Half-Step Chromatic Scale Exercise** (**page 47**)

   B. **C Scale** (**page 81**)

   C. **Note Your Naturals in C** (**page 103**)

2. **Review:** Play through your favorite music and songs in *Lesson 4* and *5* as a refresher and for reinforcement. Work on anything challenging that you still need to master... a chord change, a musical passage, whatever. Practice while reading the music. Then close your eyes and play short passages to train your memory, ears and fingers.

3. **Learn:** Each time you sit down to practice, play the following in this order...

   A. **Chords: D, E7** (**page 148**)
   Practice the **D** and **E7 chords** by learning the following chord progressions:

   1) E7 to G7 to E7 to A7
   2) C to D to Dm to G7
   4) G7 to E7 to F to G7

   B. **Music and songs:** ***Don't try to learn everything in the entire lesson at once***. Be patient and take your time to learn the music and internalize the techniques.

   1) **Select one fingerpicking pattern from page 150 and one pattern from page 152.** Practice them using the "**4. Go Tell Aunt Rhody: Fingerpicking Practice Guide" on page 154** until you can sing and play simultaneously. If you don't like to sing, play along with the Track 78 recording to get the timing right. When you learn your first two choices well enough to play slowly and in rhythm, apply them to the remaining songs in this lesson as well as to other 4/4 time songs in *Lessons 1-5*. When you have mastered the first two patterns, learn two more patterns the same way until you learn them all.

   2) **As you practice, don't forget to:**

      a) Start counting with "**one measure for nothing.**"

      b) **Continue counting** to make sure you are on the correct beat that correlates with the right hand fingers in the pattern you are learning.

Congratulations! When you finish this lesson, you will have learned:

1. The basics of reading music in the key of C in the first 4 frets of your ukulele in standard notation and tablature.

2. All the chords you will commonly find in songs written in the key of C.

Introducing the D and E7 Chords

To play all chords below: **Strum** down with the **T**humb, **I**ndex, or **M**iddle finger, or, **fingerpick** all strings simultaneously with the **T**humb, **I**ndex, **M**iddle and **R**ing fingers, T I M R.

D Chord

Two ways to fret: Depending on your finger shape and size, you have two fretting choices for this chord. Pick the one that is easiest for you.

1. **People with smaller narrower fingertips** usually prefer the 3-finger D formation.
2. **Those with wider and deeper fingertips** usually prefer the Barre D chord. The Barre D requires that you flatten out the front of the finger and lift at the knuckle to avoid muting the A string.

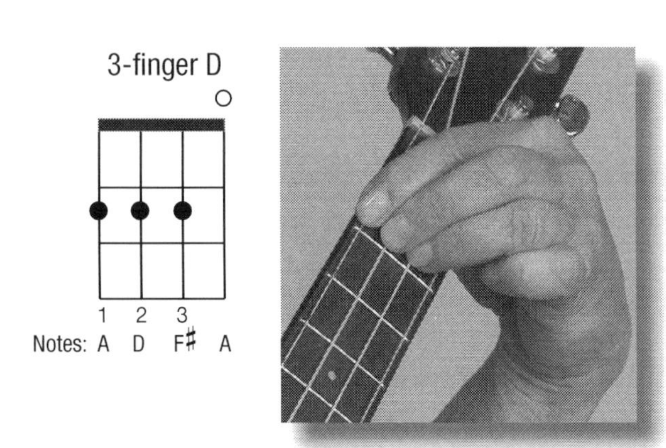

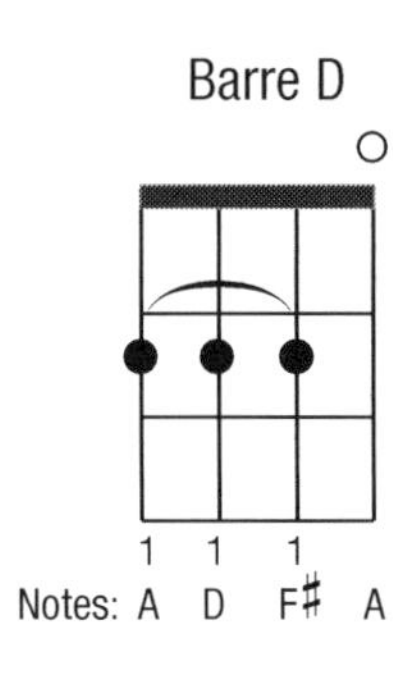

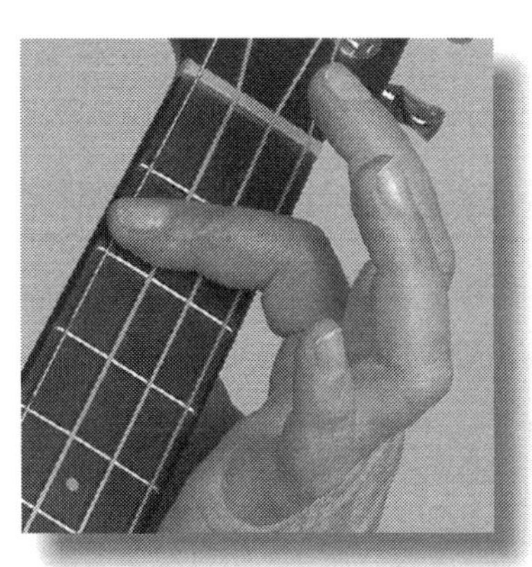

E7 Chord

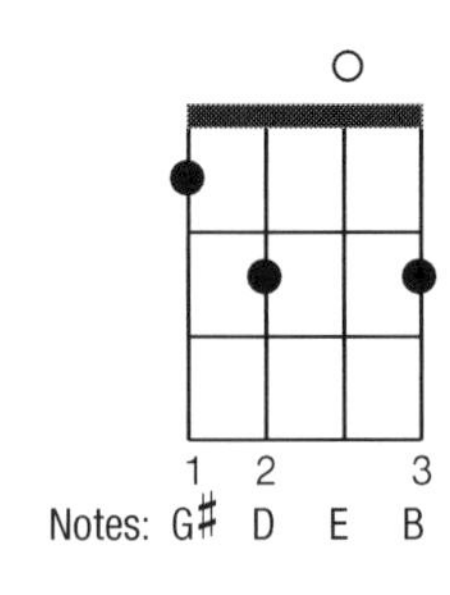

The E7 Chord:

- **Includes a G♯ (G sharp) note:** Sharps raise a note one half step in pitch. The E7 chord is spelled E–G♯–B–D. The G♯ (G string, first fret) note is one fret higher in pitch, or a half step higher than a G note (G string, open).

Roadmap for Moving Smoothly Between Chords

Moving from D Chord to G Chord

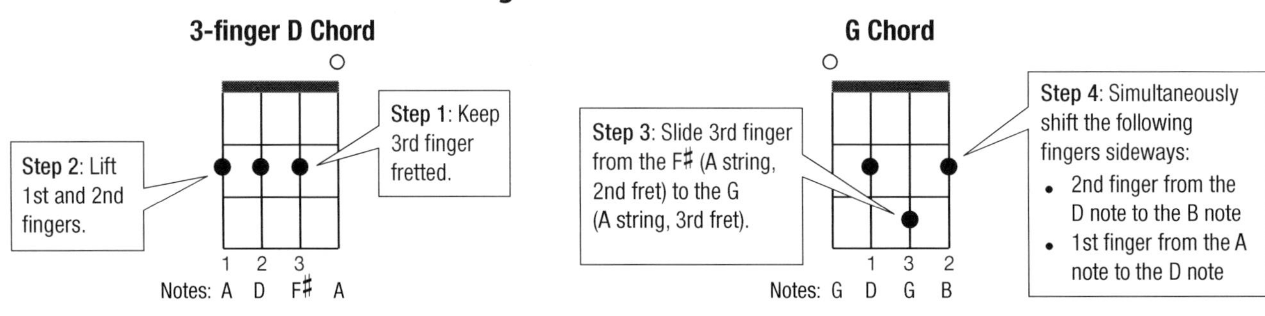

Moving from G7 Chord to E7 Chord to F Chord

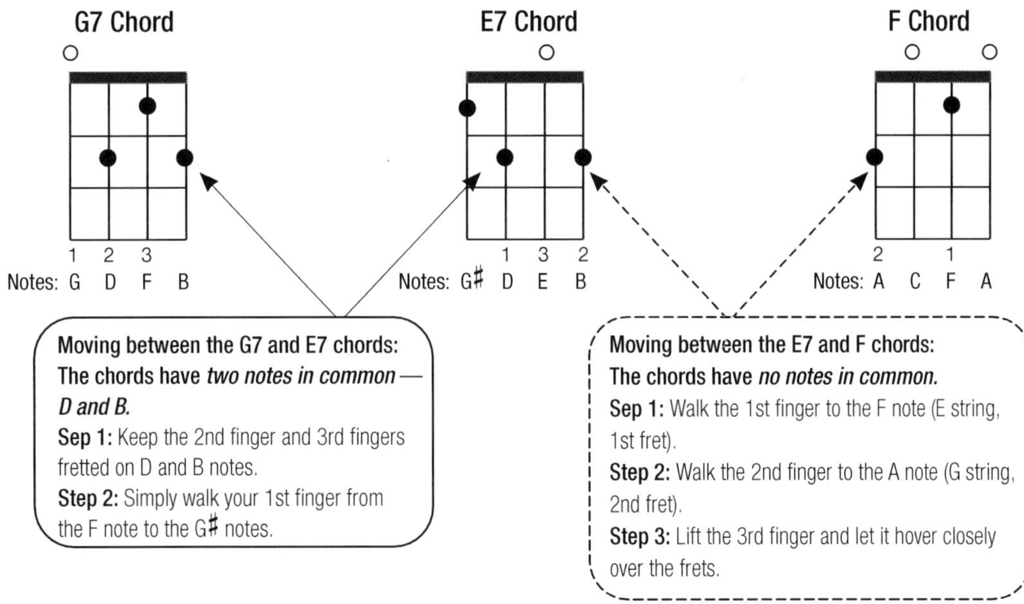

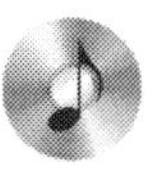

1. New Chord Warm-Up

TRACK 75

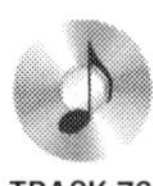

2. Double Time Fingerpicking Patterns for Songs in 4/4, C and 2/4 Time

A

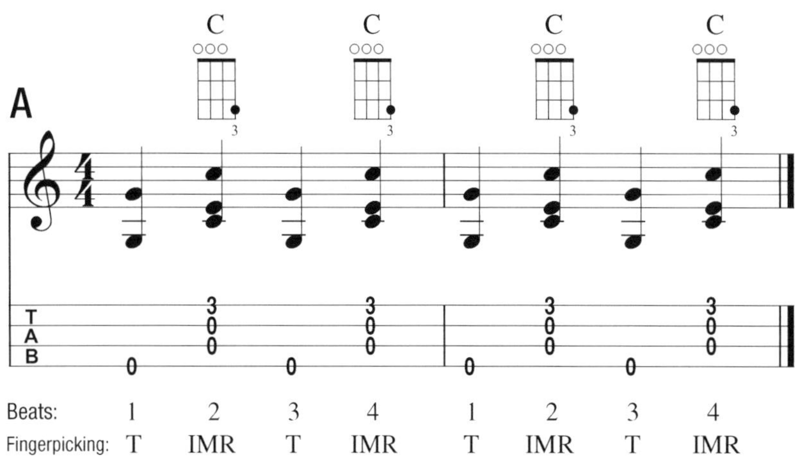

B

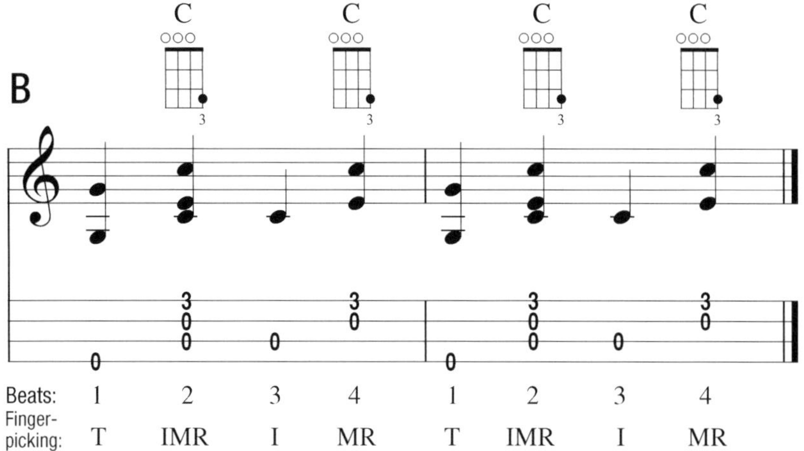

C

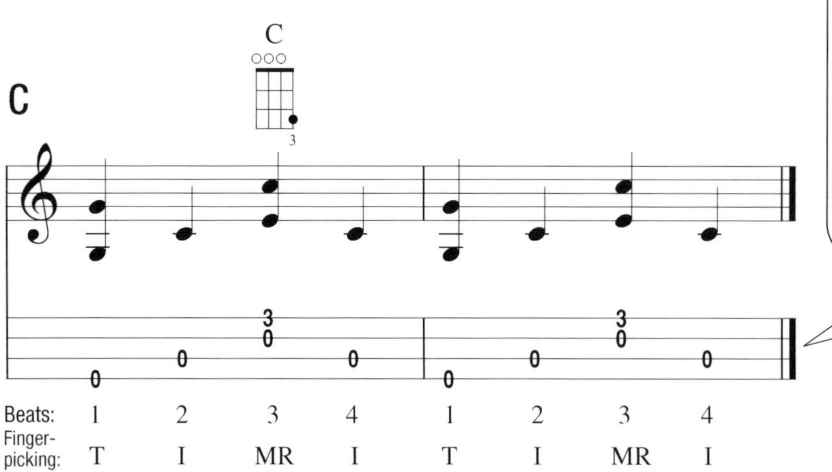

Double Time Songs That Match These Patterns

Traditional:

- Auld Lang Syne
- Aunt Rhody
- Bingo
- Blowing in the Wind
- City of New Orleans
- Country Roads
- Dock of the Bay
- Don't Think Twice it's Alright
- Go Tell it on the Mountain
- Goodnight, Ladies
- Have you Ever Seen the Rain?
- Hush Little Baby
- I've Been Working on the Railroad
- Kilgarra Mountain
- Jamaica Farewell
- Michael Row Your Boat Ashore
- Oh, Susanna
- Red River Valley
- San Francisco Bay Blues
- Shenandoah
- Skip to My Lou
- Surfin USA
- This Land is Your Land
- Waltzing Matilda
- Yankee Doodle
- You are My Sunshine

Christmas Songs:

- Little Drummer Boy
- Mele Kalikimaka
- Santa Claus is Coming to Town
- Twelve Days of Christmas

TAB:
A string top line
E string 3rd
C string 2nd line
G string bottom line

Double Time Fingerpicking Patterns for Songs in 4/4, C and 2/4 Time

VISUALS FOR PAGE 150

PATTERN A

Beat	1	2	3	4
Fingers	T 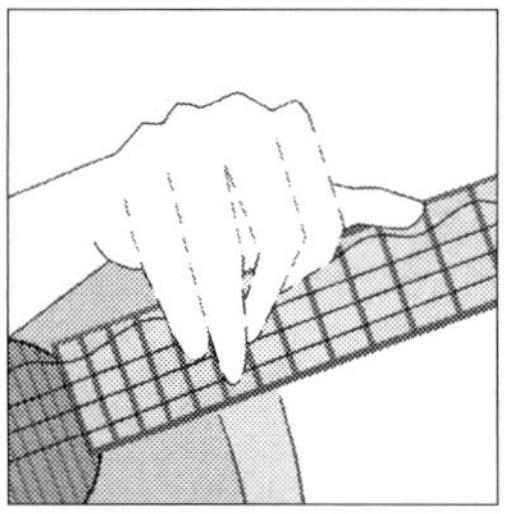	IMR 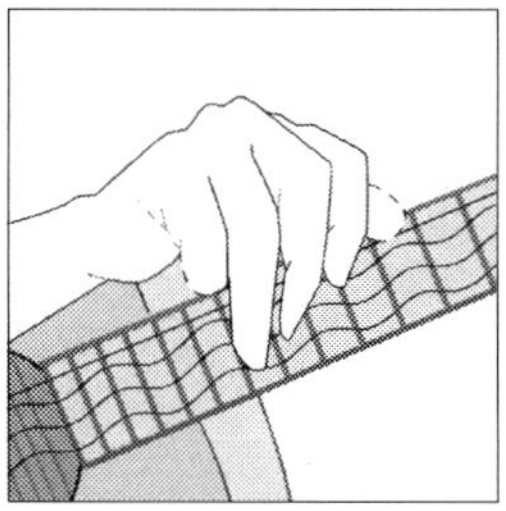	T 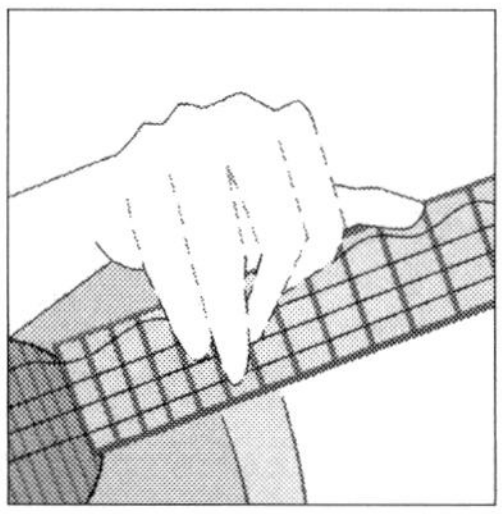	IMR 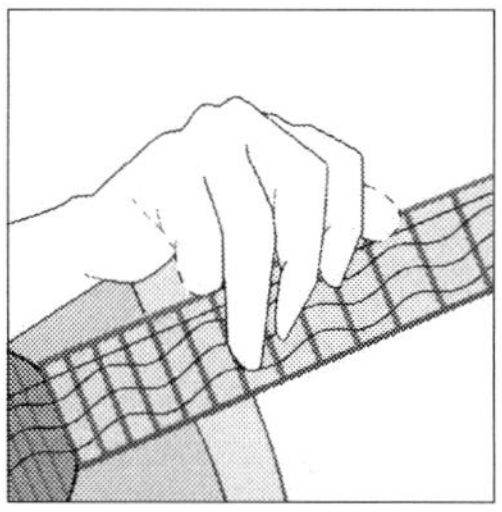

PATTERN B

Beat	1	2	3	4
Fingers	T 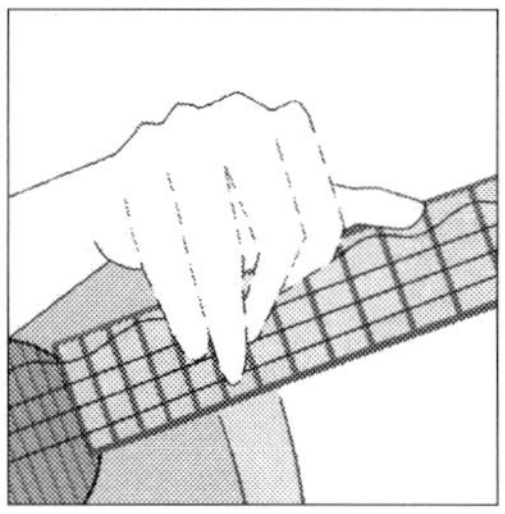	IMR 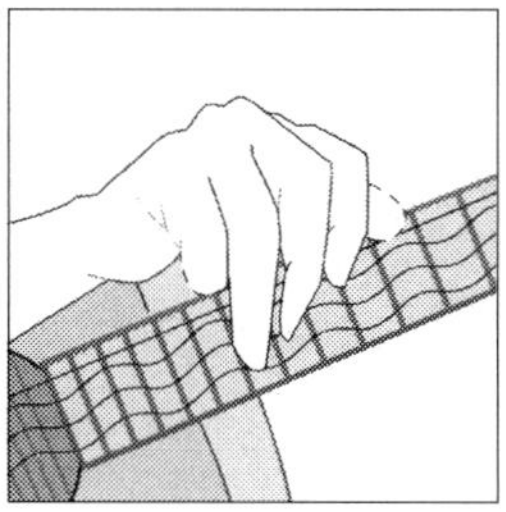	I 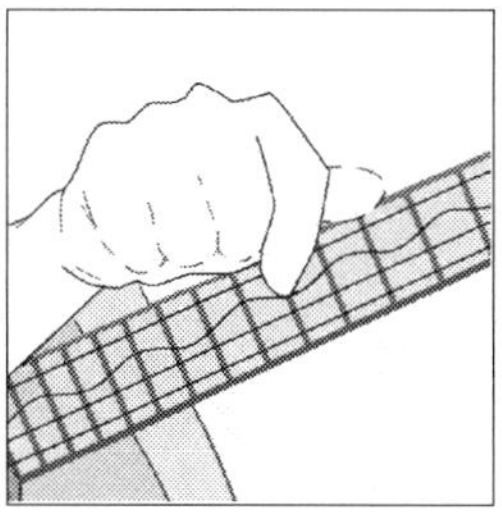	MR 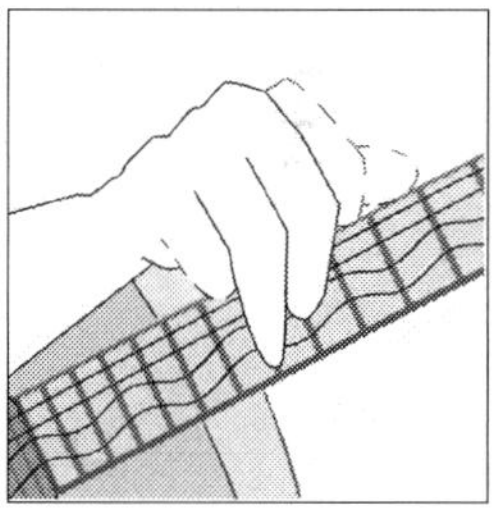

PATTERN C

Beat	1	2	3	4
Fingers	T 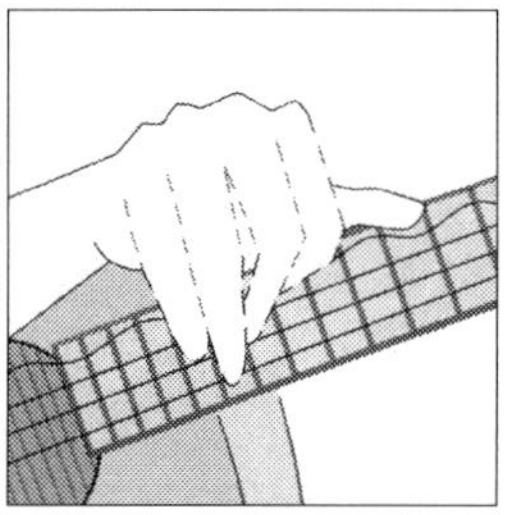	I 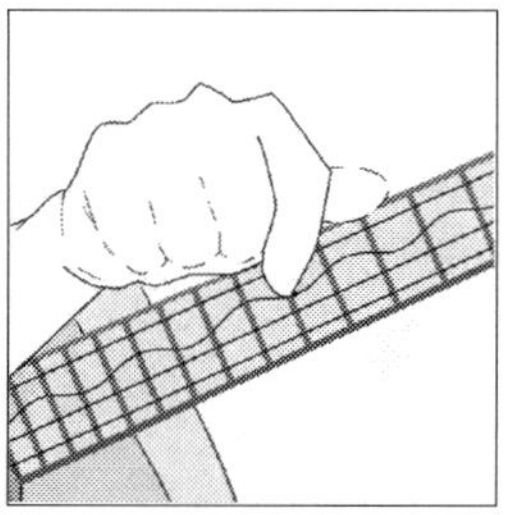	MR 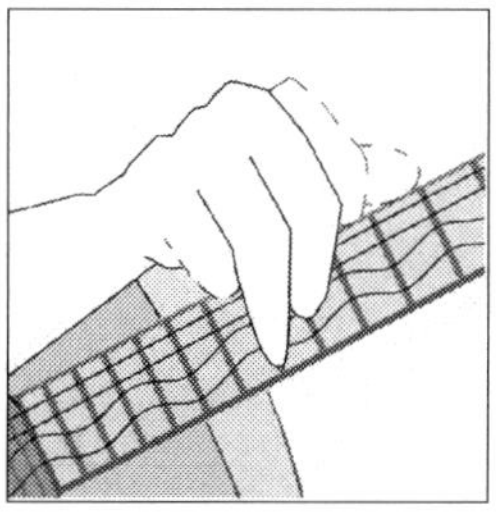	I 

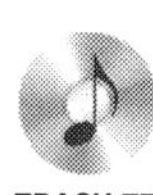

3. Double Time Fingerpicking and Brush Patterns for Songs in 4/4, C, and 2/4 Time

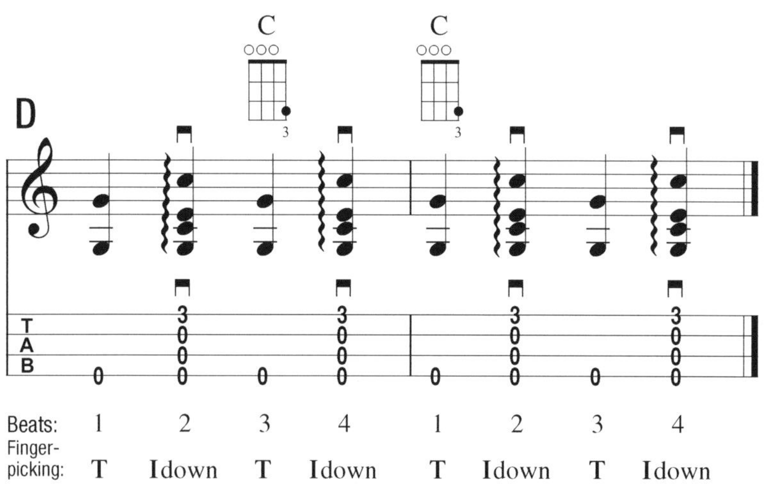

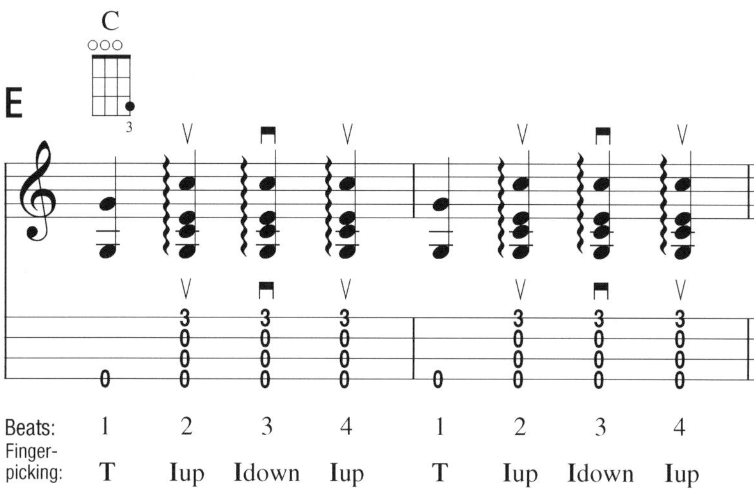

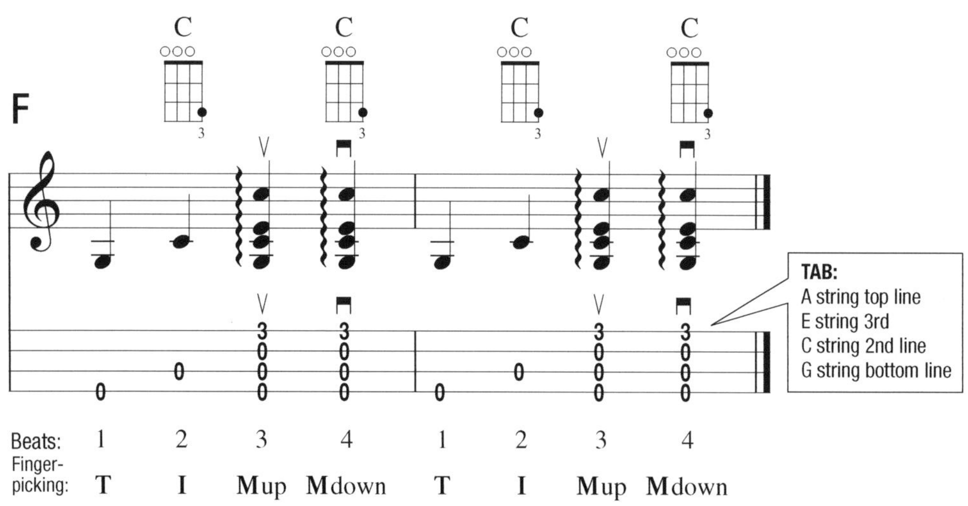

Fingerpicking and Finger Brush:

All of the patterns on this page combine fingerpicking with finger brushes.

Options for any of these patterns:

You can choose to brush with either your middle or index finger.

Down Brushes:

Use the top of the fingernail.

Up Brushes:

Use the underside of the fingernail.

Double Time Fingerpicking and Brush Patterns for Songs in 4/4, C, and 2/4 Time

VISUALS FOR PAGE 152

PATTERN D

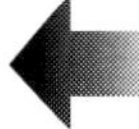

Beat	1	2	3	4
Fingers	T 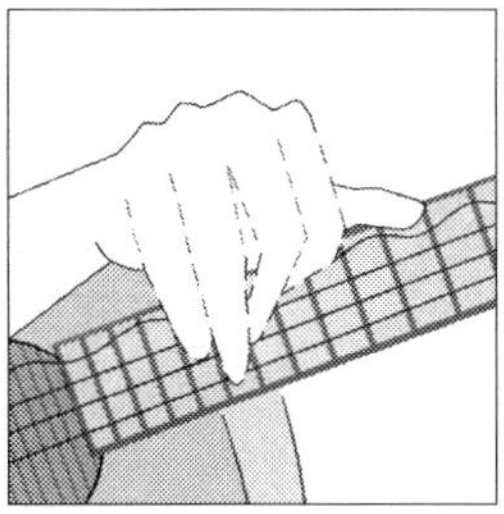	I down 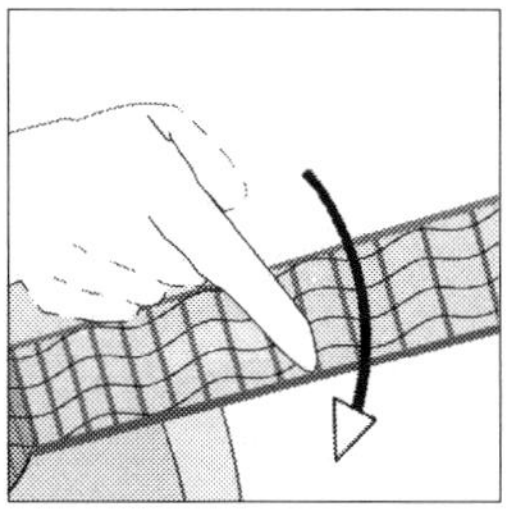	T 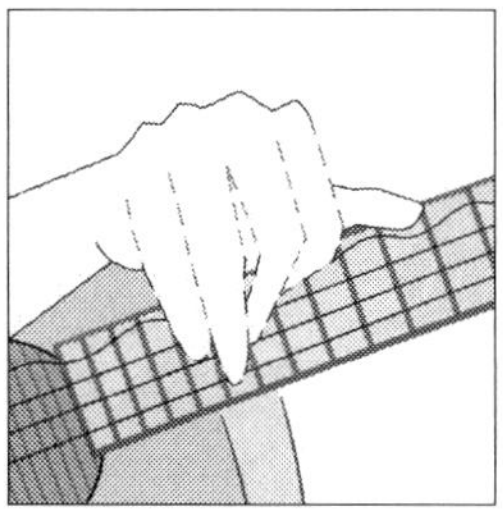	I down 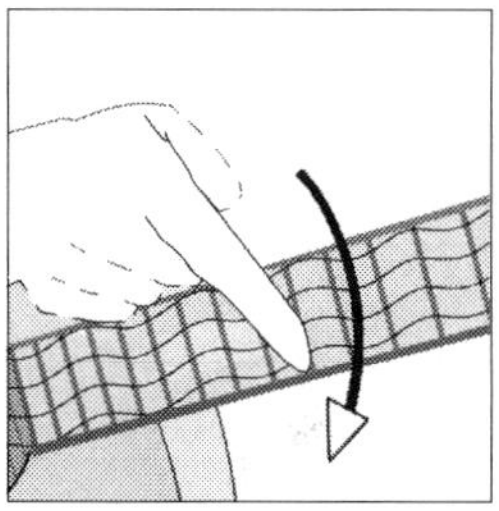

PATTERN E

Beat	1	2	3	4
Fingers	T 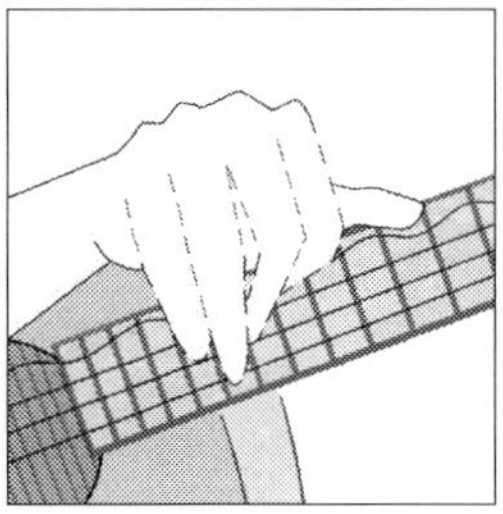	I up 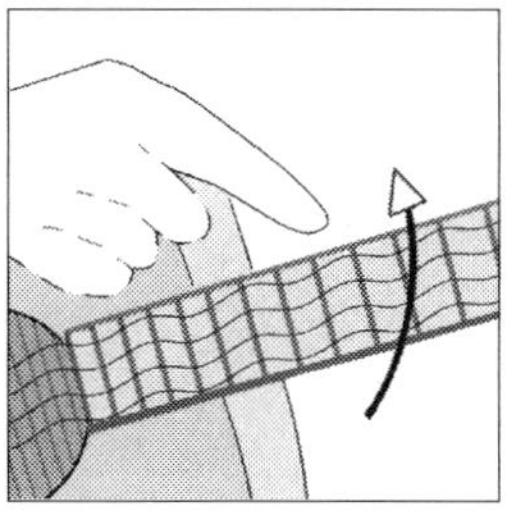	I down 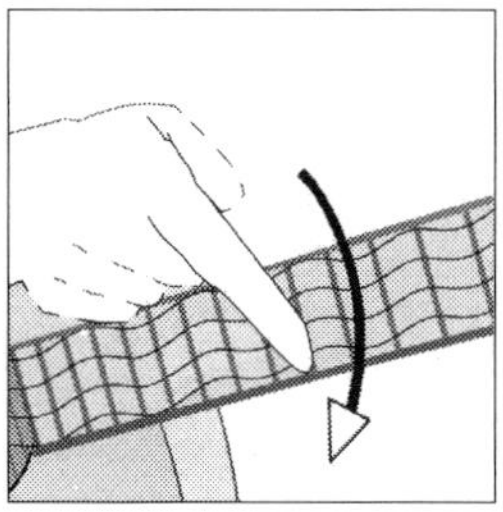	I up 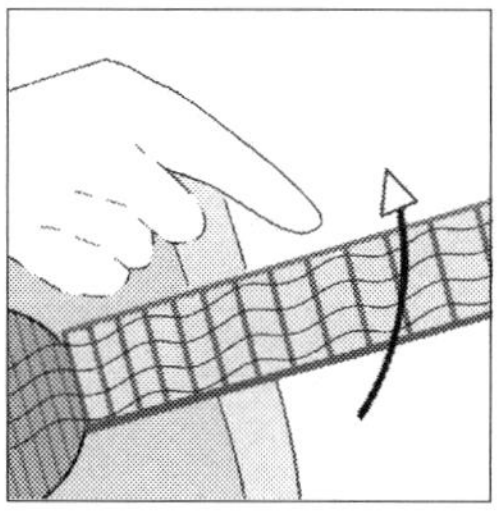

PATTERN F

Beat	1	2	3	4
Fingers	T 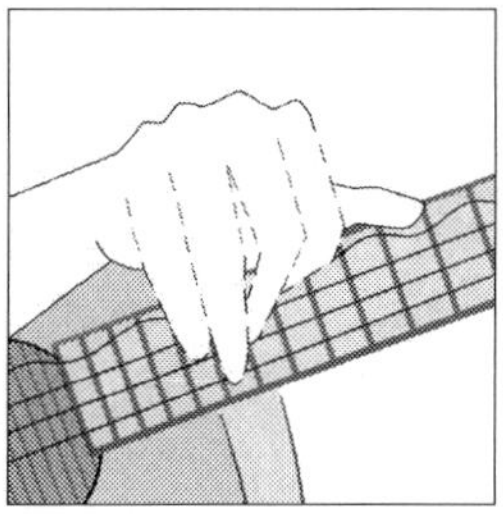	I 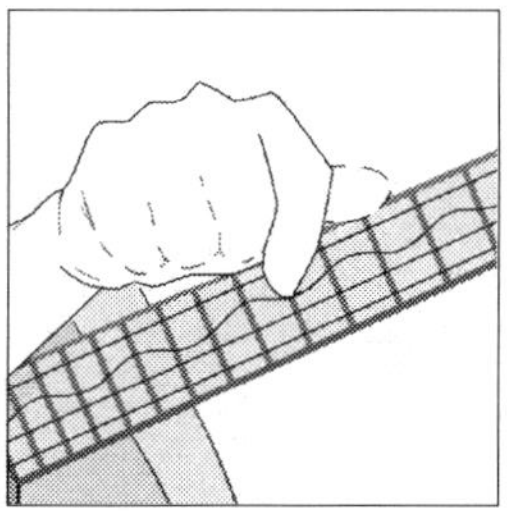	M up 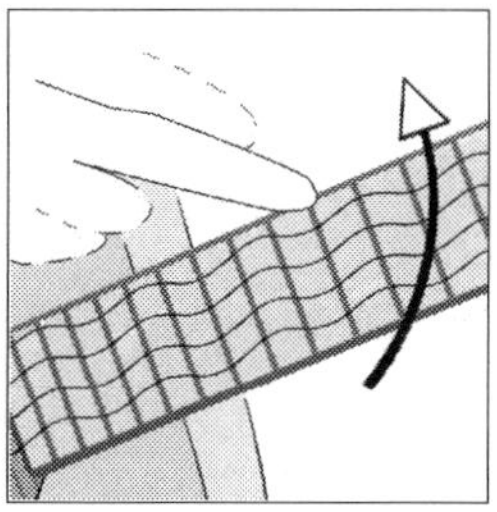	M down 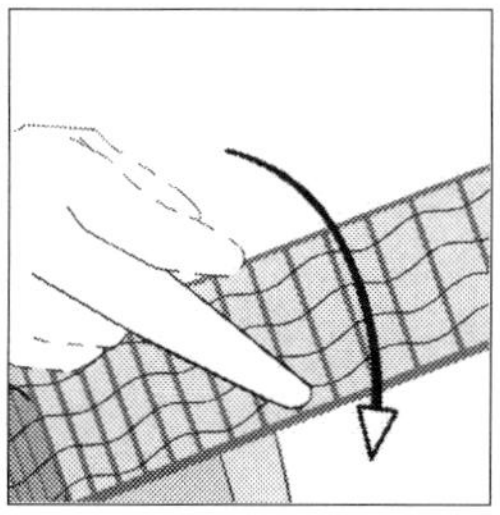

4. Go Tell Aunt Rhody: Fingerpicking Practice Guide

TRACK 78

This guide lays out all six new fingerpicking patterns and strums for easy practice.

Learning Tip—Practice playing each strum 3 ways:

1. **Count the beats** in each measure as you practice each right-hand pattern.
2. **Say** the fingerpicking patterns as you play them.
3. **Sing** the song as you practice each right-hand pattern.

Traditional

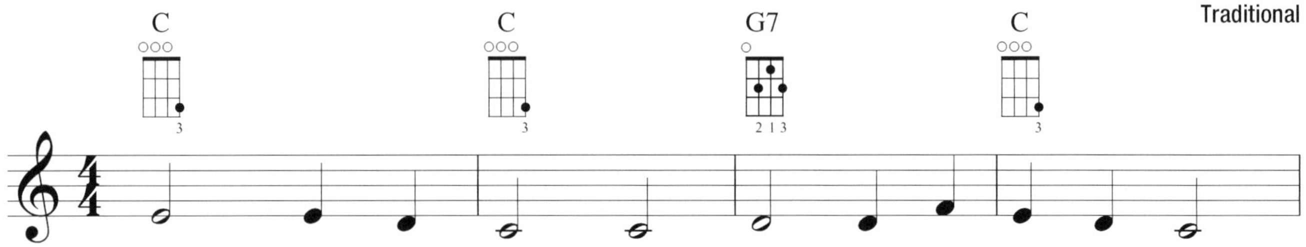

	C				C				G7				C			
Beats:	1	2	3	4	1	2	3	4	1	2	3	4	1	2	3	4
Lyrics:	Go		tell	Aunt	Rho	-	dy,		go		tell	Aunt	Rho	-	dy,	
Fingerpicking Patterns:																
Pattern A:	T	IMR	T	IMR	T	IMR	T	IMR	T	IMR	T	IMR	T	IMR	T	IMR
Pattern B:	T	IMR	I	MR	T	IMR	I	MR	T	IMR	I	MR	T	IMR	I	MR
Pattern C:	T	I	MR	I	T	I	MR	I	T	I	MR	I	T	I	MR	I
Fingerpicking + Finger Brush Patterns:																
Pattern D:	T	I(down)	T	I(down)	T	I(D)	T	I(D)	T	I(D)	T	I(D)	T	I(D)	T	I(D)
Pattern E:	T	I(down)	I(up)	I(down)	T	I(D)	I(U)	I(D)	T	I(D)	I(U)	I(D)	T	I(D)	I(U)	I(D)
Pattern F:	T	I	M(up)	M(down)	T	I	M(U)	M(D)	T	I	M(U)	M(D)	T	I	M(U)	M(D)

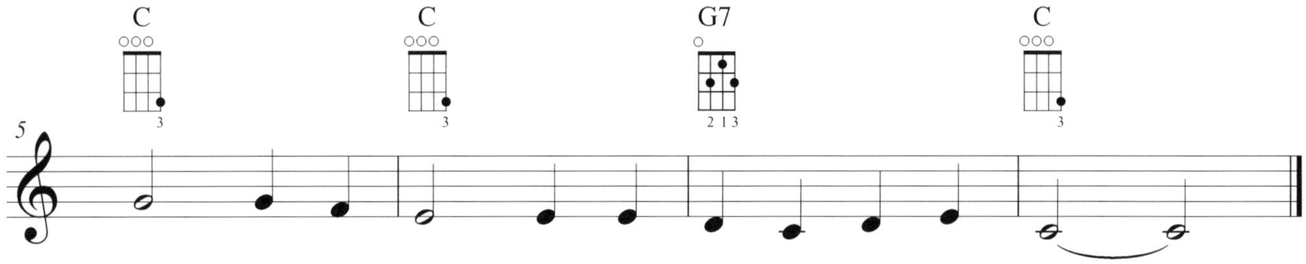

5

	C				C				G7				C			
	1	2	3	4	1	2	3	4	1	2	3	4	1	2	3	4
	Go		tell	Aunt	Rho	-	dy,	the	old	grey	goose	is	dead.________			
Fingerpicking Patterns:																
Pattern A:	T	IMR	T	IMR	T	IMR	T	IMR	T	IMR	T	IMR	T	IMR	T	IMR
Pattern B:	T	IMR	I	MR	T	IMR	I	MR	T	IMR	I	MR	T	IMR	I	MR
Pattern C:	T	I	MR	I	T	I	MR	I	T	I	MR	I	T	I	MR	I
Fingerpicking + Finger Brush Patterns:																
Pattern D:	T	I(D)	T	I(D)	T	I(D)	T	I(D)	T	I(D)	T	I(D)	T	I(D)	T	I(D)
Pattern E:	T	I(D)	I(U)	I(D)	T	I(D)	I(U)	I(D)	T	I(D)	I(U)	I(D)	T	I(D)	I(U)	I(D)
Pattern F:	T	I	M(U)	M(D)	T	I	M(U)	M(D)	T	I	M(U)	M(D)	T	I	M(U)	M(D)

Go Tell Aunt Rhody: Lyrics and Chord Chart

VERSE 2

```
    C  /          /  /
The one she's been sav-ing,
    G7 /         C  /
The one she's been sav-ing,
    C  /          /  /
The one she's been sav-ing
   G7    /      C  /
To make a feather bed.
```

VERSE 3

```
    C  /       /     /
The gos-lings are mourn-ing,
    G7 /      C      /
The gos-lings are mourn-ing,
    C  /       /     /
The gos-lings are mourn-ing,
   G7       /        C    /
Be-cause their mother's dead.
```

VERSE 4

```
    C  /       /    /
The old gander's weep-ing,
    G7 /      C    /
The old gander's weep-ing,
    C  /      /    /
The old gander's weep-ing,
   G7       /     C   /
Be-cause his wife is dead.
```

VERSE 5

```
    C  /     /  /
She died in the mill pond,
    G7  /    C  /
She died in the mill pond,
    C  /     /  /
She died in the mill pond
     G7       /     C   /
From standing on her head.
```

Repeat Verse 1

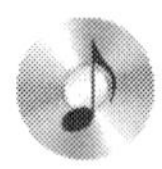

5. Au Clair de la Lune

TRACK 79

History: This French folk song dates back to the 18th century. Taught to French school children, the lyrics have a double entendre, and can be interpreted two ways. In years gone by, the song was often sung in pubs. Read the translation of the lyrics on the following page and come to your own conclusions.

Traditional French Folk Song

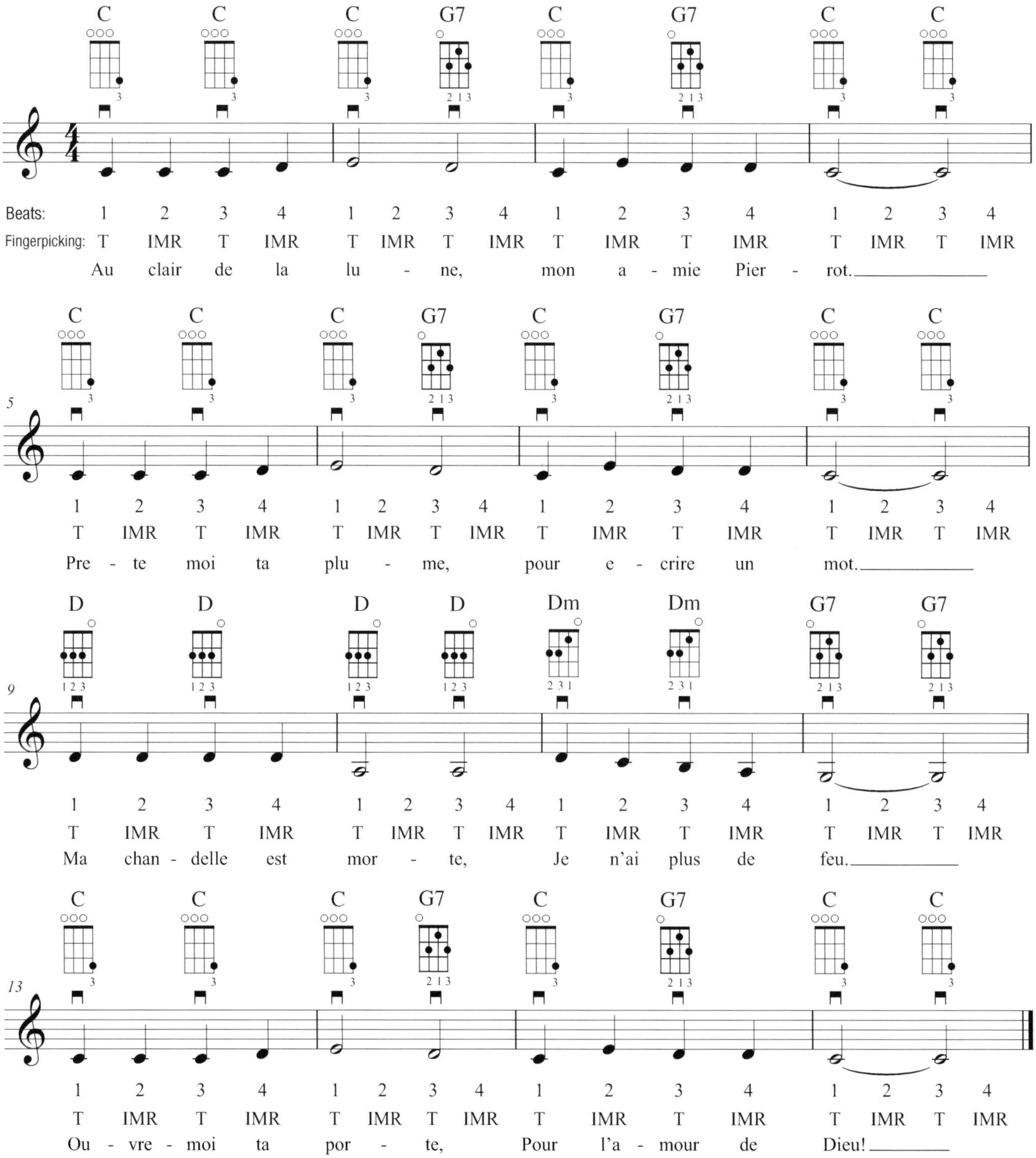

C C C G7 C G7 C C

Beats: 1 2 3 4 1 2 3 4 1 2 3 4 1 2 3 4

Fingerpicking: T IMR T IMR T IMR T IMR T IMR T IMR T IMR T IMR

Au clair de la lu - ne, mon a - mie Pier - rot.

5

C C C G7 C G7 C C

1 2 3 4 1 2 3 4 1 2 3 4 1 2 3 4

T IMR T IMR T IMR T IMR T IMR T IMR T IMR T IMR

Pre - te moi ta plu - me, pour e - crire un mot.

9

D D D D Dm Dm G7 G7

1 2 3 4 1 2 3 4 1 2 3 4 1 2 3 4

T IMR T IMR T IMR T IMR T IMR T IMR T IMR T IMR

Ma chan - delle est mor - te, Je n'ai plus de feu.

13

C C C G7 C G7 C C

1 2 3 4 1 2 3 4 1 2 3 4 1 2 3 4

T IMR T IMR T IMR T IMR T IMR T IMR T IMR T IMR

Ou - vre - moi ta por - te, Pour l'a - mour de Dieu!

Au Clair de la Lune: Lyrics and Chord Chart

VERSE 1

```
C          /     / G7  C       G7        C  /
Au Clair de la lu-ne   mon a-mi  Pier-rot,
C     /        / G7   C       G7        C  /
Préte-moi ta plu-me   pour é-crire un mot.
D          /         /   /  Dm     /         G7 /
Ma chan-delle est mor-te, Je n'ai plus de feu.
C       /        /  G7  C         G7        C    /
Ouvre-moi ta por-te,   Pour l'a-mour de Dieu!
```

VERSE 1 Translation

By the light of the moon, my friend Pierrot,

Lend me your pen, so I can write a word.

My candle is dead, I don't have any fire.

Open your door to me, for the love of God!

VERSE 2

```
C          /    / G7   C       G7      C   /
Au Clair de la lu-ne   Pierrot répon-dit:
C        /        /   G7 C       G7          C   /
Je n'ai pas de plu-me, Je suis dans mon lit.
D          /     / / Dm       /           G7  /
Va Chez la voisi-ne, Je crois qu'elle y est,
C          /       / G7   C      G7      C    /
Car dans sa cui-si-ne   on bat le   bri-quet.
```

VERSE 2 Translation

By the light of the moon, Pierrot answers:

"I don't have a pen, I am in my bed.

Go to the neighbor; I believe that she is there,

Because in her kitchen, she is lighting a fire."

VERSE 3

```
C          /    / G7    C       G7     C    /
Au clair de la lu-ne,    L'aima-ble Lu-bin
C        /       /   G7 C      G7          C   /
Frappe chez la bru-ne, Elle ré-pond sou-dain:
D            /    /   /  Dm  /      G7  /
Qui frappe de la sor-te? Il dit à son tour:
C        /    /  G7 C      G7         C    /
Ouvrez votre por-te, Pour le Dieu d'A-mour.
```

VERSE 3 Translation

By the light of the moon, likable Lubin

Knocks on the brunette's door she soon responds:

"Who's knocking like that?" He then replies,

"Open your door for the god of Love!"

VERSE 4

```
C          /    / G7    C       G7         C   /
Au clair de la lu-ne,    On n'y voit qu'un peu.
C         /       /  G7  C          G7     C   /
On cher-cha la plu-me,  On cher-cha le feu.
D         /          /  /  Dm            /          G7 /
En cher-chant d'la sor-te, Je n'sais c'qu'on trou-va;
C        /          /   G7  C      G7     C   /
Mais je sais qu'la por-te   Sur eux se fer-ma.
```

VERSE 4 Translation

By the light of the moon, one could barely see.

The pen was looked for, the light was looked for;

With all that looking I don't know what was found,

But I do know that the door was shut behind them.

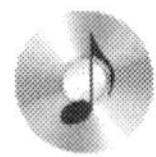

6. Bingo

TRACK 80

Performing Tip: You can choose to perform this song 3 ways:

1. Sing the melody and accompany yourself with the chords and favorite double time fingerpicking pattern on **pages 150-153** or the pattern on these pages.
2. Play the arrangement as an instrumental solo. (Next page)
3. Play the arrangement as a solo either before or after singing the song while accompanying yourself.

Traditional English Folk Song

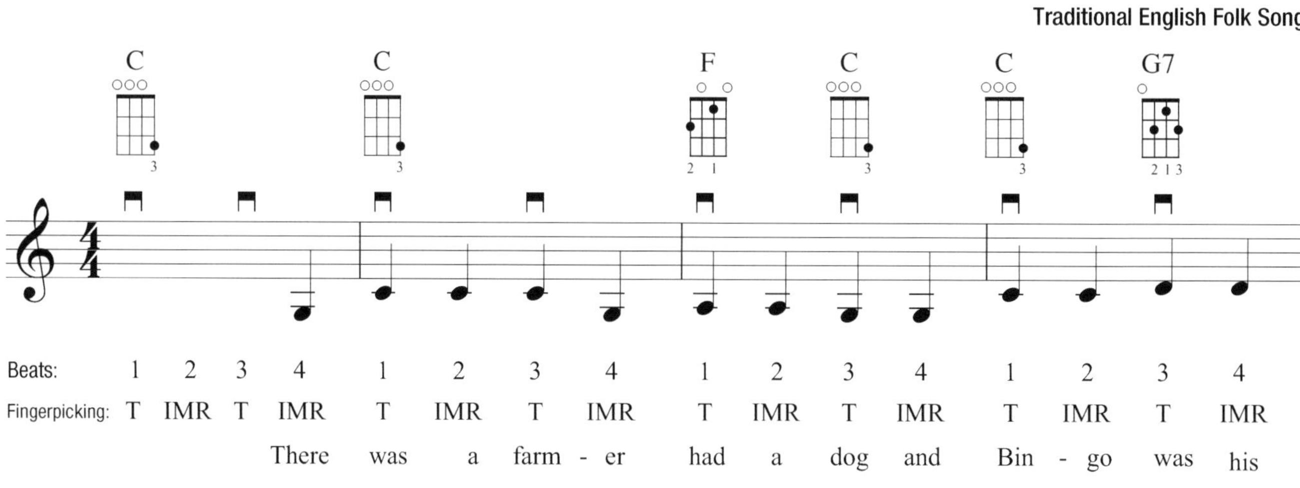

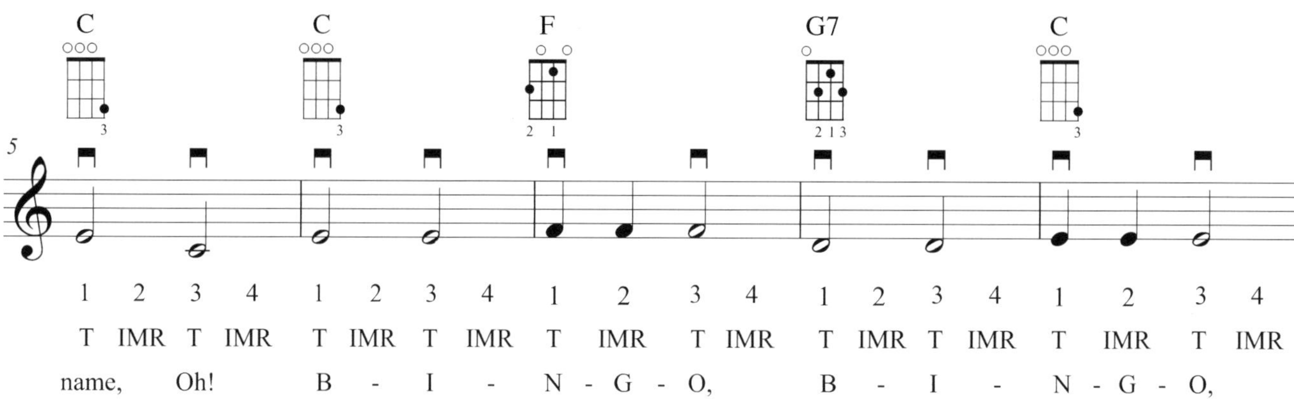

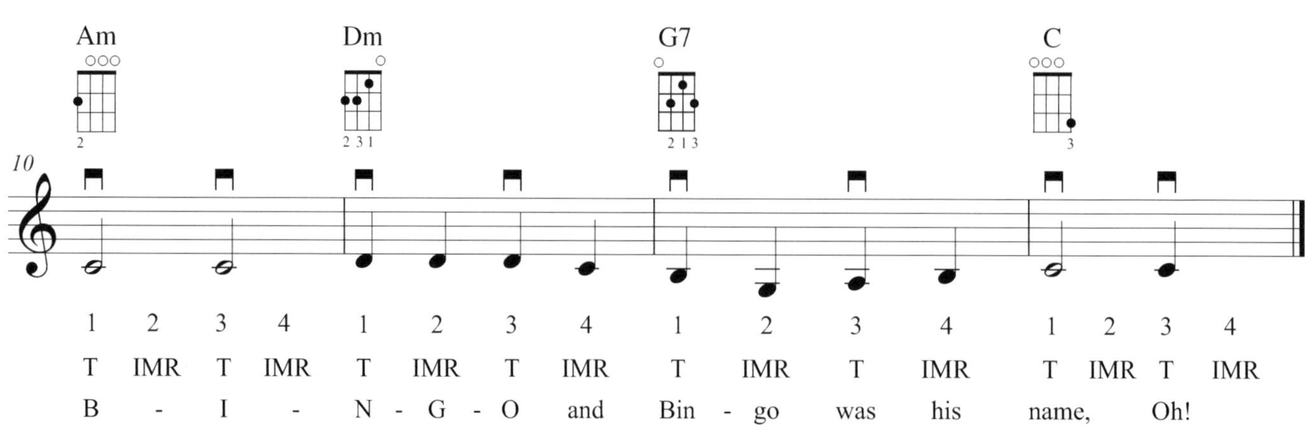

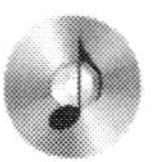
TRACK 81

7. Bingo—Instrumental Arrangement

C F C C G7

Beats: 1 2 3 4 | 1 2 3 4 | 1 2 3 4 | 1 2 3 4

Fingerpicking: T | TIMR I I T | TIMR T T T | TIMR I TIMR I

There | was a farm - er | had a dog and | Bin - go was his

C C F G7 C

1 2 3 4 | 1 2 3 4 | 1 2 3 4 | 1 2 3 4 | 1 2 3 4

TIMR I | TIMR M | TIMR M M | TIMR I | TIMR M M

name, Oh! | B - I - | N - G - O, | B - I - | N - G - O,

Am Dm G7 C

1 2 3 4 | 1 2 3 4 | 1 2 3 4 | 1 2 3

TIMR I | TIMR I I I | TIMR T T T | TIMR I

B - I - | N - G - O, and | Bin - go was his | name, Oh!

8. Red River Valley

TRACK 82

Learning Tip:

1. Practice your favorite double time fingerpicking pattern on **pages 150-153**, while singing this song.
2. Using the fingerpicking pattern below; pluck with your thumb on the 1st and 3rd beats.

Traditional Cowboy

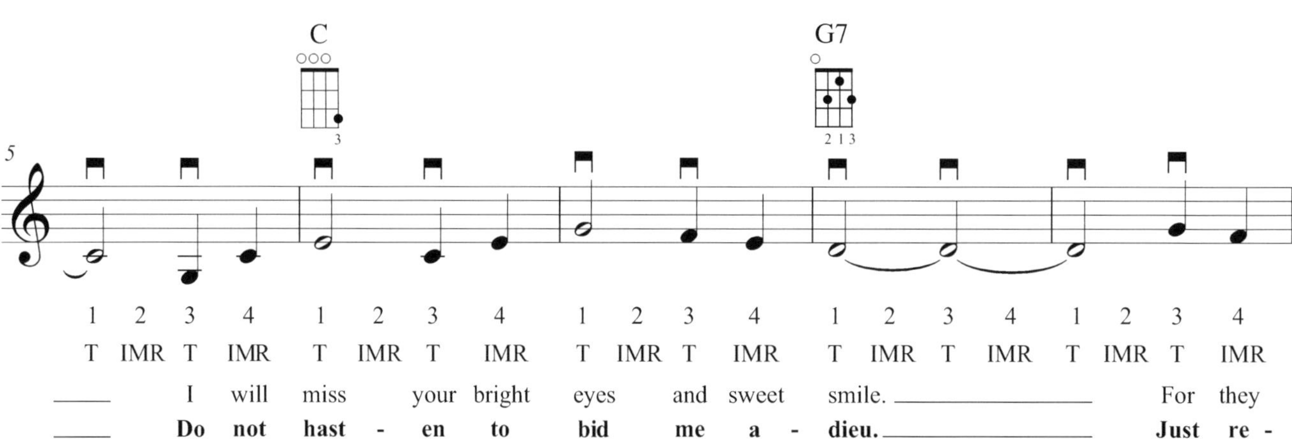

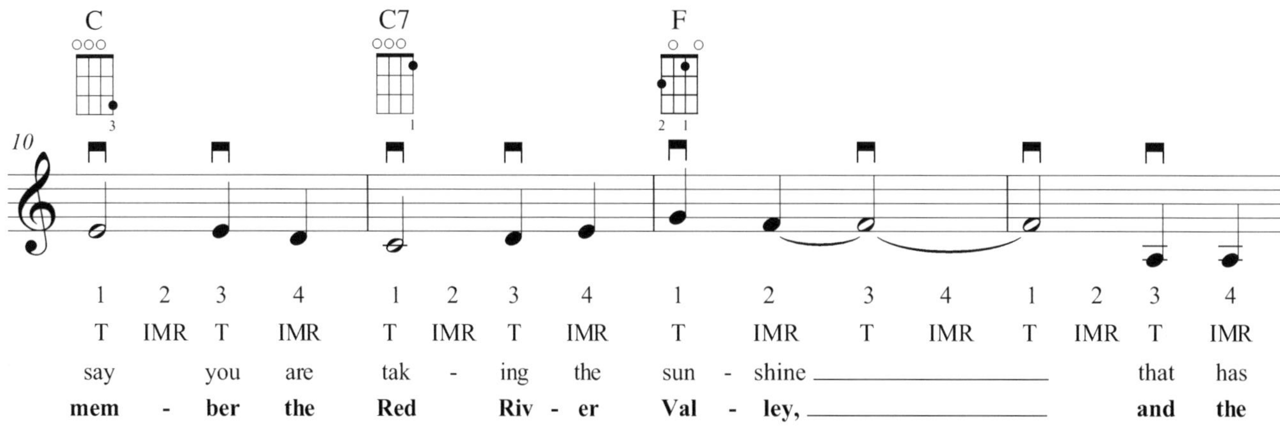

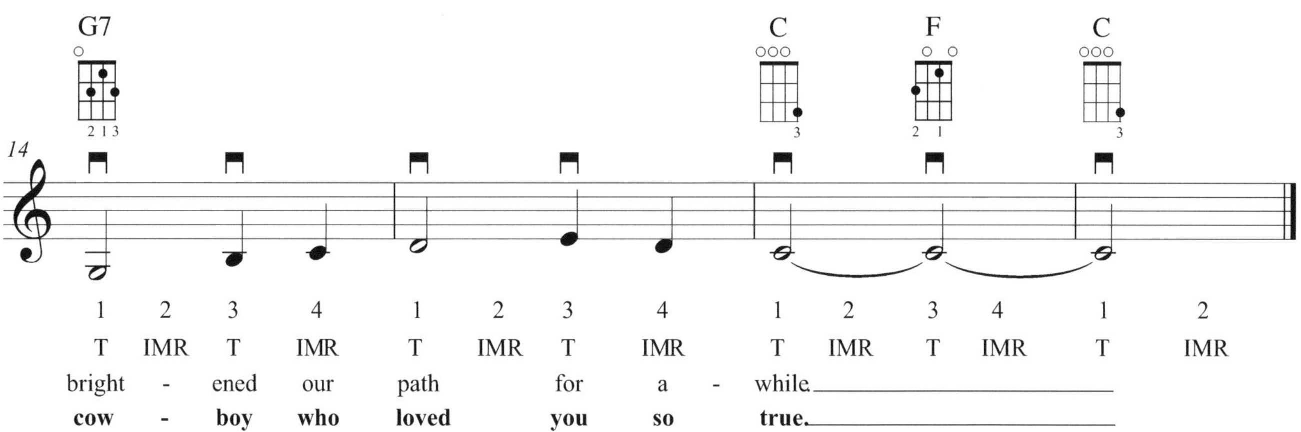

Red River Valley: Lyrics and Chord Chart

VERSE 2

C / / / / / / /
I've been think-ing a long time, my darling
C / / / / G7 / /
Of the sweet words you nev-er would say.
G7 C / C7 / F / /
Now, a-las, must my fond hopes all vanish,
F G7 / / / C F C
For they say you are go-ing a-way.
Chorus

VERSE 3

C / / / / / / /
Do you think of the val-ley you're leaving?
C / / / / G7 / /
O how lone-ly and drear-y it be.
G7 C / C7 / F / /
Do you think of the kind hearts you're breaking,
F G7 / / / C F C
And the pain you are caus-ing to me?
Chorus

VERSE 4

C / / / / / / /
They will bur-y me where you have wandered,
C / / / / G7 / /
Near the hills where the daf-fodils grow.
G7 C / C7 / F / /
When you're gone from the Red River Valley,
F G7 / / / C F C
For I can't live with-out you I know.
Chorus

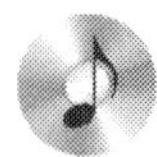

9. She'll Be Comin' 'Round the Mountain

Learning Tip:

1. Practice your favorite double time fingerpicking pattern on **pages 150-153**, while singing this song.
2. Using the fingerpicking pattern below; pluck with your thumb on the 1st and 3rd beats.

Traditional

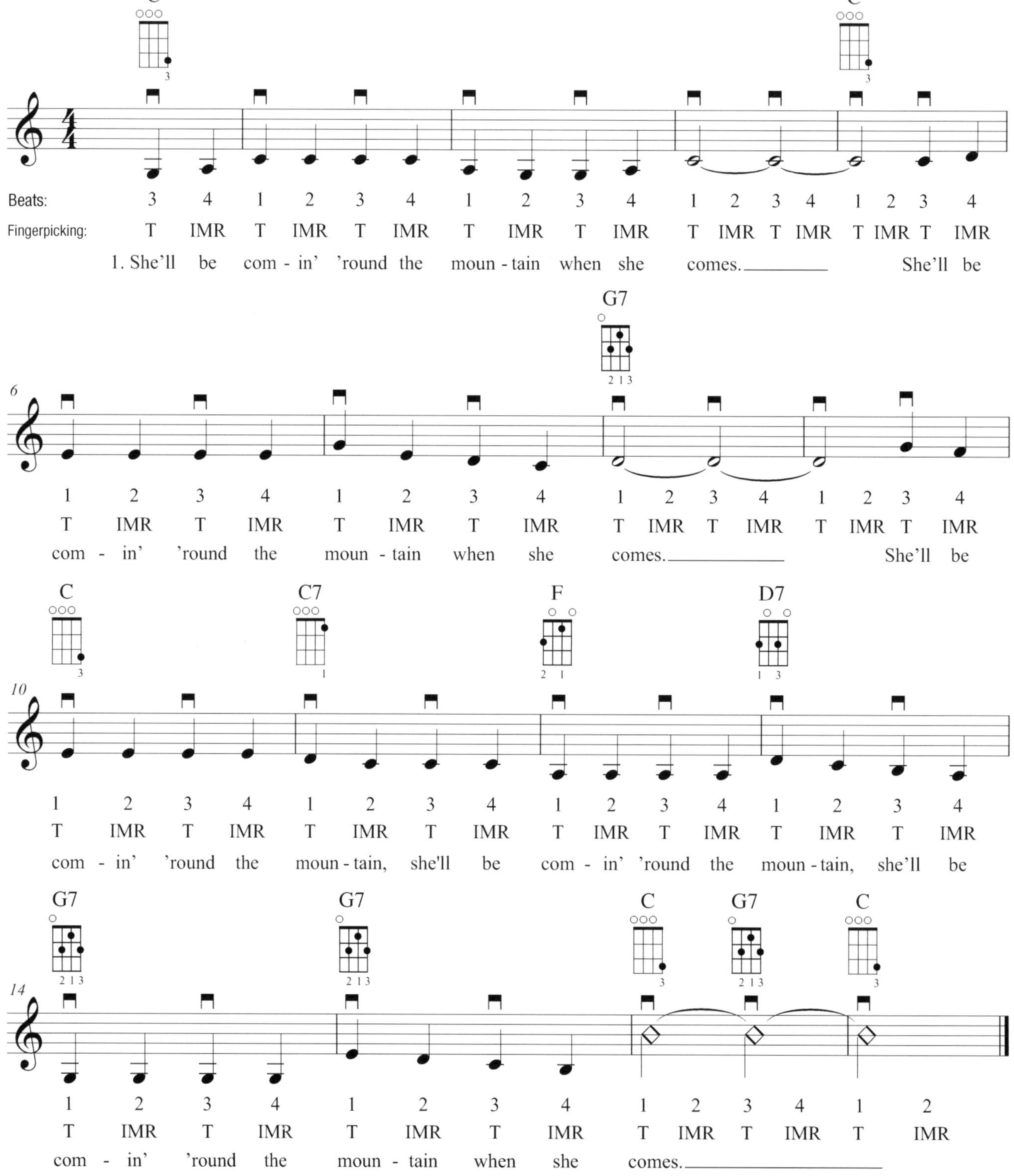

C C

Beats: 3 4 1 2 3 4 1 2 3 4 1 2 3 4 1 2 3 4

Fingerpicking: T IMR T IMR T IMR T IMR T IMR T IMR T IMR T IMR T IMR

1. She'll be com - in' 'round the moun - tain when she comes. She'll be

G7

6

1 2 3 4 1 2 3 4 1 2 3 4 1 2 3 4

T IMR T IMR T IMR T IMR T IMR T IMR T IMR T IMR

com - in' 'round the moun - tain when she comes. She'll be

C C7 F D7

10

1 2 3 4 1 2 3 4 1 2 3 4 1 2 3 4

T IMR T IMR T IMR T IMR T IMR T IMR T IMR T IMR

com - in' 'round the moun - tain, she'll be com - in' 'round the moun - tain, she'll be

G7 G7 C G7 C

14

1 2 3 4 1 2 3 4 1 2 3 4 1 2

T IMR T IMR T IMR T IMR T IMR T IMR T IMR

com - in' 'round the moun - tain when she comes.

She'll Be Comin' 'Round the Mountain: Lyrics and Chord Chart

VERSE 2

C / / / / / / /
She'll be driving six white horses when she comes.
C / / / / G7 / /
She'll be driving six white horses when she comes.
G7 C / C7 / F / D7
She'll be driving six white horses, she'll be driving six white horses,
D7 G7 / / / C G7 C
She'll be driving six white horses when she comes.

VERSE 3

C / / / / / / /
Oh, we'll all go out to see her when she comes.
C / / / / G7 / /
Oh, we'll all go out to see her when she comes.
G7 C / C7 / F / D7
Oh, we'll all go out to see her, oh, we'll all go out to see her,
D7 G7 / / / C G7 C
Oh, we'll all go out to see her when she comes.

VERSE 4

C / / / / / / /
Oh, we'll all have chicken and dumplings when she comes.
C / / / / G7 / /
Oh, we'll all have chicken and dumplings when she comes.
G7 C / C7 / F / D7
Oh, we'll all have chicken and dumplings, oh, we'll all have chicken and dumplings,
D7 G7 / / / C / /
Oh, we'll all have chicken and dumplings when she comes.

Mary Harris "Mother" Jones—In 1902 she was known as "the most dangerous woman in America," because of her success in organizing mine workers and their families against the mine owners. In 1903, upset about the lax enforcement of the child labor laws in Pennsylvania mines and silk mills, she organized a Children's March from Philadelphia to the home of then president Theodore Roosevelt in New York.

History: Pulitzer Prize winning writer, editor, and folk musician, Carl Sandburg (1878–1967) published the first printed version of "She'll Be Comin' 'Round the Mountain" in a landmark anthology of traditional American songs called *The American Songbag* in 1927. He believed that the song dates back to the late 1800s and was based on an old Negro spiritual titled "When the Chariot Comes." During the 19th century, the lyrics were transformed to the current poetry as the song spread throughout Appalachia. Sandburg believed that the "she" in the song refers to union organizer Mary Harris "Mother" Jones, who promoted the formation of labor unions in the Appalachian coal mining camps. The song was later sung by railroad work gangs in the Midwestern United States in the 1890s. Like many work songs, it was written and sung in a call-and-response style; the lead singer would shout the first line and the rest of the singers would repeat it.

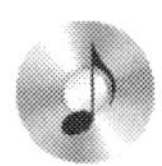

10. Auld Lang Syne

TRACK 84

Learning Tip: This song introduces the E7 Chord. Practice playing the chords with your favorite double time finger-picking pattern on **pages 150-153** while singing this song. The strum marks tell you where to play the 1 and 3 beats.

History: "Auld Lang Syne," based on a poem by the Scottish poet Robert Burns (1759-1796), is one of the best known songs in English-speaking countries, and it is often sung at the stroke of midnight on New Year's Day. The song's (Scottish) title may be translated into English literally as "old long since" or "days gone by."

C 3 C 3 G7 2 1 3 C 3 C7 1

Beats: 1 2 3 4 1 2 3 4 1 2 3 4 1 2 3 4

Fingerpicking: T IMR T IMR T IMR T IMR T IMR T IMR T IMR T IMR

Should auld ac - quaint - ance be for - got and nev - er brought to

5

F 2 1 C 3 G7 2 1 3 F 2 1 G7 2 1 3 C 3 G7 2 1 3

1 2 3 4 1 2 3 4 1 2 3 4 1 2 3 4 1 2 3 4

T IMR T IMR T IMR T IMR T IMR T IMR T IMR T IMR T IMR T IMR

mind? Should auld ac - quaint - ance be for - got and days of auld lang syne? { 1. For 2. And

10

C 3 G7 2 1 3 C 3 C7 1 F 2 1

1 2 3 4 1 2 3 4 1 2 3 4 1 2 3 4

T IMR T IMR T IMR T IMR T IMR T IMR T IMR T IMR

auld lang syne, my dear, for auld lang syne, } we'll

there's a hand my trust - y friend, and give us a hand o' thine,

14

C 3 G7 2 1 3 E7 1 2 3 F 2 1 G7 2 1 3 C 3

1 2 3 4 1 2 3 4 1 2 3 4 1 2 3 4

T IMR T IMR T IMR T IMR T IMR T IMR T IMR T IMR

take a cup of kind - ness yet, for auld lang syne.

Most Commonly Used Chords in the Key of C Major

Here is your reference guide for all of the chords you have learned. I also included a bonus chord: E major. I offer them in a music theory-style matrix in which the chords are organized via Roman numerals. Go across the matrix at the top, and you will find the chords correspond with the C scale notes C, D, E, F, G, and A. Capitol Roman numeral chords are Major, and lower-case Roman numeral chords are minor. If you go down any column, you will find chords that are sometimes substituted in music for the main chords at the top of the chart. For example, C7 may be substituted for the C chord, while D7 may be substituted for a D minor chord. I didn't include long and short forms for D7 and Em. It is your choice which forms to play.

I Major C	ii minor Dm	iii minor Em	IV Major F	V Major G	vi minor Am
3 G C E C	2 3 1 A D F A	3 2 1 G E G B	2 1 A C F A	1 3 2 G D G B	1 A C E A
C Chord Notes: C E G	Dm Chord Notes: D F A	Em Chord Notes: E G B	F Chord Notes: F A C	G Chord Notes: G B D	Am Chord Notes: A C E

Alternate Chords

- The following chords are often substituted for the **I Major**, **ii minor**, **iii minor** and the **V Major** chords.
- Hawaiian music often substitutes the II7 Major for the ii7 minor chord, particularly in Hawaiian vamps.

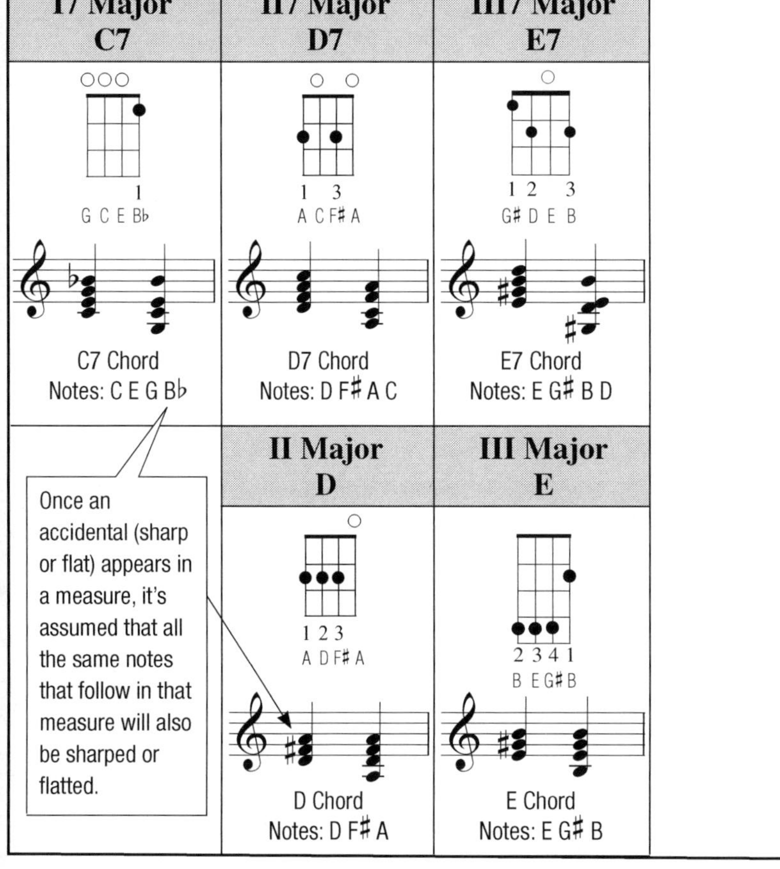

V7 Major G7	VI7 Major A7
2 1 3 G D F B	1 G C♯ E A
G7 Chord Notes: G B D F	A7 Chord Notes: A C♯ E G

11. Oh, Susanna

TRACK 85

Learning Tip: Practice playing the chords with your favorite double time fingerpicking pattern on **pages 150-153**, while singing this song. The strum marks tell you where to play the 1 and 3 beats.

History: Written by Stephen Foster in 1848, the lyrics are a good example of nonsense songs written at that time. Popularly associated with the California Gold Rush, it is probably based on a Scottish marching song, as the melody can be carried on the chanter of most bagpipes. Originally written for minstrel shows, it was first performed in northern states pre-Civil War by white singers wearing black face make-up.

Words and Music by
Stephen Foster
(1826–1864)

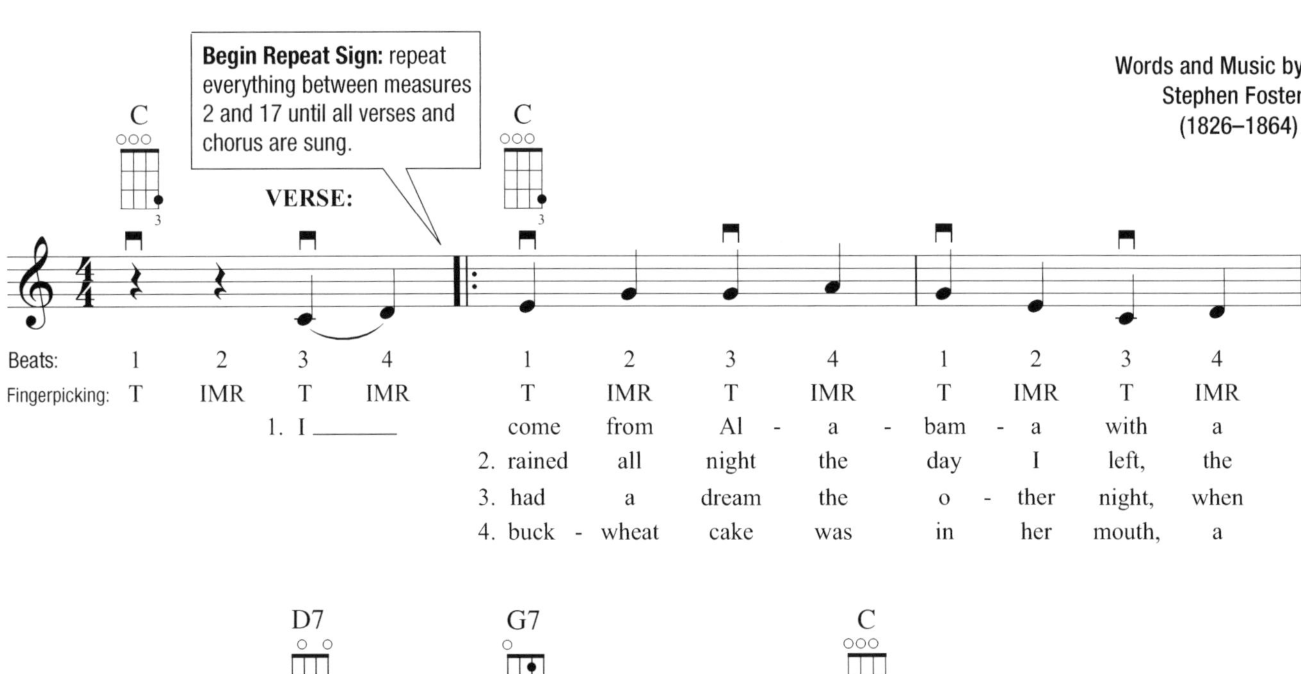

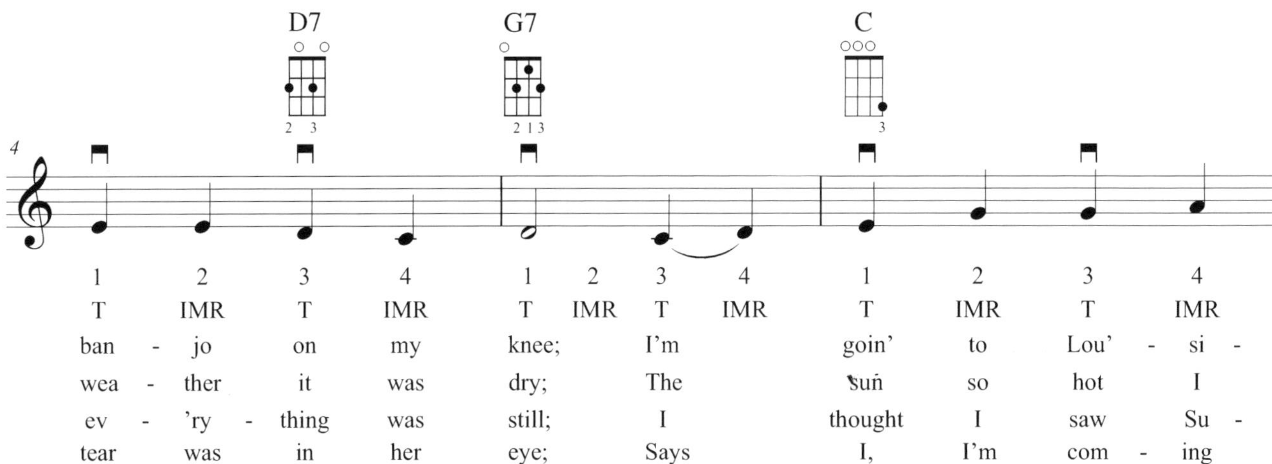

G7
C
7
1 2 3 4 1 2 3 4 1 2 3 4
T IMR T IMR T IMR T IMR T IMR T IMR
a - na, my true love for to see.
froze to death, Su - san - na don't you cry.
san - na, a - com - in' down the hill.
from the south, Su - san - na don't you cry!"
CHORUS:
F
C
D7
10
1 2 3 4 1 2 3 4 1 2 3 4
T IMR T IMR T IMR T IMR T IMR T IMR
O, Su - san - na, o, don't you cry for
G7
C
13
1 2 3 4 1 2 3 4 1 2 3 4
T IMR T IMR T IMR T IMR T IMR T IMR
me; I come from Al - a - bam - a with a
G7
C
End Repeat Sign: Return to repeat at measure 2 for more verses. Do not play measure 1 again.
Play last measure after verse 4 chorus
16
1 2 3 4 1 2 3 4 1 2 3 4
T IMR T IMR T IMR T IMR T IMR T IMR
ban - jo on my knee! knee!
2. It
3. I
4. The

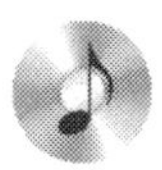

12. Good Night Ladies

TRACK 86

Learning Tip: Play the chords using your favorite double time fingerpicking pattern on **pages 150-153**, while singing the melody, or practice with the pattern indicated below.

History: Edwin Pearce Christy was an American composer, singer, actor and stage producer. He is more commonly known as E. P. Christy, and was the founder of the blackface minstrel group, Christy's Minstrels."Good Night Ladies" became the traditional "closer" for Vaudeville shows; a style of variety entertainment predominant in American theatres in the late 19th Century and early 20th Century. It is still the quintessential song for Barbershop quartets. Barbershop singing originated in African American communities in the U.S. around the turn of the century, where barbershops were, and remain today, social gathering places. The tight, four-part harmony is "a cappella," or unaccompanied vocal music, and has its roots in the Baptist church, where close harmony has a long tradition.

Composed by Edwin Pearce Christy
(1815–1862)

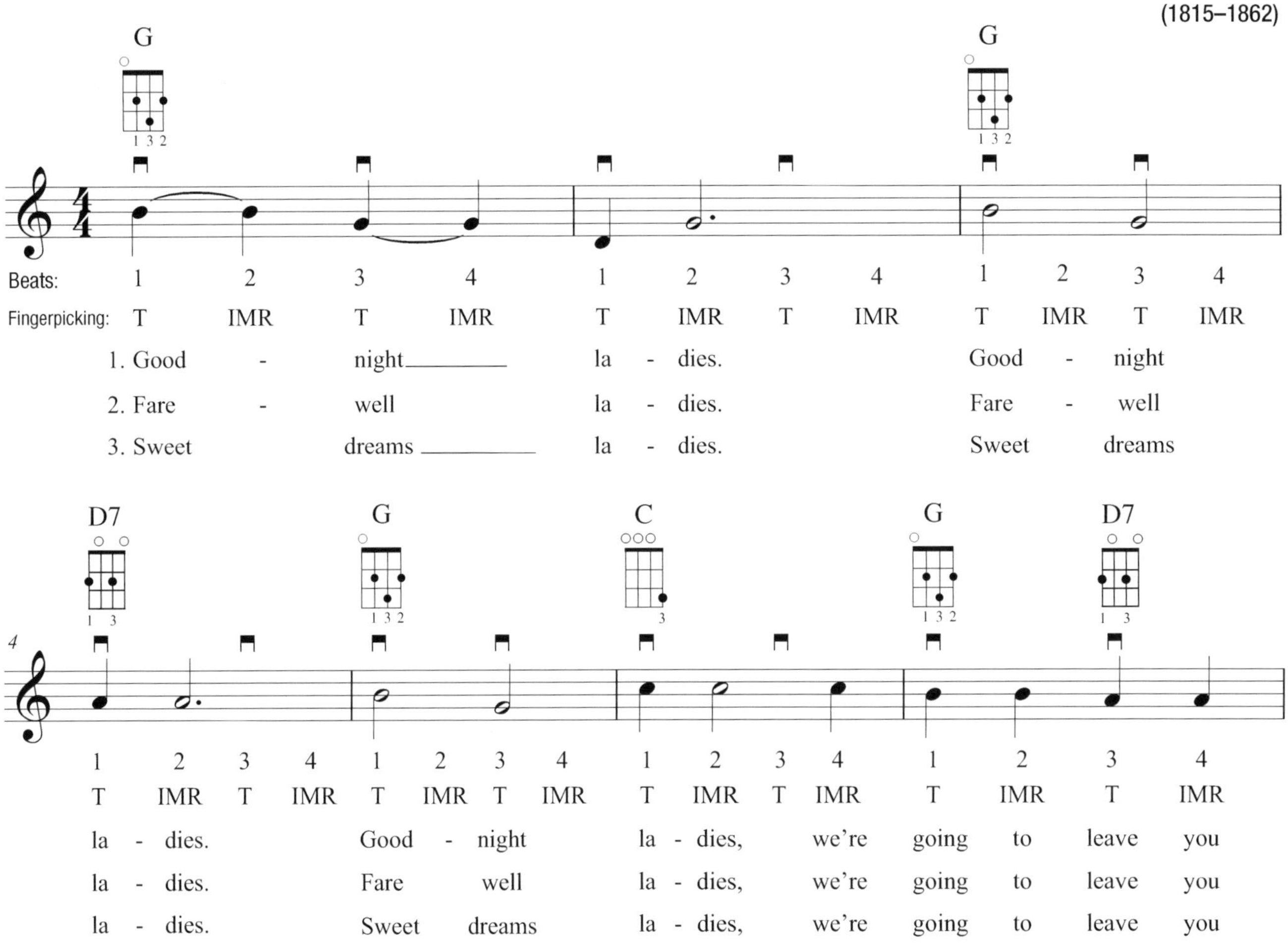

G 1 3 2 — G 1 3 2

Beats:	1	2	3	4	1	2	3	4	1	2	3	4
Fingerpicking:	T	IMR	T	IMR	T	IMR	T	IMR	T	IMR	T	IMR
	1. Good	-	night_____		la	- dies.			Good	-	night	
	2. Fare	-	well		la	- dies.			Fare	-	well	
	3. Sweet		dreams _____		la	- dies.			Sweet		dreams	

4

D7 1 3 — G 1 3 2 — C 3 — G 1 3 2 — D7 1 3

1	2	3	4	1	2	3	4	1	2	3	4	1	2	3	4
T	IMR	T	IMR	T	IMR	T	IMR	T	IMR	T	IMR	T	IMR	T	IMR
la	- dies.			Good	-	night		la	- dies,		we're	going	to	leave	you
la	- dies.			Fare		well		la	- dies,		we're	going	to	leave	you
la	- dies.			Sweet		dreams		la	- dies,		we're	going	to	leave	you

8

G				G				G			
1	2	3	4	1	2	3	4	1	2	3	4
T	IMR	T	IMR	T	IMR	T	IMR	T	IMR	T	IMR
now!___				Mer -	ri -	ly	we	roll	a -	long,	
now!___				Hope	you	had	a	hap -	py	time,	
now!___				Mer -	ri -	ly	we	roll	a -	long,	

11

D7				G				G			
1	2	3	4	1	2	3	4	1	2	3	4
T	IMR	T	IMR	T	IMR	T	IMR	T	IMR	T	IMR
roll	a -	long,		roll	a -	long.		Mer -	ri -	ly	we
hap -	py	time,		hap -	py	time.		Hope	you	had	a
roll	a -	long,		roll	a -	long.		Mer -	ri -	ly	we

14

G				D7				G			
1	2	3	4	1	2	3	4	1	2	3	4
T	IMR	T	IMR	T	IMR	T	IMR	T	IMR	T	IMR
roll	a -	long,		o'er	the	deep	blue	sea.			
hap -	py	time;		had	a	good	time	too!			
roll	a -	long,		o'er	the	deep	blue	sea.			

Appendix

UKE BASICS: Let's Talk Story!

This little, four-stringed dynamo is the great grandson of a Portuguese instrument called the "braguinha" or "machete de braga," meaning "small piece of wood" in Portuguese. The first braguinhas were manufactured in the province of Braga, Portugal (located on the Iberian Peninsula) in 139 B.C. by a tribe called the Lusitani. The braguinha became the instrument of choice for Portuguese mariners who introduced it to the world over centuries of travel.

The *braguinha* lands in Hawai'i

The first braguinha landed in Honolulu Harbor in August 1879 on the ship Ravenscraig with a boatload of immigrants from the Portuguese island of Madeira recruited to work in the Hawai'ian sugar cane fields. Portuguese folksinger, João Fernandez, who arrived on the boat, soon delighted Honolulu locals by singing and strumming his "baby guitar" around town.

"Ukulele" in Hawai'ian means "Jumping Flea"

Historians maintain that when the native Hawai'ians saw Fernandez's fingers jumping quickly over the strings, they nicknamed the little instrument a "ukulele." "Uku" in Hawai'ian means "flea" and "lele" means "to jump"... hence the nickname "jumping flea."

Three cabinet makers from the Madeira Islands also arrived on the Ravenscraig with Fernandez: José do Espirito Santo, Augusto Dias and Manuel Nunes. All three set up separate cabinet-making shops where they also made stringed instruments. By the mid-1880s, the braguinha had entered the local marketplace and evolved into the Hawai'ian-style ukulele. Nunes and his sons started the first ukulele production company around 1910, and are credited as being the first mass producers of the instrument. His advertisements of the period call him the "inventor of the ukulele."

According to the Ukulele Guild of Hawai'i (**www.ukuleleguild.org**), the first published use of the word "ukulele" appeared in an 1891 travel guide by Helen Mather.

What are the different types of ukes?

(Listed from smallest to largest):

- **Soprano**: Considered the standard, about 20 ½" in length with 12 to 17 frets.
- **Concert:** 23 ¾" in length with 12 to 19 frets.
- **Tenor:** 27" in length with 18 to 22 frets. With more frets, the tenor offers more versatility.
- **Baritone:** 29 ½" with 18 to 22 frets. This instrument has a larger body, offering a fuller, richer sound. Usually tuned D, G, B, E, like the last four strings on a guitar, the baritone uke is played exactly like a guitar, but without the first two strings (E and A).

- **Specialty ukes**: Many ukulele luthiers manufacture specialty ukes in all of the above sizes with more than the four standard strings. Some of these ukes have 8 strings, or double strings (like a classical guitar). Some have six strings with the G and C strings doubled. You can also find five-stringed ukes.

What woods are the best ukuleles constructed from?

Koa is the most popular wood for ukulele bodies, although mahogany, monkey pod, Sitka spruce, red cedar, mango, claro and walnut are also popular. More important than the wood when choosing a ukulele is how it sounds. Does it sound dull when the strings are strummed, or bright and vibrant? Is the tone deep and round, or strident?

Usual Uke Note Range:

- **High G String**—Most new ukes are strung with a high G string that matches the G note above middle C. This G string, or string 4, is actually a higher pitch than the C string, or string 3.
- Strung this way, the notes that can be played on the uke's frets range from "Middle C" to "D above high C." This tonal range is over 2 octaves, or 16 notes.

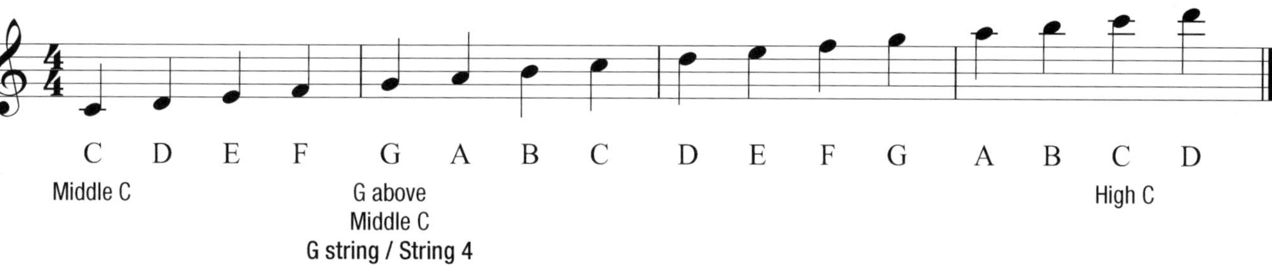

You can increase your Uke Note Range!

- **Low G string**—Instead of a high G string you can choose to replace it with a low G string. The low G string matches the G below middle C and is a lower pitch than the C string, or string 3. Many people choose to string their uke with a low G string, to increase the musical range by 3 notes. Those extra three low notes give more depth of sound and the ability to play a wider range of melodies.
- When the uke is strung with a low G string, the tonal range is 2 and 1/2 octaves, or 19 notes.

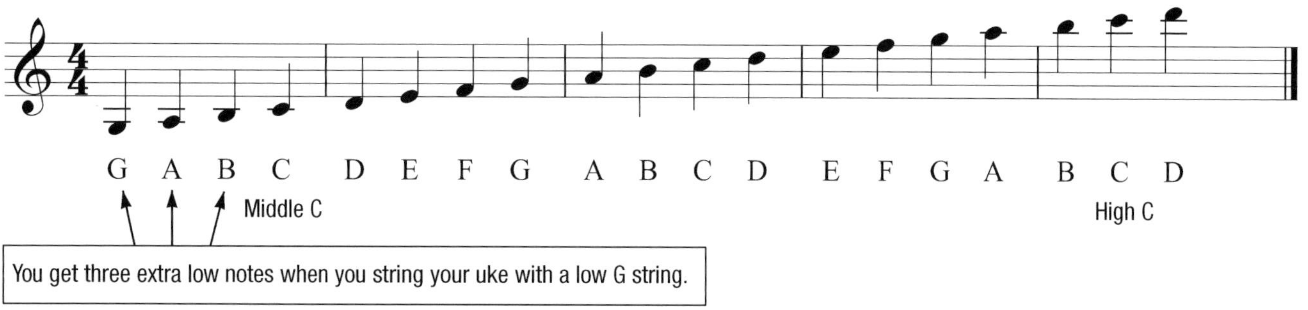

Full Ukulele Fretboard

For Soprano, Concert, and Tenor Uke:

1. This diagram represents your ukulele as if you are holding it at arm's length with the fretboard facing you.
2. Even though the focus in this book is on the first four frets, here is a chart of all the notes in the first twelve frets of the ukulele.

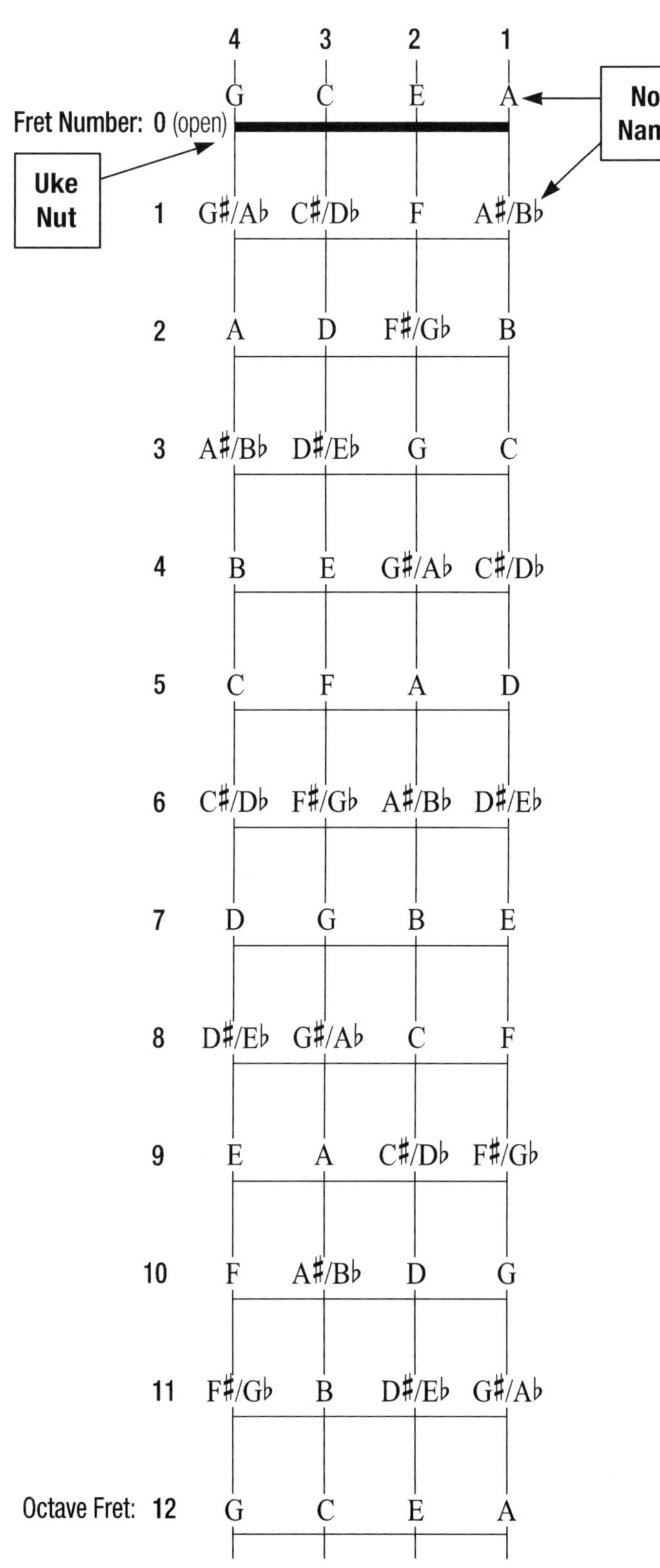

Note, Rhythm and Rest Values

Reference Chart

Read across this chart to compare and learn the different notations for corresponding note, rest and chord rhythmic values.

Pitch Rhythm Notation	Rest Notation	Chord Rhythm Notation
Quarter Note = 1 Beat (Hold each **note** for 1 beat)	**Quarter Note Rest = 1 Beat** (Hold each **rest** for 1 beat)	**Quarter Note = 1 Beat** (Hold each **chord** for 1 beat)
Half Note = 2 Beats (Hold each **note** for 2 beats)	**Half Note Rest = 2 Beats** (Hold each **rest** for 2 beats)	**Half Note = 2 Beats** (Hold each **chord** for 2 beats)
Dotted Half Note = 3 Beats (Hold each **note** for 3 beats)	**Dotted Note Rest = 3 Beats** (Hold each **rest** for 3 beats)	**Half Note = 3 Beats** (Hold each **chord** for 3 beats)
Whole Note = 4 Beats (Hold each **note** for 4 beats)	**Whole Note Rest = 4 Beats** (Hold each **rest** for 4 beats)	**Whole Note = 4 Beats** (Hold each **chord** for 4 beats)

String, Finger, and Note Reference Chart

Right Hand Fingers	Strings	Notes in the open, first fret position
T or **Thumb** **Position:** Is extended and points toward the head of the uke.	Low G	G, A, B G A B TAB 0 2 4
I or **Index** finger **Position:** Fingertip points toward your wrist. Knuckle aligns with underside of Thumb knuckle joint.	C	C, D C D TAB 0 2
M or **Middle** finger **Position:** Fingertip points toward your wrist. Knuckle slightly behind Index finger knuckle.	E	E, F, G E F G TAB 0 1 3
R or **Ring** finger **Position:** Fingertip points toward your wrist. Knuckle slightly behind Middle finger knuckle.	A	A, B, C A B C TAB 0 2 3

Tune Me Up and Turn Me Loose!

Relative Tuning Method: This is the tuning method to use if you would like to tune your uke "by ear." It is called *relative* tuning because you tune the G string to a pitch source—either a pitch pipe, piano, tuning app, or digital tuner. Then you tune the rest of the strings "relatively" to the tuned string. Everything is relative!

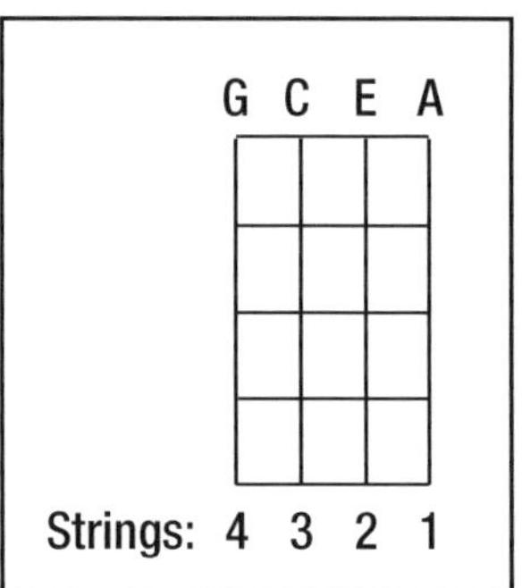

STEP 1: Memorize the names of strings

- **String 4: G**ood
- **String 3: C**ats
- **String 2: E**at
- **String 1: A**pples

STEP 2: Tune the G string using a *pitch pipe, digital tuner, tuning app*, or *piano* as a reference:

1. **High G string:** Tune to G above middle C key on the piano or with various tuning devices. (You can also tune the rest of the strings to the corresponding keys on the piano diagram below, if you choose.)

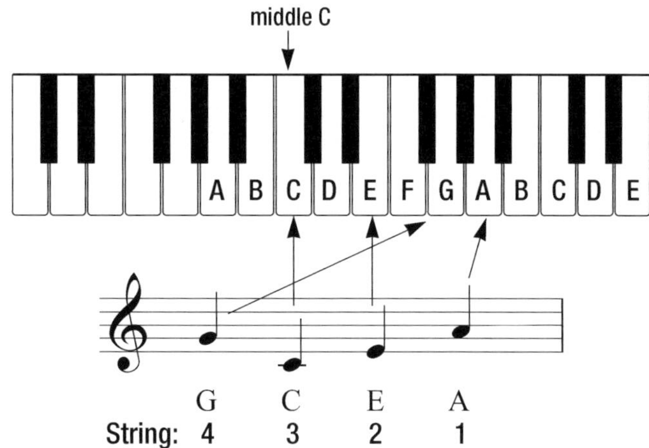

2. **Low G string:** Tune to G below middle C key on the piano or with various tuning devices. (You can also tune the rest of the strings to the corresponding keys on the piano diagram below.)

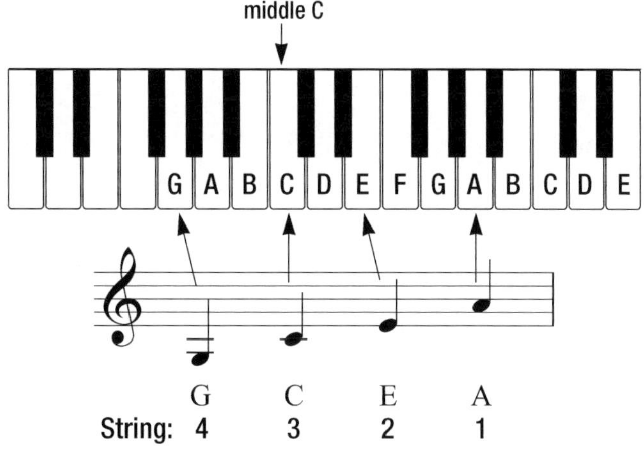

STEP 3: Tune the A string

1. On the G string (4th string), hold down the A note (2nd fret) and play it.
2. Use that pitch as a reference to tune the A string (1st string). If you are tuning with a High G string, the pitches are identical. But, if you are tuning with a Low G string, the A string is 8 notes higher in pitch than the A note on the G string (2nd fret).

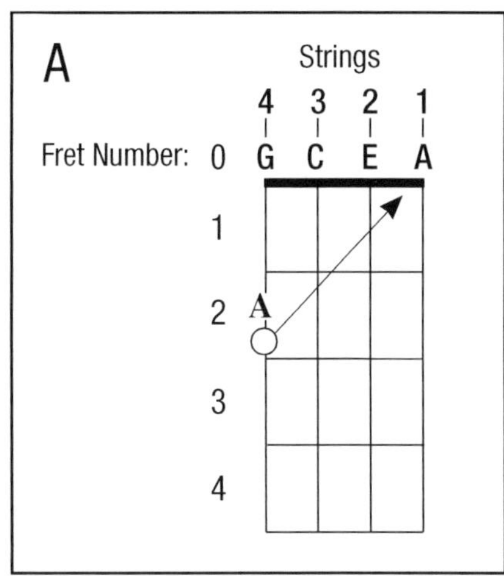

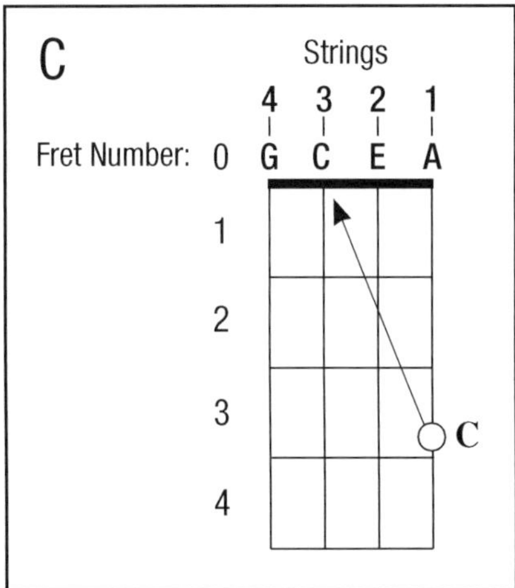

STEP 4: Tune the C string

1. On the A string (1st string) hold down the C note (3rd fret) and play it.
2. Use that pitch as a reference to tune the C string. The C string is 8 notes lower in pitch than the C note on the A string (3rd fret).

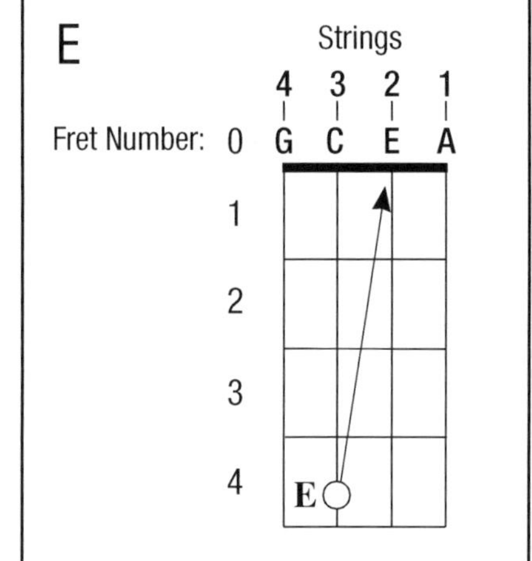

STEP 5: Tune the E string

1. On the C string (3rd string), hold down the E note (4th fret) and play it.
2. Use that pitch as a reference to tune the E string.

More Tuning Advice

My new uke goes flat the moment I tune it! What am I doing wrong?

Nothing! Just keep tuning it. New nylon strings will make you crazy before they finally hold their pitch. If you tune them consistently, they will finally stretch into the right pitch. It can take a couple of weeks.

My tuning keys are slipping, what should I do?

Your tuning keys may be loose. First, look at the tiny screws at the end of the tuning key (friction tuners), or on the gear at the back of the head (geared tuners) to see whether your tuning key needs a petite straight edge or a petite Phillips-head screwdriver. (Be sure to keep the appropriate screwdriver in your uke case for emergencies.) Whichever type of tuning key you have, use the screwdriver to tighten the tiny screws by giving them a 1/4 turn clockwise. If the strings still continue to slip, tighten another 1/4 turn until they hold. If the tuning key gets too hard to turn, then you have tightened the screw a bit too much.

Accidentals

This book focuses on the key of C, which contains only "natural" notes. Natural notes are designated in music simply with a note in a line or space. But, you will see "accidentals" in a few songs and chords in this book and in other music. So here's the information on how accidentals work.

The basic unit of musical measurement is a half-step. Accidentals raise or lower each note by a half step. Each fret on your uke represents a half step. There are three types of accidentals:

- Sharp ♯ raises a note one fret, or one half-step higher.

- Flat ♭ lowers a note one fret, or one half-step lower.

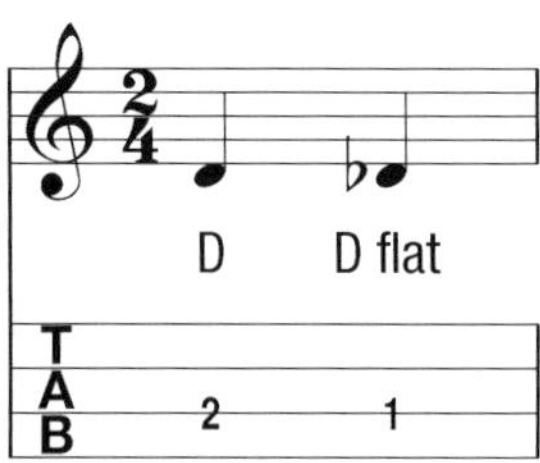

- Natural ♮ cancels a sharp or flat and returns the note to its original position.

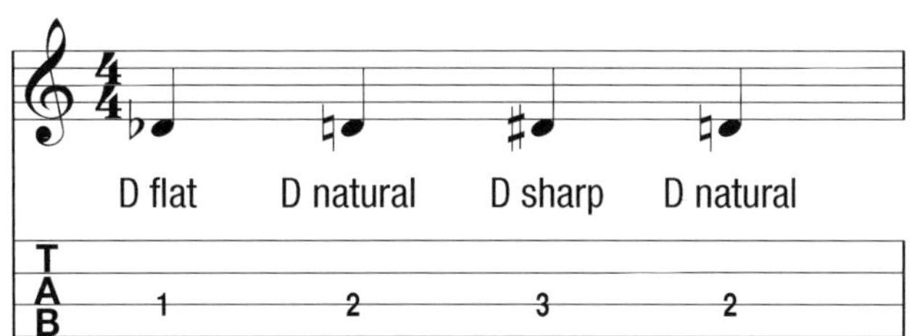

Dynamics Markings in Music

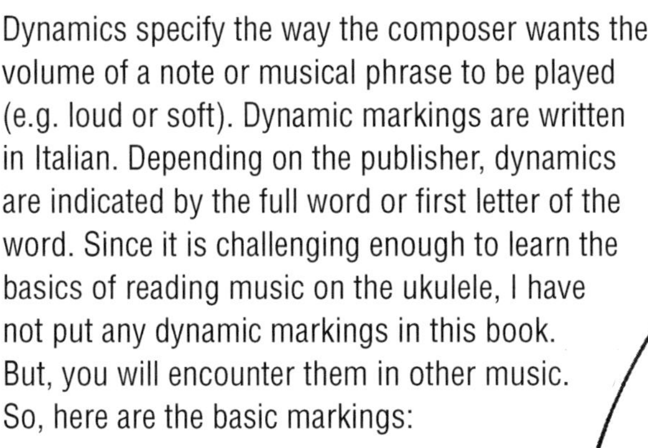

Dynamics specify the way the composer wants the volume of a note or musical phrase to be played (e.g. loud or soft). Dynamic markings are written in Italian. Depending on the publisher, dynamics are indicated by the full word or first letter of the word. Since it is challenging enough to learn the basics of reading music on the ukulele, I have not put any dynamic markings in this book. But, you will encounter them in other music. So, here are the basic markings:

p, or piano = soft

pp, or "pianissimo" = very soft

mp, or mezzo-piano = moderately soft

f, or forte = loud

mf, or mezzo-forte = moderately loud

ff, or "fortissimo" = very loud

More String Stuff

How often should I change my uke's strings?

Beginners, or those who just play for fun, might want to change them once a year. Pros or semi-pros usually change them every couple of months.

If I have friction tuning pegs on my uke can I change them to geared tuning pegs?

If you have a beginner quality uke, something under $100, it doesn't pay. You might want to invest in a second uke of a different size (e.g., consider purchasing a tenor if you have a soprano or concert size) that has geared pegs. That way you can learn to play two different sizes and learn to tune using the different peg types. If your uke is a higher quality instrument and has friction pegs, take it to a luthier for a consultation to install geared pegs.

Can I put metal strings on my ukulele?

Never! They will warp the neck and can tear off the bridge. Ukes are designed to support the weight of nylon strings.

Why are some nylon strings wound with metal?

This increases the weight of the string while keeping the flexibility of a smaller string and provides a vibrant sound. Strings that are too thick have a dead, muddy sound.

Why are some tenor string sets available with "no wound"?

Some musicians don't like metal wound strings because they make a hissing sound when a finger rubs the winding. Both metal and "no wound" are acceptable, but remember that metal can wear out the wood between the fret bar.

Why does my uke body buzz when I play it?

There may be a "Do Not Eat" (silica gel) packet inside. Shake your uke to find it, then remove it through the sound hole.

Why does one string buzz when I play it?

The groove where the nut holds the string in place above the fretboard may be either too deep or too wide. An incorrect groove depth or shape positions the string too close to the fret bars and causes buzzing as the string vibrates when played. You may also have a loose brace inside the uke that has come unglued, or you may have a loose electric pickup.

Do strings go bad?

Yes. Some strings can get stiff or over stretched, which makes them sound dull. Listen carefully to your instrument before changing strings.

Is there a difference in the sound of different brands of strings?

Yes, but there is no universal string for all ukuleles or all music played on ukes. You have to be the judge. Also bear in mind that a quality set of strings may make an inexpensive ukulele sound like a million bucks!

Protect Your Investment

Is a case or gig bag the best protection for my uke?

- Hard shell cases are thicker and harder, giving maximum protection for your instrument. Many come with both shoulder straps and back-pack straps for easy carrying.
- Gig bags are lighter, take up less room and are easier to carry, but give minimal protection.

Is it okay to leave a uke in a locked car?

The most important thing to consider before leaving your uke in your car is the weather. If it is hot, your uke can warp, and worse, the glue holding your uke together can fail causing the instrument to literally fall apart. If it is too cold, your strings can break and warping can also occur. Whenever possible, take your uke with you whenever you get out of your car.

Does humidity and dryness affect my uke?

All fretted instruments made of natural wood (ukulele, guitar, mandolin, etc.) need some moisture to maintain their shape and sound quality. A relative humidity level between 45% and 55% is recommended to prevent shrinking or distortion.

Here are some simple tips to keep your ukuleles and other stringed instruments made of wood in good condition:

- **Room humidifier:** If your house is dry or if you live in a dry climate, use a room humidifier to raise the humidity level to 45-55%.
- **Instrument humidifier:** If you're in a dry environment, use an instrument humidifier to add moisture to your uke on a regular basis. They are easy-to-use, reasonably priced, and are available at most well-stocked music stores.
- **Just in case:** If you don't use a room humidifier and monitor the humidity level, keep your ukes in their cases when not in use. A case or gig bag will help preserve your uke.
- **Stay away from heat:** Don't store your ukulele near any form of heat. This includes a direct source of heat, sunlight, or near outside doors where the room temperature is likely to change often.
- **Keep the thermostat down:** Store your uke in a reasonably cool place.
- **Digital hygrometer:** Use a digital hygrometer to measure the relative humidity level in your home. These sell at most music stores, hardware stores or home electronics stores for around $25-$30.

Hawai'ian Musical Terms

If you play regularly with an ukulele group that plays Hawai'ian music, you need to know the following Hawai'ian words:

Hana hou—encore, do it again

Kani—to sound or strike; to play a musical instrument

Kani ka pila—play the stringed instrument. Today means musical jam session, or "let's play music." ("ka" means "the")

Mele—melodic song or chant. Ancient mele were chanted songs often accompanied by rhythm instruments and by hula dances. Traditionally, mele is how Hawai'ians preserve their legends, traditions, family, and social history. Today mele can also mean songs accompanied by instruments.

'Oli—Chant

Pa`ani—to play, "horse around," sport, amusement; also means joking, playful, amusing. Used by musicians for taking an instrumental break in a vocal piece.

Pane—*verb:* to answer, to reply; *noun:* an answer, a reply. Also used by musicians as a term for an instrumental break in between the vocal verses of a song, as the instrumental break is answering the vocal verses.

Pau—finished, ended, all done

Pila—a musical instrument, originally a fiddle; today means any stringed instrument.

Keep a Weekly Practice Log

Writing down your musical goals and the work you have done to achieve them helps you:

- **Maintain a regular practice schedule**—helps you make faster progress
- **Set goals that are realistic yet challenging**—songs, chords, chord progressions, and solo pieces you want to learn, but are not so far beyond your current capabilities that they are unattainable.
- **Organize your practice session**—this enables you to:
    - remember everything on your practice list
    - logically order the exercises and music you want to practice
    - break down your work into manageable amounts that can be spread out during the week.
- **Determine how long it takes you to learn something new**
- **Write down questions for your teacher at your next lesson**

Students: Use the following two sheets as an example for creating your own practice log.

Instructors: Use the following sheets as a template for creating a log that compliments your particular practice curriculum.

Name ______________________________ Date ______________

Ukulele Monthly Music Goals

This month, I will work to master the following:

- Finger Exercises:

- Scales/ Chords/ Chord Progressions:

- Instrumental pieces—memorize the melody line and chords:

- Songs—memorize chords and lyrics:

Name ______________________________ Date ______________

Ukulele Weekly Practice Log

Practice any five days during the week to make maximum progress.

WEEKDAY	PRACTICE TIME
Monday	
Tuesday	
Wednesday	
Thursday	
Friday	
Saturday	
Sunday	
Total time for the week →	

WARM-UP

1. Finger Exercise(s):

2. Scales:

3. Chords / Chord Progressions:

PLAY MUSIC

4. Uke Book: Work on Lesson ________, pages______

5. Songs:

Made in the USA
San Bernardino, CA
03 February 2019